Handbook
of Diversity
in Parent Education

Handbook of Diversity in Parent Education

The Changing Faces of Parenting and Parent Education

Edited by

Marvin J. Fine

Department of Psychology and Research in Education
University of Kansas
Lawrence, Kansas 66045

Steven W. Lee

Department of Psychology and Research in Education
University of Kansas
Lawrence, Kansas 66045

ACADEMIC PRESS

A Harcourt Science and Technology Company

San Diego   San Francisco   New York   Boston   London   Sydney   Tokyo

Academic Press
A Harcourt Science and Technology Company
525 B Street, Suite 1900, San Diego, California 92101-4495, USA
http://www.academicpress.com

Academic Press
Harcourt Place, 32 Jamestown Road, London NW1 7BY, UK
http://www.academicpress.com

Library of Congress Catalog Card Number: 00-102241

International Standard Book Number: 0-12-256483-9

PRINTED IN THE UNITED STATES OF AMERICA
00   01   02   03   04   05   EB   9   8   7   6   5   4   3   2   1

Contents

3 *Teaching About Sexual Diversity: A New Frontier for Parenthood Educators*

Donna Swall and Forrest Swall

4 *Parenting and Ethnicity*

Diane McDermott

5 *Parenting in the Global Community: A Cross-Cultural/ International Perspective*

John Bennett and Liam K. Grimley

6   *A Psychoeducational Program for Parents of Dysfunctional Backgrounds*

Marvin J. Fine and Katherine F. Wardle

9 Grandparents Raising Grandchildren
Oliver W. Edwards

10 Parenting Emotionally Disturbed Children
Eric M. Vernberg and Anabella Pavon

14 Education Programs for Parents and Families of Children and Youth with Developmental Disabilities

Earle Knowlton and Douglas Mulanax

15 Educating Parents to be Advocates for their Children

Michelle L. Moriarty and Marvin J. Fine

16 *Managing Crisis: Intervention Skills for Parents*
K. C. Lazzara and Scott Poland

Preface

The contemporary history of parenting and parent education was given impetus by the development and dissemination of organized parent education curricula, such as P.E.T. (Gordon, 1970), STEP (Dinkmeyer & McKay, 1973), and Active Parenting (Popkin, 1993). This has occurred against the background of debate over family values, which was highlighted by the Murphy Brown vs. Dan Quayle debate. What has emerged is a clearer picture of the great diversity of family life and concomitantly, of the expanded and diverse needs of parents. David Elkind's recent book has examined families in the postmodern era, underscoring the confusion and stress that parents experience in balancing two-income families, pseudomature children, and meeting their own needs.

While there may be some set of parenting values and skills that are heuristic, the diversity of family life and issues besetting specific parents has established the need for specific and tailored programs designed to meet the need of the ecology of each parent's situation. This volume intends to identify such programs and, in light of the contemporary scene, to examine other related issues. The chapters include an examination of the family of the 1990s, implications of national policy on families, and the implications of ethnicity on Black and Hispanic parenting. Gender issues are also addressed as well as parenting at different developmental levels. The status of parenting and parent education is addressed from a cross-cultural and international perspective.

A large number of chapters describe narrowly targeted parenting programs such as parenting programs for fathers, grandparents, parents of emotionally disturbed and chronically ill children, parents of learning disabled and brain-injured children, for parents from dysfunctional backgrounds, and parents of children with various special needs. There are chapters on training parents in crisis intervention skills, training and certifying parent educators, on federal, state, and community resources for parents, as well as supportive and informational websites.

This book represents the total comprehensive coverage of parenting programs and issues in diverse populations and should be of value to both applied clinicians and educators as well as researchers and college instructors.

REFERENCES

Gordon, T. (1970). *Parent effectiveness training*. New York: Wyden.
Dinkmeyer, D., & McKay, G. (1973). *Raising a responsible child*. New York: Simon & Schuster.
Popkin, M. H. (1993). *Active parenting today: For parents of 2 to 12 year olds*. Marrietta, Georgia: Active Parent Publishing.

Contributors

Numbers in parentheses indicate the pages on which the authors' contributions begin.

Cynthia M. Anderson (253)
Department of Psychology
West Virginia University
Morgantown, West Virginia 26506

Lauren Ayers (15)
Research Associates
Albany, New York 12203

John Bennett (97)
Organization for Economic Co-operation
   and Development
Paris, France

Oliver W. Edwards (199)
Department of Educational Psychology
University of Florida
Gainesville, Florida 32611

Marvin J. Fine (133 and 315)
Department of Psychology and Research
   in Education
University of Kansas
Lawrence, Kansas 66045

Liam K. Grimley (97)
Deceased
Department of Educational and School
   Psychology
Indiana State University
Terre Haute, Indiana 47809

Thomas P. Guck (277)
Creighton Family Health Care
Creighton University School of
   Medicine
Omaha, Nebraska 68124

Dennis H. Karpowitz (1)
Department of Psychology
University of Kansas
Lawrence, Kansas 66045

Earle Knowlton (299)
Department of Special Education
University of Kansas
Lawrence, Kansas 66045

Paula E. Lancaster (231)
Center for Research on Learning
University of Kansas
Lawrence, Kansas 66045

K. C. Lazzara (337)
Department of Psychology and Research
  in Education
University of Kansas
Lawrence, Kansas 66045

Steven W. Lee (277)
Department of Psychology and Research
  in Education
University of Kansas
Lawrence, Kansas 66045

Sheila Le Gacy (155)
The Family Support and Education
  Center
Transitional Living Services
Syracuse, New York 13202

Diane McDermott (73)
Department of Psychology and Research
  in Education
University of Kansas
Lawrence, Kansas 66045

Michelle L. Moriarty (315)
Department of Psychology and Research
  in Education
University of Kansas
Lawrence, Kansas 66045

Douglas Mulanax (299)
Lawrence Public Schools
Lawrence, Kansas 66045

Anabella Pavon (213)
Clinical Child Psychology Program
University of Kansas
Lawrence, Kansas 66045

Scott Poland (337)
Psychological Services
Cypress-Fairbanks Independent School
  District
Houston, Texas 77040

Stephen T. Sirridge (179)
Department of Educational Psychology
Avila College
Kansas City, Missouri 64145

Donna Swall (37)
Social Worker (retired)
Lawrence, Kansas 66049

Forrest Swall (37)
School of Social Welfare (retired)
University of Kansas
Lawrence, Kansas 66049

Eric M. Vernberg (213)
Clinical Child Psychology Program
University of Kansas
Lawrence, Kansas 66045

Katherine F. Wardle (133)
Affiliated Psychological Services
Latham, New York 12110

William J. Warzak (253)
Department of Pediatrics
Munroe-Meyer Institute for Genetics and
  Rehabilitation
University of Nebraska Medical Center
Omaha, Nebraska 68198

CHAPTER 1

American Families in the 1990s and Beyond

Dennis H. Karpowitz

Department of Psychology, University of Kansas, Lawrence Kansas

This chapter overviews trends in American families as we move quickly toward the 21st century. Strengths and problems are identified. There is a strong commitment to prevention of problems and early intervention rather than to intervention after the problems are well developed. Much of what is suggested here opposes strong zeitgeists of our time, including materialism and individualism. The author is an advocate for children, for they are least able to care for themselves and assert their own needs relative to the needs and wants of adults. Measures of children's success should not just be defined as the absence of negatives. Most parents want more for their children than that the children are not in prison or are not on public welfare. I believe it is the responsibility of parents and adult society to provide opportunities for the maximization of children's capacities. It is within this context that this chapter unfolds.

This chapter does not reexamine the history of families and typical family developmental phases. A review of those areas can be found in the previous edition of this chapter (Karpowitz, 1980).

American families are diverse in both membership and functioning (Lauer & Lauer, 1997). Families include two-parent families in which the children are the biological offspring of these parents, two-parent, remarried families in which one or more children come from a previous relationship, and single-parent families resulting from never-married individuals, divorced individuals, and widows or widowers with children. In single-parent families about 90% are female-headed households, 10% male-headed households. Where a divorce has occurred, the parent with residential custody defines the above statistics. Many children live in more than one family. For example, a child may spend weekdays with mom and weekends with dad or some other time distribution. In more than half of all families with children, both parents work outside the home. Both parents may be employed full-time. One parent may be employed full-time and one part-time or both may be employed part-time. These families vary greatly in terms of functionality, that is, the ability of the family to meet the physical, emotional, and spiritual needs of each member of the family (Walsh, 1993).

This diversity does not imply that all family types are equally successful in maximizing children's growth and development. For example, it is clear that men and women parent differently and that children benefit from parenting of both mother and father (Lamb, 1996). Children also learn much about relationships by observing the relationship between their mother and father. Single-parent families are disadvantaged in these respects.

Much has been written about the importance of quality time between parent and child (Farber & Mazlish, 1991), but quality time also requires quantity time. Parents have only so much energy. When both parents are working long hours in high-stress jobs, there may be little energy left over for children. Some have said, "I want it all," but the reality is that there is only so much time and energy available. If we want to maximize children's potential, they must be high on the time and energy priority. Specific studies that demonstrate the relationship between parental neglect and child problems are cited below. I'm advocating for parents who will make the time and have the energy to really invest in their children's development.

The family is a very complex system with subsystems such as the marital dyad, parent child dyads, and often sibling dyads. Outside systems such as the school, employment, neighborhood, community, religious organization, subculture, and society all influence family functioning (Heatherington & Parks, 1999). In the past two decades there has been a continual shift in research paradigms away from single-variable individual or dyadic studies toward more complex, multivariable, multiperson system examinations.

TRENDS

Two trends are evident in American families. The first trend is positive and functional (Beavers & Hampson, 1990). Many men and women are placing more emphasis on family life and demanding of themselves the time and energy that it takes to create healthy, functional families. These families have higher standards for both the marital relationship and the parent–child interactions. There is a balance of work, education, and play. Spiritual values add strength to the individual and the relationship. Children flourish and grow in these families and become better prepared to continue this growth in the families they develop as adults. They are most likely to maximize their developmental possibilities.

The second trend is negative and alarming. Many families are breaking down, falling apart, and not coping with life effectively. These families have greater violence of all types, marriages that are consistently tense or disengaged, children who grow up with little parent or adult supervision, few lasting relationships, and little emotional stability on which to build their own future marriage and family relationships. At times the frustration and rage built into these families not only destroy the family but adversely affect the whole community. The children in these families manifest greater psychopathology (Lindahl, 1998).

Few, if any, families remain static. Either they are moving toward greater stability and functionality or they are moving toward greater dysfunctionality and breakdown. Like the second law of thermodynamics (things left unattended fall apart), the pressures of modern society push toward family breakdown. We are not a family-oriented society. It takes effort and commitment—"swimming up stream," if you will—in order to build family strengths.

It is not clear that as a society we are we willing to really work at prevention. What has been empirically found to work is not always popular, e.g., moms who stay at home to raise children, dads who are involved as parents, and spiritual values (Hoffman, 1989, 1963; Lamb, 1996; Beavers & Hampson, 1990). So much of our applied literature focuses on intervention long after the problem has become overwhelming. We seem to have a difficult time saying what is obvious, such as it takes the full efforts of two conscientious adults to raise a child with opportunities to maximize that child's potential. All of our efforts to assist single-parent families will not produce the equivalent of the functional two-parent home. Unless we say this loud and clear, how will young people have the facts to make informed decisions about starting a family?

Are we willing to provide disincentives for those who create problems? For example, should it become law that the biological fathers and mothers have a legal responsibility to provide for their children through the child's 18th year whether or not the parents are married, whether or not they live under the same roof? If the parents are under 18, should the paternal and maternal grandparents be made financially responsible until the parents are 18?

CHANGES IN DEMOGRAPHICS SINCE 1978

The following points are summarized from *America's Children: Key National Indicators of Well-Being, 1998* and *Statistics for the U.S. Bureau of Census, 1995.*

- Children living in poverty represent 20% of all children and 40% of all those living in poverty.
- Eighty-one percent of U.S. children are healthy, and 65% of children in poverty are healthy. Twenty-three percent of children 19 to 35 months old are not up-to-date on their immunizations.
- Low-birth-weight babies are at the highest rate in 2 decades.
- Fourteen percent of youths 18 to 24 years of age have not graduated from high school. However, 32% of young adults have obtained bachelor's degrees.
- There is a continuing rise in the number of mothers of young children who work outside the home. Sixty percent of children not yet in kindergarten are receiving some type of child care or education on a regular basis from persons other than their parents.
- Age of first marriage is increasing and with it a leveling off and slight decline of the divorce rate.
- Youth violence is increasing for both boys and girls. An even greater rise in youth violence perpetrated by young women and girls though is still well below that of boys.
- Young adults are increasingly choosing to live together and become parents but not to marry or else to postpone marriage. These relationships seem to be less stable and lack continuity.
- There are increasing high rates of alcohol and drug use in all segments of society.
- There are large expenditures on luck-oriented activities such as lotteries and other forms of gambling. These expenditures are inversely relat-

ed to income. In other words, those that have the least, spend the most on chance.

• Gang membership and violence are very high but not increasing.

MYTHS VERSUS REALITIES THAT AFFECT FAMILY LIFE

1. Money brings happiness. The pursuit of financial success justifies the behavior. "It's sensible to work 60 hours a week because I make more money and I need the money to be happy." In business, "It's okay to fire people because the stockholders need greater profits even in already profitable businesses." Myers and Diener (1995), in their review of hundreds of studies looking at who is happy, find very little relationship between income and happiness once individuals have food, shelter, and safety.

2. I can have it all. I can have a full-time career, raise children, be involved in the community, accumulate massive wealth, have considerable leisure time, and do all of these things well. Small amounts of "quality" time can magically take the place of greater amounts of "quality" time, which has always been associated with effective family functioning. Most people who accumulate significant wealth sacrifice much, if not all, of family life to spend the time necessary to accomplish their material goals. One of the most common clients I see in my private practice is a divorced man of 50 plus years who is wealthy but unhappy. He has lost his family along the way to gaining wealth. Now as he begins to look toward retirement, he not only is unhappy, but doesn't know how to enjoy life and form long-term meaningful relationships.

3. Relationships are easily replaceable and at very little cost. Every meaningful relationship involves an investment of time and energy. Moving from one relationship to another is costly to our ability to trust and invest in others. I have seen many teenagers and young adults hurt and grieved over relationships in which they invested a lot, but this was not reciprocated by their friends.

4. Moving from one place to another every 3 or 4 years will not affect children. In reality, moving can have devastating effects on children. Studies of military families who move on the average of every 3 years indicate that children either become very successful at developing new relationships or give up trying to form close friendships. Unfortunately, the latter is more common.

5. Children will not be too hurt by the divorce of their par-

ents. Because divorce is so common, we want it to have little adverse effect on children, but that just isn't the case. In families where there has not been abuse, children often suffer long-term effects of the divorce of their parents. Even their own chances of sustaining their marriage are lessened compared to adult children whose parents have not divorced.

6. I can take advantage of my friends and family to get what I want without much thought of how that behavior affects others or the relationships. Friendships are vital to health and happiness. Myers and Diener (1995) conclude, "People who can name several intimate friends with whom they share their intimate concerns freely are healthier, less likely to die prematurely, and happier than people who have few or no such friends" (p. 14).

7. If it's scientific, it's true and right. Empirical studies sometimes make sweeping conclusions while using minimum measures that support the conclusions. For example, some studies report that children are not hurt by many years of full-time day care and actually function better than children in families raised at home. Sometimes better is only measured by a lack of gross negative factors, minimum educational standards, and social assertiveness (sometimes dubbed social skills). Often the control groups lump together functional and dysfunctional families whose children are not in full-time day care. Noted child developmental psychologists such as Harvard's Burton White have spoken directly and succinctly about the dangerous effects of long-term, full-time day care on such personal characteristics as the ability to maintain relationships, to compromise for the good of the group, to give of oneself to others, and to enjoy an inner sense of self-worth and inner peace (see Meyerhoff & White, 1986).

Too often social scientists avoid discussing the importance of character, values, and morality in the development of a child. However, Beavers' longitudinal study of families clearly found that spiritual values were linked to optimal family functioning (see Beavers & Hampson, 1990). Batson, Schoenrade, and Ventis (1993) report that religious people (those who attend church regularly) are much less likely to abuse drugs or alcohol, become delinquent, be divorced or unhappily married, or commit suicide than those who are involved in less religious practice. Some of the highest correlations to life satisfaction have to do with attributes of faith (see Inglehart, 1990).

8. You can't be too thin. There is a national obsession with being thin (Abraham & Llewellyn-Jones, 1992; Cooper & Stein, 1992)—not just being average weight, but being thin. This obsession has reached into families and affects many adolescents. Average-weight children and adolescents, especially girls and young women, are told by peers and adults that they have "fat thighs," "big butts," etc. Individuals are judged almost solely on their physical appearance, and much less value is given to important characteristics such as the ability to communicate, caring and concern for others, and the ability to form lasting friendships. Children are put under pressure to diet to the point of meeting the criteria for eating disorders.

9. It is important to have power, and power in the family is based on how much money one earns. Power is often defined as the ability to control others, but in functional families power is distributed to all family members (see Beavers & Hampson, 1990; Kantor & Lehr, 1975). Each family member feels he or she is heard and understood by other family members. Each family member feels that he or she has some things "his way" some of the time. Roles are distributed across family members. Such power may have nothing to do with who makes the most money. A related confusion is between equality and sameness. Individuals can be very different but still be equal, be equally valued, and have equal rights, equal responsibility, and equal opportunity. Families, like a larger organization, function more effectively when roles are distributed across family members. This includes roles that are valued as well as roles that are necessary but not enjoyed. Equity in marriage relationships can be found in families with a stay-at-home mom, two full-time working parents, and one full-time and one part-time working parent. Children can and should have both rights and responsibilities. For all family members these roles, rights, and responsibilities may be distributed according to individual preferences, individuals skills, individual capacities, and the needs of the family.

PARENTING STYLES AND CHILDREN'S MENTAL HEALTH

There is a burgeoning literature examining family functioning, marital harmony or conflict, and parenting styles and their effects on children's mental health. Substantial evidence suggests that ineffective parenting, coercive parenting styles, inconsistency, and lack of parental responsiveness or involvement are all associated with greater psychopathology in children (Frick & Jackson, 1993; Lindahl, 1998; Patterson & Dishion, 1985). The relationship of coercive parenting styles and violent families to conduct disorder, delinquency, and antisocial behavior has been documented over several decades (Jouriles et al., 1987; Kazdin, 1987; Patterson, 1982). Lindahl (1998) has extended these findings by examining the relationship between parental patterns and attention deficit hyperactive disorder (ADHD), oppositional defiant disorder (ODD), or both. She examined family functioning in ADHD, ODD, or both in normal 7- to 11-year-old boys. Marital and parent child interaction variables were able to correctly classify the boys into the appropriate groups with 90% accuracy. High parental coercion separated the problem groups from the controls. For the problem groups, parental responsiveness and consistency in parenting were higher for the ADHD group and lower for the ODD or combined groups.

Since the late 1960s effective parenting styles have been empirically validated (Baumrind, 1967). Simply stated the basic elements are parental communication of warmth, clear verbal explanations, moderate and realistic limit setting, consequences other than physical punishment, reasonable consistency, and involvement. Children who are the recipients of these parenting characteristics manifest higher self-esteem, greater school achievement, more likable social skills, and more personal happiness than children whose parents use either permissive or authoritarian parenting styles. Child development texts reiterate these same findings (e.g., Heatherington & Parks, 1999).

OPTIMAL FAMILY FUNCTIONING

Beavers (in Walsh, 1982) summarized his longitudinal study of families with optimal functioning. In his well-known "Timberlawn Study" eight characteristics of effective functional families were found.

1. A systems orientation. Optimal families recognize that each individual needs a group, a human system, for identity and satisfaction. In family interactions causes and effects are interchangeable, and much communication is circular in nature. These families understand that any human behavior is the result of many variables rather than one "cause"; therefore, simplistic solutions are questioned. They express the attitude that human beings are limited and finite. No one is absolutely helpless or absolutely powerful in a relationship.

2. Clear boundaries. Optimal families are involved in the world beyond the family. There is an openness to other viewpoints. There are clear boundaries between family members and clear generational boundaries. Respect for individual boundaries invites intimacy. Negotiation is acceptable and practiced.

3. Contextual clarity. There is clarity about who is being addressed. Oedipal issues have been resolved. There is clarity about the nature of the relationship between the speaker and the audience.

4. Relatively equal power and the process of intimacy. Individuals in optimal families seek power in one of two ways: (1) the power of a loving relationship with others—the experiencing of closeness without coercion and (2) the power of control—control over one's inner self and one's own behavior. There is a clear hierarchy of power with parents first in an equal coalition and children with less power but clear influence in the family. Parents have complementary roles. There is little sexual stereotyping. Family members manifest a high degree of emotional energy, drive, and performance level.

5. The encouragement of autonomy. Family members in optimal families were found to accept responsibility for their thoughts, feelings, and behavior. They express thoughts and feelings clearly. There is a lack of blame, personal attacks, and scapegoating. They also accept the reality of uncertainty in life.

6. Joy and comfort in relating. Family members regularly express warmth, empathy, optimism, and affiliation. They see human beings as essentially benign and are thus open to others. Appropriate sexual expression, intimacy, and assertiveness are possible without apprehension.

7. Skilled negotiation. Family members organize themselves effectively, share tasks, accept direction, and negotiate differences. They are able to reach closure coherently and effectively. Parents function more as coordinators than directors.

8. Significant transcendent values. Optimal families recognize values and philosophies beyond themselves. They accept and adapt to change. They also accept the inevitable risks and losses that come with loving and being close. Twenty-five percent of the families Beavers studied were in this optimal group. The children in these families were most able to maximize their developmental potential.

VIOLENCE IN THE FAMILY

In 1990 the U.S. Advisory Board on Child Abuse and Neglect declared a national emergency in the field of child protection. Although much effort has been made to deal with this multifaceted complex problem, most experts admit that the crisis still exists (Melton, 1998; Straus & Gelles, 1986). Gorey and Leslie (1997) reviewed 16 cross-sectional studies. They estimated the rates of child sexual abuse for females to be 22.3% and for males to be 8.5% for North American populations. Beardslee et al. (1997) reported rates of physical abuse among 9953 individuals surveyed in North America to be 31% for males and 21% for females. In this same sample 10% of both men and women reported severe physical abuse when they were children. The negative consequences of abuse have been documented in many studies and include lower self-esteem, higher depression, greater alcohol abuse especially among females, greater physical and mental health problems of many types, poorer educational attainment, less income-producing employment, and less life satisfaction (e.g., Hartgers & Langeland, 1998; Gutierres & Todd, 1997; Boney-McCoy & Finkelhor, 1995). Treatment for abuse is not available to all, and results of many programs are mixed. Thompson and Wilcox (1995) summarize the research support findings succinctly, "The recent history of federal support for child maltreatment research paints a mixed picture of inadequate funding and uncertain administrative guidance against a backdrop of growing public concern about the prevalence of child abuse and neglect" (p. 789).

Marital violence is also staggering in its prevalence. Jouriles et al. (1987) report that physical marital violence, defined as physical assault on a partner's body, is very prevalent among families in the United States. Up to 50% of married couples experience spousal violence at some point during their marriages (Straus & Gelles, 1990). The relationship between physical marital violence and children's behavior problems has been investigated, and empirical evidence clearly indicates that children growing up in families marked by marital violence are at increased risk for clinical levels of behavior problems (Jaffe, Sudermann, & Reitzel, 1992; McDonald & Jouriles, 1991). Children who observe violence in their parent's relationship are thus abused and suffer consequences not dissimilar to those who suffer direct physical abuse.

Treatment programs for family violence must involve a wide array of community resources including police, courts, physicians and hospitals, child welfare agencies, and mental health professionals. Safety is the first concern. To this end, perpetrators, not the victims, should be removed from the home. Mandated treatment by courts should require clear indications of behavior change, not just a certain number of sessions. Treatment should include individual therapy, couples therapy, parenting education, and family therapy. Programs with this more comprehensive perspective are much more likely to reduce future abuse (Osofsky, 1997; Berghorn & Siracusa, 1982).

ALCOHOL AND DRUG USE

As noted earlier, alcohol and drug addiction among children and youth continues to rise. Alcohol and drug overuse directly affects between 1 in 5 and 1 in 10 American families. Cohen et al. (1993) report that 5% of adolescents have alcohol use disorder. Brody et al. (1998) found that as parental alcohol and drug use became more liberal so did the alcohol and drug use of their teenage children. Many studies have linked alcohol overuse with high conflict in the marital dyad and in the family (see Senchak et al., 1995). When parents abuse alcohol and have high conflict in the marriage and family, adolescents tend to have more significant problem behaviors (Barrera & Stice, 1998). Alcohol and drug abuse by any family member has an adverse affect on the development of the child and the adolescent. Children and adolescents in such families are less happy and have more behavioral and emotional problems.

CONCLUSIONS

Some American families are raising the quality of their family functioning and making the effort that it takes to maximize children's development and potential. The parents in these families use an authoritative parenting style, which includes the communication of warmth, verbal explanations of why things are as they are, moderate limits with reasonable consequences for inappropriate behavior, little or no use of physical punishment, and consistent engagement with the child. These families have a systematic view of life, clear boundaries, and understood and flexible roles. There is relatively equal power in the marital dyad. They communicate and negotiate effectively, encourage autonomy, enjoy one another and family life, expect benign rather than negative reactions from others, and have transcendent spiritual values. These families have organized their time and priorities to express their value of children and family life.

A second large group of families is breaking down, falling apart, and becoming more dysfunctional. Parents in these families tend to use either authoritarian or permissive parenting styles. They are often overwhelmed by the demands of life and do not devote the time and energy necessary to help their children maximize their potential. Many of these families experience high conflict that is consistently associated with lower family life satisfaction and happiness. Where violence is common, children suffer immensely. Drug and alcohol abuse further cripples these families. Children in these families manifest many more behavioral and emotional problems. Although intervention programs are often worthwhile, they often do too little too late. Much of the damage has already occurred. Too often our national response is to stick one's thumb in one hole in the dike after another rather than to build a much stronger dike. In my opinion, it is essential that we communicate loudly and clearly what has been found to work in and for families and what has been found to be ineffective or even cause further problems. Every child has the right to be wanted and to be cared for by parents who have matured and developed the skills necessary for effective parenting. If our only interest were economic, we would be much further ahead in investing in more prevention because prevention can do so much before problems ever develop and/or become very expensive in terms of both dollars and happiness. Such simple principles as delaying marriage until the mid 20s, having clear roles in the marital dyad, planning for and desiring each child, and providing near full-time parental care during the first 5 years of life have demonstrated effectiveness. Also respecting and encouraging each member of the family, avoiding any type of abuse, learning and practicing good communication and problem-solving skills, and living and encouraging transcendent values will do much to alleviate many of the difficulties so challenging to our children who will be the leaders and contributors for much of the 21st century.

REFERENCES

Abraham, S., & Llewellyn-Jones, D. (1992). *Eating disorders: The facts* (3rd ed.). New York: Oxford University Press.

Barrera, M., & Stice, E. (1998). Parent–adolescent conflict in the context of parental support: Families with alcoholic and nonalcoholic fathers. *Journal of Family Psychology, 12*(2), 195–208.

Batson, C. D., Schoenrade, P. A., & Ventis, W. L. (1993). *Religion and the individual: A social–psychological perspective*. New York: Oxford.

Baumrind, D. (1967). Child care practice anteceding three patterns of preschool behavior. *Genetic Psychology Monographs, 75,* 43–88.

Beardslee, W. R., Boyle, M. H., Fleming, J. E., MacMillan, H. L., Offord, D. R., Racine, Y. A., Trcme, N., & Wong, M. (1997). Prevalence of child physical and sexual abuse in the community: Results from the Ontario Health Supplement. *The Journal of the American Medical Association, 278*(2), 131–136.

Beavers, W. R., & Hampson, R. B. (1990). *Successful families*. New York: Norton.

Berghorn, G., & Siracusa, A. (1982). Clinical approaches to family violence. IX. Beyond isolated treatment: A case for community involvement in family violence interventions. *Family Therapy Collections, 3,* 139–157.

Boney-McCoy, S., & Finkelhor, D. (1995). Psychosocial sequelae of violent victimization in a national youth sample. *Journal of Consulting & Clinical Psychology, 63*(5), 726–736.

Brody, G. H., Flor, D. L., Hollett-Wright, N., & McCoy, J. K. (1998). Children's development of alcohol use norms: Contributions of parent and sibling norms, children's temperaments and parent–child discussions. *Journal of Family Psychology, 12*(2), 209–219.

Cohen, P., Cohen, J., Kasen, S., Velez, C. N., Hartmark, C., Johnson, J., Rojas, M., Brook, J., & Streuning, E. L. (1993). An epidemiological study of disorders in late childhood and adolescence. I. Age- and gender-specific prevalence. *Journal of Child Psychology and Psychiatry, 34,* 851–867.

Cooper, P. J., & Stein, A. (1992). *Feeding problems and eating disorders in children and adolescents*. Switzerland: Harwood Academic Publishers.

Faber, A., & Mazlish, E. (1991). *How to talk so children will listen & listen so children will talk*. New York: Avon.

Frick, P. J., & Jackson, Y. K. (1993). Family functioning and childhood antisocial behavior: Yet another reinterpretation. *Journal of Clinical Child Psychology, 22,* 410–419.

Gorey, K. M., & Leslie, D. R. (1997). The prevalence of child sexual abuse: Integrative review adjustment for potential response and measurement biases. *Child Abuse and Neglect, 21*(4), 391–399.

Gutierres, S. E., & Todd, M. (1997). The impact of childhood abuse on treatment outcomes in substance users. *Professional Psychology, Research and Practice, 28*(4), 345–355.

Hartgers, C., & Langeland, W. (1998). Child sexual and physical abuse and alcoholism: a review. *Journal of Studies on Alcohol, 59*(3), 336–349.

Heatherington, E. M., & Parks, R. D. (1999). *Child psychology: A contemporary viewpoint*. Boston: McGraw-Hill.

Hoffman, L. W. (1989). Effects of maternal employment in the two-parent family. *American Psychologist, 44*(2), 283–292.

Hoffman, L. W. (1963). Mother's enjoyment of work and effects on the child. In F. I. Nye & L. W. Hoffman (Eds.), *The employed mother in America*. Skokie, IL: Rand McNally.

Inglehart, R. (1990). *Culture shift in advanced industrial society*. Princeton, NJ: Princeton University Press.

Jaffe, P. G., Suderman, M., & Reitzel, D. (1992). Child witnesses of marital violence. In R. T. Ammerman & M. Hersen (Eds.), *Assessment of family violence: A clinical and legal sourcebook* (pp. 313–331). New York: Wiley.

Jouriles, E. N., Barling, J., & O'Leary, K. D. (1987). Predicting child behavior problems in maritally violent families. *Journal of Abnormal Psychology, 15,* 165–173.

Jouriles, E. N., Norwood, W. D., McDonald, R., Vincent, J. P., & Mahoney, A. (1996). Physical violence and other forms of marital aggression: Links with children's behavior problems. *Journal of Family Therapy, 10*(2), 223–234.

Kantor, D., & Lehr, W. (1975). *Inside the family*. San Francisco: Josey-Bass.

Karpowitz, D. H. (1980). A conceptualization of the American family. In M. J. Fine (Ed.), *Handbook on parent education*. New York: Academic Press.

Kazdin, A. (1987). Treatment of antisocial behavior in children: Current status and future directions. *Psychological Bulletin, 102,* 187–203.

Lamb, M. (Ed.) (1996). *The role of the father in child development.* New York: John Wiley and Sons.

Lauer, R. H., & Lauer, J. C. (1997). *Marriage & family: The quest for intimacy* (3rd ed.). Madison, WI: Brown & Benchmark.

Lindahl, K. M. (1998). Family process variables and children's disruptive behavior problems. *Journal of Family Psychology, 12*(3), 420–436.

McDonald, R., & Jouriles, E. N. (1991). Marital aggression and child behavior problems: Research findings, mechanisms, and intervention strategies. *The Behavior Therapist, 14,* 189–192.

Melton, G. B. (1998). Personal communication.

Meyerhoff, M. K., & White, B. L. (1986). Making the grade as parents. *Psychology Today, 20*(9), 42–45.

Myers, D. G., & Diener, E. (1995). Who is happy? *Psychological Science, 6*(1), 10–19.

Osofsky, J. D. (1997). Community-based approaches to violence prevention. *Journal of Developmental and Behavioral Pediatrics, 18*(6), 405–407.

Patterson, G. R. (1982). *Coercive family process.* Eugene, OR: Castalia.

Patterson, G. R., & Dishion, T. J. (1985). Contributions of families and peers to delinquency. *Criminology, 23,* 63–79.

Senchak, M., Leonard, K. E., Greene, B. W., & Carroll, A. (1995). Comparisons of adult children of alcoholic, divorced, and control parents in four outcome domains. *Psychology of Addictive Behaviors, 9*(3), 147–156.

Straus, M. A., & Gelles, R. J. (1986). Societal change and change in family violence from 1975 to 1985 as revealed by two national surveys. *Journal of Marriage & the Family, 48*(3), 465–479.

Straus, M. A., & Gelles, R. J. (1990). *Physical violence in American families: Risk factors and adaptations to violence in 8,145 families.* New Brunswick, NJ: Transaction.

Walsh, F. (Ed.) (1982, 1993). *Normal family processes.* New York: Guilford

CHAPTER 2

Gender Issues in Parenting: Parenting Teenage Girls

Lauren Ayers

Research Associates, Albany, New York

INTRODUCTION

In a new study of adolescent females, girls worry much more than their mothers about their future as women. They are anxious about financial security, abusive relationships, unemployment, college acceptance, and general life success in the future (Moore, 1999). How could this be so? After so much effort to produce healthy daughters, after a feminist revolution, and after pages of antidiscrimination laws, how is it that girls feel so fragile?

For parents and professionals concerned about girls, there is limited wisdom available in the form of parenting programs. This chapter is a review of current guidance materials and should be of help to those interested in finding their way through the maze of parenting literature. The findings, suggestions, and concepts presented can be infused in different ways into programs for parents of teenage girls.

Increases in premature parenting, rape, sexually transmitted disease, and other problems of female adolescence have led to the development of parenting programs that have paradoxically underscored girls' fragility without finding ways to strengthen young women. The popular parenting book *Reviving Ophelia* (Pipher, 1994) suggests that, following the metaphor of the Shakespearean figure who drowned herself out of love for the mad Hamlet, girls today need to be saved from their own self destructiveness, perhaps by more efficient parents.

The following presentation, as indicated, can serve as a resource for those concerned about the development of teenage girls and the crucial role that parents can play in their lives.

INFORMATION ON TEENAGE GIRLS

Although there are data on the status of teen girls in today's culture, there is comparatively little analytic material to explain the unique character of female development. Exceptions to this include the longitudinal research by Gilligan and colleagues at Harvard (Brown & Gilligan, 1992; Gilligan, 1982; Gilligan, Lons, & Hammer, 1989; Gilligan, Rogers, & Tolman, 1991), which looks at how girls relate and how that relating changes during adolescence. Gilligan finds that girls come up against what she calls the "stone wall" of Western culture when they reach puberty, when they must choose between spontaneous emotional expression and group acceptance.

A second source of research on girls, the American Association of University Women's Research Projects, including the Landmark Research Project (American Association of University Women, 1991, 1992, 1993) and the Positive School Climate Series (American Association of University Women, 1995, 1996a, 1996b, 1998a, 1998b), have included studies and summaries which extensively explore the status of girls in today's culture and do so in the critical arena of education.

As girls reach adolescence, they experience a significantly greater drop in self-esteem than boys do, and girls are systematically discouraged from entering math and science careers. The overall conclusion of the nationwide poll of students in grades K–12 in *Shortchanging Girls, Shortchanging America* (American Association of University Women, 1991) is that American girls receive an education inferior to that of boys throughout the first 13 years of school. In schools, 85% of girls experience intimating sexual harassment and poor preparation in technology.

Clear information on adolescent girls is relatively hard to find, except from commercial sources like Youth Intelligence, a New York consulting firm, which gathers information for companies such as Sprint, Polo Jeans, and Coca-Cola on what is popular in the teen market. With revenues of

$1.5 billion last year, the group publishes the Cassandra Report, which tracks teen trends through street interviews and focus groups and reports to the industry, in order to build sales to teens (Furchgott, 1999).

THE STATUS OF PARENTS

Changes in the culture have made parents themselves a more vulnerable group, with less help from the extended family, the courts, religious organizations, and schools. The extended family once served to reinforce parental values, as grandparents, aunts, and uncles could offer nurturing and guidance to girls, but geographical separations, divorce, and other factors have reduced this form of support for families. Although the courts have traditionally supported parental authority and effectiveness, the complexity of modern problems in child development often appears to overwhelm the resources and the wisdom of law enforcement, with problems such as juvenile delinquency, custody/visitation, child support, and child abuse rarely receiving adequate attention.

Good parenting is generated by a host of factors, however, and cannot be imposed from above. Religious institutions and the public school systems have been eclipsed by such influences as television, the Internet, and other sources in transmitting values, many of which reflect the commercial needs of the society rather than cultural norms.

PARENTAL OBJECTIVES

Professionals seem ill at ease with a focus on the unique problems of teen girls and struggle to find equivalent problems in boys. Parents are often disarmed by the admonitions of parenting literature to see the two genders as interchangeable. The result is a good deal of confusion over practical decisions, for example, guidance for the girl who wants to walk home alone from the library late at night. A parent's reaction is likely to involve an awareness of all of the crimes, particularly rape, abduction, and murder, which target young females, and an absence of similar reports of young males. However, the requirements of the age are that parents ignore these distinctions, and the result is often that girls do not receive the protection that they need and are left to fend for themselves. Cultural changes in gender expectations sometimes leave adolescent girls more vulnerable than supported.

With a sensitivity to the cultural prohibition on sexist choices, a girl may deliberately make decisions as though she were a boy, which endanger her while supporting the principle of gender equivalence. Observing her own vulnerabilities may seem like "giving in" to sexist influences. Vietnam-era parents, echoing an earlier generation's demands for "emotional space," can be trapped in their own history, which fails to acknowledge the new world in which girls grow up. This is best illustrated by the current dilemma of college campuses, where the student revolutionaries of 2 decades ago won the right to lives without rules and restrictions, but teenage girls of today live in an unstructured setting where they are easily the target of criminal predators.

Do mothers and fathers parent differently when they raise teen girls, or are they merely different forms of the same thing, a chocolate–vanilla pairing of adult behavior? Men and women have distinctly different communication styles in American culture, with women striving for emotional connection and men working to establish a position of dominance (Tannen, 1990).

The emotional sensitivity of the mother–daughter relationship may reach an exquisitely painful peak during adolescence when a girl's need to establish ties outside the family and a mother's sense of exclusion, betrayal, and loss may produce explosions and, more ominously, estrangement. A father–daughter relationship, more focused on issues of power and control, may become a struggle for dominance. Family dynamics can become triangulated as a girl shifts alliances between parents, sometimes daily, but these tensions usually recede as she approaches maturity.

THOSE WHO HELP PARENTS

The idea of giving advice to parents is not new, but the professional development and marketing of parenting programs are no more than a few decades old. Part of the belief that science can improve all aspects of human life, this movement has become a major industry, and all of the new developments in electronics have come to be incorporated in it.

Some of the approaches reflect the needs or ambitions of those more focused on advancing their own gain rather than the welfare of girls. When the **Girlz World!** Netlink and the **HipMama Magazine Homepage** (http://www.hipmama.com), an alternative parenting magazine, offer information about the anti-welfare reform protests, this seems like an attempt to involve girls in activity which benefits others, rather than improving their developmental course.

In a far more sinister vein, an enormous wealth of information is available on teenage girls in the area of pornography. A recent Internet search using major search engines turned up 2800 references on parenting teenage girls and over *four million* references that offered pornographic material on teen girls, much of it of the rawest kind.

MODERN PARENTING PROGRAMS

Traditional parenting programs are still available to parents, but, because most consumers are women, and teenage girls have a larger range of pitfalls than boys, these materials tend to be about teenage girls and be read by women. An example of this type of program is the **Positive Parent Workshops** offered by Denver's Family Advocacy, Care, Education, Support Inc. (http://www.health.aclin.org/cinch/profiles/00034.htm), which teach parents new skills and confidence.

In a similar vein, **Partners in Parenting** (http://health.aclin.org/cinch/profiles/00123.htm) aims at reducing risky behaviors in female adolescence by mobilizing community support through the use of public awareness campaigns, speakers, education exhibits, newsletters, etc. The difficulty with this type of program is the same as with many programs, that is, the premise that societal problems develop because of a lack of information and that by providing proper factual information the problem will solve itself. In a media-soaked culture, elemental information is disseminated quickly. Most parents know, for example, that to prevent teen pregnancy requires that a girl be given a great deal of adult supervision and companionship and that she become involved in social activities (other than romance) during the teen years. However, both of these require a good deal of adult time, which a parent may be unable or unwilling to extend to a girl. The peer connection facilitates the building of rapport, but it makes the help given only as good as the particular skill of the available volunteer.

Long-standing programs seem to have an established utility, at least for certain types of problems or situations. **Tough Love** (York & Wachtel, 1983), a self-help program for parents dealing with troublesome teenage behavior, consists of support groups for parents and provides a process for change that parents can use as a guide.

There has been considerable controversy over the harsh responses recommended by the standard group to severe teen misbehavior and over the AA format that the meetings resemble, although, for truly severe behavior problems, the alternatives to the tough love approach may be much worse and disastrous for a teen in trouble.

For very severe adolescent behavior problems, programs such as **Street Law, Inc.** (http://www.streetlaw.org/comm.html) work to prevent legal violations as well as to help young people deal positively with the law. As part of the Street Law program, the derivative **Save Our Streets** and **Street Law Leadership Camp** projects teach conflict resolution skills for community violence and help young people to stop peer problems from coming before the courts as legal violations. At the very least, programs such as these keep kids "off the streets," and they are likely to put kids into contact with good role models in the form of law enforcement personnel, social workers, and others who can establish caring relationships and offer good guidance.

The great majority of parenting programs currently available are problem focused and are directed toward preventing or dealing with specific problems of female adolescence. The **Pregnant and Parenting Teen Program** (http://www.bakersfield.org/ydc/girls.html), for example, strives to help parents help a pregnant daughter through pregnancy and parenthood by mobilizing the family's energy and reducing the stigma of extramarital pregnancy.

The **Go Girls** (http://www.health.aclin.org/cinch/profiles/00881.htm) program in Aurora, Colorado, a pregnancy prevention program, offers "healthy alternatives" for teen girls, including trips, sports, food fights, fashion tips, luncheons, and dance theater, on the assumption that girls become prematurely pregnant when sex is used recreationally.

GOVERNMENT-BASED PROGRAMS

In his 1995 State of the Union Address, President William Clinton called for a national campaign to address the issue of teenage pregnancy and charged the Department of Health and Human Services with developing appropriate programs and services.

The late-20th-century trend for governmental responsibility for parenting failures has produced programs based on the premise that information and education can control teen behavior and offset inadequate parenting.

The impetus to develop such initiatives has reached all levels of government, and the political popularity of creating social programs to help youth, through substitute parenting, has a great deal of public support. At a state and local level, such activities can be funded from federal mandates, making them more attractive.

Most state agencies have information networks that provide home-grown information and tie into wider databases and services on the Web. **Arkansas's Parent's Web** (http://www.ark.org/kidz/parents.html) is an example of this type of service, offering links to commercial information sources about child care, education, and children's health care.

The appeal of programs available through the Internet is that they can reach a wide geographical area, they can be constantly updated, and they take advantage of popular trends in computer usage. They link to other information sources, saving public funds, and require little overhead, but they are limited to the computer savvy and they assume that information changes behavior without human contact.

To provide an interpersonal connection, some communities have emphasized the development of street programs that aim to bring teenagers into contact with helpful and guiding individuals. The New York City Community Action Program is a broad-based service network that builds on neighborhood development areas in 44 New York City communities and tries to build a web of services which will function in place of missing parental guidance. The program includes such established entities as the **Crown Heights Youth Collective, Inc.** (http://www.ci.nyc.ny.us/nyclink/html/cap.html), a program designed to provide comprehensive crime and violence protection to young people.

GIRL-FOCUSED PROGRAMS

Programs aimed directly at teen girls, distributed directly through schools and mailings, are used by women's colleges to recruit girls or to remediate deficiencies that might later handicap a girl's educational strivings. These programs include a focus on an array of skill areas, including college-level writing, ethnic awareness teaching, leadership skills, and general academic preparedness. Some substitute parenting programs are more generic and offer a broader life-skills curriculum to girls.

Web sites continue to be the most popular form of information exchange, with communications aimed at parents and at girls separately. Perhaps because of the novelty of this form of communication, designers of *in loco parentis* programs for girls see the Web as a communication form that girls are more likely to utilize, making them more reachable. Such programs as the **Baby Think It Over** Web page (http://btio.com), a parenthood simulation, pregnancy prevention program, **Know the Rules** (http://www.missingkids.com/html/ncmec_default_know_the_rules_main.html), a safety instruction program, and **McKenzie and Co.** (http://family.go.com/Categories/Computing/Features/family_0202_01_01/f...famp020201_fpmcken), a video game that offers role playing in a high school social context, attempt to work directly with adolescent girls.

TRADITIONAL PARENTING PROGRAMS

School-based programs such as **STEP Teen,** part of the Systematic Training for Effective Parenting of Teens series (Dinkmeyer & McKay, 1982), a 12-week program for parents that uses a group discussion format to improve parent–teen relations, produce more responsible teen behavior and increase everybody's self-esteem. **Parent Effectiveness Training** (Gordon, 1970) is even older than the STEP programs, and it works to change communication patterns in the home as a way to develop more effective parenting. It is particularly useful in clarifying the complex emotional messages that often complicate problem resolution in the home and reduces communication to its most logical and compassionate form.

When these programs were introduced, they represented a new initiative, in that they were the products of private industry and offered a training sequence to parents. Until this time, parenting information had developed as a by-product of the child guidance movement, which provided more generic information through books and lectures out of an academic context.

Technology has added new dimensions to these programs. **The Interaction Network for Children and Families** (http://www.positive parenting.com/commong.html), for example, provides courses in a number of cities that parents and teens attend together for 2.5-hr sessions over 6 weeks. Advances in electronic media also allow wider distribution of visual material, reflected in **Whole Persons Associates** (http://www. wholeperson.com/wpa/ghb/fi/fi.htm), which has developed a video program for parenting adolescents. The videos cover an hour of practical parenting tips from family therapists and include discussion guides and worksheets. Newer parenting programs concentrate on sound bites and catchy phrases and promise to make parenting easier and quicker, with little exploration of the motivations and complexities of female adolescence.

In marked contrast to traditional programs are the promotional/guidance overtures to girls: **Don't Be a Ditz, Get Rid of Your Zits** (http://www.girlzone.com/html_98-07/insideout.html), for example, is a production of the e-zine **Girl Zone,** and **Girl Talk** (http://www.playtextampons.com/girltalkhtm) by Playtex gives advice directly to girls. Less commercially motivated, **Girls Incorporated** provides research-based education programs in math and science education, pregnancy prevention, media literacy, adolescent health, substance abuse, and sports participation. The **Dare to Dream Program** (http://www.daretodream. org/mentors.htm) is a mentoring program for girls that uses adult female models to help girls develop productive approaches to living. **Girls Count** (httpwww.girlscount.org/programs.html) helps adults develop the skills needed for helping girls, and it does so in a training format, with print and other components.

Not-for-profit agencies and political organizations are also involved in the offerings of parent substitute materials, often to gain public service credits. Planned Parenthood, the March of Dimes, and the American Medical Association all offer net links for girls on issues such as sexual activity, pregnancy, and body health.

The Internet has changed American life in many ways, and parenting programs reflect this change. An example of the resources now available to parents through this source is the **Mining Company Guide to Parenting of Adolescents** (http://parentingteens.miningcocom), which offers parents links to Web sites that cover virtually every concern a parent could have in raising a teenage girl. Subjects such as getting into college, depression, drug use, eating disorders, HIV/AIDS, and a mass of other topics are listed with a series of Web sites for each.

Higher-income, better-educated parents may have access to electronic parenting programs, but the sparseness of screen solutions and the absence of human contact may indicate more packaging than content.

Human contact is available through chat lines on the Internet. **Moms Online** (http://www.momsonline.com), offers bulletin boards, real-time chat connections, advice columns, first person stories, and advice sections. Harder to find are detailed discussions of parenting, although **Parenting Today's Teen** (http://www.parentingteens.com/GerlachN96.html) is an example of an online magazine that covers subjects in depth. In dealing with the construction of stepfamilies, for example, the site offers many connections and links that cover specific problems. The orientation is that of pop psychology, with lots of "inner child" references, but the format is a new one for parents.

This same source offers detailed material on raising teen girls, some of it geared to teen girl readers themselves. It often seems as though girls are being instructed to raise themselves on the Internet, which they may be if there is a nonfunctional parent in the home.

RELIGIOUS PROGRAMS

With the resurgence of religious movements at the end of the 20th century has come the introduction of parenting programs based on spiritual approaches. The programs of religious groups reflect the diversity of religious belief in the advice they offer parents. Some of these organizations concentrate on the totality of a youth's life and attempt to provide educational, social, emotional, and spiritual support to young people as an act in keeping with their religious values. Others are more directly evangelical in nature and aim primarily at religious conversion or belief intensification with problem solving of teen issues as a means to this end. These programs are aimed primarily at young people, not at parents, and serve in place of parents in offering guidance and a good deal of emotional interaction as well.

An example of this type of program is the **Lutheran Ministries of Florida** (http//www.naples.net/social.db.37.htm), which aims at helping families with problem teens. Situated in Collier County, Florida, the organization offers various programs to families in crisis, including parenting groups, a mediation service for conflicts between parents and teens, and combined teen/parent groups. It also operates an adolescent runaway shelter for young people.

Crisis services are often a part of religious-based parenting programs, perhaps because pastoral counseling can be easily overwhelmed by the needs of families in crisis. **Denver Area Youth for Christ** (http://www.webcreations.com/denveryfc/callus.htm) ministers to at-risk youth, including kids in danger of committing a crime, becoming pregnant, committing suicide, or running away from home.

Some of the religious-based parenting services are clearly evangelical in focus, and they aim to provide help as a means of recruiting followers. **The Caring Touch** (Heartlight Magazine, 1999), for example, an off-shoot of the Heartlight Magazine and the Westover Hills Church of

Christ, advises parents that they need to look to religious guidance in finding answers to parenting problems.

NEED FOR COMMUNITY FOUNDATION OF PARENTING

What is the impact of parenting programs on raising teenage girls? Parenting programs exist to help parents who perceive that their daughters are not doing well, and so parents, for the most part, select themselves to participate in training programs. However, if the experience of the public schools is any index of parenting behavior, then it is those parents who are most in need of help who avoid those services that might be most useful.

Does this apply to programs aimed directly at teen girls, those which serve *in loco parentis*? Program outcomes probably depend on the changes in environment and living arrangements that such programs bring to a girl's life. There is an enormous difference, for example, between a program that provides a weekly hour of group discussion to girls involved with drugs and a residential treatment program that relocates a girl to a new school and community.

A second factor in program success is the opportunity for a girl to develop a caring, continuous relationship with adult caregivers in any helping program. These adults often replace parents and can counteract the negative or absent influences that shape a girl's behavior and choices. What shapes parents' behavior and turns a mother or father's focus to a girl and her needs? The most powerful forces are those embedded in the community, which exert their influence through the normal channels of social influence. The institutions of communities, including extended family networks, schools, neighborhood groups, commercial businesses, voluntary organizations, and religious centers, all have a powerful effect in supporting effective parenting behavior. When changes in a parent's life cause disruptions in community belonging, this can have profound implications for a girls' development, but community influences have the potential for buffering these difficulties.

Girls whose parents divorce and remarry, for example, and who experience both a school and a residence change are at increased risk, as family tensions lead to a girl's withdrawal from participation in a changed family life. When parents divorce and remarry, but a girl remains in the same school and house, then all of the other adults who have participated in peopling her life, and exerting their values, continue to do so and can help to offset the dilution of the family's influences. However, when these wider adult influences are also removed, most girls find it extremely difficult to recreate a community network for themselves at the same time that they are trying to find a new place in a changed family.

In the worst case, the result can be a rebellious, angry teen girl who sleeps first at friends' houses to avoid home, and then in parked cars, eventually sliding into prostitution and victimhood, which is more directly the result of a loss of community than a loss of family. Economic pressure makes it difficult for parents to draw on a surrounding community for support. The final report of the National Commission on Children, *Beyond Rhetoric* (National Commission on Children, 1991a), reports that more than sixteen million children, or 25% of all American children, lived with only one parent in 1989, about twice as many as in 1970. Often these families are poor, which further isolates them from community help. How do these parents connect to the broader community around them, and how are they received? Parents who struggle for income often have no time to participate in community organizations, and may be so burdened with work and household maintenance chores that this participation is seen as a luxury that they cannot afford.

Geographic change is often overlooked as having lasting psychological implications for parenting success. Population mobility has been a powerful social force over the past decades because it has become commonplace for parents to leave a community and settle in a new one, sometimes repeatedly. The need to grow new emotional relationships at short intervals may prevent the development of attachment of sufficient depth to direct a girl's behavioral choices, forcing her to cast about for an emotional anchor. Equally potent is the loss of relatives who may have shored up a troubled parent's efforts to raise a girl: the grandmother whose house is always open, the uncle who coaches soccer at school, or the cousin who operates a local business near the school. Genetic connections give a girl a sense of belonging and may help her respond to parental direction in a fruitful manner.

A mother's employment and time away from home become more significant with a change in community because there is less support for a girl on her own in these circumstances. When a family lives in a community that has a strong sense of integration, a working mother can draw on many sources of known support in raising a daughter, including familiar teachers at school, neighbors, and other community figures. More importantly, a girl feels less abandoned since she can also depend on these people who are more likely to be familiar with her circumstances. However, a move to a new locale obliterates all of these touchstones and may give a girl a sense of free-falling. Even when there are caring people, they are not familiar enough with a girl's life for her to readily turn to them.

Girls themselves have difficulty sorting out the elements of a new community of peers, and the risks and dangers therein. Good judgment is difficult in a new town, with a new peer group, and when girls enter a new middle school or high school it may be easier to connect with the fringe elements of the school and more difficult to become accepted by the well-adjusted kids. Although substance abuse is a complex and many-faceted problem, it is probably best considered in a social context, and a girl without roots is more vulnerable to unhealthy behaviors which gain her peer acceptance.

Perhaps most critical is the effect on a girl's overall life satisfaction, her happiness. When community ties are lost and a girl is isolated without the power to regenerate the setting she needs to thrive, the situation can become critical. The rate of adolescent suicide doubled in the 1960s and 1970s, and by 1986 it had increased another 30%. Suicide is the second cause of death among adolescents, following accidents (which may or may not represent a disregard for one's own life). The rate of misery in adolescence is high, with eight times as many young people attempting suicide as those who complete the act (National Commission on Children, 1991b).

COMPONENTS OF A SUCCESSFUL PARENTING PROGRAM

The major shortcoming of most current parenting programs is that they are parentcentric, in that they represent a parent's earlier relationship with a daughter, when she was dependent on the adult for solutions to life's challenges. However, this arrangement changes with puberty, and parents are relegated to the role of bystanders. At this time, life's problems must be solved by a girl, with data that she, rather than her parents, has gathered. Although most parents pay lip service to this objective, few find it easy to enact.

Building a stronger family is a parent's goal at a time when most adolescent girls have little interest in family life. They have typically spent the first 12 years of life trying to understand parents, and generally lose interest by puberty, or rather their interest has been transferred to the far more intriguing workings of their peers. So when parents set out to try to build peaceful, close relationships with girls, they are generally acting out of their own need, rather than as part of a joint wish for such arrangements.

Many parenting programs are aimed at helping adults win conflicts with girls, through conversation, sensitive listening, discipline, or education. Implicit in many parenting programs is that they will show parents how to win the adult–adolescent war. However, when adults win, girls lose, and when adults lose, girls lose as well, because the fundamental realignment in the relationship must be recognized in the solutions to any problems. This is why programs like Outward Bound are generally successful, because they throw a girl on her own resources, where the power struggle is with herself, rather than with the adults in her life.

The parent–daughter relationship changes at puberty because of something that parents notice, but try to hide from a girl, namely, that she has become more powerful than they are. At 13, a girl can no longer be physically overpowered, restricted to the house, made to eat, sleep, study, or go to school, although in earlier years, she could have been. It is not only that girls develop adult bodies in these years, but they are far more daring and worldly, and their social connections give them many more options outside the home.

Parents, alarmed by what seems to be physical growth without parallel growth in maturity and judgment, suffer a good deal of anguish in these years, often more than the situation seems to warrant. The distraught character of this period may have more to do with adult life changes, middle age, than with the challenge that teens present.

The great difficulty parents find in dealing with a daughter's adolescence is changing their view of the family to one that includes all members as equals. Parents see their youngsters as continuing through childhood endlessly and parental behavior often reflects this. This is perhaps why parents have such difficulty with a teen girl's all-knowing attitude, need for privacy, relationships with the opposite sex, time with friends, emotional swings, lack of respect (which in an adult/adult relationship would be called disagreement), challenging rules, and different values. Changes in a girl's subordinate position make all of these areas seem out of control to a parent.

What if girls were writing the parenting programs? Most girls have little interest in their parents' values, goals, and experiences, as they plan to redefine the world according to their own preferences, which they share if asked. How much time does anyone spend exploring their parents' philosophy of childrearing? By the time girls reach adolescence, parents are peripheral in their thinking, unless parents are very bad, for other influences have begun to dominate a girl's life.

There is a human time line that girls follow in their growth and development, and by the time girls are 13, the major shaping by parents has been completed and a girl is less open to family influences. The parents who decide to attend church or teach a sport when a girl is 13 will have far less impact than they would have had when she is 7.

A girl is shaped by the culture she lives in, including the community, neighborhood, television, peers, and other factors. American girls spend an average of 21 hours a week watching television, and far less time in thoughtful conversation with parents. The influence of her family involves more than parents, as brothers and sisters, particularly if they are older, can have a large impact.

Too many parenting programs are built on winning the parent–daughter power struggle by teaching parents techniques and strategies, an interesting experience for the generation that learned to mistrust anyone over 30. The strategies taught often involve sarcastic or clever remarks, keeping a girl off balance so that she doesn't become arrogant or overpowering or "push a parent's buttons." However, if we saw a daughter as a future world leader who might one day save the human race from disease, warfare, and poverty, parenting programs might instead develop approaches that would deliberately teach girls to be more powerful and more productive.

A successful parenting program needs to involve both teen girls and adults because girls need to change behavior for parenting to succeed. What are the elements of such a program? They involve the teaching of four attitudes, or habits of thought, which can be brought out in any exploration of everyday problems or major crises with girls (Ayers, 1994). When these attitudes are repeated in many situations, and a variety of contexts, a girl will begin to internalize them and apply them automatically. In teaching these to a girl, a parent internalizes these four constructs as well, which shapes adult behavior in a productive manner.

1. *Focus on herself.* In parenting teen girls, it is easy to become involved in power struggles that energize a girl's creativity and intelligence in defeating or outwitting parents. The format of this type of battle generally follows a predictable sequence: A parent makes rules, a girl breaks rules, and a parent reacts. Both parent and daughter look at all problems defensively, in terms of innocence and blame, with self-righteousness abounding. The difficulty with this situation is that a girl becomes preoc-

cupied with parental disapproval and her own anger and defensiveness, and she fails to make independent judgments on her own behalf.

The long-term effects of power struggles are to divert a girl's attention from the issues important to her development and well-being. As an adolescent, her attention needs to be upon those things that have long-term consequences, the decisions that she makes about her future, and how to use her time and her talents. She can use her abilities in outwitting a parent, so that she is able to score overt or sneaky victories in fights, but this does little to pave the way to a fulfilling adulthood.

A focus on herself, in contrast, continually brings a girl back to the center of her life's course, which is her own decision making for herself. It forces her to examine what is beneficial to her, what is best for achieving her dreams, and what fits with her personality, preferences, and competencies. Girls rarely fight with parents over substantive issues, such as career choices; rather, the struggles are over household irritations, such as messy rooms, irregular hours, discourteous behavior, and poor study habits. A strong parenting program needs to return the focus of these problems to developing a girl's ability to make sound choices for herself rather than listening to a parent's directives.

Perhaps the most graphic illustration of the need to control one's focus is the case of a teenage girl who had recently gotten her driver's license and had constant quarrels with her parents over the use of the car, which she drove too fast and never cleaned. One evening in the midst of an uncontrolled argument, she grabbed the keys, jumped in the car, and floored the accelerator while screaming insults out the window at her parents. She hit a large tree in a head-on crash that left her with lifelong facial scars. Maintaining a focus on her needs and goals in the teen years is essential to a girl's welfare and her future.

2. *Raise her self expectations.* Parenting programs aimed at adolescent girls generally present the image of a girl as a vulnerable person apt to fall into mischief or disaster. Girls are seen as high risk because of the unique pitfalls of their gender—pregnancy, abortion, premature parenting, anorexia, bulimia, rape, etc.—and these are problems powerful enough to cause parents serious life disruptions.

The difficulty with this view of girls is that to see them as potential problems not only is discouraging for girls, but also is discouraging for the wider community, as this group is then seen as a drain on the community's resources rather than as a source of strength. Historically, young females have been the mainstay of American culture, and they have been essential in every advance of the society. In the movement westward, the settling of the great plains, and the continental expansion of the new nation, it was teen girls who formed the backbone of the drive westward and the communities that emerged.

However, the place of young females is very different in today's culture. They have become a marketing target, not only as a large potential consumer market, but as the object of predatory gratification. The culture seems to have little use for girls as intelligent, energetic, principled human beings and so the problems described above sink girls, because the society can find no better way to integrate them.

In response to the disparity between males and females in math and science education, for example, programs have emerged to draw females in, but the emphasis on these has been the need for fairness, not the need for a feminine perspective in these areas. The impetus is not to employ the talents of females in service of the culture and community, but rather to provide equal rights to all. This accomplished, a self-satisfied American society apparently has little other use for young female human beings.

To a girl, these messages are denigrating, and few girls see themselves as essential to the broader society. The result is that they often act as though they were disposable, not as though they saw themselves as indispensable to the nation's future. On a practical level, this perspective produces a very different conclusion for a youngster making choices. The decision to engage in risky sexual behavior can be based on whether it will upset parents and peers, or it can be based on discarding the alternatives for an exhilarating future. However, if society has little interest in the much needed contributions a girl might make, then parenthood may not seem like a bad choice.

As the culture changes its estimate of the value and utility of its young female population, girls will raise their self-expectations. What is needed is a great debate over the value of girls to the culture. Are they frivolous accessories to the harder necessities provided by other groups, or are they critical to cultural progress?

3. *Develop judgment.* The ability to make choices with sound reasoning, strong self-knowledge, and an appropriate set of values takes many years to grow. It requires continual experimentation, trial and error, and an assessment of the success of one's choices. A parent's job is to help a girl decide when and how to experiment and to evaluate the results of her trials, with errors that are hopefully not too lasting in their consequences.

This can be a breathtaking experience as a parent watches from the sidelines while a girl learns all those things that a parent already knows. However, life skills require learning anew in each generation, and a youngster benefits from having a steady hand to be able to see the causative factors that make up experience. A parent needs to help a girl choose those experiences which are good experiments and rule out the small number which are not. To experiment with drinking while driving, or with keeping a suicidal friend's secrets, can have dangerous and far-reaching consequences, whereas to experiment with studying for a test, skipping breakfast, and leaving a room messy do not.

Adolescence must be a time of experimentation, for it is during this period that a girl has loving helpers who can rescue her when her experiments go awry. In adulthood, the effects of trial and error learning, for example, in choosing a marital partner or in deciding to have a child, are far too profound for a woman to develop her judgment skills at this late date. Girls who fail to experiment enough in youth may feel compelled to do so as adults, thus prolonging dependency and short-circuiting a healthy life.

Helping a girl to experiment puts the energy of parenting into teaching instead of protecting and changes the information that parents need to have. Instead of offering parents and girls all of the data on risks to girls, the focus of parenting programs in this orientation then becomes teaching strategies for reaching girls in ways that develop their judgment. Power struggles are less central in this approach, since both parent and daughter are on the same side, working for a girl's safety and fulfillment.

In the protecting scene, a parent's job is to keep a girl safe and to ensure her future, and a girl is the major source of resistance or the obstacle. This approach generates the struggle between a parent who wants to protect a girl, and a girl who wants to have a life. A parental teacher, however, struggles for whatever it is that a girl wants and helps her to use her experiences to develop her talents and the abilities necessary to reach her goals, the idea being that these will transfer to new ambitions as she matures.

How can parents help to develop a girl's judgment? Remembering that pride of authorship plays a critical role in adolescent behavior changes, it is important to develop critical thinking in a girl, so that she arrives at her own, logical conclusions. How can parents clear up the messy thinking so characteristic of the young? The following can help:

1. *Be quiet.* Listen attentively to what she says. Don't argue or point out the flaws in judgment. Make eye contact. Nod occasionally. Don't make faces. Let her listen critically to her own voice, undistracted by yours. When she says: "This is stupid We have math

homework every night and the teacher is really dumb. She doesn't know what she's doing. And she hates me. That's why she's always picking on me for not getting my work done." Don't point out the obvious. Unless she is seriously impaired, she hears what you hear, and it sounds just as foolish, but *don't point it out to her*. Let her notice for herself.

2. *Ask questions rather than giving opinions.* Questions remain in thinking longer than declarative statements, and stir less defensiveness. Thus, "That skirt is much too short!" becomes, "Do you think that skirt is the right length for school?"

3. *Act like you like her and that you generally approve of her.* Smile at her. Nod positively. You don't have to feel it to communicate it. When you have to disagree or correct, do it gently. Say it with love. Be encouraging and optimistic about her future. Downplay her mistakes. Enlarge on her achievements, no matter how small. Give her hope in herself.

4. *When you have to put the brakes on her, do it clearly and forcefully and don't back down.* Make sure that you can win in those very few instances where you truly must. Don't tell her she can't drive the car if you know she has an extra set of keys somewhere. Be loving and kind but don't give an inch, and remind her that you care about her more than anybody on earth. Fight for what's good for her and make sure that you both win.

Developing judgment also requires that a parent work to strengthen a girl, rather than comfort her when she encounters difficulties. This is not to suggest that a parent abandon sympathy and compassion, but rather that a parent raise her expectations of a girl and see her as the first line of response to challenges. A parent here steps back, as an observer, and lets a girl attack a problem, offering encouragement and an occasional suggestion when asked, but remaining outside the fray. The conditioned response of comforting a helpless and confused child is avoided, and a parent sees a girl as an adult ready to solve her own problems.

4. **Find the good in her.** Adolescent girls rely on adults for an honest evaluation of themselves. Even with all of the argument and challenge, teenage girls still look to the adults around them to assess their advancement to adulthood. The trials and disappointments of this period, however, can easily lead to frayed tempers and gloomy predictions of a girl's future. Self-fulfilling prophecies operate for girls in trouble, and can lead to a girl's abandoning her dreams out of a sense of hopelessness.

A parenting program that teaches parents to have relentless optimism for a girl's future offers a powerful message because girls cannot find this encouragement in the culture, and they are are often discouraged in looking at themselves in their progression to adulthood. Because the culture generally skips childhood with girls, and moves them from childhood to adulthood, girls are apt to judge themselves as either successful adults or foolish children, with no gray areas, and no adequate time for development. It helps to reassure a girl that youth is not a failure, and that all human beings must traverse the long learning period of adolescence.

It also helps to soften the harsh judgments that girls sometimes make of themselves, so that they give themselves enough leeway to learn from errors, and reason through to more effective choices. This will require a similar softening of the way that parents evaluate themselves.

Currently, parents are seen as responsible for how girls turn out, and it is primarily mothers that bear the blame for a girl's failures. However, a parent does not control all of the factors which influence a girl, and it is wise to forestall judgments about a girl's success until she reaches 30, and all parental influences have had an opportunity to exert themselves. Conclusions about a girl's development before that time are apt to be too shortsighted and parent focused, and they may easily overlook all of the influences outside the family that have so strong an effect on a girl's well-being.

However, girls themselves need a much more solid source of guidance than parents are often able to exert. We need to find ways to bind parents into the community of residence so that all of the positive parental exertions are strengthened. The culture itself too easily becomes a source of undermining in childrearing, and rather than merely neutralizing it, we need to structure it to serve as a foundation that supports parental initiatives with teenage girls.

SUMMARY AND CONCLUSIONS

This chapter has attempted to highlight issues related to the development of teenage girls and the challenge faced by their parents. A number of important resources have been identified, along with components of effective parenting programs for teen girls.

Parent educators interested in supporting parents of adolescent girls should find useful resources within this chapter. It is recognized that each program offered to parents will have its own context and agenda; for example, a program might be offered parents of inner city teenage girls with a strong focus on pregnancy prevention and personal goal setting. Other programs will be provided to other parent/teen populations in different contexts. Parent educators will need to organize their programs accordingly, integrating literature, concepts, and skills, so that they are appropriate for the target population.

REFERENCES

American Association of University Women (1991). *Shortchanging girls, shortchanging America.* Washington, DC: AAUW.

American Association of University Women (1992). *The AAUW report: How schools shortchange girls.* Washington, DC: AAUW.

American Association of University Women (1993). *Hostile hallways: The AAUW survey on sexual harassment in America's schools.* Washington, DC: AAUW.

American Association of University Women (1995). *Growing smart: What's working for girls in school.* Washington, DC: AAUW.

American Association of University Women (1996a). *The influence of school climate on gender differences in the achievement and engagement of adolescents.* Washington, DC: AAUW.

American Association of University Women (1996b). *Girls in the middle: Working to succeed in school.* Washington, DC: AAUW.

American Association of University Women (1998a). *Separated by sex: A critical look at single sex education for girls.* Washington, DC: AAUW.

American Association of University Women (1998b). *Gender gaps: Where schools still fail our children.* Washington, DC: AAUW.

Ayers, L. (1994). *Teenage girls: A parent's survival manual.* New York: Crossroads Publishers.

Brown, L., & Gilligan, C. (1992). *Meeting at the crossroads.* New York: Ballantine Books.

Dinkmeyer, D., & McKay, G. (1982). *The parents handbook: Systematic training for effective parenting.* Circle Pines, Minnesota: American Guidance Service.

Dinkmeyer, D., & McKay, G. (1998). *Step teen—Systematic training for effective parenting revised.* Circle Pines, MN: American Guidance Service.

Furchgott, R. (1999). *On my desk, the cassandra report. The New York Times,* January 10, 2.

Gilligan, C. (1982). *In a different voice: Psychological theory and women's development.* Cambridge: Harvard University Press.

Gilligan, C., Lons, N., & Hammer, T. (1989). *Making connections: The relational worlds of adolescent girls at Emma Willard School.* Troy: Emma Willard School.

Gilligan, C., Rogers, A., & Tolman, D. (1991). *Women, girls & psychotherapy: Reframing resistance.* New York: The Haworth Press.

Gordon, T. (1970). *P.E.T. [parent effectiveness training].* New York: The New American Library.

Heartlink, Inc. (1999). *The caring touch.* Austin: Heartlink, Inc.

Moore, B. Study finds teenage girls worry more than their mothers. *The Daily Gazette,* January 18, 1999, 6.

National Commission on Children (1991a). *Beyond rhetoric: Final report of the National Commission on Children.* Washington, DC: 101st Congress.

National Commission on Children (1991b). *Speaking of kids: A national survey of children and parents.* Washington, DC: 101st Congress.

Pipher, M. (1994). *Reviving Ophelia.* New York: G.P. Putnam.

Tannen, D. (l990). *You just don't understand.* New York: Ballantine Books.

York, P., & Wachtel. (1983). *Toughlove.* New York: Bantam Books.

CHAPTER 3

Teaching About Sexual Diversity: A New Frontier for Parenthood Educators

Donna Swall

Social Worker (retired), Lawrence, Kansas

Forrest Swall

School of Social Welfare (retired), University of Kansas, Lawrence, Kansas

INTRODUCTION

Why should parents be taught about sexual diversity? What and when should parents be taught about sexual diversity? How can resources be made available to parents to assist them in learning about the fact and nor-malcy of sexual diversity? Where can parents of today and tomorrow learn about sexual diversity issues?

Most parents, even before the birth of their child, assume that their child will be a "normal" heterosexual boy or girl. However, for as many as one family in four and one child in ten, this assumption will be incor-rect (PFLAG, 1995). By the time a child and his parents discover the false-ness of this assumption, unnecessary emotional pain and confusion for both the child and his parents will most likely have occurred.

Most often a parent's realization of their child's differing sexual orienta-tion and their child's ability to name their differentness occur at different times in the life of the family. The parents' expectation of their child's heterosexuality will have shaped all of their behavioral interactions with the child. Meanwhile, the child, from an early age will have experienced confusion and discomfort due to the incongruity between his and his parents' expectations (e.g., Anderson's fairy tale of "The Ugly Duckling"). This incongruity will be experienced by the child in most of his other significant relationships such as with siblings, at school with classmates and teachers, at church, with other family members, and in the larger community or wherever the child is.

PURPOSE

The purpose of this chapter is to address the need for including issues concerning sexual diversity in the education of all those who are or will become parenthood educators, whatever their professional discipline. Although sexual diversity can be understood quite broadly, this chapter will concern itself with individuals who are gay and their families. Not to have access to information on sexual diversity as a part of the curriculum is a serious gap in the professional training of parenthood educators. The phenomenon of gayness occurs in as many as one in four families (PFLAG). Thus, it is imperative for educators to know, understand, and teach about sexual diversity issues. Until this begins to happen many children and families will be hurting unnecessarily.

Unfortunately, until the last ten years, accurate information about differing sexual orientations was ignored. Even now few parenthood educators are making use of available information. In a recent study of secondary school health educators "only 46% teach about sexual orientation at all, and 91% of those devote less that two class periods to the topic." As many as 33% of those who make sexual orientation information a part of their teaching were doing so with the attitude "that gay and lesbian rights are a threat to the American family and its values" (Kennedy, 1999). An example of the unavailability of information about sexual diversity in professional literature for parenthood educators as recently as eight years ago is demonstrated in the table of contents and the index of the second volume of this series on parenthood education (Fine, 1991). In the 1995 edition of the Merriam-Webster dictionary—self-described as "the voice of authority"—the concepts of "heterosexism," "transgender," and "transsexual" are not listed. (Merriam-Webster, 1995)

EXTENT OF NEED FOR SEXUALITY
DIVERSITY EDUCATION

The enormity of the need for sexual diversity education to be a part of professional training across the spectrum of training for human services providers has been brought home to us repeatedly in the last five years. The need has become evident to us with our active involvement in PFLAG (Parents, Families and Friends of Lesbians, Gays [Bisexuals and Transgenders]). Beginning in September, 1996, the PFLAG Lawrence-Topeka, Kansas Chapter has presented more than 35 workshops about the unmet needs of sexually diverse school-age children and their families. The workshops have been presented at conferences and as continuing education for school social workers, school psychologists, librarians, teachers, and other public school staff and public health department staff. The workshop participants, human services professionals, come from more than ten midwest states. Presentations have included classes for social work students in the School of Social Welfare at the University of Kansas and the Social Work Department of Washburn University in Topeka.

Every workshop participant's evaluation indicates that this is the first time information about sexual diversity had been presented as part of their graduate professional training or continuing education opportunities. Their written comments address the need for every teacher, administrator, and other staff in the public schools to receive sexual diversity information.

In every workshop discussion, one or more participants has invariably talked about a student in their school who is gay or struggling with his/her sexual orientation or about someone they know who has died from an AIDS-related infection. One college student said he had become estranged from his sister following her coming out to him as lesbian. He said he hadn't stopped loving her but hadn't known how to talk with her and had cut himself off from having any contact with her. He wrote in his class log following the workshop presentation that he had reconnected with his sister and that it felt really great for both of them! The expressed wish of all the people referred to above has been to be able to respond in helpful and supportive ways to students they care about whose sexual orientation is different, regardless of whether they are a friend, teacher, or family member.

Clearly, there has been little or no opportunity for professional educators and human service providers to learn about sexual diversity. Even the concept, "heterosexism" was not included in the vocabulary of the Windows 95 program. We have added it to the spell check in our PC vocabulary!

WHY ISN'T THE ISSUE OF SEXUALITY DIVERSITY INCLUDED IN PARENTHOOD EDUCATION?

There are many reasons professional training of future providers of human services fails to include information about sexual orientation. One clear reason is that the information has not been readily available. A second reason, information that is available has been ignored. A third reason is the homophobia which pervades society. Faculty, as well as parenting educators, are affected by the cultural influences which have made sex education virtually taboo in most of the public schools.

Our society is permeated with homophobia, the irrational fear, dislike, or hatred of lesbians, gays, or bisexuals (see Appendix A). Homophobia manifests itself in varying ways in a person's behavior, including physical and emotional distancing or ignoring kinds of behaviors at one end of a severity scale to verbal abuse and physical attacks that could lead to physical injury or even death at the other end. All of us in America are more or less homophobic, depending on our life experiences and openness to differences. "It is reasonable to expect that just as all persons reared in our culture have internalized some elements of racism, homophobia has been internalized as well" (Mallon, 1998, p. 42). The intensity of homophobia may depend in part on what we have learned about respect for differences in people around us.

Anyone teaching about or advocating for those who are sexually different needs a period of sensitization and introspection, individually or in a group, in order to become aware of where the homophobia lies within him/herself. Mallon points out that "it is imperative that professional social workers challenge their own attitudes and beliefs about sexual orientation through a process of systematic self-exploration." (Mallon, 1998, p. 42). Our social work training prepared us to accept homosexuality in our work with others. However, we realized that homophobia was part of who we were when our daughter "came out" (see Appendix A) to us in 1984. The institutional roots of homophobia are strong and run deep.

WHAT BRINGS US TO THIS DISCUSSION

As parents of a daughter who is lesbian, we believe that parents of today need to be prepared for the possibility of one or more of their children growing up to discover he or she is sexually diverse. "Current researchers point to the difficulty of determining the number of people who are lesbian, gay, bisexual, or transgendered (LGBT). Kinsey's study published in 1947 estimated that 10% of the male population and 8% of the female population were exclusively homosexual" (Lipkin, 1999, p. 77). From our experience, most parents are unaware or, if they have heard that statistic, are confident it won't happen in their family.

Parenthood educators, whether pediatricians or nurses, teachers, or other human services providers, are in key positions and must be prepared to provide accurate information about sexual diversity. When this has occurred, we believe the fear and shame young people now experience will be greatly diminished. The stigma of being gay will diminish. Young people will be far less inclined to resort to self-destructive behavior, including suicide, because of their homosexuality. The shock parents now experience will be lessened along with a reduction in rejection of their sons and daughters along with outbursts of violence or feeling they need to kick their sons or daughters out of their homes when they learn of their homosexuality.

Teaching parents about parenting is what parenthood education is all about. When parents are informed about sexual diversity, they are able to understand the variations of normal sexual development from the time their child is born.

INFORMATION ABOUT ANOTHER ASPECT
OF SEXUAL DIVERSITY

Some children will have a parent or parents who acknowledge their own gayness only after an extended period of marriage and parenthood, as they realize that being married and having children has not changed their gayness. (White, 1995; Norman, 1998). More and more, spouses or parents prior to marriage and parenthood, aware of their possible gayness, but who hoped that having a spouse and a family would change them from gay to straight, are deciding they can no longer live a lie to themselves or their families. Additionally, some spouses or parents come to the realization that they are gay only after a period of marriage and parenthood. These spouses and parents, in fairness to their families and themselves, painfully decide they can no longer live and function as if they were heterosexual in their sexual orientation (Norman 1998).

It is our view that educators need accurate information about sexual diversity and this information must be included in their teaching. When what is presently known about the implications of sexual diversity in our lives, caregivers such as teachers, social workers, counselors, therapists, physicians, priests or ministers, and others will be prepared to help parents and children respond positively to the challenges they face in a world of sexual diversity. This is happening already for some human services providers as exemplified by the PFLAG Lawrence-Topeka, Kansas Chapter workshop experiences.

We are confident parents want to succeed in raising children who will take pride in who they are, feel good about themselves, and become productive and contributing citizens in their communities. We know from our interactions that many young men and women who are happy in their adult gay relationships have a sense of emptiness because their parents do not accept their sexual orientation nor acknowledge their adult child's significant relationships. Parents who are informed about sexual diversity are far more likely to be accepting and supportive.

Based on our experience, informing parents about sexual diversity issues is at least as important as informing parents about major childhood illnesses, birth defects, or developmental variation possibilities. The obvious significant difference between major childhood illnesses or developmental issues and sexual diversity issues is that the former are usually known early in a child's life, whereas awareness of a growing child's differing sexual orientation most often surfaces, at the earliest, when a child enters puberty.

In the case of birth defects or childhood illnesses, there is a well-informed community of health professionals available to guide and support parents in caring for their children. A similar support system is not available to the parents of children, or the children themselves, who are in the sexual minority. Fortunately, there is a growing number of groups and individuals available to assist and support parents and children after parents learn that their child's sexual orientation is different from what they had assumed.

As a child takes the initiative to come out or as parents realize their child's sexuality, different reactions are experienced. Some parents react with calmness and acceptance. At the other end of the continuum, parents may respond violently, literally kicking their child out of the home. There are many variations of parental reaction between these two extremes.

Children whose sexual orientation is different from the majority of their peers may be physically assaulted by those who are not accepting of sexual diversity, i.e., the beating and subsequent death of Michael Shepherd in Wyoming in 1998. They may experience rejection by fellow students, teachers and their minister, as well as community youth service groups such as the Boy Scouts. However, other youth organizations have quietly accepted and embraced sexual diversity, i.e., 4-H and Girl Scouts. This is good news!

Happily, we see other instances of positive change. There are now more than 400 local chapters of PFLAG, with more than 70,000 members in 50 states (PFLAG, 1995). There is GLSEN, a national organization of public school educators who are gay, lesbian, and bisexual and their straight allies in 70 chapters in our country. We are beginning to see proactive behavior on behalf of gay children and adults by thoughtful people in churches, local city governments, even state governments. Governors of California, Massachusetts, and Iowa and some state-level boards of education now include sexual orientation language as part of their antidiscrimination policies. Massachusetts is a forerunner of these changes where Governor Weld signed into law "An Act to Prohibit Discrimination Against Students in Public Schools on the Basis of Sexual Orientation" on December 10, 1993. The bill was the first of its kind in the nation—protecting lesbian and gay public school students from harassment and discrimination (Woog, 1995, p. 366).

Even with the progress being made, too many parents are not prepared to help their child or themselves deal in a helpful way with the knowledge of their child's sexual orientation. It is not uncommon for parents who lack an understanding of sexual diversity to retreat into a state of "denial" at the time their child comes out. Too often by the time the child and the parents are cognizant of the need for having appropriate information about sexual diversity as well as knowledge of useful resources, considerable emotional pain associated with their lack of knowledge and understanding are manifest in the child's negative or low sense of self-esteem and the parent's sense of having failed in being available to their child at a time of great need.

In addition to preparing parenthood educators to include accurate information about sexual diversity in their work with parents, some of whom will have children who are LGBT, parents need to know that their children will encounter sexual diversity-related issues throughout childhood. These events are another reality about which most parents nor teachers give much, if any, serious thought. In our conversations about sexual diversity with parents of children who are gay as well as with parents of children who are straight, we have learned that they wish they would have known about sexual diversity earlier in their parenting experience or even before becoming parents. Thus, it becomes increasingly important for professionals to take responsibility for educating and training future parent educators to be knowledgeable about issues of sexual diversity.

EXPERIENCES CHILDREN WILL ENCOUNTER AS THEY ARE GROWING UP

How can parents help their children successfully navigate the sexuality issues of childhood experiences? Parents need to be aware of the kinds of experiences their children are likely to encounter as they are growing up. Parents need to have accurate information in order to counter inaccurate and negative information. More importantly, from a positive educational perspective, parents need to know early in their parenting in order for their parenting role to be enhanced.

Parents want to be and can be their children's most significant teachers. In matters of sexuality parents may be the only informed source for their children. Children face a barrage of myths and misinformation about sexual diversity. The reluctance to include sexuality and sexual diversity means that students will receive little if any constructive education regarding sexual diversity in their schools. Consequently if children are to acquire needed information about their sexuality and sexual diversity it must come from their parents. In the absence of parental guidance in matters of sexuality children face a barrage of unchallenged myths and misinformation.

Educational materials on sexuality and faith prepared by the Unitarian Universalists and the United Church of Christ echo what many professional educators recognize: that parents are their children's most important sexuality educator. The authors state that "the primary responsibility for educating children about sexuality rests with the parents" (Hoertdoerter et al., 1999, p. 9).

In general parents know about the variety of experiences children encounter in their neighborhoods and communities. This knowledge provides an incentive for parents who want to be proactive in their child's sexual education. The following list encompasses some of the experiences that we think compels the inclusion of sexual diversity in parenting education curricula and programs:

1. **Learning about friends, classmates, neighbors, and others who are or perceived to be LGBT.** People who are sexually diverse are increasingly visible. Movies and television programs include gay situations and roles in comedy and drama. Openly sexually diverse persons who hold elective positions in government and receive considerable media attention.

A decade ago Rock Hudson and Liberace were prominent movie and television celebrities and were gay men who died of AIDS. Today Cher Bono and her daughter, Chastity, who is lesbian, are often in the news. Chastity has written her story titled *Family Outing* (Bono & Fitzpatrick, 1998), and she makes frequent public appearances on radio and TV talk shows as well as meeting with various groups and organizations across the country talking about her growing-up experiences.

Children are exposed at a young age to the language, people, and issues of sexual diversity. Even young children in day-care and kindergarten hear and sometimes use pejorative names. As children will do, they call each other names, including "fag," "dyke," "queer," or "fairy." They may not know what the names mean but they learn early that these labels or names are meant to hurt or put down another person. The professional training of educators responsible for parenting education must include comprehensive and accurate sexual diversity content so that parents can respond appropriately and helpfully to their children when these names and experiences are told about at home.

2. **Children will have classmates and will be making friends with classmates whose parents are LGBT.** There are increasing numbers of families with one or two parents who are gay. There are over 4 million lesbian, gay, or bisexual parents who have 8 to 10 million children in the public schools. These youth are often fearful of responses from classmates and teachers. Parents in many of these families feel disenfranchised from the school community (Vaughn, 1999).

There is a growing acceptance in society for gay men and women to parent their own children and to sometimes provide foster and adoptive homes for children in need. Parents with a more traditional background in human sexuality are often reluctant for their children to be in contact with children of parents who are gay or lesbian, fearful that their child may become homosexual because of the association. They may prevent their child from playing with a child of a gay parent. Even more, they will be reluctant for a child to stay overnight in a household with a parent who is gay or lesbian.

The following is an example of a parent's reluctance to allow even visual contact with gays or lesbians. A few years ago at a Pride Parade a mother was observed hurrying her two young daughters into their car. She was overheard saying "I don't want you to see this parade; these are bad people!" The negative attitude about gay people was very clear.

In contrast, our daughter living in Colorado overheard a different kind of interaction between a friend and her 4-year-old daughter. The daughter asked if girls could marry girls while she and her friend were staging a wedding with only their female barbie dolls. The mother responded with, "Yes, girls can marry girls;" and the little girls went on playing with their dolls. The message of acceptance was clear. If one of these young girls were to grow up realizing that she was lesbian in her orientation, what would she feel about herself as a result of her parents' attitude about sexual diversity?

As professionals develop accurate knowledge about the realities of sexual diversity they will create parenting education programs that enable parents to understand sexual diversity. Increased understanding will enable parents to provide information and guidelines for their children about relationships with all children, even children of gay parents.

3. **Children are aware of aunts, uncles, cousins, close friends, or co-workers of parents who may be gay or lesbian.** The data indicate that one in four families has a family member who is gay. Almost everyone knows of someone in their extended family or a family friend who is gay.

In the past, and even now, many families remain closeted about a family member who is gay. As happens so often the fact of gayness is rarely a secret. When the subject of a cousin's or uncle's homosexuality is brought up, the response by many parents is to ignore or suppress the conversation. As a consequence, the opportunity is lost for a parent to use the situation as a basis for an informative conversation with their child. Most parents are just not prepared to have a conversation about sexual orientation with their children.

Recently a good friend who is in a committed lesbian relationship related a conversation with a long time close personal friend. The conversation had to do with her pre-adolescent daughter and how she wanted to be careful about what her daughter learned about "those kinds of people."

4. **More and more children have important adults in their lives who are LGBT.** These may include school teachers, Sunday School teachers, youth leaders, ministers, coaches, and others. We have always had teachers and staff in the public and private schools who were gay. We have always had ministers and youth leaders who were gay. However until recently, and even now, most of us were unaware of their sexuality. In most cases, in the absence of information, we assume that they are straight "just like us."

In the past, the sexual orientation of adults who were LGBT was simply not discussed in families. Occasionally the information would come out and the teacher, or minister, or youth leader would resign or be asked to leave. Except for occasional situations, the matter would be handled "quietly," with little or no discussion. Children would often never know why they "left." If an explanation was given, it was at best a partial truth, avoiding the issue of sexual orientation.

5. **Children and youth of every age are now exposed to media information about people who are gay from TV, radio, newspapers, periodicals, the Internet, and more.** These include public figures who are LGBT, that is, church and government leaders, persons in the entertainment field, such as recording artists or movie or television personalities, and others. There is no escaping our children's contacts with sexual diversity in our culture.

It is not that there are more people who are gay; rather, we are more aware of people who are gay. People who are gay are feeling more free to be open and feel less need to hide their sexual orientation. Ministers, teachers, physicians, lawyers, police officers, fire fighters, and all kinds of people in communities across the country are known to be gay. There is news of clergy performing Holy Unions or commitment ceremonies for gay couples.

Because of the increased openness, people of all ages, including preschool children, are exposed to the reality of sexual diversity. This openness gives parents many opportunities to inform and educate their children.

6. **Religious denominations are engaged in discussions about sexual diversity.** Some religious denominations are in the process of reviewing their policies and practices regarding people who are diverse in their sexuality. The considerable media attention being generated is increasing public awareness of sexual diversity.

In nearly every major religion and religious denomination there are organizations consisting of people who are LGBT. Some of these organizations have standing with the religious body and some do not.

7. **Gay youth are acknowledging their sexuality differences at young ages.** Recent studies show that ages of coming out vary; however, there apears to be a drop in the age of coming out for both boys and girls. According to Jill Vaughan the average age of first identification for gay males is 13.3 and for lesbian girls 13.9 (Vaughan, 1999).

Our daughter has told us she was aware that she was different as early as kindergarten. She had no words to describe her difference other than to know that when other girls talked about growing up and marrying their "boyfriend" she wanted to grow up and marry her "girlfriend."

Early childhood dreams may remain just that as children grow older. However with our daughter, and others who have shared their stories with us, their dreams did not fade. Clearly, many young people become aware in their early teens that their yearning for love is with someone of the same sex.

As PFLAG educators and advocates for families where sexual diversity exists, our experience suggests that most of today's parents, even educators, received minimal formal education in elementary and secondary school about human sexuality, much less sexual diversity. The education they received about sexual diversity was most likely incomplete at best and at worst, often inaccurate, negative, and destructive. As was true for us, over the years they will have heard stories from peers, older children, and adults that continue the negative and destructive stereotypic themes or anecdotes about persons who are gay or lesbian. As a consequence, most parents carry homophobic feelings themselves and are not prepared to help their children understand the normalcy of sexuality diversity in others or themselves. To the extent these observations are valid, the challenge for colleges and universities is to develop curricula that includes sexual diversity content in its course work for the wide variety of students who will be parenthood educators, formally or informally.

Education about sexual diversity takes place in a wide variety of settings: university and college classes across many disciplines such as education, social work, psychology, medicine, etc., and in public and private school classrooms; places of worship, such as the church, synagogue, mosque, or temple; hospital or health department birthing and parenting classes; continuing education workshops—wherever people gather to learn about themselves and others. We believe the cycle of misinformation, lack of information and distorted and stereotypical information may best be corrected by incorporating accurate and comprehensive human sexuality information in a continuum of parenting education venues, wherever students may be found, including the public schools.

OUR FAMILY STORY

We are parents of three children: a son born in 1956; a daughter born in 1961 and a second daughter born in 1963. Tara, our older daughter, "came out" to us—revealed her diverse orientation—the summer of 1984, just before her 23rd birthday. She had told her brother and his wife approximately 6 months earlier. However, even with their assurance that Mom and Dad would be okay about it, she could not bring herself to tell us. She was too fearful of a negative response.

We had thought Tara's periods of continuing deep depression were related to her bipolar mental health disorder diagnosed two years earlier. She was inconsistent in taking her medication and we thought adjustments needed to be made in the amount or kinds of medication she was taking. For several years, all of us were on an emotional roller coaster.

We became increasingly concerned about the possibility that Tara would attempt suicide as the frequency and severity of her depressive periods increased. We thought she needed more support than what we could give her to help her understand that the mood swings she was experiencing were the result of a biochemical imbalance and were not amenable to even her strong will power. We were relieved when with our encouragement, she found a social work counselor with whom she felt she could talk.

However, even with consistent medication and counseling, her periods of depression continued. With our continuing concern about a possible suicide attempt, we were especially worried when she failed to return on the afternoon following an overnight camping trip with a friend at a near-by county park. When we reached Tara's friend by telephone later the next afternoon, she told us Tara had decided to stay a while longer at the campground. The day wore on without a word from Tara. Her delay and lack of contact were inconsistent with her usual pattern of behavior.

It was after 8:30 p.m. when the telephone rang. Tara, 200 miles away, was calling to tell us she was on her way to see her sister in Washington, D.C. Following a brief exchange that included firm instructions from us to return home with the car, it became clear that Tara, in tears, was profoundly distressed. We feared for her safety. It was nighttime, she was alone and 5 hr from home.

Our initial insistence to return seemed only to increase her distress. As we groped for alternatives, we encouraged her to contact long-time close family friends living near where she was calling. She agreed to drive to their home, promising to call us when she arrived and perhaps plan to spend the night with them. We had no way of knowing if our friends would even be at home! However, we knew that, if they were, Tara would be welcomed with open arms and unconditional love.

Our prayers for her safety were heard! Two hours later, our friends called to tell us Tara had arrived, that she was okay, and she had something important to talk about with us. Tearfully, Tara told us that she was lesbian!

In an emotional conversation, Tara told us of her fear that now we would stop loving her, that we would hate her, that we would not want to claim her as our daughter! She had heard of these kinds of things happening to other young people as their parents learned of their child's gayness! After assurances of our continuing love for her and wanting her home safely with us where we could talk face to face, she agreed to stay overnight with our friends and return home in the morning.

We talked together most of the following day, with Tara volunteering information about herself and freely answering our questions. What a relief it was for us to have Tara so obviously relaxed, in good spirits and smiling. It was a good day for all three of us as knowledge and understanding replaced the hurt and confusion of the months and years that had led up to this day.

We knew that Tara had been struggling with the earlier unwelcome diagnosis of a bipolar mental health disorder. Now we realized she had felt the need to hide the truth from us about her sexual orientation for an even longer period of time. It is no wonder that she had felt at times as if she wanted to die!

Fortunately, with support from her social work counselor and our mutual family friends, Tara had decided to tell us about her sexual orientation because hiding the truth about herself from us was no longer a viable option to her. She no longer wanted to keep her "secret" to herself. She wanted to be honest with us, to have us know who she was, regardless of the pain in the telling, for us as well as herself. We marvel and applaud her courage and her honesty! We also came to better appreciate the agony of her struggle about accepting the reality of her sexual orientation, and we became painfully aware that we had not been there for her when she was in so much pain that she wanted to just stop living!

The events immediately surrounding the revelation of her secret were dramatic! We later came to realize that the drama that had been played out in our family was not that unusual for most families when a child finally gathers up the necessary courage to come out to his/her parents.

As with many parents when their child comes out of the closet, we slipped into the closet's empty space. We experienced a range of negative feelings about her sexuality very much like those she had experienced and had prevented her from telling us what she knew about herself. We experienced guilt. Where had we gone wrong? What had we done to cause her to "choose" to be a lesbian? We feared for her personal safety, that friends and family might turn away from Tara and from us, that Tara would be rejected or vilified or physically hurt because of her gayness. We grieved the loss of our dreams for her to marry and give birth to a child who would be our grandchild.

We found ourselves reluctant to talk about Tara with family and friends. We talked proudly about her outstanding professional work in special education in a distant state, but we avoided discussing her personal life in any way other than to casually answer from time to time, when asked, "Oh no, there was no special young man in her life right now."

Looking back we recognize our lack of knowledge, our limited comfort level in discussing sexual orientation, the insecure feelings, and at times the inappropriate behaviors that accompanied our newly found knowledge about our daughter. It took time for us to fully discover that she was still the same person whose birth had brought such delight to us and realize that her differing sexual orientation was simply another part of who she is that we have come to know and appreciate. Our daughter, who happens to be lesbian, is a truly wonderful person. We are grateful that we met the challenge to put aside our initial homophobia and now voice our pride and love for our daughter and her partner, Kasey.

Eleven years after Tara's "coming out," she and Kasey decided they were ready to hold a public celebration of their decision 10 years earlier to be each other's companion for the rest of their lives. On a hot and windy but beautiful day in Lawrence our friends and families gathered to publicly witness and support Tara and Kasey's exchange of vows and rings. Our daughter and daughter-in-law have now lived together in a loving and monogamous relationship for more than 15 years. Each holds responsible positions as teachers in their community, and in March 1999 they purchased their first home. We are as proud of our two daughters in California as we are of our other two children and their families in Kansas and Colorado!

WHAT PARENTS SHOULD KNOW ABOUT SEXUAL DIVERSITY

Fortunately, the positive road our family has been able to take is the way it is for an increasing number of families. Even so, many families are unable to respond with love and compassion or support for their son or daughter who has just revealed their differing sexuality.

Where there is strong family support, there is the possibility for positive outcomes for youth who are LGBT. These good outcomes are measured in terms of students completing school, developing positive friendships, entering responsible life careers, establishing committed relationships, forming families, and having rewarding life experiences.

In families where youth are rejected when they come out as LGBT, the young people are at risk of such negative outcomes as suicide, homelessness, living on the streets, prostitution, violence, and abuse. Knowing what the possibilities are for good outcomes along with the potential risk of negative outcomes compels including sexual diversity in parenting education.

Based on our family experience, it is our firm belief that receiving quality information early in the parenting process can prepare parents for accepting diversity in their children's sexuality. Experience through our PFLAG chapter reveals that parents have seldom been exposed to information concerning possible sexual diversity in their children. Although some have had an academic exposure to the issue of homosexuality, seldom has this resonated in terms of their own children being gay, until after the fact. This was true for us and has been true of other parents with whom we have become acquainted across the country.

We are both social workers. We have long had friends and colleagues who are gay, and friends who have children who are gay. Even so, we expected our three to be "normal' heterosexual children. We simply did not contemplate the possibility that one of our three children would be gay. As a consequence, when our daughter came out, even with all of our academic sophistication we experienced much of the same surprise, shock, sense of guilt, and loss felt by most other families when their children come out to them.

So, what is it that parenting educators should know in order to be able to develop parenting education instruction or programs that would help parents achieve positive outcomes for their families when, within that small but significant percentage, some children will be gay, lesbian, bisexual, or transgendered? A fundamental and comprehensive education for educators is essential in developing and implementing education for parenthood.

Ten essential concepts are the building blocks for useful parenting education:

1. **Sexuality is diverse.** Not all children grow up heterosexual. Most children grow up to be heterosexual and some exclusively heterosexual. Studies now provide us with indications that 10% males and 8% of females grow up to be exclusively homosexual (Woog, 1995). Other children grow up with some variations between heterosexuality and homosexuality. Most children whether straight, gay, lesbian, bisexual, or transgendered have the potential for a normal childhood and for becoming "normal" adults. The single most critical factor in the process is that of informed and supportive parents.

2. **Understanding sexual orientation.** Sexual orientation is an enduring emotional, romantic, sexual attraction to another person. It exists along a continuum that ranges from exclusively homosexual to exclusively heterosexual orientation and includes varying degrees of bisexuality. Persons with a homosexual orientation are often referred to as gay (both men and women) or as lesbian (women) (see Appendix B) (APA brochure, 1998).

3. **Sexual orientation is not a choice.** Human beings do not choose to be either gay or straight. Sexual orientation emerges for most people in early adolescence without prior sexual experience. Although we can choose to act on our feelings, psychologists (and social workers and psychiatrists) do not consider sexual orientation to be a conscious choice that can be voluntarily changed. (APA, 1998).

4. **A person's sexual orientation is not caused by being near someone who is gay.** A young person who comes out to his or her parents has not been contaminated through associations with adults or other teens who are gay. Sometimes parents make an effort to keep their children away from people who are LGBT for fear that association will somehow result in determining their child's sexual orientation. "Most social and behavioral scientists assent to the view that same-gender sexual orientation results from a complex interaction of factors that is not well understood" (Hunter et al., 1998, p. 177).

5. **Sexual orientation is becoming evident at earlier ages.** Children as early as ten or eleven sometimes express an awareness of their "gayness." The Allegiers in their 1995 edition of *Sexual Interactions* report that "Most men come out at age 19 or 20; however, women tend to come out somewhat later, in their early 20s" (Allegier & Allegier, 1995, p. 495). The earlier ages cited indicating age 13.3 for boys and 13.9 for girls (Vaughn, 1999) suggests a decline in age for males and females coming out.

6. **A homosexual orientation is not attributable to a problem or pathological relationship between the father and mother.** This notion that homosexuality was a mental illness and connected to pathological relationships with one or the other parent was a commonly held belief until recently. Increasingly, studies indicate that sexual orientation represents a combination of biological, genetic, and environmental factors. Orientation is not considered a function of the relationships of boys and girls with their parents nor is it considered a mental illness.

> Historically, most hypotheses that have been advanced to explain sexual orientation have included the notion that people are gay because of defects: inherited disorders, deviant hormonal exposure, harmful family patterns, early sexual experiences, or gender-role nonconformity. If not for negative influences, it was thought, the individual would be heterosexual (Allgeier & Allgeier, 1995, p.500).

7. **Forms of sexual orientation are increasingly accepted as normal by society whether gay, lesbian, bisexual, or transgendered.** Units of government at all levels, corporations, churches, educational, and charitable organizations are incorporating sexual orientation language in their anti-discrimination policies. Many public schools are responding positively to "Safe-School" campaigns designed to create safe learning and teaching environments for students and staff of all diversities. All of the major mental health professions have joined in reversing earlier positions categorizing homosexuality as a mental health problem. They have now joined in an effort to reduce the stigma associated with people who are LGBT.

As recently as November 1999: "a coalition of the nation's leading education, health and mental health organizations strongly urges educators and school administrators to better understand sexual orientation development, support lesbian, gay and bisexual students, and reject efforts to bring "ex-gay" messages into the nation's schools" (Youth Advocates, 1999). The coalition included the American Academy of Pediatrics, American Counseling Association, American Association of School Administrators,

American Federation of Teachers, American Psychological Association, American School Health Association, The Interfaith Alliance Foundation, National Association of School Psychologists, National Association of Social Workers, and the National Education Association.

8. **A homosexual orientation is not a barrier to having a family and children.** Through the use of modern technologies, more and more single parent and same-sex couple families have and rear children. Although people who are gay, lesbian, or bisexual may be less apt to choose to have children, having children is becoming more the norm. In addition, gay singles and couples are rearing foster and adoptive children. However, some state and federal laws continue to act as barriers to gay persons serving as foster or adoptive parents (Hunter et al., 1998, pp. 122-124).

9. **Young people often experience great difficulty in telling parents that they are gay.** Because of the continuing pervasive social stigma associated with homosexuality, there is often a fear of disapproval and rejection. Young people often report that they think they are the only students in their schools who are gay. They are afraid to talk with their parents, fearful that they will disappoint or arouse their parents' anger. When the topic is rarely or never discussed they only know what they feel about themselves. Too often there are no indications of anyone in their school, including counselors, willing to talk with them about their sexuality.

In our workshop contacts teachers and other school staff report the need to be particularly careful about talking with students because of potential charges of "recruiting." In addition there is a constant fear of dismissal of teachers and staff because of the level of homophobia in their schools.

10. **The possibilities for positive outcomes for normal homosexual children are as good as with normal heterosexual children.** The diverse sexual orientation of children can be a positive and fulfilling family experience. People who are gay are like the rest of the population, in that they are gifted, talented, creative, and are contributing members to their families and to society. This may be especially true for our gay and lesbian children who still bear the burden of the need to excel hoping for acceptance through accomplishment (Hunter et al., 1998, p. 124).

Including these ten fundamental concepts in parenting education programs can open the door for parents to prepare their children, whether they may or may not be gay, for healthy sexual development. Elsewhere in this paper there is a discussion of the contacts with other children and adults that children have in the normal course of growing up. Families who are able to convey a positive, accepting attitude about people who are LGBT are preparing their children to be caring and accepting of their peers. In the event that one, or more, of the children in their family is gay the groundwork for acceptance and support is established.

Parenting education programs can make a contribution to parents that will result in increased openness and acceptance. Although we emphasize the positive in the preceding ten fundamental concepts, there is a need to call attention to the range of myths that, in the absence of sound information, condition parental attitudes and behaviors in rearing their children. The following set of "myths and facts" is important in preparing parents for parenting:

1. **Myth:** *I don't know any people who are gay, lesbian, or bisexual.*

Fact: *Actually,* people do! Many people are just not aware that they know any gay, lesbian, or bisexual people. Kinsey's study, published in 1947, estimated that 10% of the male population and 8% of the female population were exclusively homosexual (Kinsey, A.C. et al., 1948). Many people now view sexual orientation on a continuum, where most people are not exclusively either gay or straight during their lives. Further, Judd Marmor, Professor of Psychiatry at USG Medical School, has calculated that one in every four families has a close family member, parent or child, who is lesbian or gay (Marmor, 1996).

2. **Myth:** *Gay people can be identified by their mannerisms, appearance, or choice of occupation.*

Fact: Gay, lesbian, and bisexual people are as diverse as the greater population to which they belong. There are gay, lesbian, and bisexual people of all races, religions, economic classes, and occupations. To name just a few: National Lawyers Guild Gay and Lesbian Caucus, National Education Association Gay and Lesbian Caucus, Gay Nurses Association, and the Gay and Lesbian Association of Scientist and Engineers.

3. **Myth:** *Gay, lesbian, and bisexual people shouldn't be parents. Their children will be poorly adjusted.*

Fact: To date, no research supports the notion that having gay parents causes children to be poorly adjusted. On the contrary, numerous studies indicate that children of lesbians and gays grow up to be as well adjusted as their peers who are raised by heterosexual parents. This myth suggests that the difficulties these children may face is the fault of the lesbian or gay parents. Any difficulty experienced by children of gays and lesbians is more likely to be the result of anti-gay bigotry present in society.

4. **Myth:** *Gay people shouldn't be teachers. They will molest students or try to convert them to homosexuality.*

Fact: The truth is that the vast majority, up to 95%, of child molesters are heterosexual men. Gay men and lesbians are attracted to adults of the same gender, not to children. Second, it is not possible to convert individuals into homosexuality. Sadly, the people who are in the best position to support gay and lesbian students are gay and lesbian teachers because they understand the stresses caused by discrimination. Unfortunately, due to the misconceptions caused by the myth of "converting," gay and lesbian teachers are often hesitant to advocate for gay and lesbian youth.

5. **Myth:** *If a child grows up with gay or lesbian parents, that child will most likely grow up to be gay or lesbian.*

Fact: As mentioned earlier, children raised by gay men or lesbians do not differ significantly in any way from their peers raised by heterosexual parents (Mallon, 1998, p. 159). In addition, if this myth were true, then how does one explain that that so many gay men and lesbians raised by heterosexual parents did not grow up to be heterosexual?

6. **Myth:** *There are no gays or lesbians in my school. Most gay men and lesbians don't realize their sexual orientation until after they reach 18 years of age.*

Fact: Many gay men and lesbians report sensing something "different" about themselves as early as age four or five. The average age at which youth presently realize their sexual orientation, or come out is age 13 [13.3 for boys and 13.9 for girls] (Vaughan, 1999).

7. **Myth:** *Homophobic put downs are rare in high schools.*

Fact: Ninety-seven percent of students at Lincoln Sudbury High School in Massachusetts reported hearing homophobic language regularly at school. Fifty-three percent of students in 12 Massachusetts gay-straight alliances reported hearing teachers use homophobic language at school (Woog, 1995).

RISKS FACED BY GAY AND LESBIAN YOUTH

Youth are at risk when their parents have little or no preparation for parenting children who may be LGBT and lacking acceptance and support. The following information provides some indications of the risks they face (PFLAG 1995).

1. Fifty percent of all gay and lesbian youth interviewed in one study reported that their parents had rejected them for being gay.
2. Twenty-six percent of gay and lesbian youth are forced to leave home because of conflict with their families concerning their sexual orientation.
3. Forty-two percent of homeless youth identify as gay or lesbian.
4. Studies show that gay and lesbian youth comprise up to 30% of all completed youth suicides annually.
5. Gay and lesbian youth are two to three times more likely than heterosexual youth to attempt suicide.
6. Forty-five percent of gay males and 20% of lesbians experience physical or verbal assaults in high school. Twenty-eight percent of these young people feel forced to drop out of high school due to harassment based on sexual orientation.
7. Fifteen percent of lesbian, gay, and bisexual youth have been injured so badly in a physical attack at school that they require medical care, even hospitalization.

WHAT WILL PARENTS BE ABLE TO DO BETTER WHEN SEXUAL DIVERSITY AND SEXUAL ORIENTATION ARE INCLUDED IN PARENTING EDUCATION PROGRAMS?

Just as a child may be aware that he is different, parents are sometimes aware that their child is different, too. This awareness by parents may come early in their son or daughter's childhood, or much later: for some like us, not until our daughter actually told us in her early twenties.

So, what difference could it make in parenting if parents are aware that their child might be gay?. . . or what difference would it make if parents are more aware that their child will be encountering people who are gay?. . . or will be getting information about people who are gay through the media, friends, school, etc.? From our experiences and literature review we think it could make a significant difference and we believe the following represent only a few of the possible outcomes for parents. As a result we strongly believe parents will be better able to:

1. Talk comfortably with their children about matters of sexuality and sexual diversity.
2. Listen and hear their children's stories, concerns and questions about their sexuality.

3. Parents will be able to talk with their children about homosexuality in age-appropriate terms and in ways that are comfortable for them.
4. Parents will be able to recognize inappropriate behavior in their child's peers, at school and will be able to address these situations in constructive ways.
5. Interrupt inappropriate name calling by their child or their child's friends and use the experience for constructive teaching rather than unnecessary punishment.
6. Recognize and address the inappropriate use of sexual language and sexual epithets and will be able to engage constructively with school personnel or other youth leaders about their concerns.
7. Discuss matters of sexual diversity and sexual orientation with their children; also talk about the meaning of being gay and the value of accepting people who are different.
8. Respond constructively, with support and acceptance, when a son or daughter of any age reveals questions or concerns about their sexuality.
9. Make use of resources for themselves, as well as their children, when or if their child confides to them that they are unsure of their sexuality or that they are gay.
10. Serve as a resource to other parents who confide in them about their child's sexuality.

Based on our experience, we see enormous value for parenting education programs to include sexual diversity and sexual orientation information. We believe it should be part of the formal teacher training curriculum as well as a subject for specialized workshops in the field for parent educators.

In our work with the PFLAG Lawrence-Topeka Chapter, we have developed a workshop program that includes educational content and an interactional process useful for teacher preparation. See Appendix B.

SUMMARY

The chapter emphasizes the urgent need for educators and all of the professional human services providers to include sexual diversity content in parenting education programs that teach parents about parenting.

Information is included about the ways children are learning about sexual diversity and ways parents can help their children understand their experiences. Information is included about ways parents can help their children understand that sexual diversity is simply another part of life and not something inherently bad. Rather, sexual diversity is a part of human sexuality and, as such, is to be expressed in a responsible manner.

It is the our view that parents must receive accurate information, early in a child's life about sexuality, including sexual diversity. We are convinced that the more this happens, parents as well as children will see sexual diversity as nothing to fear. For this to happen, preparation for parenting educators must include content on sexual diversity.

An example of a PFLAG workshop is included (Appendix B) as an illustration of one way for parenthood educators to become informed of the need as well as the opportunities to make a difference for families.

Our family story illustrates the need for parents to have information that prepares them to teach their children about sexual diversity. Whether or not families will have a child who is gay, accurate information will enable their child to learn, grow and behave in more responsible ways regarding their sexuality and that of others.

Our hope is that sexual diversity content will be included in formal as well as informal educational presentations. We think sexual diversity content in teacher preparation courses is long overdue. Professionals in family life education as well as health educators have an ethical responsibility to include this critical content in their course materials.

Information about sexual diversity needs to be presented in classes for parents and children, where the children have an opportunity to learn, in their parents' presence, about their changing bodies in the maturation process. For children to grow up understanding their bodies and develop a responsible appreciation for people who are different, an understanding of sexual diversity is necessary. We think it is important for information about sexual diversity to be presented even in the school setting in health classes as well as in social studies classes.

APPENDIX A: GLOSSARY

The terms included are intended to clarify language used in sexual diversity literature and speech. Because of widespread misinformation it is important to provide professional educators as well as human service providers with accurate definitions.

Androgynous   having both feminine and masculine feelings and behaviors regardless of sexual orientation or gender identity.

Bisexual   a positive term referring to both men and women who identify themselves as bisexuals and having accepted with pride their affectional attractions towards both genders.

Breeder   a negative term used to stereotype heterosexuals.

Bulldyke, fag, queer   negative terms sometimes used to refer to gay men and lesbians. These are equivalent to hate terms or epithets used against racial and ethnic minorities.

Closeted   refers to someone who is not open about his or her sexual orientation. The person for personal reasons chooses to hide his or her orientation from others, and sometimes denies their orientation to him or herself.

Coming out   a developmental process of a gay or lesbian individual who is accepting ones affectional and sexual orientation; initial involvement with others in the gay and lesbian community; a metaphor for telling people about one's sexual orientation.

Disclosure   the point at which a lesbian or gay person openly identifies his or her sexual orientation to another. It is inappropriate to use terms such as discovered, admitted, revealed, found out, or declared to describe this phenomena. These are pejorative terms that suggest judgement and should be avoided by professional educators and members of the helping professions.

Dyke   usually a negative term applied to stereotypypical "masculine" women, much as "fairy" has been used to stereotype "feminine" men.

Faggot   a negative term used to stereotype "feminine" males. Applied to homosexuals during the inquisition when they were burned along with "witches," (from Latin meaning "a bundle of sticks").

Gay   a positive term referring to males who identify themselves as homosexual and have accepted with pride their affectional and sexual orientation. Most women who are homosexual prefer the word "lesbian" because "gay" generally refers to men.

Gender role   the characteristics of an individual who is culturally defined as masculine or feminine.

Heterocentism   denotes the assumption that everyone is heterosexual unless otherwise indicated; also a system of advantages bestowed upon those who are heterosexually oriented.

Heterosexual   affectional and sexual attraction primarily toward members of the opposite sex; a clinical term.

Heterosexism   the assumption that everyone is or should be heterosexual because it is assumed to be the only acceptable and viable life option; this assumption often leads to discrimination based on sexual orientation; a form of homophobia. It constitutes an ideological system that denies, denigrates, and stigmatizes any nonheterosexual form of behavior or identity, relationship, or community. Heterosexism operates principally by rendering homosexuality invisible and when this fails, by trivializing, repressing or stigmatizing it.

Homoignorant a term developed to describe individuals who possess a very limited knowledge about gays, lesbians, bisexual, and transgendered individuals.

Homophobia the irrational fear, dislike, or hatred of lesbians, gays, or bisexuals; can be both personal and institutional prejudice and often results in acts of discrimination, avoidance of homosexuals, or the subject of homosexuality; the personal fear of being homosexual. Homophobia is used to refer to a wide variety of negative feelings, attitudes, and behaviors directed toward homosexuality and gay men and lesbians.

Homosexual affectional and sexual attraction primarily towards members of the same sex; a clinical term.

In the closet a homosexual who cannot or will not "come out" to themselves, peers, parents, family, or others.

Lesbian a positive term referring to females who identify themselves as homosexual and have accepted with pride their affectional and sexual orientation (from Greek Isle of Lesbos, where the lesbian poet, Sappho, had a school in 400 B.C.).

Lover/life partner/companion identifies the partner or significant other of gays or lesbians who are in a committed relationship.

Outing a relatively new and controversial phenomenon where lesbians and gay men are forced "out of the closet" without their consent. The term has gained popularity with the outing of celebrities who are believed to be gay and lesbian.

Questioning a term used with particular reference to young people who may be genuinely exploring issues of sexual orientation in their lives. Some of these young people will ultimately identify as gay, lesbian, or bisexual; others will identify as heterosexual.

Sexual identity an individual's sense of self as male or female from the social and psychological perspective. Identity is the culturally informed process of expression of desires in a social role and with socially shared cultural practices within a social context.

Sexual minority a term used to identify persons who self-identify as homosexual, gay, lesbian, transgender, or transvestite. Although it is true that all gay and lesbian persons are members of a sexual minority, not all sexual minority persons are gay.

Sexual orientation the range of feelings of affection and sexual attraction toward members of the same sex (homosexual), opposite sex (heterosexual), or both sexes (bisexual); how one perceives oneself fitting in the above categories.

Sexual preference   a term often misused to mean sexual orientation. Sexual preference suggests that sexual attraction, including same gender attraction, is a matter of conscious choice. Current research indicates that sexual orientation is not a matter of choice, therefore sexual orientation is the more accurate term.

Stonewall   the site where, in 1969, gays and lesbians fought police for 5 days. This event marks the Independence Day of gay and lesbian culture. Although it is generally accepted that the Stonewall Rebellion marks the start of the Gay and Lesbian Movement, two other liberation organizations preceded this event—Mattachine Society begun in 1950 and The Daughters of Bilitis in 1955.

Straight   a term referring to heterosexuals; non-gay.

Transgender   refers to the constellation of persons who differ from traditional gender norms. The "transgender community" is made up of support groups, advocacy agencies, activists, publishers, and information services.

Transsexual   a person whose gender identity is different from his or her anatomical sex; a sense of being a woman or a man which differs from their anatomical sex.

APPENDIX B: PFLAG WORKSHOP: THE INVISIBLE AND SILENT MINORITY: MEETING THE NEEDS OF SCHOOL-AGE CHILDREN WHO ARE GAY, LESBIAN, BISEXUAL, AND TRANSGENDERED

The workshop goals:

1. To sensitize human services personnel to the fact of gay, lesbian, bisexual, and transgendered children among those they serve;
2. To teach about the needs of these children and their families; and
3. To provide information about the available resources.

The workshop presenters include ourselves and other parents of children who are gay.

Young people in high school and college also participate by telling about their experiences in growing up gay. The participation of parents and young people puts a "face" or humanizes what it means to be gay. The format of the workshop follows:

Workshop Objectives

Participants will be able to

1. Relate to the impact of prejudice and discrimination directed at people who are gay, lesbian, bisexual, or transgendered (GLBT).
2. Engage with clients who are GLBT with greater effectiveness by knowing the nature of societal prejudice in its various ramifications.
3. Participate in organizations whose purposes are to bring about changes to reduce and eliminate institutional prejudice and discrimination toward people who are GLBT.
4. Appreciate the value of a society free of prejudice and discrimination against people who are GLBT.

Presenters: Members of the Lawrence/Topeka PFLAG Chapter

Introduction: The commitment to the invisible and silent minority.

"Straight from the Heart": Video 27 min. Family stories with an emphasis on fairness and equal rights for people who are gay, lesbian bisexual and transgendered.

Experiences of Parents and Families: A parent panel of PFLAG families (5 min each parent couple, 10 min discussion)

Experiences of Youth: A panel of gay high school and college youth. (5 min each, 15 min discussion)

It's Elementary!: Talking about gay issues in school. Video, 87 min (depending on time frame a 10 min segment.) Followed with 15 min discussion.

Legal developments: legislation and court decisions. An attorney who specializes in issues of concern to individuals and couples who are gay, lesbian, bisexual, and transgendered.

Questions/discussions

Conclusion and workshop evaluation

Information packet: workshop participants are provided with a substantial resource packet with the emphasis on "safe schools."

The workshop is modified for the particular audience and time frame provided. The complete workshop fits well into a half day conference time period. By using short clips of the videos most of the material can be presented to a college or university class in a 2-hr class period.

The two panels, parents and youth, become the galvanizing part of the workshop (or class). Parents and youth interacting with workshop participants stimulates interest and questions and creates an environment more supportive of learning than teaching by lectures or assigned readings alone.

There are increasing resources, such as video tapes, biographies, and popular and academic periodicals. Use should be made of these which relate to the objectives of the courses or programs. Some of these are listed at the end of this chapter. In addition, there are a number of organizations in the community that stand ready to supply additional resources and, in some cases, people to talk about their "journeys" and experiences.

APPENDIX C: RESOURCES

Little has been written that focuses on parenting education or that provides information related to sexual orientation content for parenting education programs. As a consequence, the books, articles, and videos presently available relate to families and young people after the fact of disclosure. More material needs to be developed which will prepare parenting educators and families to address the eventualities of sexual diversity among children.

Books

Lesbian and Gay Youth: Care and Counseling, Catlin Ryan and Donna Fetterman, 1998. A comprehensive guide to health and mental health for LGBT youth and an excellent resource for educators, counselors, parents, and providers.

Homosexuality: The Secret a Child Dare Not Tell, Mary Ann Cantwell, 1996. Without words, without warning, without knowing it, we teach many of our children that there is something wrong with them. We teach them so well that they hide themselves to protect us from discovering that they are something unacceptable to us. This book sheds light on the truths and insights that homosexual individuals knew as children and offers a compassionate and healthy view of new possibilities and awareness for parents of gay children.

The Family Heart—A Memoir of When Our Son Came Out, Robb Forman Dew, 1994. "A reflective exploration of a mother's struggle with her attitudes toward homosexuality and a family's negotiation of difference." — Kirkus Reviews.

Now That You Know—What Every Parent Should Know About Homosexuality, Betty Fairchild and Nancy Hayward, 1989. First published in 1979, this is one of the early publications written to help parents understand what a son or daughter who is gay or lesbian is trying to tell them. The update includes a new chapter on "AIDS and the Family." As one reviewer suggested, this book "can spare all concerned needless anguish, unproductive guilt and/or accusations of blame." — Publishers Weekly.

Foundations of Social Work Practice with Lesbian and Gay Persons, Editor; Gerald Mallon, DSW, 1998. This book represents a scholarly work designed especially for social workers, but is also a rich resource for professionals in related educational and human services fields. Of special value is the chapter on the application of values and ethics. As one reviewer noted, "This book avoids romanticizing and convincingly debunks the mythology and stereotyping of gay and lesbian people."

The Best Little Boy in the World, Andrew Tobias. 1998. First published in 1973 under the pen name of John Reid, now, with the change in times, published under his real name. This is an unusually frank account of a young man coming to terms with his sexuality. "An enlightening portrait of growing up gay in a straight world". — Chicago Tribune.

My Child is Gay—How Parents React When they Hear the News, Edited by Bryce McDougall. 1998. "A remarkable, compassionate and extraordinary balanced book, where ordinary parents speak simply and from the heart. For any parent of teenagers, the book is illumination; for those who have gay or lesbian family members of any age, it will ease the path and help to keep communication open." — Steve Biddulph

Straight Parents, Gay Children, Robert A. Bernstein. 1995. "Through personal stories, Bob shows the ability and indeed the necessity of parents to not only accept their children but to become their advocates as well. Nothing speaks more loudly or passionately than a parent who simply wants a fair and equal life for his or her child." — Candace Gingrich

School Experiences of Gay and Lesbian Youth—The Invisible Minority, Editor Mary B. Harris, Ph.D. 1997. ". . . a valuable collection of research and commentary on the experiences of lesbian and gay youth in the classroom. The combination of a qualitative and quantitative research provides hard data, but more importantly, poignantly reflects the lives, the challenges, and the spirit of young people who are lesbian and gay. This book is a useful resource for professional and lay people who are concerned about the quality of education for sexual minority youth." — Margaret Schneider

Lesbian, Gay, and Bisexual Youths and Adults—Knowledge for Human Services Practice, Ski Hunter, Coleen Shannon, Jo Knox, James Martin.1998. This book is at once a scholarly work and a practical guide for understanding lesbian, gay, and bisexual persons. It provides a valuable social and historical context of lesbians, gay men, and bisexual men and women as well as exploring the oppressive responses of the heterosexual world. This is one of few texts which addresses the challenges of the turbulent adolescent life stage.

The Classroom Closet—Gay and Lesbian Students, Teachers and Curricula. Editor: Karen Harbeck, Ph.D., J.D. 1991. The book is a collection of well-rounded research articles related to homosexuality and education. It will be especially useful in preparing materials focused on parenting education.

The Beloved and Bent—Families Learning to Accept Lesbians and Gays. Pam Allen-Thompson and Di Allen-Thompson, LPCC. 1996. Educators focused on parenting education will find this to be a valuable tool in understanding the dynamics of families confronted with a child or sibling who is gay, lesbian or bisexual. ". . . a valuable tool for building bridges." — Mandy Carter

. . . And Then I Became Gay—Young Men's Stories, Ritch Savin-Williams. 1998. The stories told serve to demolish the stereotypes of gay male development, replacing them with real life experiences. Letting youth speak for themselves provides a valuable insight for professional educators engaged in preparing teachers for front-line parenting education roles.

Family Outing, Chastity Bono. 1998. A coming-out story by a young woman well known to the public because of the celebrity status of her parents. Her story is unique yet instructive. Chastity provides insight into childhood experiences of value to the development of parenting education materials. The story of Cher's response to Chastity's coming out is especially useful in addressing a parent's reaction to discovering that their child is gay or lesbian.

School's Out—The Impact of Gay and Lesbian Issues on America's Schools. Dan Woog. 1995. "Whether America wants to admit it or not, its schools are filled with gays and lesbians among the students, teachers, principals, coaches and counselors. And each day they face enormous challenges." (from the book cover). A compelling confrontation with the reality of sexual diversity and sexual orientation, and a valuable resource for students in preparation for an educational role in schools.

Sexual Interactions, Albert and Elizabeth Allgeier. 1995. This text is a study guide, and it or another of comparable scope is a must for the serious student of sexual diversity and sexual orientation. The chapter on "Sexual Orientation" provides a comprehensive overview of concepts and knowledge related to homosexuality. The material is fundamental to acquiring a sound grasp of homosexuality in today's society.

These are but a few of the books available. During the 1980s and 1990s there has been a substantial increase in publications, books as well as articles which have a significant bearing on developing materials for parenting education. On-line Internet services provide a wealth of listings of additional publications: books, articles, and documents.

Video Tapes

The decade of the 1990s has seen the production of a number of valuable video resources. Here are but a few of the outstanding publications:

Always My Kid: A Family Guide to Understanding Homosexuality. 1994, 74 min. Triangle Video Productions, 550 Westcott, Suite 400, Houston, TX 77007; (713) 869-4477; Fax: (713) 861-1577.

Straight From the Heart: Stories of Parents' Journeys To A New Understanding of Their Lesbian and Gay Children. 1994, 26 min. Dee Mosbacher, producer. Motivational Media, 8430 Santa Monica Blvd., Los Angeles, CA 90069; (800) 848-2707.

Queer Son: Family Journeys To Understanding and Love. 1994, 48 min. Vickie Seitchik, 19 Jackson Street, Cape May, NJ 08204; (212) 929-4199; Fax: 884-0264.

It's Elementary: Talking About Gay Issues In School. 1996, 87 min. Women's Educational Media, 2180 Bryant Street, Suite 203, San Francisco, CA 94110; (415) 641-4616.

Teaching Respect for All—Why Teachers, Administrators, Parents and Schools Need to Care About Issues of Sexual Orientation. 1995, 52 min. GLSTN, 122 W. 26th Street, Suite 1100, New York, NY 10001; (212) 727-0135; e-mail: GLSTEN@glstn.org; http://www.glstn.org/respect/

Additional titles and sources are available through the Internet on-line resources.

Organizations and Agencies

PFLAG, Parents, Families and Friends of Lesbians and Gays provides a wealth of resources that focus on families. In addition the organization has links to a wide range of collateral agencies and organizations some of which are noted below.

The PFLAG address: 1101 14th Street, N.W., Suite 1030, Washington DC 20005; (202) 638-4200; Fax: (202) 638-0243; e-mail: PFLAG@aol. com.

Organizations, Corporations, and Agencies

American Airlines
American Civil Liberties Union (ACLU)
American Library Association Gay, Lesbian and Bisexual Task Force
American Psychiatric Association
American Psychological Association
BiNet USA
The Blackstripe
Cathedral of Hope, world's largest gay & lesbian church
Children of Lesbians and Gays Everywhere (COLAGE)
Digital Queers
Dignity/USA
Ex-ex gays
Family Pride Coalition
Gay and Lesbian Alliance Against Defamation (GLAAD)
Gay Financial Network
Gay, Lesbian and Straight Education Network (GLSEN)
Gay Parent Magazine
GayScribe Listing of G/L Publications
Human Rights Campaign (HRC)
Institute for Gay & Lesbian Strategic Studies
Lambda Legal Defense and Education Fund
Licensed to Kill (documentary)
Intersex Society of North America
More Light Presbyterians

National Black Lesbian & Gay Leadership Forum
National Consortium of Directors of LGBT Resources in Higher Education
National Gay and Lesbian Task Force
OutProud! The National Coalition for Gay, Lesbian, Bisexual and Transgendered Youth
People for the American Way
PFLAG-Talk
Rural Gay & Straight Spouse Network
Scouting for ALL
T-SON Transgender Special
Outreach Network
Youth Resource

REFERENCES

American Psychological Association. (1998). Pamphlet: *Answers to your questions about sexual orientation and homosexuality.*

Allgeier, A. R. & Allgeier, E. R. (1995). *Sexual interactions.* Lexington MA: D.C. Heath and Company.

Blumfield, W. J. (1992). A theory of How Homophobia Hurts Everyone. *A matter of justice and compassion, addressing the needs of lesbian, gay, bisexual, transgendered youth.* Wichita KS: PFLAG Chapter.

Bono, C., & Fitzpatrick, B., (1998). *Family outing.* New York, NY: Little Brown and Company.

Griffin, C, Wirth, M. J., & Wirth, A. G. (1986). *Beyond acceptance, parents of lesbians and gays talk about their experiences.* Englewood CA: Prentice Hall.

Hoertdoerter, P, Morris, M. E., Barrett, J. M., & Johnson, F. A. (1999). *Sexuality and our faith.* Boston MA: Unitarian Universalist Association.

Hunter, S., Shannon, J. K., & James, I. M. (1998). *Lesbian, gay, and bisexual youths and adults.* Thousand Oaks CA: Sage Publications, Inc.

Kennedy, D. (1999). The New UUA Sexuality Curriculum. *World, The Journal of the Unitarian Universalists Association.* Boston MA: Unitarian Universalists Association.

Lipkin, A. (1999). *Understanding homosexuality, changing schools.* Boulder CO: Westview Press.

Mallon, G.P. (1998). Social Work Practice with Gay Men and Lesbians Within Families. In G. Mallon (Ed.), *Foundations of social work practice with lesbians and gay persons.* Binghamton NY: The Harrington Park Press.

Marmor, Judd, (1996). Non-Gay Therapy With Gay Men and Lesbians: A Personal Reflection. In: Ed.: Colby, Robert P. & Stein, Terry S. (1996). *Text book of homosexuality and mental health.* Washington D.C.: American Psychiatry Press, Inc.

Merriam Webster's collegiate dictionary. (1995).

Norman, T. L., (1998). *Just tell the truth, questions families ask when gay married men come out.* Kansas City, MO: Prehension Publications.

PFLAG. (1995). *Our daughters & sons, questions and answers for parents of gay, lesbian and bisexual people*. Washington DC:Parents and Families of Lesbians and Gays, Inc.

Vaughn, J. (1999). *Creating safe schools for all students, what educators need to know about gay, lesbian and bisexual Students*.

White, M., (1995). *Stranger at the gate*. New York, NY: Penguin Books USA Inc.

Woog, D. (1995). *School's out, the impact of gay and lesbian issues on American schools*. Los Angeles: Alyson Publications, Inc.

Youth Advocates hail Education, Health, mental Health Groups for Unprecedented Collaborative effort in Support of lesbian, Gay, Bisexual Students. (November 23, 1999). *GLSEN News*.

CHAPTER 4

Parenting and Ethnicity

Diane McDermott

Department of Psychology and Research in Education, University of Kansas, Lawrence, Kansas

INTRODUCTION: THE IMPORTANCE OF THE TOPIC

Over the past 80 years the fact that there are cultural differences in the many facets of life with which mental health professionals and educators deal has become increasingly important. There are several reasons why, at this time in history, those who hope to provide successful services to parents of diverse cultures and ethnicities must avail themselves of information about a wide variety of populations. The following two vignettes serve to illustrate the importance of having and using information about the cultural group for which the service is intended.

Ms. Whitely and the Parent Education Program

Sue Whitely has been a teacher in her school district for the past 20 years and has developed a good working relationship with her school's parent organization. Recently, the town in which her school is located has attracted many immigrants from Mexico and Cambodia. These families have come to make a better life for themselves with the steady employment they have in a local industry. Although the city has been receptive to these newcomers, many parents have expressed concern, albeit from lack of information, that these children may not be a desirable influence in the schools and neighborhoods. The school board has asked Sue Whitely to develop and conduct a parent education program for the parents in her school. The purpose of this program would be to educate all parents, but especially those from Mexico and Cambodia, about parent effectiveness.

Sue is a gentle and well-meaning person who is also an excellent teacher. She has not, however, had dealings with individuals from other cultures, whether foreign born or from the United States. Her upbringing and adult life were spent in a middle class, white suburb, and her current living situation is very similar. Sue has never considered her values, which are those of the dominant culture, to be different than anyone else's, let alone to be less than absolutely correct. When she determines which parenting values to present, she naturally turns to those of the culture in which she was raised.

Sue decides to base her program on issues concerning parent–child communication, the importance of students bonding with the school, parent participation in school events, and parent supervision of homework. From the research she has read, these subjects are all important ways parents can help their children become successful in school. She decides to have the parent education sessions in the afternoon when many children are in after-school activities. She sends a notice home with each child announcing the program, content, and hours. Twenty parents attended the first meeting, all of them white and middle class. Clearly she has not reached her target audience.

Before we examine a more successful attempt, let's review some of Sue's errors. To begin with, Sue did not know the life situation or the family values of her target audience. Rather, she made the assumption that, even though their values and situation may be different from the majority of her students, they would all aspire to be like the dominant culture. The topics she had selected, although very important for all families, may have seemed impossible to achieve, or even less important than other life issues, for the newly immigrated families she had hoped to reach.

In addition to the subject matter, the time Sue chose for the meetings and the method she used to announce the program was unrealistic. Many immigrant children do not have organized after school activities, but rather may be needed at home. In many of these families both parents work so that neither could take time to attend a parenting program. In addition, for these ethnic groups the role of the oldest male in the family is highly important, and such a meeting time precludes his participation. Last, and very important, in many immigrant families English is not spoken or read in the home, so announcements sent home that are written in English may not be understood. There are things Sue might have done differently that would have increased the likelihood that her target audience would have attended. Useful information is presented later in the chapter as each ethnic group is discussed. By contrast, the parent education program designed by Mr. Delarue is presented.

Mr. Delarue's Teen Substance Abuse Program

Joe Delarue taught for a number of years at the high school level and recently became the director of student services for his school district. One of the problems in this district is substance abuse, with students bringing drugs into the schools. The city in which this district is located has a large percentage of students who are African American and Hispanic, although their rate of substance use is no greater than that of white students. Joe Delarue has been teaching students from all cultural backgrounds and has come to know many of their parents over the past 15 years. He has learned a great deal about the problems and concerns that face these parents as they raise their children.

The program Joe offers is geared for students who have been discovered with drugs for the first time. Normally, this offense would require a 3-day out-of-school suspension, a punishment that may be more troublesome for the parents, who usually work, than for the students, who see it as a chance to "hang out" with friends. Rather than the suspension, this program requires the student and a parent or other relative, to attend a 2-hr meeting one evening each week for 10 weeks. The content of the meetings will be substance abuse, drug education, prevention, and family communication.

When a student is discovered with illegal substances, the counselor will call the home and describe the program to a parent or other guardian. Joe Delarue's program has been successful in reducing subsequent offenses, and the number of suspensions for first-time offenses significantly decreased over the previous year. Furthermore, a number students and interested family members regularly attend meetings that take place in the administration building once a week.

Joe Delarue's knowledge of the lives of the district's diverse population helped him to develop a program that could be used by the families of problem students. The meetings were set in the evenings so that many working parents could attend. Any adult who was interested and available to the student could attend—not only a parent, because many students live with other relatives or in an extended family. Personal contact was made with the home regarding the student's problem. Such individual communication is important to be certain the parents or others understand the purpose of the program and the magnitude of the concern.

WHY LEARN ABOUT CULTURAL DIVERSITY?

These two situations illustrate how the effects of having or lacking knowledge about diverse cultures can affect the success of our work. There are very specific reasons why issues of ethnic diversity are growing in importance, and will continue to do so in the future. Population projections estimate that within the next decade white Americans will be in the minority in many areas in the United States, with substantial growth taking place in the Hispanic and Asian American groups (U.S. Bureau of the Census, 1996). The dominant culture may no longer be preeminent and we may all need to re-examine our values with respect to the lives of our students and their families. Even standard American English as the language of choice for all schools has come into question with issues such as the bilingual classroom or the validity of Ebonics (A Case for Ebonics, 1997).

Increasing ethnic populations is not the only reason for developing an understanding of other cultures. Ethnic minorities, especially those individuals who have recently emigrated to the United States and those who live at or below the poverty level, constitute an undeserved group (Cheung & Snowdon, 1990; Sue & Sue, 1990). Although substance abuse, crime, school attrition, teen pregnancy, unemployment, and a host of other problems afflict all groups, the poverty and living conditions of many minority individuals make these groups especially vulnerable. It is imperative that parent education be suited to the values and culture of the specific groups for which it is aimed.

It also appears that many minority individuals in need of assistance do not access services even when they are available (Cheung & Snowdon, 1990). Many ethnic minorities either fear or distrust people whom they view as representative of a system that has been oppressive toward other members of their group. Additionally, some ethnic groups, such as Asian American, may believe that admitting problems within a family would be shameful (Yao, 1985).

When, for example minority individuals seek professional mental health consultation, 50% stop treatment after the first visit, compared with a 30% drop-out rate for Caucasian clients (Sue & Sue, 1990). Within the mental health field, specifically psychology, there has been a concerted effort to train individuals to be more sensitive to issues of diversity. In 1981 minority representation among psychologists was 3.2, and by 1991 it was 4.2 (Prochaska, Norcross, & Farber, 1993). McDermott and Stadler (1984) also found that a majority of counseling students in programs across the United States was Caucasian and middle class and had very little experience with minorities. It is clear that we cannot rely on minority professionals to serve the growing numbers of culturally diverse individuals or families. Caucasian professionals in all branches of human services must become familiar with diversity issues in order to provide effective services to families and their children.

The focus of this chapter is on the family, specifically cultural diversity in parenting and family issues. Not only is there is a wide range of parenting styles unique to specific cultural groups, but there are also situations and concerns unique to these groups that must be understood in order to provide effective services. Although no specific cultural diversity curricula are suggested here, the information presented is designed to provide a framework to assist those who establish programs for parents and children of diverse cultural and ethnic backgrounds.

The format for presenting cultural information will examine each group separately, beginning with Caucasian, or European American. It is this group that constitutes the dominant culture, the values of which have been those commonly accepted as the norm for the United States. It has been suggested that all diversity training begin with an examination of the dominant culture, for it is these values against which other values may come to be seen as different, or even abnormal (Kiselica, 1983; Sue & Sue, 1990). Dominant culture values are so thoroughly ingrained in most Caucasian Americans that they are often not recognized as actual values. People from other ethnic groups, however, are well aware of the differences and recognize that they will be judged on the basis of how well they conform to the values of the dominant culture.

A FEW CAVEATS

Before proceeding to a description of each group and its cultural values it is important to insert a note of caution concerning generalizations. Although it is possible to speak of general characteristics of a group, any given member of that group may not fit the description. There are many factors that mediate culture and may be stronger in determining what the lifestyle of the individual will actually be like (Atkinson, Morten, & Sue, 1993). For example, socioeconomic level may determine an individual's place of residence, educational attainment, and referent group. Related to this, the level of education achieved greatly determines employment and lifestyle, among other variables. There may be more similarity between a poverty level Caucasian family and a poverty level African American family than between the low socioeconomic and high socioeconomic families of either ethnic group.

Gender must also be taken into account when making generalizations about culture (Hays, 1996). Both sexes have commonalties within their own group that transcend ethnicity, or even socioeconomic factors. For example, women who have children can usually relate to other women with children, regardless of their social or economic situation. Similarly, men can be seen fraternizing in the sports arena regardless of whether or not they would have much in common in any other context.

Age is an important variable that mediates the way in which individuals in a group (Baruth & Manning, 1991) may manifest culture. For example, among first generation Asian Americans there appears to be a stronger desire to acculturate than among their foreign-born parents. Native American elders may manifest more traditional ways than their much younger offspring. African American youth appear to have a very different attitude about racism in the United States than their parents who grew up during the days of Martin Luther King.

Do these caveats indicate that we cannot make any generalizations about the values of ethnic groups in the United States? We nonetheless are shared by enough individuals that they are helpful in our understanding. The best advice for any human service worker who is communicating with parents and children from a different ethnic group is, when in doubt, ask.

THE PLACE TO BEGIN: EXAMINE YOUR OWN VALUES

As previously noted, it is necessary first to understand one's own values before it is possible to understand those of another. Accordingly, we begin with a presentation of values that comprise the standard for the dominant culture. Although these values are so commonly accepted that they are usually unquestioned by members of the dominant culture, it is important to remember that they are not shared by all, and that we often use them as the yardstick to measure the adequacy of others.

EUROPEAN-AMERICAN VALUES AND THE DOMINANT CULTURE

The dominant culture is identified as European-American because the majority of its peoples originally emigrated from countries in western, central, northern or southern Europe. Although each part of Europe contributed variations to the cultural milieu, some central themes have developed that characterize the dominant culture. It is those themes we present here. Although there are other values that may be important to take into account in specific instances, these values are the ones most likely to be problematic when the human service worker assesses the life style of a minority client. The values presented here are adapted from the work of Katz (1985).

Individual as the Primary Unit in Society

The United States was founded on ideals of rugged individualism and the concept that each person is responsible for his or her own life and achievements. Within this framework the concepts of independence and autonomy are important. Most dominant culture youth have goals of establishing their lives separate from that of the their families, often moving great distances from their parents. Yet other cultures place a higher value on the group rather than the individual, and family/community ties may be binding.

Competition

Generally speaking, the dominant culture is a competitive group. Even though lip service is given to how the game is played, winning is still a driving force for many individuals. Parents urge their children to compete in sports, for scholarships, and a variety of other achievements about which the parents brag.

Communication Standards

In the United States people are expected to speak Standard English, to stand an appropriate distance from others, and to make direct eye contact. Although personal space variations occur within the dominant group, eye contact is important in connoting sincerity. The correct use of English is often used to judge social class and education. Those who work with ethnic minority families need to be aware not only of potential language barriers, but also of the variety of nonverbal communication styles that may be used.

Action Orientation

An important value of the dominant culture is its view that something must be done about every situation, no problem can be left unsolved; a "doing" versus "being" orientation to life (Ho, 1987). The dominant culture demonstrates this action orientation, as well as the competitive drive, by structuring many activities for children, insuring that they will never have "idle hands."

Time Orientation

In the dominant culture we value punctuality and live by the clock. We are a scheduled nation and value time as if it were a commodity; "time is money," we say. We communicate this value to our children by scheduling their days, in and out of school, giving the impression that their lives should parallel their parent's lives in activity.

Another implication of time orientation concerns whether individuals focus on the past, present or future. The dominant culture focuses on the future, and we instill this in our children by encouraging them to delay gratification, earn good grades for scholarships, save their money, and a host of other exhortations.

Work Ethic

The importance of hard work, sometimes referred to as the Protestant work ethic, is a value that is stressed in the dominant culture. This country was built upon a principal that it is possible to "pull one's self up by the bootstraps" and that hard work will pay off. For many people this is simply not the case. By virtue of birth, many people of color or unfortunate circumstances cannot work hard enough to see any appreciable gain in their status. The United States, once the land of opportunity, now has serious social problems that affect an unfortunate number of individuals. The Protestant work ethic remains a desirable value; however, there is an inherent danger in basing judgments upon it. Not all successful individuals have gained their success through their own initiative, and, in the reverse, not all unsuccessful people have failed because they did not work hard enough.

Family Structure

For a good part of the 20th century the dominant culture has favored the nuclear family as the structure of choice. As the country became more affluent and more mobile the establishment of smaller families, rather than extended families became the norm. No longer was there a need for the large family to work together for survival. Economic conditions, in addition to autonomy and independence, dictated the desirability of establishing separate homes.

For other cultures within the United States, however, the extended family is the norm. For immigrants and others living in disadvantage situation it is obviously desirable to pool resources in order to survive. A lack of understanding of the importance of family structure can produce problems in effectiveness for the human service worker.

SUMMARY VIEW OF EUROPEAN-AMERICAN VALUES

Developing a composite picture of a member of the dominant culture we see an individual who values his or her individuality and autonomy, views hard work as the route to success and along with that, may be competitive in work or play. This person is likely to take action in the face of difficulties and places a premium on time. The communication style of this person is likely to be standard English, and he or she may be uncomfortable with indirect eye contact. It is likely our composite person lives in a nuclear family, probably with a spouse of the opposite sex.

As we view our composite person we cannot limit group membership on the basis of ethnicity, race, skin tone, gender, age, or socioeconomic status. Membership in the dominant culture, although most accessible to those of European-American heritage, is also open to any who accept and live according to the dominant culture's credos. By the same reasoning, simply because an individual is white, does not guarantee he or she will fit the mode of the dominant culture.

The purpose of this chapter is to present issues of ethnicity as they relate to parenting. A basic assumption is that most professionals working in the areas of parent education, school counseling, school psychology, family counseling, or other related professions are members of the dominant culture, and therefore share the European-American value system. Minority group members who are professionals are also likely to share this value system but, in any case, it is unlikely that they would be conversant with the values of all other major cultures within the United States (Atkinson, Morten, & Sue, 1993).

The important values that impact parenting for each ethnic group will be presented first. Next, brief descriptions are given, based on actual cases, to illustrate the lifestyles and concerns of each group.

AFRICAN-AMERICAN VALUES AND PARENTING

About the Group

The term "African-American" is used here, rather than black American; however, it is important to recognize that the group is made up of individuals whose heritage is from places other than Africa (e.g., Haitians, West Indians). According to the U.S. Census Bureau (1996), there were over 34-million African-Americans in the United States, constituting the largest minority group. Of this number over 86% live in urban areas (Sue & Sue, 1990.) There are approximately two million more women than there are men, and the mean age for the entire population is 29.5 years, compared to 35 years for whites. The average socioeconomic conditions for African-Americans are well below those for whites. High unemployment, especially among young African-American men, limited educational opportunities, and a generally inequitable system all contribute to oppressive conditions for many members of this group (Young, 1988). It is against this backdrop that cultural values, as they may affect parenting, are presented.

There are several noteworthy characteristics of the African-American family that have a profound effect on parenting, and that should be understood by any professional hoping to work with that group. First in importance is the family structure. The extended family, rather than the nuclear family, is the norm for this group (Hale-Benson, 1986; Lum, 1986). From an expediency point of view, with over 5070 of African-American households headed by single mothers, having other relatives or friends in the home to help with childcare is beneficial. However, the extended family also has historical roots, dating back to slavery, and before that to Africa (Lum, 1986). The extended family is a close-knit system that serves as both security and identity for the individuals within it.

Consistent with the concept of extended family, are the values of mothering expressed by African-American women (Blum & Deussen, 1996). These mothers see their children as belonging to the entire group, not only to themselves. Siblings, relatives, and even friends and neighbors are encouraged to discipline and care for children. African-American neighborhoods are often close knit communities where children may come under the purview of any adult who happens to be watching. In a dominant white culture neighborhood this might be considered "nosiness" and interference with the family's right to manage its own children.

By dominant culture standards the discipline meted out in the African-American family appears to be harsh. Corporal punishment is the norm, with strapping and hitting common (Spurlock, 1985). Historically, African-American children, especially young men, were punished as a means of protection and to teach them their place in white society (Bell-Scott & McKenry, 1986).

The role of the church in African-American family life is important to note. The church often comprises the community that serves a social as well as spiritual function (Hale-Benson, 1986; Nye, 1993). A description of church services provide a clear example of some of the differences between African-American and dominant culture values. For example, although most Protestant or Catholic services begin and end at regular times, the African-American service is likely to begin when enough people arrive and continue on into the day. African-American spiritual music tends to be less formal, and the congregation is encouraged to participate spontaneously in the service to a greater extent than would be found in most dominant culture churches.

Any consideration of the African-American family must take into account the social and economic conditions previously mentioned, because these contribute numerous problems with which the family must cope. There is high unemployment, especially among young men, low wages, crime and drugs in many neighborhoods, and poor health care for low-income African-Americans (Atkinson, Morten, & Sue, 1993). Racial discrimination, despite the many improvements over the past 50 years, continues to be a powerful influence on the identity development and success of African-American youth (Williams & Kornblum, 1994). The following vignette is a description of the life situation common for a low-income African-American family. This example is not meant to be generalized to the entire group, but rather, to illustrate some common values.

Dorothea's Family

Dorothea Jackson is a 30-year-old single parent with three children. She, her children, her mother, her sister and her two children live in a large old home in an urban area that is mostly African-American. Dorothea's mother is partially disabled from diabetes but is able to watch over the children after school while her daughters are at work. The children's fathers, who are frequently unemployed, are not in the home but make financial contributions when they can.

Dorothea and her sister are hard workers. Both women hold jobs in the dietary department of a local hospital, and Dorothea attends night classes at the community college in order eventually to obtain a better paying job. This schedule does not allow her to spend much time with her children, but she knows they are well cared for by their grandmother and aunt.

For social interaction, and because they are deeply Religious, the entire family attends church every Sunday. The values Dorothea hopes to instill in her children are also reinforced through the church. These values are hard work, respect for family and community, and faith in God. She fears however, that a peer group that does not share these values will tempt her children as they grow into adolescence. There are drugs and crime in her neighborhood, and she sees young people with seemingly nothing to do lounging on street corners drinking and smoking.

Although Dorothea wants her children to attend college, she also knows they must work especially hard to obtain scholarships. She urges her children to do well, but wonders if she is pushing too hard. Already her oldest son, who is 11, tells her he doesn't need to work hard because there are no jobs for black men out there anyway.

This brief vignette illustrates some of the positive values of the African-American family. For many young people these appear to be in conflict with social reality! creating frustrating and angering situations. Another source of conflict is the discrepancy between what behavior may be expected in the home and what is expected at school (Locke, 1995). African-American children may experience more emotional expression, and less restriction on motion and noise than dominant culture children. The dialect spoken in the home may also be different than that required at school for African-American children. Professionals who hope to be successful with this group must recognize the legitimacy of all the stresses impinging on African-American families.

ASIAN-AMERICAN VALUES AND PARENTING

About the Group

The term "Asian" encompasses a number of groups including Chinese, Japanese, and Korean, which have been the largest groups in the United States. Asians who are also immigrating in larger numbers are from the many countries in Southeast Asia, from India and from the Pacific Islands (U.S. Bureau of the Census, 1996). Each of these groups has a culture and values that differ from the other, making generalizations difficult (Atkinson, Morten, & Sue, 1993). It is important not to group all Asians together but rather to determine the country of origin and what specific concerns the individual family may have.

Socioeconomically, the most recent immigrants experience the most disadvantages. They must cope with language differences and often can obtain only low paying employment. Those from Southeast Asia seldom immigrate with any substantial resources of their own, having come from third-world countries ruptured by war. Contrasted with this poverty however, is the notion of the model minority, the Japanese, Chinese and Korean groups who are out-stripping Whites in success (Kao, 1995; McLeod, 1986). Although it is true that a number of Asian-Americans have been very successful, a closer examination shows large groups of Asian-Americans living in sub-standard housing, ghettoized, and living at or below the poverty level (Atkinson, Morten, & Sue, 1993). For this group, there are a number of social problems adversely affecting the family with which human service professionals must become familiar.

Providing a general picture of Asian values with respect to parenting since Asians and Pacific Islanders make up over 25 distinct groups (Sue and Sue, 1990). However there are values, such as familial interdependence and group orientation, that appear to be represented in nearly all groups (Atkinson, Morten, & Sue, 1993). It is these, as they affect families that are presented here.

A composite of parenting values for this group highlights family structure, group orientation, work ethic, respect for elders, and the concept of "face." The extended family is important to Asian-Americans, with grandparents and other relatives often living in the home or nearby. The structure of the Asian family is patriarchal with the oldest male garnering the most respect and obedience. Male children are valued more than female children, but all are expected to work hard and be successful. Hard work and achieving financial stability is important for members of this group. Although education is acknowledged as the road to success, children may be expected to work to help support the family rather than pursuing higher education (Atkinson, Morten, & Sue, 1993).

Discipline may be verbally harsh involving name calling and shaming if children disobey the head of the family (Itai & McRae, 1994). Children are exhorted to work hard and put family interests before individual wishes. As immigrant children begin to acculturate the family discipline becomes increasingly disparate with the values of the dominant culture (Sue, 1980). A common problem occurs when a young person wishes to pursue a career other than that desired by the father. The young person is caught between the value of respect for the parent, possible loss of face for the family if the parent is disobeyed, and personal wishes for a career.

The story of Lee and her family describe a situation commonly experienced by Vietnamese immigrants. Although the description might be somewhat different if Lee were of another Asian culture, or male rather than female, the story serves to illustrate those values that can generalize best across groups.

Lee's Family

Lee is a young Vietnamese woman who lives with her husband and daughter in the suburbs of a large western city. Lee's husband owns a beauty supply warehouse, and Lee owns and operates a nail care salon. Their daughter is in the first grade and attends public school.

Lee, her parents, two older brothers, and a younger sister emigrated from Vietnam when Lee was 7 years old. The family came first to central California where Lee's parents worked as farm laborers in the orchards. All the children began public school immediately, learning English quickly. Lee attempted to teach her parents the new language, but because they continued to speak Vietnamese in the home, her parents never became proficient in English.

An important value for Lee's family was the benefit of hard work. After school, on weekends, and each summer, all the children worked in the orchards. Lee can remember many summers when she was quite small, working long hours picking fruit in 100° weather. As tiring as that was however, no one in the family complained because the income was needed if the family was to survive and prosper.

By the time Lee was ready for high school the family had amassed enough money for her father to buy a small grocery store. The family moved to a Vietnamese community in a coastal California town where both parents and children worked in the store. Lee's father expected all his children to be successful, but his plans for his oldest son were to continue in the family business. The second son was to become a professional, which she did by entering law. A small family crisis was generated when Lee announced she was not going to college, but rather to cosmetology school. When she married, however, and her husband was a merchant, Lee's father was satisfied that she would be in good hands. Lee maintains the family value placed on education by encouraging her younger sister to continue in college, even paying some of her tuition. Lee hopes her own daughter will become a doctor, thus bringing prestige and money into the family.

The daily life of Lee and her family is not unlike the life of her own family when she was a child. She works long hours in her salon, and her daughter plays and watches television there when not in school. Unlike the many after school activities favored by the white middle class for their children, Lee believes her daughter is just as well off spending her afternoons where her mother works. Her daughter will soon by old enough to work in her father's warehouse and become a contributing member of the family.

Professionals who work with parenting issues, and who are themselves imbued in dominant culture values, may judge Lee to be neglectful of her daughter's needs. They must come to understand the values instilled by the family of origin and view the strong work ethic in its survival context.

What this vignette does not describe is the struggle between acculturation and tradition and the promise of a better life as opposed to social realities. Lee's story is one of success, but many immigrants do not fare so well. Unemployment is high in crowded areas, identity confusion is common between the generations, and youth may turn to drugs and gangs (Atkinson, Morten, & Sue, 1993). There may be strife within the family when the value of respect begins to break down as children begin to take on the values of the dominant culture. Older Asian Americans are confused when their children act in ways they never would have considered (Baruth & Manning, 1991). It behooves parenting specialists to become aware and sensitive to the wide variety of stresses upon the Asian-American family.

LATINO-AMERICAN VALUES AND PARENTING

About the Group

As with Asians, the term Latino is a composite one including people whose heritage includes Mexico, Spain, Cuba, Puerto Rico, Central and South America, and the Dominican Republic. However, unlike Asians, there is more homogeneity among people whose heritage is Hispanic (Casas & Vasquez, 1989). The U.S. Bureau of the Census (1996) reports a population for this group of over 29 million, approximately 50% of each gender, with a mean age of approximately 27 years of age. Nearly 90% of this group live in the Pacific Southwest, Illinois, New Jersey, New York, or Florida. According to the U.S. Census (1996) over 28% of Latinos live in poverty.

Immigration of Latinos has been high, causing a number of social problems. As with other immigrant groups, there is a tendency to cluster where there are others of the same country of origin and who speak the same language. This ghettoization can produce high unemployment, lowered wages, crowded classrooms, and a variety of problems for young people such as drugs and gangs (Atkinson, Morten, & Sue, 1993). A thorough knowledge and understanding of the social conditions in which Latinos live is necessary if the helping professional expects to be successful.

As with Asian- and African-American peoples, the extended family is central to the values of Latinos. The family may include parents, grandparents and other relatives, and often Godparents as well as honorary aunts and uncles. The Latino family is patriarchal, with the oldest members of the family commanding the most respect (Falicov, 1982). Respeto, respect for one's elders and members of one's family is an important traditional value taught in the Latino family (Atkinson, Morten, & Sue, 1993). The roles of women and men in the Latino family are often traditional, with the responsibility for rearing the children belonging to women. The role of the church is important in the Latino family, and most often the religion is Catholicism. The church reinforces the dominance of men and the childbearing role of women, and advocates for large families. Another value, fatalism (Rotter, 1966), appears to be consistent with Latino Catholic beliefs.

Within the Latino family children are treasured and discipline may be relaxed. Loyalty to the family is expected, however, as well as obedience to the father or oldest male member. This value, termed familismo, ensures that the individual's first concern will be the welfare of the family, and, through that, he or she will find comfort and identity (Fialicov, 1982).

As with other ethnic groups described, social problems are integral to an understanding of the Latino family. Because so many individuals and families have emigrated from Mexico to the southwestern part of the United States, that unemployment is high and wages are low, housing is insufficient, and health care is inadequate. Many migrants are illegal, and therefore not eligible for social services, placing a further strain on families. Many young people, recognizing these problems and with little hope for the future, drop out of school or turn to drugs or gangs, further alienating them from their families (Atkinson, Morten, & Sue, 1993).

The story of Manny describes a family in better circumstances than those found in the barrio. However, even a family living in a semirural community encounters difficulties in maintaining its values in the face of changing times.

Manny's Family

Manuel, called Manny by his friends, was born in Colorado to parents who had emigrated from Mexico in the 1950s. His parents had settled in a small community in Colorado because his father had obtained a job at a local meat processing plant. There were seven children in the family and never enough money to meet expenses. In high school Manny was a good student and would have liked to graduate. However, the family needed the income, so he quit school in his sophomore year and went to work in the meat processing plant alongside his father.

When Manny was 18 he met the love of his life, Maria. They were married, and, soon after, she became pregnant. Because they had little money, the young couple lived with Manny's parents, where Maria helped his mother with the housework and took care of the younger children.

Living in the large family was comfortable and congenial, but extremely crowded. As soon as Manny was able to save enough money, he and Maria rented a house very near his parents. Children continued to come for Manny and Maria, and each one was considered a special gift from God.

Each Sunday, the entire family including grandparents, parents, children, aunts, uncles, and cousins could be seen dressed in their best clothes attending the Spanish-language Mass. The church played a central role in the life of the family. Manny and Maria's boys served with the priest at the alter, Maria took care of the alter flowers, and her daughters cleaned the church. One of Manny's cherished dreams was that one of his children would be called to a vocation in the church.

As contented as Manny and Maria were with their own lives, their children could not envision spending their lives at the meat processing plant. They were becoming restless and eager to move to a larger city either to find different work or to attend college. As important as Manny knew a college education to be, he dreaded the influences of a larger city and, most important, he feared the dissolution of his family and the loss of values so important to him.

The story of Manny and his family illustrates the values of respeto, familism, and fatalism. Unfortunately, many who come the United States to seek a better life must leave their families behind. The disruption of the values that characterize the Latino family can only have a negative effect on Latino children.

NATIVE-AMERICAN FAMILY VALUES

About the Group

As with the other ethnic groups discussed, Native-Americans are a diverse population. There are 511 federally recognized native entities, 365 state-recognized American Indian tribes, and there are 200 tribal languages spoken (Manson & Trimbel, 1982). The population numbers over two million, with more than half being women and a mean age of 27.7 years (U.S. Bureau of the Census, 1996).

The socioeconomic conditions of Native-Americans has been well documented (U.S. Senate Select Committee on Indian Affairs, 1985). Unemployment is high, ranging from 20% to 70%, depending on the reservation and location. For the most part there is substandard housing and inadequate health care, resulting in a shortened life expectancy. Suicide rates are also high for this group, possibly reflecting a loss of hope for the future. Formal education is low with the mean number of years of schooling for those over 25 being S.6 (Brod & McQuiston, 1983). Nearly one third of all Native American Adults is classified as illiterate (Price, 1981). It is against this backdrop that parenting issues are presented.

The extended family, central to the Native-American culture as with the other ethnic groups described, takes on a somewhat different meaning. Because of the tribal system and its diversity, family is difficult to describe. Every individual in a tribe has some relationship to every other and could be considered family. Children may live in a nuclear family, or they may live with many family members, even in a number of different homes (Red Horse, 1982). Members of the Indian community, much as with the African American-neighborhood, watch and care for all the children belonging to their group. Because it is estimated that approximately 30% of Native American households are headed by women, and 25% are receiving some type of public assistance (Staples & Mirande, 1980), the extended family is an efficacious means of insuring adequate child care.

Native-Americans tend to be noncompetitive and nonacquisitive (Sue & Sue, 1990). These values can cause Indians to be labeled as lazy by the dominant white culture, in which acquiring property and competition are considered admirable traits. Sharing, rather than coveting, is the norm for Native-Americans. These values, as well as that of humility, can convey the faulty message that Indian people do not care about the way they live, or are not interested in improving themselves. This may be especially true in school, where Indian students hesitate to put themselves forward at another student's expense. The values of the family and community reinforce quietude and a self-effacing behavior that is at odds with what is commonly expected in public school.

Discipline in the Native-American family tends to be relaxed and consistent with the values children are taught. Among those values are sharing, cooperation, harmony with nature, noninterference, respect for elders, loyalty, and a present, rather than future, time orientation (Herring, 1996). Children are encouraged to participate in tribal ceremonies, and it is common to see children dancing alongside their parents in full dress at a pow-wow.

Native Americans have their share of social problems, and it would be impossible to discuss family values without also presenting the problems and concerns with which these families cope. In addition to poverty, poor health care, boredom, and a host of other ills, alcoholism features high on the list. The rate of alcoholism is far higher for the Indian population than it is for the dominant culture (Anderson & Ellis, 1980). Although there may be a hereditary component, the poverty, boredom, and lack of opportunity may also be a reason why many Indian people drink. Youthful drinking is also a problem, and may stem from a general lack of hope for the future. In a recent study of 146 Native-American students, it was found that they scored significantly lower in hope on a validated scale, than did White or African-American students (McDermott, et al., 1998).

The story of Ben White Cloud, although not generalizable to all Indian people, illustrates some of the family values that are important for those who work with Native American parenting issues to understand.

Ben White Cloud's Family

Ben was born on the Crow reservation in Montana in 1946. As soon as he was old enough for school he was removed from his family and taken to a boarding school run by Catholic nuns. The purpose of Ben's education, and that of the other students who spent their school years away from their families, was to acculturate them in the ways of the dominant White culture, and to ensure that the only language they spoke fluently was English. During the few visits each year that Ben was allowed with his family, he and they felt an increasing alienation from each other. Although all the tribes abhorred removal of Indian children from the family and the reservation, the Federal Government that mandated the policy was too powerful to fight.

When Ben turned 16 he decided he had had enough of school and moved to Billings, Montana to seek his fortune. He had no skills and no high school diploma, so the only work available to him was a low paying service industry job. After working for some time as a dishwasher, Ben decided to return to his people on the reservation. Once there, the alienation he had felt as a child returned, and he began to drink for solace. Ben drank heavily for several years while living with his parents and drawing a government allotment. Ben's parents did not like his drinking, but said nothing about it in the hope that he would recognize he had a problem on his own.

Despite his frequent bouts with alcohol, Ben began to learn more about his Crow heritage and, as he became more comfortable with his identity as a Crow, he began to drink less. He regularly attended ceremonies, and it was at a pow-wow that he met Sharon. She was several years younger than he and had a child from another relationship, but they continued to spend time with each other, and finally were married.

After Sharon and Ben began their lives together, Ben stopped drinking completely and obtained a job with a ranch just off the reservation. The salary was small, but Ben enjoyed working with the cattle and riding the fence lines during the day. They continued to have their government allotments, and with game and fish plentiful, they were satisfied with life.

Ben encouraged his stepson to go to school, and to learn the ways of the Crow people by spending time with the elders. Their family life was a good one, but Ben and Sharon both knew the temptation of alcohol and the dangers of poverty and boredom. They had tried to instill in their son a sense of balance between all the forces of nature, and a reverence for their culture. However, would these values be enough to protect him from the hopelessness that infected Indian people all around them?

SUMMARY AND CONCLUSIONS

This chapter has presented values as they influence the parenting of European-Americans, African-Americans, Asian-Americans, Latinos, and Native-Americans. There are a number of commonalities and differences both between and within these groups. Professionals who work with children and their families must familiarize themselves with the characteristics of each group, examine their own values for any pejorative judgments they may be inclined to make, and then respond to each individual family as unique.

It is important to take into account the specific group membership within the larger ethnic group, the ages of the family members, their varying stages of acculturation, and the way in which gender influences the role with in the family. A sampling of the social problems experienced by families has been presented in this chapter, but it behooves us to identify problems that may be unique to specific environments and geographical locations.

As a final note, remember that one individual cannot know all there is to know about any ethnic group. It is important to know your limitations and then ask the families for help in learning what you do not know about their ethnic and cultural backgrounds. This simple guideline will be appreciated, and will enhance your program's effectiveness.

REFERENCES

A case for Ebonics: An interview with Norma Le Moine, (1997). *Curriculum Review. 36,* (7), 5–6.

Anderson, M. J., & Ellis, R. H. (1980). Indian American: The reservation client. In N. A. Vacc & J. A. Wittmer (Eds.), *Let me be me* (pp 105–127). Muncie, IN: Accelerated Development, Inc.

Atkinson, D. R., Morten, G., & Sue, D. W. (1993). *Counseling American minorities: A cross-cultural perspective.* Dubuque, IA: Wm. C. Brown.

Baruth, L. G., & Manning, M. L. (1991). *Multicultural counseling: A lifespan perspective* (2nd ed). Upper Saddle River, NJ: McMillan.

Bell-Scott, P., & McKenry, P. C. (1986). African adolescents and their families. In G. K. Leigh & G. W. Peterson (Ed.), *Adolescents in families* (pp. 410–432). Cincinnati, OH: South Western.

Bernal, G., & Gutierrez, M. (1988). Cubans. In L. Comas-Diaz & E. E. H. Griffen (Eds.), *Clinical guidelines in cross-cultural mental health.* New York: John Wiley & Sons.

Blum, L. M., & Deussen, T. (1996). Negotiating independent motherhood: Working class African American talk about marriage and motherhood. *Gender and Society, 10,* 199–211.

Brod, K. L., & McQuiston, J. M. (1993). American Indian adult education and literacy: The first national survey. *Journal of American Indian Education, 1,* 1–16.

Casas, J. M., & Vasquez, M. J. T. (1989). Counseling the Hispanic client: A theoretical and applied perspective. In P. B. Pederson, J. G. Draguns, J. Lonner, & J. E. Trimble (Eds.), *Counseling across cultures* (3rd ed., pp. 153–175). Honolulu: University of Hawaii Press.

Cheung, F. K., & Snowdon, L. R. (1990). Community mental health and ethnic minority populations. *Community Mental Health Journal. 26,* 277–291.

Falicov, C. J. (1982). Mexican families. In McGoldrick, M., Pearce, J. K., & Gordiano, J. (Eds.), *Ethnicity and family therapy* (pp. 134–163). New York: Guilford Press.

Hale-Benson, J. E. (1988). *Black children. Their roots. culture. and learning styles.* Baltimore, MD: Johns Hopkins University Press.

Hays, P. A. (1996). Addressing the complexities of culture and gender in counseling. *Journal of counseling and development. 74,* 332–338.

Herring, R. D. (1996). Synergetic counseling and Native American Indian Students. *Journal of Counseling and Development. 74,* 542–547. 25

Ho, M. K. (1987). *Family therapy with ethnic minorities.* Newberry Park, CA: Sage.

Itai G., & McRae, C. (1994). Counseling older Japanese clients: An overview. *Journal of Counseling and Development. 72,* 373–377.

Kao, G. (1995). Asian Americans as model minorities: A look at their academic performance. *American Journal of Education. 103,* 121–159.

Katz, J. H. (1985) The sociopolitical nature of counseling. *The Counseling Psychologist, 13,* 615–624.

Kiselica, M. S. (1998). Preparing Anglos for the challenges and joys of multiculturalism. *The Counseling Psychologist, 26,* 1, 5–9.

La Fromboise, T. (1988). American Indian mental health policy. *American Psychologist, 43*(5), 388–397.

Lock, D. C. (1996). Counseling interventions with African American youth. C. Lee (Ed.), *Counseling for Diversity.* Boston, MA: Allyn & Bacon.

Lum, D. C. (1986). *Socialwork practice and people of color: A process-stage approach.* Monterey, CA: Brooks/Cole.

Manson, S. M., & Trimbel, J. E. (1982). American Indian and Alaskan Native communities: Past efforts and future inquiries. In R. L. Snowdon (Ed.), *Reaching the underserved: Mental health needs of neglected populations.* Beverly Hills, CA: Sage.

McDermott, D., & Stadler, H. A. (1984). Attitudes of counseling students in the United States toward minority clients. *International Journal of Counseling. 11,* 61–71.

McDermott, D., Gariglietti, K., & Hastings, S. (1998). An investigation of hope in minority school children. Unpublished manuscript. University of Kansas, Lawrence, KS.

McLeod, B. (1986 July). Success story: Outwhiting the Whites. *Psychology Today,* 48–52.

Nye, W. P. (1993). Amazing grace: Religion and identity among elderly black individuals. *International Journal of Aging and Human Development, 36,* 103–114.

Price, J. A. (1981) North American Indian families. In C. Mendel & R. Habenstein (Eds.), *Ethnic families in America.* New York: Elsevier. 245–268.

Prochaska, J. O., Norcross, J. C., & Farber, J. (1993). Contemporary psychotherapists: A national survey of characteristics, practices, orientations, and attitudes. *Psychotherapy. Theory, Research and Practice, 20,* 161–173.

Red Horse, Y. (1982). A cultural network model: Perspectives for adolescent services and professional training. In S. M. Manson (Ed.), *New Directions in Prevention among American Indians and Alaskan Native Communities* (pp. 17–18). Portland, OR: Health Sciences University.

Rotter, J. B. (1966). Generalized expectancies for external and internal control of reinforcement. *Psychological Monographs, 80,* 609.

Spurlock, J. (1985). Assessment and therapeutic intervention of Black children. *Journal of the American Academy of Child Psychiatry, 24,* 168–174.

Sue, D. W., & Sue, D. (1977). Barriers to effective cross cultural counseling. *Journal of counseling psychology, 24,* 42–429.

Sue, V., Bernier, J., Durran, A., Feinberg, L., Pedersen, P., Smith, E., & Vasquez-Nuttal, B. (1982). Position paper: Cross cultural counseling competencies. *The Counseling Psychologist, 10,* 4–52.

Sue, D. W., & Sue, D. (1990). Counseling the culturally different: *Theory and Practice.* New York: John Wiley & Son.

U.S. Bureau of the Census. (1996). *Statistical Abstracts of the United States* (116th ed.), Washington D.C.: U.S. Government Printing Office.

U.S. Senate Select Committee on Indian Affairs. (1985). *Indian Juvenile alcoholism and eligibility for BIA schools.* (Senate Hearing 99-286). Washington, D.C.: U.S. Government Printing Office.

Williams, T., & Kornblum, W. (1994). *The uptown kids: struggle and hope in the projects.* New York: Putnam.

Yao, B. L. (1985). Adjustment needs of Asian American immigrant children. *Elementary School Guidance, 19,* 223–227.

Young, C. (1988). *State of Black America 1982–1988.* New York: National Urban League.

CHAPTER 5

Parenting in the Global Community: A Cross-Cultural/ International Perspective

John Bennett

Organization for Economic Co-operation and Development, Paris, France

Liam K. Grimley★

Department of Educational and Social Psychology, Indiana State University, Terre Haute, Indiana

INTRODUCTION

In considering parenting issues in the context of the global community, we will discuss in this introduction the importance of cultural awareness in cross-cultural/international studies. We will then identify some factors which have made parenting more complex and difficult in different countries, before discussing contrasts in parenting conditions between developed and developing countries.

In the second section we will present some cultural–ecological models, such as the ecological theory of Bronfenbrenner (1979), which provide a framework for better understanding of parenting issues in the global community. In the third section, we discuss Lifestart projects in five different global environments, all of which are based on "Growing Child," a parent education program developed in the U.S. In the fourth section, we present some successful parenting programs in different countries, including France, Turkey, The People's Republic of China, and the Philippines. Last, we present some concluding comments on parenting in the global community.

★Deceased.

Handbook of Diversity in Parent Education

The Importance of Cultural Awareness

A cross-cultural/international perspective on parenting must immediately confront the issue of cultural diversity in our world. Parenting is perceived and defined differently in different cultures of the global community. Definitions of parenting are, of course, intimately related to varying perspectives on the nature of childhood. Each culture—and indeed each age within a culture—either implicitly or explicitly redefines the nature of childhood and parenting within its own sociohistorical framework (Ambert, 1994).

In the Western world, for example, the concept of what constitutes a family has recently been undergoing change due to recent court decisions pertaining to same sex marriages, palimony in the case of unmarried couples, and more fathers than ever before being granted custody of children in divorce cases. In comparison with a few decades ago, an increasing number of children are also now spending more time, during their early childhood years, with paid caregivers than with parents. What constitutes the "ideal" family structure is therefore a matter of continuing debate (Hughes, 1989).

A cross-cultural perspective helps to underscore the reality that parenting as a cultural phenomenon is an evolving construct in both time and place. Ambert (1994) has noted that "parenting is constantly being constructed according to the ideologies and the paradigms of those sciences and professions that happen to dominate at any point in time in terms of dictating what is good for children." (p. 530)

In this context, it may be noted that most of the research on children and parents has been dominated by paradigms from Western culture. Brazelton (1991) has pointed out that our ethnocentric research models tend to limit our observational techniques as well as other forms of data gathering. Although this Western dominance is widely recognized (Kessen, 1993), the results of research studies are too frequently presented as though they were universally applicable to all cultures.

Conceptualization of our world can be so influenced by Western thought that it may be difficult for us to comprehend how other cultures, such as tribal societies in Africa and Asia, developed their own parenting and child-rearing practices. Among the Habakushu bush tribe of Botswana in southern Africa, for example, once young children are weaned, the boys are raised in the men's village and the girls in the women's village. The same word "father" applies to all men of the village responsible for the boy's upbringing, just as the one word "mother" applies to all those involved in the girl's upbringing. Older children develop responsibility by supervising younger children in daily activities, with well-regulated societal proscriptions related to sexual behavior and procreation.

Although tribal customs and practices might appear primitive to an outside observer, they are generally highly functional within their own cultural context. In cross-cultural study, one is obliged to break the molds of one's own narrow "certainties" in order to gain deeper insight into the complexities of human behavior.

Our own involvement in planning and programming of parenting programs in different countries has convinced us that cultural awareness is an essential prerequisite for the success of such programs (Grimley & Bennett, in press). Reproductive patterns, family formation, and child-rearing practices differ widely in the global community. They are not just expressions of individual will but are often determined by deep-rooted religious and cultural world views from the past, as well as by social and economic conditions in the present.

Some cultural differences are so deep rooted that they are difficult to discern. Others can be identified at an observable level. It has been observed, for example, that there are differences between ethnic groups in proxemics, the nonverbal language of social space. When Caucasian Americans engage in conversation, they generally stand about 21 in. apart. In contrast, Asians, Indians, Pakistanis, and Northern Europeans prefer to maintain a greater distance, whereas Arabs, Latin Americans, and Southern Europeans are accustomed to being closer to one another when they talk (Gollnick & Chinn, 1998).

Language also reflects differences between cultures. When translating from one language to another, for example, one finds that a concept that is taken for granted in one culture may not even exist in another. In Spanish, for example, there is an important distinction between the words "ser" and "estar," yet both are translated by only the one verb "to be" in English. In translating the English word "cross-cultural" to the French word "interculturel" part of the English meaning is lost because the term "interculturel" refers to a comparison *between* cultures, thereby losing the connotation of a possible common ground among those cultures.

Complicating Factors in Parenting

Cultural awareness is an important first step in developing a cross-cultural perspective on parenting in the global community. Throughout the world the role of the parent has become more difficult and more complex. Three factors that make the task of parenting in the global community considerably more difficult are poverty, war, and migration. The negative impact of poverty on children, and on family life in general, has been well documented. These families often lack adequate nutrition, medical care, and proper housing. Children in poverty exhibit the entire gamut of physical, emotional, and behavioral problems and often perform poorly in school (McLeod & Shanahan, 1993).

A second factor that makes parenting more complex and difficult in the global community is the impact of war and violence on the lives of children. A recent study by the National Academy of Sciences (1994), for example, has documented some of the devastating effects of war on children in the countries of the former Yugoslavia. Even in countries that have not experienced war, there is evidence of a dramatic increase in violence to which children are exposed. Schools can no longer be considered safe environments for children. There is evidence to indicate that schools have become, in some instances, a breeding ground for antisocial behavior (Bronfenbrenner & Weiss, 1983).

Immigration, either as a result of war or because of adverse economic conditions, is a third factor negatively affecting many families throughout the world. Even the change from an agrarian to an urban environment can adversely affect parent–child relationships, with the children more likely to become an economic liability as consumers in their new environment rather than being economic producers.

As waves of immigrants and refugees move from one country to another, a key variable in the process of adaptation is the degree of similarity between the old and the new cultural environments. Where the cultural differences are extreme, it is not unusual to find immigrant children who attend school rejecting the language of the home as well as traditional customs, practices, and other family values. LeVine and LeVine (1985) have suggested some reasons why children are generally less respectful and obedient to parents in a new cultural environment, namely, because, through schooling, they are more influenced by the culture of the host society and are constantly exposed to peer influence. Parents, on the other hand, lose, in their new cultural setting, the communal social support for child-rearing practices and the traditional family values of the home society that they have left.

All of the factors we have considered underscore the complexities and difficulties experienced by parents in the global community. Other problems become apparent when we consider contrasts between developed and developing countries.

Contrasts Between Developed and Developing Countries

In the industrialized world, family education programs have generally fo-cused on parenting and child-rearing, understanding human development including sexuality, supporting children's learning, and improving inter-personal relationships and family processes. Matters of health care, re-source management, and even children's education are often left in the hands of providential government authorities who are expected not only to provide such services but to set and maintain stringent high standards in these areas.

Salaried, nuclear families rarely if ever experience the social and eco-nomic constraints imposed on those in the poorer countries of the devel-oping world. Despite widespread reporting of child abuse cases in West-ern societies, attitudes toward children are also, in general, very different from those in developing countries. In Western societies, generating of children is generally seen, not as a destiny to be accepted, but as a freely chosen means of fulfilling the couple's happiness. Children born from unions of choice are generally treated with love and consideration. Few obstacles are placed in their way, unless their desires are seen to interfere with their health, schooling, or future happiness. Appeals to authority, family honor, not to mention harsh confrontation with superior physical force, are rarely resorted to, and conflict is negotiated as among adults. In short, the child is treated as a subject of desire, with full rights to respect and equal treatment.

Nevertheless, some economic, educational, and socialization challenges still exist. In many Western countries, children are still expected to work long hours at school, in directive, authoritarian classrooms, so as to forge them into the disciplined workforce of the future. They are seen by many policy makers as units of human resources, the future guarantors of pensions, social values, even of nationhood and other ideologies. Despite lip-service paid to developmentally appropriate practices, schools often fail to encourage and help children to be creative, to make choices, to learn prosocial behavior and engage in real problem-solving skills that may better serve the work force of the future. As a result, children and families may find it difficult to bend to reality and may need assistance through parenting programs to do so. In general, however, despite these challenges, the main preoccupation of families in Western societies is not basic survival, but rather the pursuit of happiness.

By contrast, in parts of the developing world where survival is a daily concern, family well-being is generally defined in terms of the satisfaction of fundamental human needs, such as food, shelter, health, and basic education. The satisfaction of these needs depends to a great extent on basic life skills, that is, on information and behaviors necessary for survival and family development. These include food production skills, home-building, and basic infrastructure skills such as the ability to manage resources, nutrition information, family planning, and reproductive health information. Given the nature of the situation and the content of the above life skills, family education programs in developing countries frequently emphasize community solidarity and cooperation.

In most countries of the developing world, reproductive health is a critical issue in parent education because of AIDS or threats to the health of child-bearing women. Maternal health is also endangered by multiple pregnancies, which lead often to chronic morbidity in mothers and to malnutrition and neglect of children, especially girls. In the case of the infant, it is the compounding of poor maternal health in pregnancy with postnatal malnutrition that conspire to cause the greatest ravages on an infant's brain and bodily development. The roots of school failure—poor health, vision and hearing defects, and low learning ability—are often implanted during the crucial period from conception to 2 years of age.

In the survival societies of the developing world, family organization and attitudes toward children are based—as was also the case in Europe a century ago—on the iron law of necessity. To survive, all members of the family, including children, must work and place family interests before their own. In such a model, parents or adult caregivers play a predominant role. Children may be loved as much or as little as in the West, but once generated they are socialized according to traditional views of family solidarity and along strict gender lines. In poor, rural societies where children are still seen as the property of the parents, they are valued above all for their work value, and later on as the caregivers for parents in their old age. In extreme, patriarchal settings, in which boys are considered to have greater work use, girls can be overprotected to enhance their marriage value or are abandoned, neglected, or sold. By Western standards, children of both sexes are often treated harshly, even abusively, by uneducated parents living under duress. Unwanted children are among the most vulnerable and the most likely to be at risk of dying at an early age.

In contrasting developed and developing countries, it is obvious that parenting programs—if they are to be useful—will differ radically according to the situation. In the developing world, parenting education—or, family life education, as it is more commonly called—focuses on family planning, child survival, nutrition, and reproductive health education. Because of the danger that overpopulation poses for human ecology, economic growth, and the development of education systems, family planning for both men and women is considered a priority in family life education programs.

In contrast to Western countries, developing countries have also typically focused child-related programs on child survival: maintaining nutritional and primary health by providing children with adequate food and protecting them against disease or other dangers. A change has been taking place, however, over the past few years, as the shortcomings of concentrating on physical well-being alone have been pointed out (Myers, 1992). As health care, feeding, and the personal development of the child are intimately connected, mothers are encouraged to use moments of care to interact with their children in developmentally appropriate ways and thus promote psycho-social and cognitive growth as well. The focus is on child development and parent education, which has been defined as a range of educational and supportive measures that help parents and prospective parents to understand themselves and their children and enhance the relationships between them (Pugh & De'ath, 1989). The aim of such programs is to empower parents by training them to access and improve statutory services, sensitizing them to support child development, and providing them with the means to support child learning. Already, sufficient indications have been given to show that such programs depend on the economic and social context and, in particular, on parents being freed from survival tasks so that they can concentrate on family related developmental issues. In general, national economy, public health, and education improve when there is a better match between resources and the population base. As a result, mothers are healthier and have more time to invest in the care and education of fewer children, who, in turn, are more robust, better nourished, and more likely to succeed in school.

Having considered the importance of cultural awareness, the complicating factors of poverty, war, and migration, as well as contrasts between developed and developing countries, we need now to consider some theoretical models that provide a helpful framework for better understanding of parenting issues in the global community.

A CULTURAL–ECOLOGICAL APPROACH

Bronfenbrenner's Ecological Model

Bronfenbrenner (1979, 1986, 1995) has proposed a socio-ecological model of child development that is helpful in considering child-rearing practices in different cultural contexts. Although the model has recently been expanded to include biological influences (Bronfenbrenner, 1995; Bronfenbrenner & Morris, 1997), we will limit consideration to the socio-ecological model as shown in Figure 1. The four systems in this model are the microsystem, the mesosystem, the exosystem and the macrosystem.

At the center of the microsystem is the child with his or her unique individual characteristics (age, gender, physical capacities, etc.). The microsystem is the setting in which the child experiences direct interactions with others, including family, school, church, etc. Bronfenbrenner has pointed out that most of the research on socio-cultural influences in a child's life has focused on microsystems. He also points out that the interactions within a microsystem are two-way influences, with the child as active participant, and not—as is sometimes wrongly assumed—as though the child were merely a passive recipient of these influences (Marjoribanks, 1996).

As children grow up, they become involved in an increasing number of

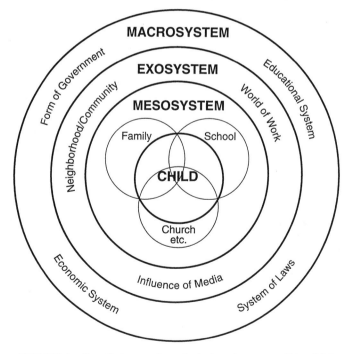

FIGURE 1   Bronfenbrenner's ecological environment of the child.

microsystems, all of which form part of what Bronfenbrenner has termed the mesosystem. The mesosystem involves the interconnectedness of all the various microsystems. For example, there are connections among family, school, and work. Children who grow up in an enriched family environment are more likely to begin school ready to learn, and those who do well in school are more likely to be successful in seeking a job. Likewise, children who grow up in a disadvantaged family environment are likely to experience repercussions in other areas of their lives.

The family, including its child-rearing practices, is an important element of the mesosystem. There have been many recent comparisons between parenting practices in different countries (Bornstein 1991a, 1991b; Bronstein, 1994; Clark 1980; Davison, 1989; Gfellner, 1990; Keller, Chasiotis, & Runde, 1992; Keller & Scholmerich, 1988; Kelley & Tseng, 1992; Mizuta, Zahn-Waxier, Cole & Hiruma, 1996; Tulloch, 1997). Other studies have focused on parenting practices in just one country, such as India (Sharma, 1996), Malaysia (Yaman, 1996), Taiwan (Chung, 1994), and the People's Republic of China (Liang & Sugawara, 1992).

The importance of considering interaction between variables within a mesosystem can be illustrated by the results of a study by Best, House, Barnard, and Spicker (1994). They compared the impact of gender on parent–child interactions in France, Germany, and Italy. They found that French girls and Italian boys were more affectionate toward their parents than were the other groups of children. French and Italian parents and children were found to be more interactive, in general, than the German dyads. It was also found that French and Italian fathers engaged in more playful activities than mothers, but the opposite was found among the Germans. In this study, both gender and ethnicity proved to be important and interconnected variables when comparing parent–child interactions in these countries.

Studies of school achievement and the development of literacy skills in children have also shown that wider systemic variables are involved, including health-related issues (Puchner, 1993), and maternal care during pregnancy (Negussie, 1990). Hence the importance in cross-cultural comparisons, of considering the interconnectedness of many different variables within the mesosystem.

The next layer, exosystem, includes a wide range of elements, which, though not directly experienced by the child, can have a significant impact on the microsystems which affect the child. For example, a parent's workplace is not an immediate concern of a child as long as the parent's work provides a means of support for the family. However, if a parent loses a job, which is part of the exosystem, it will inevitably impact the child and other family members. Likewise, the lack of public daycare and early education services have a negative impact on child rearing, particularly in socieites in which parents are expected to participate in the labor market.

The macrosystem in Bronfenbrenner's model is a still larger cultural context in which the previous systems are embedded. A country's form of government, system of laws, and economic and educational systems form part of the macrosystem. Though an individual child may seem to be far removed from government policies or international agreements, they can and often do have some impact on the child's life. For example, as indicated previously, a study sponsored by the National Academy of Sciences (1994) documented the tragic effects of war on the lives of children in the countries of the former Yugoslavia. Brofenbrenner's model is focused on the child, but with slight modification one can create a parallel family

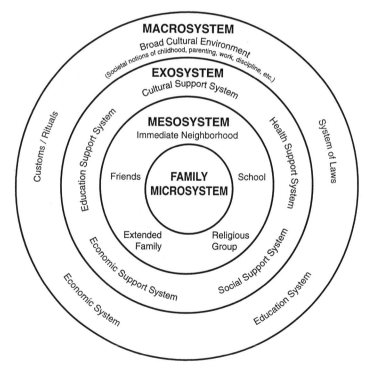

FIGURE 2   An ecological model of the family system.

model which can serve as a conceptual tool for planning family programs or parenting interventions in a country, or locality.

In this revised model, the family, with its internal processes and resources, is at the center. However, as in Brofenbrenner's original model, it is linked in turn with ever larger environments, on which parenting professionals must also act if they are to be effective in supporting families. For this reason, it is unrealistic, for example, to blame individual families for failure or treat antisocial behavior as if it were a question only of individual psychology. This is not to deny that frequently, and not least with families at risk, the careful, individual accompaniment of the family through its internal processes is absolutely necessary. Educators cannot afford, however, to be unaware, of the influence of the immediate community (the mesosystem) in which the family is inserted nor of the larger sociocultural and economic support system (the exosystem) that hold a particular society together, nor indeed of the overarching system of laws, state institutions and the broader cultural representations of the child (the macrosystem) that inform the actions of societies and their governments (McGoldrick, Giordano, & Pearce, 1996).

Two conclusions may be drawn from the above model. First, that a general, parent education program, no matter how expertly developed, needs adaptation if it is to fit different milieus. The homes in our cities and countryside are nested in larger, more powerful relationship systems which differ considerably, particularly at meso-system (neighborhood) and exosystem (socio-economic context) levels. Second, the nesting of homes in neighborhood and socio-economic systems indicates that parent education cannot by itself solve the problems posed by poverty and demoralized communities. Parent education needs to be supported by adequate health, social and public education services, caring schools, outreach to parents, as well as by pathways into the mainstream economy.

The Developmental Niche

While Bronfenbrenner's socio-ecological model provides a useful framework in which to consider parenting issues in different cultural contexts, the model of the developmental niche, developed by Harkness and Super (1993), focuses more specifically on the importance of cultural context in understanding child development. The developmental niche consists of three interrelated subsystems: the physical and social settings in which the child lives, the culturally regulated customs and practices of child care and child rearing, and the psychology of the caretakers, including parental eth-notheories (Figure 3).

The physical and social settings of child-rearing include the physical aspects of the child's home. Is there running water, indoor plumbing, electricity, etc.? It also includes family size and structure. How many siblings? What is the child's birth order? Is it a single parent or a two-parent home? What are the physical and social characteristics of the neighborhood? What are the regular daily activities of both adults and children?

Observation of children's settings leads to the discovery of the second subsystem: culturally regulated customs and practices of child-care and child-rearing. These customs and practices are so thoroughly integrated into the larger culture and so commonly practiced by members of the community that they are perceived as the "natural" way to behave. They generally have no need for justification or rationalization within a community and are often not even given conscious thought. They are simply assumed to be the "right way" to raise children.

A leading role is assigned to the third subsystem, namely, the psychology of the caretakers, including parental ethnotheories or belief systems. These belief systems are specialized cultural models derived from broader cultural influences. In China, for example, Confucianism underlies parents' attitudes to their children (Ekblad, 1986). Filial piety, whereby children are expected to show reverence for their elders and to satisfy their

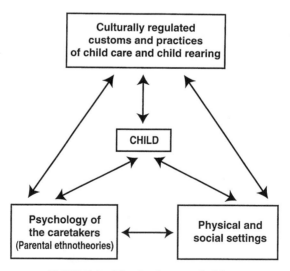

FIGURE 3   The developmental niche.

parents in all things, is an important Confucian concept for both parents and children (Hsu, 1981).

Studies examining parenting in immigrant Chinese families provide a unique opportunity to observe how parental ethnotheories gradually change from the culture of origin to the new culture. Kelley and Tseng (1992) examined differences in parenting techniques and goals between immigrant Chinese American mothers and Caucasian American mothers. They found that, whereas both Chinese and Caucasian mothers had similar child-rearing goals (morality, concern for others, etc.), immigrant Chinese mothers relied on traditional Chinese methods of socialization (more physical punishment, yelling, etc.) to achieve these goals.

In comparing differences across generations among Chinese families in Hawaii, Lum and Char (1985) found that families did not consider themselves fully assimilated—taking on the characteristics of the host culture—until the third or fourth generation. First and second generation families usually maintained strong bonds to their culture of origin, having their children participate in Chinese language programs and attending a church in which Chinese was the language of worship.

Eldering's Culture–Ecological Model for the Study of Child-Rearing in Bicultural Settings

The culture–ecological model proposed by Eldering (1995) is basically a combination of Bronfenbrenner's socio-ecological model and the framework of the developmental niche developed by Harkness and Super. The culture–ecological model seems particularly appropriate for studying changes in child-rearing practices in bicultural settings as a result of immigration.

Prior to World War II, few European countries experienced large scale immigration comparable to that in the U.S. In recent years, however, many European countries have been experiencing massive immigration of families (Eldering, 1995). These families can be categorized broadly into four groups:

- Immigrants from former colonies that are now independent (from India, Pakistan, Ireland, and the West Indies to the United Kingdom; from North Africa to France; from the Moluccas, Indonesia, Surinam, and the Antilles to the Netherlands)
- Migrant workers (predominately from Greece, Italy, Spain, and Turkey)

- Refugees from countries experiencing war or political unrest such as the countries of the former Yugoslavia
- Families experiencing job-related dislocation as a result of the establishment of the European Union.

Those immigrating from developing countries experience particular difficulty because they usually differ in several respects from the indigenous population. They not only experience culture shock related to their values, language, and religious beliefs, but they generally have low socioeconomic status in their new environment.

Children of immigrant families face particular problems, which, until recently, received little attention from researchers—other than to document their frequent failure in their new school settings. Although the parents sought to maintain strong links to their country of origin and to preserve the only traditional cultural values they had ever known, the children were expected somehow to be successful in a totally new cultural environment.

It has been found that immigration leads to a long process of interaction between the immigrants and the receiving society. The outcome of this bicultural interaction—and the ultimate impact on parenting practices—depends on many factors within the immigrant communities and the receiving society. In a study of the migration of Hindustani's from India to Surinam and later to the Netherlands, Eldering (1995) has identified some of the more salient factors. Between 1873 and 1916 about 34,000 Hindustanis—most of whom had been living in poverty or deeply in debt—emigrated to Surinam, which was a Dutch colony where slavery had been abolished in 1863. Because of an acute labor shortage, these immigrants came as indentured plantation workers. About 80% of these immigrants were Hindu and 20% Muslim. On board the ships which transported them to Surinam, customs related to their caste system could no longer be observed. On the plantation, employers considered all Hindustanis as field workers, irrespective of caste. In private life, however, the Hindustanis preserved much of their traditional culture. Marriages were still arranged by parents and celebrated according to Hindu or Muslim rituals. Although egalitarian principles applied when working on the plantations, traditional values and customs were preserved in private life by living in close-knit villages of rural Surinam.

In the 1970s, many Hindustanis decided—mainly for political reasons—to emigrate from Surinam to the Netherlands. Here they encountered the Dutch policy regarding immigrants from former colonies, namely, that they be widely dispersed across the country in order to be more fully integrated into the dominant culture. As a result, the Hindustani community lost its cohesion and social control. Among the Hindustani community in the Netherlands, researchers have found many problems, including a high divorce rate, a high percentage of female-headed households, and many conflicts between parents and children (Eldering, 1995).

This study of the migration of Hindustanis to Surinam and to the Netherlands indicates a difference in impact on families in the public and private domains. By living together in communities in Surinam, Hindustanis continued to maintain social cohesion and family control. Those who emigrated to the Netherlands in the 1970s, however, lost their cultural cohesion. This ultimately led to the erosion of traditional family values and the disintegration of family life as they had known it.

CULTURAL ADAPTATIONS OF A PARENT EDUCATION PROGRAM, "GROWING CHILD", IN FIVE DIFFERENT GLOBAL ENVIRONMENTS

In this section we will describe how a parent education program, *Growing Child*, has been used in five very different ethnic and cultural environments. Although the goal remained the same in all settings, namely, to provide parents, month by month, with practical understanding of their child's development, throughout the early childhood years, each of these different global contexts provided unique problems and challenges requiring specific cultural adaptations.

The "Growing Child" Model of Parent Education in the United States

How does a parent education program come into existence? *Growing Child*, a parent education program that has reached over 3.5 million families in the U.S., is somewhat unique in that it's a program that began with the identified needs of just one family. Realizing that other families with young children must be experiencing similar needs for education on child development, this family decided to act. This is the story of how the *Growing Child* parent education program began:

> *Growing Child* began with a boy named Phillip, who was experiencing learning problems in school. Phillip was enrolled in a special remedial learning program at the same time his parents were being trained to fill in the gaps in his earlier childhood learning experiences. Even though the outcome of Phillip's remedial training was positive, his parents became aware that other children were experiencing similar problems—problems that did not have to happen if parents had more knowledge about early childhood development. Since Phillip's father was in the publishing business, it was a logical step to engage a team of child development specialists to develop a monthly newsletter that would identify for parents the early childhood experiences important for future learning. The team included specialists in fields such as child psychology, language development, pediatrics, visual development, learning disabilities, motor development, speech pathology, special education, and family counseling. The newsletter was developed with a focus on stimulation of normal growth and development and on the prevention of unnecessary problems that may result from parents' lack of knowledge of child development. (Grimley & Robinson, 1986, p. 82)

Growing Child provides parents with information on child development, month by month, from birth through 6 years of age. Each month parents receive the specific issue geared to their child's age in months. Parents are also made aware that children vary in their development. Usually a child may be ahead in some areas, a little behind in others, and "typical" in still others. The concept of the "typical" child describes the characteristics one would expect to find in children at a particular given age. By being aware of developmental milestones, parents can thus assess their child's individual strengths, weaknesses, and other characteristics.

Besides describing developmental characteristics, parents are informed in each issue of *Growing Child* about simple activities in the home which can facilitate their child's development. For example, the parents of a 3-month-old baby read in the "3 Months" issue:

> By the time Baby is three months old she has become quite social. She coos and smiles at you as you approach her. When you lean over her playfully and talk to her, she responds by smiling, gurgling and even chuckling.
>
> She may still prefer to turn her head part way to the side, but more and more often brings it to mid-position. She promptly looks at a dangling toy, and if you move it slowly from one side to the other she turns her head and follows it with her eyes.
>
> Baby's hands are no longer tightly closed. Her fingers have started to relax, and if you place a rattle in her hand, she will hold it and glance at it. (*Growing Child*: 3 Months, p.1).

In evaluating *Growing Child*, three basic assumptions underlying the program's goals were identified: (1) Because parents are viewed as the central and most important persons in a child's development, parent education should aim to support the parents rather than become a substitute for the parents' role; (2) Better parenting is more likely to occur when parents are provided with age-appropriate information about their child's developmental stage; and (3) A sound educational program for parents is one of the most effective methods of early childhood intervention and prevention of unnecessary developmental problems.

The results of a survey to determine the characteristics of *Growing Child* readers and the extent to which the material was read and applied by parents has been reported elsewhere (Grimley & Robinson, 1986). In summary, it was found that an overwhelming majority of the respondents to the survey (97%) were from two-parent homes. A majority of the fathers (56%) had a university degree, which was also the case for more than half (52%) of the mothers.

One of the most encouraging aspects of the survey results was that 99% of the mothers reported reading some or all of the material each month, 85% of the mothers read all of it, and 67% of the fathers read some or all of it. Another important finding was that, whereas only 14% of the readers reported discussing the child development information in *Growing Child* with their pediatrician, 95% reported that they discussed this information with one another. In other words, parents were not only receiving important information in *Growing Child*, but this newly acquired knowledge was helping to stimulate discussion about child development in the home.

The First Lifestart Project in the Connemara "Gaeltacht"

In 1985 the Lifestart Foundation was established. Using the *Growing Child* materials,[1] the first project was planned for the economically-disadvantaged but culturally-rich region of the Connemara *Gaeltacht* in the west of Ireland where Irish (Gaelic) is the native language.

To understand the cultural adaptations in *Growing Child* that needed to

---

[1]In light of the fact that the *Growing Child* materials have been made available free of charge to all Lifestart projects so far, it seems appropriate to note that a recent book written by the publisher is entitled *Every Child Is Our Child* (Dunn, 1992).

be made, it is important to understand some of the characteristics of the region.

Although the region is classified as economically disadvantaged, the Irish-speaking families along the west coast of Ireland have preserved, over a period of centuries, a very rich cultural heritage. Traditional Irish music, dance, and song—as exemplified recently in performances of *Riverdance* around the world—have been passed from generation to generation by means of a strong informal educational system. This system was in existence long before the advent of the formal educational system of state-supported schooling. Likewise poetry and literature have been transmitted by bards and storytellers by means of strong oral traditions within the community.

In establishing the first Lifestart project, *Oiliúint Baile* (Home Education), in the Connemara *Gaetacht*, it was decided not to present the material in written form but to rely on the culturally familiar custom known as "cuartaíocht" (an Irish word, which, loosely translated, means "visitation"). It had long been a practice in this region for experienced mothers in the community to visit and provide support for the mother of a newborn baby. By training a group of *"cuairteóirí"* (visitors), through this project, it would be possible to present the new mother with the information in the *Growing Child* materials. However, first those materials needed to be translated into Irish and adapted to the local cultural setting.

The Connemara Lifestart project known as *Oiliúint Baile* was developed in two phases. During Phase I, 1985 to 1989, a first draft of the Irish translation of the *Growing Child* materials was prepared. A group of 20 parents who had already successfully raised children in the region were selected as consultants to review, evaluate, and recommend changes in the materials. The criteria used in this evaluation included the appropriateness of the material to the cultural environment, the clarity and simplicity of the language used, and the practicality of the recommended parental interventions. During this phase, the *cuairteóirí* were trained to provide this age-appropriate child development information to parents.

Phase 2, implementation of the program, began in February, 1989. During this phase the *cuairteóirí* who had been trained began to visit mothers of newborn babies in the community on a monthly basis. They spent approximately 1 hr with each mother, month by month, sharing the age appropriate information on child development and responding to concerns or questions the mother might have. A copy of the age-appropriate materials was then left with the parents each month.

In an Evaluation Report on the project prepared by the Center for Health Promotion Studies at University College Galway in 1994, some of the issues of cultural adaptation involved in the project were identified:

> "The educational purpose of the Lifestart materials, which are standardized in each project location, is to inform and enrich the parent–child relationship. In this aspiration, Lifestart moves away from the centre periphery model of education which tends to impose a dominant educational agenda from outside and which arguably values standardized educational attainment and abilities at the expense of personal or cultural characteristics. Homes that are culturally different such as the Gaeltacht are most at risk from such "cultural totalitarianism." (McNelis & Kelleher, 1995, p.21)

Sensitivity to the cultural environment in which the program is developed became a hallmark not only of the *Oiliúint Baile* project but of all subsequent Lifestart projects. In the next section, further details of the Evaluation Report will be presented.

The Ballymagroarty Project in Northern Ireland

How can one take a parent education program which has been successful in one cultural environmental (i.e., the U.S.), then adapt it to meet the needs of parents in a second very different cultural environment, (i.e., the Connemara *Gaeltacht*) and then further adapt it to a third very different cultural environment, namely, Ballymagroarty in Northern Ireland?

Ballymagroarty is a new housing development in Derry, a city in Northern Ireland which has experienced much sectarian strife in recent years. At the time it was decided to initiate a Lifestart project in Ballymagroarty in October 1989, this particular housing estate, according to the Interim Report of the Family Centre Project (1990), had the highest percentage of children to population in the United Kingdom. Although it was classified as a working class housing estate—with a male unemployment rate of 87%—"it would not be unfair to classify it as a nonworking working class area" (McNelis & Kelleher, 1995, p. 29). It has also been noted that many of the parents were having their first child at a young age and that 32% of the households in the area were single-parent families (Ballymagroarty Development Group, 1993).

A two-phase process, similar to what took place in the Connemara

Gaeltacht, was developed. During Phase I, under a grant from the Northern Ireland Department of Economic Development, a group of 6 workers rewrote and adapted the *Growing Child* materials. Although the language of this project was English, differences in terms of unemployment, limited income and educational achievement became important issues for consideration. For example, although the setting was urban, the newly adapted materials did not encourage or even mention the use of store-bought toys, focusing instead on the educational uses of items readily available in the home. (McNelis & Kelleher, 1995). During this phase, the newly prepared materials were distributed to a group of experienced parents for evaluation purposes, using a questionnaire of the same format as had been used in the Connemara *Gaeltacht* project. Based on this input from parents, further changes and adaptations were made.

Although parents served as consultants to the project in Phase I, during Phase 2 the parents who were consumers in the project became the evaluators. Following the monthly home visits, during which the young child's development was discussed, parents received not only the materials but also an Evaluation Questionnaire, which, as in the Connemara *Gaeltacht* project, was collected by the visitor at the next visit. It should be noted at this point, that, because the *Growing Child* materials are in loose-leaf rather than book form, adaptations, revisions, and updates can easily be made in a very short period of time.

An evaluation of the Lifestart projects in the Connemara *Gaeltacht* and in Ballymagroarty, conducted by the Centre for Health Promotion Studies at University College Galway, reached this conclusion:

> Both projects, but most particularly the *Oiliúint Baile* project, faced a considerable challenge in adapting the *Growing Child* materials for an audience that was geographically, culturally, socially and financially removed from the original American clientele. In doing so, consideration had to be taken of not only the language and cultural differences, but also of family relationships, financial difficulties, personal and community self esteem, and levels of motivation that could impinge on the reaction to and use of the materials.
>
> Both projects rose to this challenge, and produced materials that were appropriate to the user audience, and which vary slightly from the message of the original text. While the Family Centre in Ballymagroarty did excellent work on presenting the original text in a shorter and cleaner style, *Oiliúint Baile* had greater handicaps in their adaptation. Yet they have produced a text that is very much in keeping with the natural environment of the area and its cultural heritage, while providing much supplementary information that would not be available in a straight translation of the American text (McNelis & Kelleher, 1995, p.39).

The El Raval Project in Barcelona, Spain

In January 1994, with encouragement of the European Commission, a delegation from Fundacio Esco in Barcelona, Spain, visited the Lifestart projects in the Connemara *Gaeltacht* and Ballmagroarty to determine the feasibility of starting a similar project in the Catalan-speaking area of El Raval in Barcelona. According to the Lifestart Programme Report in 1995:

> El Raval has for some considerable time been a 'slum' where poverty is endemic. There is large scale prostitution, drug taking, alcoholism and crime.
>
> The core of the problem is seen as the disintegration of the family and the marginalization of the individual. Problems are handed down from parents to children who do not have elementary schooling and job training, which in turn has a direct impact on the unemployment levels which are very high. The children often suffer from serious problems of malnutrition, lack of medical assistance, abuse and irregular schooling.
>
> Poverty is especially visible in housing with most flats lacking basic facilities such as water, sanitation, electricity. Many flats are rented without official contracts leaving the renters open to exploitation (Rowan, 1995, p. 8-9).

Unlike the previous Lifestart projects, this program of early childhood parent education would become an additional component of a larger ongoing program funded by the Esco Foundation. Some of the other components that were already in place included programs such as, "*Casal*" (a summer program) and "*Equip Tutories Juvenils*" (youth monitoring teams), "*Accompanyment de Families*" (a family visitation program), and "PIRMI" (a state-funded program to integrate the resources of various agencies tailored to the needs of individual families that had been socially excluded through lack of employment, alcoholism, drugs, and prostitution).

All of these Esco Foundation programs were highly integrated with one another. For example, a parent might become part of the family visitation program, *Accompanyment de Families*, as a direct result of a child being identified as high risk during the *Casal* summer program for children. This in turn could lead to access to the State-funded PIRMI program, which integrates socially excluded families into the labor force. Likewise, a child identified as high risk during the *Casal* summer program could be helped throughout the year in the youth monitoring program, *Equip Tutories Juvenils*, in which an individualized program would be developed for each high risk child. The location of the meeting with the child would depend on individual circumstances. For some students who need after school remedial classes, the Esco foundation offices might be the most appropriate site. For others, the city streets might be the only possible meeting place.

The Lifestart early childhood parent education program therefore not only needed to be translated into Catalan and adapted to this particular cultural environment, but it also needed to be designed in such a way that it could successfully enmesh within and build upon an already-existing integrated service delivery structure. In addressing the cultural adaptations which would need to be made, in comparison with what had been accomplished in the *Oiliúint Baile* and Ballymagroarty projects, the Lifestart Programme Report 1995 stated

> The situation in Barcelona (El Raval) is considerably different. The differences include: immigrants with different cultural backgrounds, more fragmented family patterns, considerably more deprivation in terms of housing and education, greater poverty, greater disintegration of families, high levels of prostitution, drugs, alcoholism, crime and homeless persons (Rowan, 1995, p. 10).

Because of the complexity of the problems to be addressed, it was decided to pay particular attention to the training of the family visitation teams. The training would include development of core competencies including (1) product knowledge (i.e., familiarity with the adapted *Growing Child* material), (2) instructional skills, (3) demonstration skills, and (4) group leadership skills. In addition, newly trained team members would be required to complete an internship in the program under direct supervision of an experienced team leader. It was planned that the vocational skills acquired would ultimately lead to certification by national bodies and would have "direct transferability into the workplace whereby visitors who are on work placement schemes can seek employment as training instructors in any industry sector" (Rowan, 1995, p. 11). In this way, if workers in the project experienced "burnout" because of the problems being faced, they would have acquired competencies and skills which would readily transfer to other employment settings.

Because the program in El Raval has been implemented so recently, evaluation data are not yet available. Needless to say, unlike neatly controlled laboratory studies, the evaluation of the project must take into account the migratory nature of the population and other complicating environmental factors.

The Lifestart Project in the Former Yugoslav Republic of Macedonia

Following a fact-finding UNESCO mission to the Former Yugoslav Republic of Macedonia (FYROM) in 1997, it was decided to provide

UNICEF funding for a new Lifestart project in Bitola, the country's second largest city. This particular project differs from previous Lifestart projects not only in terms of cultural differences but also because of the impact of war on the lives of children in the countries of former Yugoslavia. A recent study by the National Academy of Sciences (1995) has identified some of those consequences. This study, which was based on information gathered from professionals in many different specialty areas and from various geographic regions of former Yugoslavia, concluded that "mental health and psychosocial problems were among the paramount problems facing children throughout this region" (p. 24). The study also concluded that the psychological well-being of the majority of these children and adolescents has been negatively impacted by the effects of war, whether or not they have been exposed to direct conflict situations.

Prior to the war, a well-developed framework for providing mental health services had been in place throughout the country. Professionals providing mental health service must now, however, contend with an overwhelming variety of new problems, including the disruption of traditional care, increased caseload of war-related mental health problems, physical destruction of many treatment facilities, as well as a dire shortage of needed resources. The National Academy of Sciences Report (1994) notes that under such difficult circumstances, "many local physicians and psychiatrists themselves have depressive symptoms, creating a need to broaden the scope of professional effort focused on mental health" (p. 26).

Because the FYROM is the only country to emerge peacefully from the break-up of former Yugoslavia, it has, in recent years, experienced a dramatic influx of thousands of refugees, including many families with young children. The UNICEF Annual Report for FYROM (1996) indicates that "ethnic conflicts and political-economic crises . . . have displaced almost 1.5 million people in the Caucasus and Central Asian countries. In the region as a whole, an estimated 6 million to 8 million people have fled their countries or become displaced from their homes as a result of conflict" (pp. 33–34).

Among the nationality groups to be served in the FYROM Lifestart project are Macedonians, Albanians, Turks, Vlachs, Serbs, Croatians, and Greeks. The one common element of the parents in this Lifestart project is that they all have children under the age of 6 years and are in need of help in raising these children. Faculty at the University of Saint Kliment of Ohrid in Bitola are directly involved in the evaluation of this project. It must be noted, however, that the migratory nature of the population makes accurate research data gathering not only difficult, but almost impossible. It must also be understood that in evaluating the effectiveness of the program, service to families in need must take precedence over considerations of "purity" of research data. Nevertheless, the researchers will attempt to provide as accurate an evaluative report as possible on the effectiveness of the Lifestart project in this unique and challenging cultural setting.

Discussion

What these five early childhood parent education programs indicate is that a program such as *Growing Child*, which has proven to be successful in one cultural environment, namely, the U.S., could be used in a very different cultural context, provided appropriate adaptations and accommodations were made. That challenge was first addressed in the adaptation of *Growing Child* to *Oiliúint Baile* in the rural economically disadvantaged but culturally rich environment of the Connemara *Gaeltacht* in the west of Ireland. From there, the next step was to adapt it to the newly developed urban housing estate of Ballymagroarty in Derry, Northern Ireland, where there has not only been sectarian strife over the past 25 years, and where male unemployment was as high as 87%.

Having taken the *Growing Child* parent education program in the U.S. and adapted it to two such different cultural environments in Ireland, it remained to be seen if the program could be implemented elsewhere in the global community. The ghetto neighborhood of El Raval in Barcelona, Spain, offered some unique challenges. By incorporating the Lifestart project within an already existing service delivery structure established by the Esco Foundation, it was possible to add an important new parent education component to meet the unique needs of families with young children in that region. Last, the Lifestart project in Bitola, in the Former Yugoslav Republic of Macedonia, provides a totally different ethnic context in which to provide early childhood parent education.

Despite the distressing circumstances in which many of these Lifestart projects have been operating, it is encouraging to note that, not only international organizations such as UNESCO and UNICEF, but more and more national governments, both in developed and developing countries, are recognizing the importance of early childhood parent education programs. It is also encouraging to note that, no matter how complex or challenging the problems may be, more and more early childhood parent education programs are being developed around the world in order to try to break an otherwise unending cycle of poverty, suffering, and misery experienced by young children and their families. In the next section we will briefly describe some successful parent education programs which have been developed in other parts of the global community.

PARENTING PROGRAMS IN DIFFERENT COUNTRIES

In this section we provide some examples of other successful parenting programs in the global community. Although each of these programs has a unique and different focus to address the needs of specific populations, they were all designed for the purpose of providing parents with better knowledge and understanding of the importance of family life and child development. Parents are thereby empowered to fulfill their parenting role in a more competent and rewarding manner.

ACEPP Programs for Immigrant Families in France

Although day-care services in France are generally of good quality, their lack of outreach to parents has sometimes been noted. For immigrant parents, this issue was particularly acute because of their poor language ability in French, their lack of education, and their low socioeconomic status. Although the child-care services provided by the local municipalities were of some help, each morning the parents experienced a sense of disempowerment, as they entrusted their children to an institution whose culture and organization was foreign to their own cultural background.

In 1986, ACEPP (L'Association des collectifs enfants, parents et professionels) was founded in France to promote parent involvement of immigrant families in day-care services for their children (Combes, 1994). In ACEPP projects, immigrant parents are directly involved in the planning and setting up of child-care services. When the child is brought to an ACEPP center each morning, the educational and nursing staff—who are specially trained in multicultural issues—welcome the parents. They discuss with the parents their hopes for their child as well as any difficulties they may be experiencing in child-rearing. The discussions take into account the parents' educational level as well as their socio-economic condition.

Parents are actively encouraged to become involved in the child-care activities. Flexibility in program management enables parents to involve themselves as much as possible in the care of their children. Even when neighborhood problems arise, working groups of parents and professionals are established to explore and deal with these problems. As a result of the ACEPP programs, immigrant families in France now experience greater social integration into the broader community.

The Mother–Child Education Program in Turkey

In Turkey, early childhood parent education programs must be both low-cost and large-scale, if they are to reach large numbers of children from disadvantaged backgrounds. Only in this way can the gap be bridged that exists between the majority of children and their more advantaged peers when they begin school. Furthermore, because of the relatively low status of women in Turkey, there is a need for programs which meet the needs of mothers who have low levels of education and who can make little formal contribution toward economic life.

The Mother–Child Education Program in Turkey aims to meet simultaneously the needs of children and mothers. In so doing, it offers real solutions to the social problems of the country (Kagitcibasi, 1995). The dual focus of the program is the positive development of the child and the empowerment of the mother. From the beginning, great attention was paid to making it community-based and culturally sensitive to women's needs. Involving both early childhood and adult education, it has now become a major governmental program, sponsored by the Ministry of Education.

An empowerment model—in contrast to a deficiency model which stresses the milieu's shortcomings—underlies the Mother-Child Education Program. The goal is to offer both children and mothers enrichment by providing support for their already existing strengths and by building on those strengths at both the personal and family levels. The mother is the center of the intervention as she is the key not only to her own development but also to her child's growth and social integration.

The basic approach and method is to provide community-based intervention by capitalizing on women's networks and by using group discussion methods. The training program involves a weekly group meeting of 2 hr over a period of 25 weeks. Each group is made up of approximately 20 mothers who are guided by a trained group leader during the first part of the discussion. The topics of the discussion focus on sensitive communication between mother and child; increasing awareness of the child's developmental needs; promotion of child health, education and play; and maternal and reproductive health. The second part of the discussion—conducted in small groups led by mother aides—involves role-playing based on the exercises and work sheets in the Training Manual, as well as storybooks which the mothers will later use during the week with their children.

In 1991, a major breakthrough occurred when the program was adopted into the Adult Education Program of the Turkish Ministry of Education. Group leaders from the Adult Education Section of the Ministry of Education make home visits on a regular basis to ensure that the cognitive training materials are being used correctly. In the same year, the revised Training Manual was published by UNICEF. In 1993, a private bank, the Finance Foundation, was set up the Mother-Child Education Foundation to fund these programs and to provide training of group leaders and para-professionals. During 1994–1995, the program was expanded to 20 provinces across Turkey and today provides service to over 4000 mother–child pairs.

The results of an evaluation of the program are impressive. Children have been tested by researchers from Bogazici University, Istanbul, on various cognitive measures: IQ scores, school grades, standardized tests of academic achievement, and subtests of the Wechsler intelligence scales. The results show striking differences in cognitive development between children whose mothers have undergone training and those who have not. The benefits of the program are also reflected in the behaviors of the mothers. Mothers who had been trained valued autonomous behavior of their child more than non-trained mothers and were more cognitively stimulating when interacting with their children. They were more likely to share decision making with their spouses on subjects such as birth control and child discipline. They also enjoyed a greater degree of communication and role-sharing with their spouses—the latter being evident, for example, in husbands helping with household chores. These effects were found to be long-term, especially in low-income households.

The children in the mother-trained group showed better school performance than the nontrained group over the 5 years of primary schooling. They also manifested more positive attitudes to schooling and better self-concept. For example, they felt that they could be the best in the class if they studied hard. Both the teachers and the children themselves were found to be proud of their performance. The children also provided more positive academic reasons for remaining in school, rather than the negative reasons given by other students, such as, "having nothing better to do" or "my parents make me go."

The cost-effectiveness of the Mother-Child Education Program makes it attractive for wide-scale use. Home intervention has proved to be a highly effective and relatively low-cost strategy for delivering the program. Being community-based and using trained paraprofessionals, it has inherent flexibility as a model while its links with the Ministry of Education guarantees core funding and the maintenance of high standards.

Parent Schools in the People's Republic of China

Recognizing that parents are a child's first and most important educators, Parent Schools were first established in the 1980s to "educate the educators," that is the six hundred million parents involved in child-rearing in the People's Republic of China. The Parent School programs have many specific goals: to provide a better understanding of family life; to emphasize the importance of the mother's role vis-a-vis children and thereby promote the status of women; to raise the general level of literacy and education in Chinese families; to promote linkages between parents, school and community; and to familiarize parents with what their children were learning in school—both content and methods—so that they could be more supportive of learning in the home.

Today Parent Schools in China number 240,000. There are four general types: (1) Parent Schools run by schools or departments of education specifically to develop parental support for children's learning in school; (2) Parent Schools run by the community to promote community values and the moral education of children; (3) Parent Schools run by research institutes to disseminate information about child development, parenting, and child-rearing practices; (4) Parent Schools run by hospitals (prenatal and childbirth classes) or other specialized institutes.

Except for the latter group, almost all parent education programs take place in the evenings at the local elementary or secondary school. In these programs many different instructional techniques are used besides classroom teaching, including radio, TV, and group discussion. Correspondence courses are also widely used as self-learning by parents is greatly encouraged in China. Many of the teachers in Parent Schools are also the teachers of their children who can explain to the parents how they can assist with school learning in their homes. The courses are usually free of charge, other than a modest fee to cover the cost of materials. Since the early 1980s more than 500 new books related to family education have been published in China for these programs. In addition, a TV lecture series "Family Education in China" is screened at prime time on every

Wednesday and Friday, and many provincial and municipal radio stations regularly broadcast lectures on family education topics.

An evaluation of Parent Schools conducted for UNESCO in 1995 by the National Institute of Educational Research in China identified many benefits of these programs:

- The importance of the three "goods"—good childbirth preparation, good child-rearing, good education—were found to be widely disseminated throughout Chinese society.
- There was greater awareness of the importance of and need for family education.
- Self-learning by parents had greatly increased.
- Parental knowledge about child development was much improved.
- Parents were experiencing greater success in raising their children, neither treating them as "Little Emperors" nor returning to traditional constraint methods.
- Graduates of the programs reported having more harmonious relationships with spouses, children, and grandparents.
- The children of program graduates generally obtained better grades in school. There was better integration between home, school, and community.
- In general, the Parent School programs were accomplishing the objectives for which they had been established.

The Parent Effectiveness Services Program in the Philippines

The Parent Effectiveness Services (PES) program was initiated in the Philippines in 1978 (Bautista, 1994). It was developed within the Social Welfare Project of the Department of Social Welfare and Development (DSWD). Small groups of parents were organized at the barangay (village) level to provide support for families with young children. Parental needs in terms of parent education were assessed through parent congresses and through village-level consultations. Within 2 years, the PES was implemented in 120 municipalities in 14 regions of the country. It has now become part of the broader framework of the "Plan of Action for Children" in the Philippines. The program has three basic modules: (1) radio programming, (2) group sessions for parents, and (3) home visits and home training. In 1992, a parent education radio program, "School in the Air" was introduced within the PES program in Maguindanao, a province in

Muslim Mindanao, in the southern part of the Philippines. It involved the production and airing of radio programs on parent education, covering 180 lessons over 3½ months. Participants had test booklets with questions to respond to as a way of monitoring their progress throughout the course. At the end of the course, they received certificates of completion. Within 2 years, a total of 10,500 parents, in three batches, had participated in the program. This program has proved to be a cost-effective way of disseminating information, considering the popularity and wide reach of radio, even in far-flung rural areas.

Responsibility for implementing, training and monitoring the PES program has resided primarily with the Bureau of Family and Community Welfare of the DSWD. Financial responsibility for the program has been shared by the Philippines government and UNICEF. A Local Government Code, enacted in 1991, provided for the devolution of national government authority to local government units. Accordingly, greater responsibility has been assigned to the local units that are now directly in charge of implementing the PES program.

There are important lessons to be learned about parent education programs based on the experiences from the PES program in the Philippines. Although PES programs are situated within the context of other child-focused programs that are government-initiated, (such as daycare centers, public school-based teacher-child-parent programs for health and nutrition, or maternal and child health programs), it is important that such programs should also be closely linked to the efforts of nongovernmental agencies. This is particularly important at the village or community level to strengthen the organizational base for PES as a parent education program which relies heavily on participation of the community. The design and content of PES programs should eventually move from a prescribed and structured format to a parent-driven agenda. That will allow for greater flexibility in terms of approaches to working with parents as learners, facilitating their own growth, and supporting the growth and development of their children.

Growing and Changing: The UNICEF Cross-Cultural Parent Education Videotape Series

The overall goal of this initiative is to enhance early childhood development by supporting parents in their role as primary caregivers. The specific objective was to design a series of short animated videotapes and accompanying print materials that provide parents across different cultures with the essential knowledge, strategies and resources for enhancing children's development during the first 6 years of life (Landers, 1990). Supported by the UNICEF Global Education Fund, the series has been designed for national television broadcast. The broadcast quality of the series and its availability in videocassette format enables use by service providers in a wide variety of community settings, including health care centers, preschools, community centers, and literacy programs. The material complements ongoing UNICEF-assisted initiatives and can be integrated into programs which provide care and education directly to the young child.

The animated video series consists of four 10-min videos and accompanying facilitators' and parents' guidebooks. These materials include fundamental information on normal child development and strategies for creating effective home learning environments. Several animated child characters illustrate progression of skills in language, social, emotional, physical and motor development. Practical suggestions for what parents can do to enhance development are portrayed by interactions between children and caregivers. The titles in the four-part child development series are (1) Off to a good start: The first year of life; (2) A time of adventure: One and two year olds; (3) Pathways to learning: Three and four year olds; (4) Ready for school: Five and six year olds.

The purpose of the animated programs is to provide universal core knowledge of human development. The goal is to build on the information contained in the animation to capture the strengths, patterns and practices that enhance development in a particular environment. The series can be used in combination with culture specific materials, and a guidebook has been prepared to assist in the development of complementary live action sequences appropriate for different cultural environments. Each video is accompanied by a Facilitators' Resource Guide as well as a set of parent materials. The purpose of the Facilitators' Resource Guide is to help facilitators, including health care workers, teachers, early childhood specialists, and community workers, explain the information contained within the video and generate viewer discussion. Facilitators are trained to use the materials in a series of ordered sequences with pauses between segments to discuss various aspects of the presentation. The parents' information package consists of a set of supplementary materials that highlight the critical information in the videos. The content is portrayed clearly and simply through illustrations that reinforce program content and objectives, and suggest activities to be done at home.

CONCLUSION

In light of what we have discussed in this chapter, these are some concluding comments about parent education in the global community. First,
any parent education program, no matter how expertly developed, needs
adaptation to the cultural milieu in which it is used (LeVine & White,
1986). Second, parent education cannot by itself solve the problems posed
by such factors as poverty, war, and the migration of families. Third, even
in developing countries, there is growing awareness of the shortcomings
of programs which concentrate solely on children's physical survival. The
other rights of children, such as the right to education and personal development both at home and in school, need also to be addressed. Fourth,
there needs to be a variety of policies and approaches to parent education
in order to meet the needs of culturally diverse populations. Fifth, parent
education needs to be adequately supported by health, public education,
and social services programs.

These conclusions are supported by the recent findings of a World
Bank Report on child-rearing in Kenya. Owing to the deterioration in
the social and economic climate in Kenya between 1980 and 1994, and
the rapid transition from communal families—in which older relatives
were available to look after children—to an urban nuclear family pattern,
a crisis in child-rearing had occurred. Among the policy recommendations made by the World Bank to the government of Kenya were the following:

- To provide parent education and actively explore other parent sup-
  port models
- To allow more flexible working conditions for working mothers
- To arrange for better health care and nutrition programs
- To provide more home-based services to parents in the form of mo-
  bile health clinics
- To lessen the costs for parents of child-rearing and schooling
- To utilize limited resources more efficiently through cost sharing in
  order to provide greater benefits to children and their families.

The example of Kenya's situation helps to underscore the reality that,
despite cultural variations, there are some basic human needs which are
common to all countries. Such universal needs include food, shelter, security, health, education, nondiscrimination, and social participation. There
are also age-specific psychosocial needs as the child and adult move
through what Erikson (1968) has called the cycle of epigenetic develop-

ment, that is the adaptations which normally occur as one moves from one stage of psychosocial development to another. Although these needs are universal, their forms of expression are culture linked: for example, the types of food, purpose of education, cognitive modes as well as community values and expectations which may differ significantly from one culture to another. In this way even universal needs and common developmental processes are molded, shaped, and expressed differently in each individual culture.

The commonality of human needs means that parenting programs can be utilized across cultural frontiers provided there is in-depth understanding of what constitutes communal values and family well-being within each specific culture. These programs must not only be provided with adequate resources and support services but they must also have extensive parental and community involvement if they are to meet the needs of children and their families in the widely different cultural environments of the global community.

REFERENCES

Ambert, A. M. (1994). An international perspective on parenting: Social change and social constructs. *Journal of Marriage and the Family 56,* August 1994, 529-543.

Ballymagroarty Development Group (1993). A project to assess the needs of the people of Ballymagroarty, Unpublished manuscript.

Bautista, F. (1994). *Parents as learners: Toward partnership and participation.* Haydenville, MA: Coordinators' Notebook.

Best, D. L., House, A. S., Barnard, A. E., & Spicker, B. S. (1994). Parent–child interactions in France, Germany, and Italy: The effects of gender and culture. *Journal of Cross-cultural Psychology, 25*(2), 181–193.

Bornstein, M. H. (1991a). *Parenting in cross-cultural perspective: The United States, France and Japan.* Bethesda, MD: National Institute of Child Health and Human Development.

Bornstein, M. H. (Ed.). (1991b). *Cultural approaches to parenting.* Hillsdale, NJ: Lawrence Erlbaum.

Brazelton, T. B. (1991). Discussion: Cultural attitudes and actions. In M. H. Bornstein (Ed.), *Cultural approaches to parenting.* Hillsdale, NJ: Lawrence Erlbaum.

Bronfenbrenner, U. (1979). *The ecology of human development.* Cambridge, MA: Harvard University Press.

Bronfenbrenner, U. (1986). Ecology of the family as a context for human development: Research perspectives. *Developmental Psychology, 22,* 723–742.

Bronfenbrenner, U. (1995). The bioecological model from a life course perspective. In P. Moen, G. H. Elder, & K. Luscher (Eds.), *Examining lives in context.* Washington, DC: American Psychological Association.

Bronfenbrenner, U., & Morris, P. A. (1997). The ecology of developmental processes. In R. M. Lerner (Ed.), *Handbook of child psychology.* (5th Ed., Vol. 1). New York: Wiley.

Bronfenbrenner, U., & Weiss, H. B. (1983). Beyond policies without people: An ecological perspective on child and family policy. In E. Zigler, S. L. Kagan, & E. Klugman (Eds.), *Children, families and government.* (pp. 393–414). Cambridge, UK: Cambridge University Press.

Bronstein, P. (1994). Patterns of parent–child interaction in Mexican families: A cross cultural perspective. *International Journal of Behavioral Development, 17*(3), 423–446.

Chung, F. C. (1994) *Parental attitudes, parent-child interaction and children's competent behavior in early childhood in Taiwan.* Unpublished dissertation, The University of Wisconsin—Madison.

Clark, A. L. (Ed.). (1980). *Culture and child rearing.* Philadelphia, PA: Davis.

Combes, J. (1994). Les crèches parentales. In S. Tessier (Ed.), *L'enfant et son intégration dans la cité.* Paris: Syros Publications.

Davison, J. E. (1989). *Parenting style and family environment of Caucasian-American versus Malaysian families.* Unpublished dissertation, Indiana State University.

Dunn, D. (1992). *Every child is our child.* Lafayette, IN: Dunn & Hargitt.

Ekblad, 5. (1986). Relationships between child-rearing practices and primary school children's functional adjustment in the People's Republic of China. *Scandinavian Journal of Psychology, 27,* 220–230.

Eldering, L. (1995). Child-rearing in bi-cultural settings: A cultural-ecological approach. *Psychology and Developing Societies, 7*(2), 133–153.

Erikson, E. H. (1968). *Identity: Youth and crisis.* New York: W. W. Norton.

Gfellner, B. M. (1990). Culture and consistency in ideal and actual child-rearing practices: A study of Canadian Indian and white parents. *Journal of Comparative Family Studies, 21*(3), 413–423.

Gollnick, D. M. & Chin, P. C. (1998). *Multicultural education in a pluralistic society.* Columbus, OH: Merrill.

Grimley, L. K. & Bennett, J. (in press). Beginning school ready to learn: An international perspective.

Grimley, L. K. & Robinson, R. (1986). Parent education in early childhood: The Growing Child Model. *Techniques, 2,* 81–87.

Growing Child (1998). Lafayette, IN: Dunn & Hargitt.

Growing Child/Growing Parent reader survey. (1981). Unpublished manuscript. Dunn & Hargitt, Lafayette, IN.

Harkness, S. & Super, C. M. (1993). The developmental niche: Implications for children's literacy development. In L. Eldering & P. Leseman (Eds.), *Early interaction and culture: Preparation for literacy. The interface between theory and practice.* (pp. 115–132). Paris: UNESCO.

Hsu, F. L. K. (1981). *Americans and Chinese: Passages to differences* (3rd ed.). Honolulu: University Press of Hawaii.

Hughes, J. (1989). Thinking about children. In G. Scarre (Ed.), *Children, parents and politics.* (pp. 36–54). Cambridge, UK: Cambridge University Press.

Interim report of the Family Centre Project (1990). Unpublished Lifestart Foundation report.

Kagitcibasi, C. (1995). *The coordinators' notebook* (No. 17). New York: UNICEF.

Keller, H., Chasiotis, A. & Runde, B. (1992). Intuitive parenting programs in German, American, and Greek parents of 3-month-old infants. *Journal of Cross-cultural Psychology, 23*(4), 510–520.

Keller, H. & Scholmerich, A. (1988). Communication patterns in adult-infant interactions in Western and Non-western cultures. *Journal of Cross-cultural Psychology, 19*(4), 427–445.

Kelley, M. L. & Tseng, H.-M. (1992). A comparison of immigrant Chinese and Caucasian American mothers. *Journal of Cross-cultural Psychology, 23*(4), 444–455.

Kessen, W. (1993). A developmentalist's reflections. In G. H. Elder, Jr., J. Modell, & R. D. Parke (Eds.), *Children in time and place* (pp. 226–229). Cambridge, U.K.: Cambridge University Press.

Landers, C. (1990). *Growing and changing.* New York: UNICEF.

LeVine, S., & LeVine, R. (1985). Age, gender, and the demographic transition: The life course in agrarian societies. In A. Rossi (Ed.), *Gender and the life course.* (pp. 24–42). New York: Aldine.

LeVine, R. A. & White, MI. (1986). *Human conditions: The cultural basis of educational developments.* New York: Routledge & Kegan Paul.

LeVine, R. A. (1980). A cross-cultural perspective in parenting. In Fantini & Cardenas (Eds.), *Parenting in a multicultural society.* New York: Longman.

Liang, S. & Sugawara, A. I. (1992). Reflections on parenting practices in urban China today. *Early child development and care, 81,* 15–24.

Lum, K. Y., & Char, W. F. (1985). Chinese adaptation in Hawaii: Some examples. In D. Y. H. Wu & W. S. Tseng (Eds.), *Chinese culture and mental health.* (pp. 215–226). Orlando, FL: Academic Press.

Marjoribanks, K. (1996). Ethnicity, proximal family environment, and young adolescents' cognitive performance. *The Journal of Early Adolescence, 16*(3), 340–354.

McGoldrick, M., Giordano, J., & Pearce, J. K. (1996). Ethnicity and family therapy. New York: Guilford.

McLeod, J. D., & Shanahan, M. J. (1993). Poverty, parenting, and children's mental health. *American Sociological Review, 58,* 351–366.

McNelis, C. & Kelleher, C. (1995). *An evaluation of the Lifestart early learning programme.* Galway, Ireland: Centre for Health Promotion Studies, University College Galway.

Mizuta, I., Zahn-Waxler, C., Cole, P. M., & Hiruma, N. (1996). A cross-cultural study of preschoolers' attachment: Security and sensitivity in Japanese and U.S. dyads. *International Journal of Behavioral Development, 19*(1), 141–159.

Myers, R. (1992). *The twelve who survive.* London: Routledge.

National Academy of Sciences (1994). *The impact of war on child health in the countries of the former Yugoslavia: A report of a workshop, Trieste, Italy, March 27–30, 1994.* Washington, DC: National Academy of Sciences.

Negussie, B. (1990). Maternity care and childrearing: Preconditions for educational achievement: Experience in a cross-cultural perspective with special focus on East Africa. Unpublished paper presented at the International Conference for Maternity Nurse Researchers, Gothenburg, Sweden, June 18–22, 1991.

Puchner, L. D. (1993). *Early childhood, family, and health issues in literacy: International perspectives.* Philadelphia, PA: National Center on Adult Literacy.

Pugh, G., De'ath, E. (1989). *Working toward partnership in the early years.* London: National Children's Bureau.

Rowan, M. (1995). *Lifestart programme report.* Galway, Ireland: Lifestart Foundation.

Sharma, D. (1996). *Child care, family and culture: Lessons from India.* Unpublished dissertation, Harvard University.

Tulloch, E. A. (1997). *Effectiveness of parent training on perception of parenting skill and reduction of preschool problem behaviors utilizing an ethnically diverse population.* Unpublished dissertation, Hofstra University.

UNESCO (1995). *Early childhood care and education: Basic indicators on young children.* Paris, France: Young Child and the Family Environment Unit, UNESCO.

UNICEF (1996). *Former Yugoslav Republic of Macedonia Annual Report.* New York: United Nations Children's Fund.

Yaman, J. A. (1996). *Patterns of caregiver interaction with infants aged 15 months among the Melanau of Sarawak Malaysia.* Unpublished dissertation, Harvard University.

CHAPTER 6

A Psychoeducational Program For Parents of Dysfunctional Backgrounds

Marvin J. Fine

Department of Psychology and Research in Education, University of Kansas, Lawrence, Kansas

Katherine F. Wardle

Affiliated Psychological Services, Latham, New York

Persons raised in dysfunctional families may carry forward into their adult lives the emotional turmoils and dysfunctional patterns of the past. The potential for these dysfunctional patterns to negatively affect their own parenting behavior is great. A number of writers have addressed this concern through the preparation of "popular" books for parents identifying pitfalls to healthy parenting and sharing models and techniques of effective parenting (Becnel, 1991; Mason, 1990; Rolfe, 1990; Wassil-Grimm, 1990). Although adult children of alcoholics in particular have been singled out, many of the characteristics attributed to these persons are shared by others who have been raised in nonalcoholic but equally dysfunctional families.

Before proceeding any further it should also be noted that a number of individuals raised in dysfunctional families have shown resilience, emotional hardiness, or at the least a kind of survivor mentality that has permitted them to ostensibly grow and develop into reasonably functional adults. Even though these persons might recall and recount with some emotionality their family experiences, they seemingly are able to function satisfactorily in employment and social relations and very importantly in a contemporary parenting role. There are others who seem to have been affected by their dysfunctional family experiences so that now in their contemporary

Handbook of Diversity in Parent Education

133

parenting role they are experiencing significant difficulties. It should also be noted that the empirical literature encourages caution in overgeneralizing from the popular thinking about adult children of alcoholics as expressed in the parenting books cited earlier (Collins, Leonard, & Searles, 1990; Steinglass, 1987; Windle & Searles, 1990). Many of the generalizations made of persons from dysfunctional backgrounds arise from clinical experiences with self-selected samples of persons with acknowledged problems.

One avenue of assistance with their current parenting problems is to participate in a parent education program. However, parenting classes offered through churches and community agencies have often been implemented as if the participants were members of an intact, two-parent family. Many of these programs also seem to have an implicit assumption that with new information and a brief demonstration, that any participant can substantially improve their parenting skills. This viewpoint ignores the psychological blocks that some parents experience when attempting to consider different tactics and different ways of understanding and responding to a child's behavior. It is not surprising that there usually are high attrition rates in such "canned" programs and that many parents upon completing parent education programs still report difficulty and unhappiness with a range of parenting tasks. Many of those parents would benefit from a parent education program that could guide them in examining the positives and negatives of their own growing up experiences, becoming more aware of what they bring to their parent role by way of beliefs, expectations, and emotional resources, and offering them a conceptualization of healthy parenting including specific skills they could practice.

This chapter describes an approach to parent education that was developed for parents whose dysfunctional backgrounds seem to be interfering with effective parenting practices. Many of these parents are concurrently in individual, group, or family treatment programs and were referred to this parenting program by their therapists or a social agency. The program is psychoeducational in nature because of its incorporation of a strong educational component in conjunction with important psychological considerations related to program structure and the dynamics that the parents bring to the program.

SOME GENERALIZATIONS ABOUT "DYSFUNCTIONAL FAMILIES"

Several years ago a cartoon appeared that depicted only one person in the audience of a meeting for persons from *functional* family backgrounds. The cartoon sends an important message that if we establish too narrow a set of guidelines for what constitutes a functional or healthy family then it may indeed be a very small minority of the population who meet those criteria. An overly narrow designation of what is "healthy" or "functional" may also miss the realities for most parents of the ongoing challenges of parenting that periodically pushes them to the "brink."

Each family labeled "dysfunctional" may vary in its dynamics, but there seem to be some common themes that can affect children and influence their subsequent parenting behavior. The following discussion derives from a rather extensive literature in the field of family psychology and family therapy, some of which is empirical and much of which is experiential (Beal & Hochman, 1991; Beavers & Hampson, 1990; Collins, et al.; Gladding, 1998; Goldenberg & Goldenberg, 1996; Steinglass, et al.). These represent a catalog of possibilities rather than a depiction of how every "dysfunctional" family operates.

1. The parents may express inappropriate age expectations for children, either demanding maturity or at other times suppressing it. This goes hand in hand with the difficulty that children experience in knowing exactly what parental expectations are and how to please their parents.

2. The family may be characterized by collusive relationships so that there is a frequency of side taking. This involves the concept of triangulation. Family members get caught up in conflicts among each other with the children put in positions of either working against the parent or on behalf of a parent and with resultant problems of divided family loyalties.

3. There may be unhealthy patterns of how affection is expressed. Some families are very cold with a kind of formality around the sharing of warm emotions. Parents in those families may insist that they love their children, but observers would note that there are unclear and very limited expressions of loving feelings. In other instances the family may be extremely effusive in the expression of warm and loving emotions to where family members become very enmeshed with each other. The children are not allowed to develop authentic feelings but instead get patterned into ways of feeling and experiencing themselves emotionally.

4. The daily life of the family may include a number of "secrets." There are things that the family does not talk about and there are issues that are never dealt with, at least openly. Again, family members, especially young children, get patterned into these ways of thinking and feeling so that these ways become an inherent part of how members function in the family without ever explicitly inspecting the family or themselves.

5. Dysfunctional families often have a tendency toward "either-or"

thinking and other cognitive distortions about cause–effect events. Because communication within these families is not open, family members seldom explicitly explore the validity of ideas so as to support modifications of ways of thinking and behaving.

6. Communication patterns, as mentioned, are not open but tend to be very circumscribed. Sometimes people talk in "code"; there are likely to be secrets about which people really have some awareness, and there are topics that just don't get discussed. Such dysfunctional families would not typically be characterized by family members talking in a relatively open and comfortable way with each other about how they feel, what's going on, and new experiences.

7. In more functional families there are usually clear generational boundaries with the parents assuming appropriate leadership roles and the children being monitored, directed, and guided accordingly. As children grow older they are allowed greater autonomy and decision making. However, for the most part until children actually become adults and leave home, there remains a fairly clear hierarchical structure within the home. In dysfunctional families the boundaries may become blurred; at times there may be a role reversal where the children shift into a parenting role with their parents. This would be more likely in instances of a parent becoming disabled or very dysfunctional, such as through drugs or alcohol or other kinds of chronic conditions, and where the child is directly or indirectly encouraged to assume more responsibility. However, it may also occur because of a parent's lack of confidence and the parent becoming more dependent on the child either in general or in specific situations.

8. Children growing up in these environments can feel vulnerable in their relationship with the outside world. There may be a sense of scare over being found out in relation to the family pathology; these children are more likely to grow up with serious self-esteem and self-confidence issues. Connected to self esteem issues would also be the presence of feelings of shame and guilt.

9. Persons from dysfunctional families often have difficulty in behaving "authentically" and instead tend to take on or to be assigned roles. These roles become a kind of typecasting to which people are expected to conform; indeed, if they don't conform other family members will exert psychological pressures to get them to conform. Such roles include the scapegoat, the enabler, the family hero, and the rescuer.

10. This last point relates to the overall organization of the family and perhaps should have occurred as the first point. That is, families are in fact systems in which persons and their behaviors interconnect reciprocally with

each other. Each family achieves some degree of homeostasis in terms of roles, relationships, patterns of behavior, communication styles; dysfunctional families are in a sense stabilized around a pattern of instability.

SOME GENERALIZATIONS ABOUT CONTEMPORARY PARENTING PROBLEMS

So how might growing up in a dysfunctional family influence a person's contemporary parenting? Once again it is important to acknowledge that there is no one narrowly defined pattern of parenting that has been associated with parents who grew up in dysfunctional families. Because the dysfunctionality plays itself out in different ways, there are likely to be different effects on members of that family as they grow up and subsequently assume a parenting role. In some instances there may appear to be a clear continuation of the pattern that the parent experienced as a child. An example would be parents who were abused as children now abusing their own children. However, there can also be dramatic variations that push the pendulum in the opposite direction. An example would be parents who are so reactive to any implication of abuse that they fail to discipline and set reasonable limits with their children.

There are a number of problem patterns or behaviors that have been repeatedly identified in the literature and reported by parents in the different parenting groups that we have led. Many of these patterns follow logically from the earlier depiction of the growing-up experiences of these parents. The following summarizations of these patterns and behaviors are not in any order of frequency or relevance; they are intended to orient prospective group leaders to the kinds of issues the participants may be experiencing and which then can be incorporated into the sessions.

1. *Explosive behavior by the parents.* There may be a number of trigger situations within the family that precipitate a flash of anger. The anger, which seems to come out of nowhere, is characterized by verbal and/or physical attack on the child or children in the family. These incidents are typically followed by remorse and attempts to make up to the child. The pattern is somewhat similar to that of abusing spouses in terms of the explosiveness, the remorse, and then attempts to compensate.

2. *Parental anguish over the child's feelings about them.* Many parents from dysfunctional backgrounds experience ambivalence about their own parents and their early growing-up experiences. Although feeling resentments against their parents there is still a neediness for their own parents to have

approved of them. They convert their longings and frustrations about their recalled hurt feelings as children into whether their own children will love them. This parental need to be loved becomes problematic as the parent attempts to discipline and set limits. The not uncommon retort by a young child that the parent is being mean or is a bad parent is usually met with understanding and good humor on the part of a strong parent. For a parent with an exaggerated need to be seen by the child as a good parent, such angry child statements are triggers to depression and the re-experiencing of bad memories, all of which undermine effective parenting.

3. *Indecision and self-doubt.* As an extension of the previous point, many parents are constantly second guessing themselves around decisions that they have made. In situations where it might be generally agreed that it was appropriate for a parent to set certain limits or enact certain consequences such as grounding a child for some repeated infraction, these parents will constantly question whether they have been too harsh or unfair. This leads to frequent ruminating over events and an exaggerated sense of responsibility for any perceived negative happening.

4. *Inconsistency.* One can readily see how with the kinds of self doubt and indecisiveness that many parents experience that it is almost inevitable that they act inconsistently. This leads to some confusion on the part of the child as to what is acceptable or unacceptable, and one might find the children of these families engaging in a lot of limit testing as a means of establishing what the parent really means and what really are the limits. The interpretations that the parent often gives to the child's limit testing is that the parent is inadequate and probably doing bad things to the child.

5. *Pendulum swings.* The confusion and anxiety over being a good parent seems to prompt pendulum swings in areas of child care. An example is where a parent becomes overprotective to the point of restricting a lot of normal activities by children. This might include not letting them go into the neighborhood to play with other kids, constant fear that if the child is not looked after closely things will go badly. However, at other times the same parent appears unaware of dangers and is almost too cavalier in allowing a child into potentially dangerous situations. The underpinning to the pendulum swing seems to be the parents' own confused emotionality regarding the parenting role and their own needs interfering with accurate perceptions of situations.

6. *Emotional overloading and withdrawal.* One can appreciate how with what has been described so far that many of these parents are in fairly constant turmoil and under constant stress in the parenting role. At times, because of what appears to be an emotional overloading, they can become

somewhat emotionally blunted and attempt to withdraw from the parenting role. This would be exemplified where the parent in exasperation yells at the child, "Do whatever you want to do," and then the parent might lock themselves in the bedroom basically leaving the child to his or her own judgments for some period of time. The awareness that they have essentially fled a situation that they believe "good" parents could have handled furthers their sense of inadequacy.

7. *Confused expectations.* As stated earlier, some parents will shift dramatically from an over- to an underprotectiveness. This may in part relate to confused expectations for what is appropriate behavior on the part of children. We find some parents in the overprotecting role laying out clothes and attempting to make personal decisions for children well into their teens, whereas other parents may expect all kinds of self-care behavior on the part of relatively young children. The consequence is that some children are thwarted in their attempts to move toward maturity, whereas other children are pushed into situations that demand greater maturity and can lead to disasters or precocious behaviors.

8. *Distorted attributions.* The parents own emotional neediness often leads to distorted perceptions around why children are doing what they are doing. In some instances the parent may insist that the child is being deliberately and knowingly malicious and is out to get the parent. In other situations the parent may deny that the child has any awareness of what the child is doing in a given situation. These misperceptions are connected to confused attributions and can then distort the parent's response to the child. This is what can occur in abusive situations where a parent feels some justification for physically assaulting the child because of the belief that a child is "choosing" to do something hurtful to the parent.

9. *Absence of bidirectional thinking.* The parent through the nature of attributions may block awareness of the way in which people interact and play off each other. They may see the child's behavior as coming exclusively from the child somehow irrespective of their own behavior, or the parent may see themselves as the total cause of the child's behavior as an expression of their sense of inadequacy in parenting, and they may ignore the child's participation in the events.

DESCRIPTION OF THE PROGRAM

The following is a description of the program that has at times been referred to as "Healthy parenting skills for parents from unhealthy backgrounds." Because the program is psychoeducational and attempts to be responsive to the needs of the participants the agenda may vary somewhat from group to group. This personalizing of the curriculum makes the program different from a "canned" program where the instructor may feel more of an obligation to adhere to the prepared curriculum.

The basic goals of the program are to increase the particpants' skills and sense of comfort and efficacy related to their parenting. It is believed that the participants can be strengthened in their capacity to think through situations and to respond more appropriately and less reactively. The participant's should also be helped to more accurately and positively assess their skills and to develop a greater sense of comfort and optimism about themselves as parents.

Organizational Considerations

Unlike more traditional parent education programs that might be advertised by the school or community, participants in the program are mainly referred by individual therapists or agencies. What this typically means is that these parents will be maintaining some kind of ongoing contact with the referral source as a locus of psychotherapeutic treatment while concurrently participating in the time-limited parent education program. There may also be communication between the instructor and the referring source. This is more often initiated by the therapist than the program instructor and requires written permission by the parent.

The program has been organized around six sessions, 1½ hr per session. This time frame was arrived at more experientially than empirically and seemed to be consonant with the time and energy availability of parents to participate in a sequenced learning experience. Some sessions have tended to run over because of participant interest. The preparedness of the group leader to draw closure and terminate the session as scheduled is considered to have therapeutic value as an example of setting boundaries.

Participation is typically limited to a maximum of eight to ten parents with no restriction on whether one or both parents attend. Our experience has been that the participants have typically been either single parents or just one of the couple with women predominating.

Cost has varied as a function of the setting. The program has been offered within the context of a private practice as well as through nonprofit agencies. There has usually been a sliding scale with insurance being tapped when possible. In some instances discretionary funds were used by a social welfare agency to assure that certain individuals could participate.

The seating is usually in a circle for purposes of encouraging discussion and face-to-face interaction among participants. There is no formal text materials, but a number of different handouts are utilized at different times. The handouts are usually summaries of aspects of parenting such as models of parenting, ways of effectively communicating, handling discipline situations, etc.

The Model of the Program

The model is psychoeducational in nature. Information on effective parenting is considered important because of the poor role models and faulty information the participants likely experienced in their own families. The cognitive-behavioral theme of the program is reflected in the emphasis on the participants learning to become more analytical and aware of their thoughts and behaviors within parenting situations (Craighead, Craighead, Kazdin, & Mahoney, 1994; Joyce, 1990; Meichenbaum, 1997).

Assumptions about the participants are that many of them might be emotionally flooded at times of parenting stress and that their cognitive skills to manage feelings, to think clearly, and to behave appropriately may become impaired. They may connect events to feelings and behavior in irrational ways, have self-defeating attributions, and in other cognitive ways undermine their functioning. Although these assumptions could apply to any parent they are likely to act themselves out more pervasively with the participants in this program.

There are numerous times in the course of the program when the participants are encouraged to observe themselves in terms of the relationship of their thinking ("self-talk"), feelings, and behavior. This might include checking out assumptions and attributions they hold in different situations. An example would be where a parent believes that a child has a family trait of stubbornness and therefore there is nothing that can be done to assist the child in becoming more compliant. Another example would be the erroneous belief that in different situations there is only one right way for a parent to respond. Because these parents often doubt their parenting skills they are quick to conclude that they have responded incorrectly.

The leader's skill in using positive refraining is an important tool in assisting the parents to see themselves as more adequate. Their self-critical attributions often cover up the skills and good judgements that they do exhibit. These parents would not be in the parenting program if they were not eager to be a positive influence in their children's lives and to avoid repeating their own negative experiences. The parents can be easily presented as survivors, heroes, and certainly as loving parents.

The didactic framework includes four emphases: (1) information giving, (2) increasing self-awareness, (3) skill-building, and (4) monitored practice. The infusion of these four emphases into each session requires skill on the part of the group leader. For example, the presentation by the leader on models of parenting is likely to prompt the participants to talk about how their growing-up experiences were in contrast to a positive model of parenting. This could then open the door to a discussion around how their parenting experiences may be influencing the way they are parenting today. This example shows how information giving and increasing self-awareness can dovetail within a session.

As another example, when focusing on a specific skill such as how to offer a child encouragement, the participants may be prompted to contrast what they are learning with the way their parents reacted to them. This would then allow for an examination of what their historic tendencies and patterns had been in this area and how they could support themselves in attempting a new pattern of behavior.

When participants have attempted to practice new procedures or strategies at home, the subsequent discussion within a session would allow for an examination of the kinds of difficulties they experienced. This often brings the focus to personal and family dynamics such as a perceived lack of spousal support, or difficulty in controlling the impulse to scream and threaten. In the ways just mentioned the four focuses can interact with each other and overlap within each session.

STRUCTURE AND CONTENT OF EACH SESSION

Session One: Introduction

The first session includes a brief introduction to the program, its goals, and very importantly, group rules and guidelines. The group needs to be seen as a safe place where each person will be accepted. The voluntary nature of sharing and participating in specific activities is emphasized as is the importance of confidentiality. Also stressed is the importance of respecting each other and appreciating each person's individuality. The group leader

is acting in part as a "good" and responsible parent by expressing acceptance of each member, clearly defining expectations, and clarifying
boundaries.

Short personal interviews or telephone conversations between the
leader and each participant typically occurs in order to establish the appropriateness of the program for that parent. This allows each parent to learn
in advance that each other participant has some parenting issues with
which they were coping and that each participant comes from a problematic background.

There is an opportunity early in the session for people to introduce
themselves in whatever way they are comfortable, describing their current
family and growing up experiences. Because a number of the group members have been in other kinds of groups there are often some members
who are fairly comfortable getting the discussion started by "telling their
story." The goal of such sharing is to establish some bonding among
group members, to break the ice, and to defuse individual members' self-
consciousness around notions that they might be different.

A very important leader function is to bring a positive emphasis to the
group in terms of pointing out how everyone is committed to becoming a
more effective parent. Following the sharing the leader can summarize information about dysfunctional families, touching on such areas as communication patterns, the way the family solved problems, how affection was
expressed, what kinds of collusions and secrets existed, and in general the
ways it was not safe to be oneself and open in those families. This encourages participants to share what they want for themselves in their current
parenting role and to identify some areas in which they are currently experiencing difficulties. Parents have commonly mentioned such areas as
communication, anger, discipline, working together with a spouse, and
feeling guilty over the perceived lack of adequate parenting skills.

The leader also needs to depict the six sessions as opportunities for the
participants to examine their parenting, to increase their level of knowledge and comfort in parenting, to commiserate with other individuals,
and to increase their parenting effectiveness. However, it should also be
emphasized that the participants need to assume realistic expectations for
what can be accomplished in six sessions, that each participant will probably continue dealing with personal issues in other therapeutic contexts,
and that they can also find opportunities to enter into other parenting experiences that might be available in the community following the completion of this series of sessions.

By way of homework the parents are encouraged to not attempt to make great changes in their parenting but rather to become an observer of themselves and their children and other family interactions. They are also encouraged to pay attention to what they think and say to themselves at different points in the parenting process. Some examples are given of how people can encourage or discourage themselves, and emotionally support or depress themselves, as a result of what they think and say to themselves. There are usually some active signs of personal recognition of their own patterns. The leader should be supportive and accepting, offer suggestions, and invite participation in certain activities rather than presenting demands and assignments that everyone is expected to do as might occur in a more structured program.

Session Two: Healthy Parenting: Healthy Families

Each session typically begins with an opportunity for people to share any afterthoughts from the earlier session as well as any events that occurred during the week that somehow connected to items of discussion. The main assignment from the first session was for the participants to practice observing interactions among family members as well as their own thoughts and feelings in different situations. This activity can assist persons to detach emotionally and become more objective in their understanding of the sequence of family events as well as to become more aware of their own reactions.

Regarding information giving, there is a brief presentation on models of parenting as described by Baumrind (1989, 1991). This includes a description of authoritarian, permissive, and authoritative parents. Additional ideas on normal and healthy family functioning are introduced (Curran, 1983; DeFrain & Stinnett, 1992; Stinnett & DeFrain, 1989) with the intent of presenting some conceptualizations in a fairly concrete and operational way but also continuing to emphasize the individuality of families and the fairly wide latitude of family functioning that could still be considered healthy.

As mentioned, there is a cognitive influence to the instructor's interactions with the group. It is deemed important for group members to think about themselves and their reactions more objectively and to consider that they have choices in different parenting situations. Queries by the instructor as to what the participants were thinking in different situations helps them to clarify their beliefs and to better recognize the relationship between cognitions, feelings, and behavior.

By the end of the session the focus shifts to ways within the context of healthy parenting that parents can encourage and emotionally support their children. This typically leads to a discussion of ways of offering encouragement or "positive strokes."

A concept that many parents have found useful is to discriminate between "conditional and unconditional strokes." Conditional strokes are similar to reinforcement, things parents do to encourage or discourage specific child behaviors. Unconditional strokes have to do with the parent's basic feelings for the child. So giving a child a hug simply because the child is there and it is a loving gesture would constitute a positive and unconditional stroke. Praising a child for making an effort at some task or earning a good grade are examples of positive and conditional strokes. Children need both kinds, conditional strokes because they are reality feedback and can encourage or discourage certain behaviors, and unconditional positive strokes because they validate the existence and worth of the child. The concept of unconditional strokes seems to hit home for many of the participants and typically prompts active sharing of childhood experiences.

By way of homework, participants are encouraged to continue observing themselves in the different parenting situations with a focus on thoughts, feelings, and behavior and also to notice the ways in which they encourage their children. Many parents leave this session expressing an intent to offer their children a lot of hugs during the week.

Session Three: Children: What to Expect? What's Normal?

Session three begins again with an opportunity for people to share carry-overs from the preceding session or to bring up events that occurred during the week. The agenda per se is to focus the discussion at some point on the normal variances of child development. This occurs through a summary presentation on temperament differences in young children (Chess & Thomas, 1987) developmental issues that children experience (Erikson, 1968), and the bidirectionality/systemic nature of behavior.

The concept of bidirectionality seems important towards helping parents understand that their interactions with children are a two-way street. The concept encourages parents to think more systemically as opposed to an absolutist and often negative view of a child's personality and behavior. Introducing parents to the concept of developmental issues can assist them in being more attuned to the internal concerns of children as they grow older, and the presentation on temperaments can lead into a discussion of the ways that children and settings can be a good or not-so-good match. This in turn allows for examining the difficulties that parents can experience in terms of children not meeting expectations and understanding what constitutes appropriate expectations.

The homework has the parents observing their interactions with their children in different situations, paying attention to how they respond differentially and how the children react to them. The intent is to continue the theme of the parents increasing their awareness of their thoughts, feelings, and behavior in parenting situations.

Session Four: Communication

As with previous sessions this one begins with a sharing of the homework experience, The leader's task is to connect the sharing with the ideas presented in the prior session and also to move on to the new topic of communication.

This session borrows heavily from the writings of Gordon (1970; 1980) and focuses on active listening, "I" versus "you" statements, roadblocks to communication and ways of working through differences. The question of "who owns the problem" is given attention and usually prompts active discussion. This concept seems especially important to parents who have difficulty with boundary issues related to "rescuing" their children in peer conflict situations and in setting appropriate expectations for children.

This unit also allows for moving back into the content of previous sessions such as styles of parenting. Many parents still struggle with what it means to be authoritative in terms of the parent being in charge and yet being sensitive and respectful of children's needs and growing competence.

The homework is for the participants to try out some of the communication techniques that were presented and role played. The parents are also cautioned regarding possible children's reactions to new and different parent techniques. A number of times parents have reported that their children identified their attempts to communicate differently with comments such as, "Oh, you've been to another parent class" and "Why are you talking funny?" The participants are helped to understand that their children may pick up on new parent behaviors, become somewhat anxious or defensive, and attempt through humor or even ridicule to discourage the parent.

Session Five: Discipline and Child Management

The session again begins with attention to things that occurred during the week or the bringing up of ideas that people have regarding past sessions. In particular, because this session follows the session on communication, there is a strong focus on the parents' experiences in trying new styles of communication and how their children reacted. The sharing typically involves success experiences as well as instances of negative reactions by children. Parents are supported in understanding that acting out new behaviors is personally challenging and that children's negative reactions can be an expression of concern that the parents are actually becoming more effective and that the children might be losing some of their power. The recurrent theme regarding communication is the importance of "practice, practice, practice."

An important theme in this session is that loving parents offer children the security of knowing that a parent cares enough to set limits and to not allow the child to engage in hurtful behavior towards self or others. The presentation on discipline looks at various problem-solving strategies and ways of understanding the behavior of children. Early on there is shared discussion of "trigger" events that prompt angry or otherwise reactive and ineffective disciplinary responses. The message here is that learning to anticipate opens the door to other options, including physically leaving the situation. The common participant notion that the parent not reacting means the child has won gets replaced with the notion that by not being reactive in the old ineffective way and by choosing when to respond, the parent can better create win–win situations.

This is followed by a presentation of selected concepts and strategies from Gordon (1970; 1980), the Adlerian/Dreikurs tradition (Dinkmeyer & McKay, 1976; Gamson, Hornstein, & Borden, 1989), and behavior modification. Dreikurs' view of "misbehaving" children as discouraged in their attempts to relate more productively with others and then turning to certain negative patterns for establishing a social identity is usually presented first. This viewpoint frames children in a positive and dynamic way as opposed to the stereotypical view a number of parents have that defines children in a more absolutist way such as "he's just bad" or "just like my uncle."

The four patterns Dreikurs discusses are the children who establish an identity and attempt to meet their needs through attention, power, revenge, or inadequacy. Dreikurs describes techniques for identifying the goals of the child's misbehavior which begin with the parent's awareness of their own feelings in response to the child's behavior. Specific intervention techniques include the use of natural and logical consequences, and encouragement.

"I" statements and the concept of "who owns the problem" (Gordon, 1970, 1989) also help parents in setting boundaries and communicating clear expectations. Useful techniques from behavior modification include selective reinforcement, consistency, and contingent responding.

For homework the participants are again encouraged to be observers of their own behaviors as they interact with their children and to tune in on their thoughts and feelings especially during trigger events. They are also encouraged to experiment with applying the techniques covered in the session that seem applicable in their situations.

Session Six: Putting It All Together

This is a summary session that while beginning again with recounting of events of the preceding week and reports of specific discipline or child management situations, attempts to have an integrative focus.

There is discussion about how the participants perceive themselves in terms of what they have learned and what concepts and skills have added to their parenting effectiveness.. They are also encouraged to identify topics, skills, etc., that did not seem useful in terms of approaches to child raising and parenting. The analogy to people starting out on a journey and moving at different paces is used to encourage the participants to evaluate themselves and their gains in a positive light, and also to continue to view themselves as ongoing learners rather than being static in their skills. Discussion around follow-up sessions or topics that they might want to pursue on a more individual basis with their own therapist are also typically covered. In addition information on other parent education opportunities in the community is presented.

The evaluation of the several sessions occurs by a group discussion in the last session, identifying what was helpful or not, what personal changes occurred, and what needs still exist. The session is also an opportunity for the leader to give positive feedback to the participants with encouragement to continue their "journey."

COMMENTARY ON PROGRAM CONTENT, STRUCTURE, AND DELIVERY

Leadership Considerations

The nature of this program places it between a more traditional educational program and a group therapy program. The ways in which educational and therapeutic components are integrated requires that the leader be familiar with both areas. The leaders of this program have typically been mental health professionals with a background in parent education rather than persons without clinical training.

From professional and ethical perspectives the leader needs to discuss boundary issues related to the educational and therapeutic dimensions of the program. The nature of the material being covered and the experiences and reactions being frequently elicited from the participants opens the door for them to move into wanting to deal more directly with their therapeutic issues. However, because all of the participants are usually involved in some kind of independent therapy program then it would seem that some differentiation between the parent program and the other therapeutic program is necessary. Otherwise there can be a blurring and confusion of the two contexts, with potential for conflict and even the sabotaging of the therapy experience by the parent program.

The balance that needs to be struck is a dynamic one because the program is based on the assumption that personal issues are interfering with effective parenting. It is desirable that some of these personal issues come out in the course of discussion so that these issues can be better understood and dealt with. However, the more in-depth pursuing of an individual's therapeutic issue may side-track the group, still not adequately resolve the issue, and leave the participant vulnerable. The leader may point out that a particular issue could be better dealt with more extensively between the participant and her therapist.

On occasion some of the strategies for coping with a child may heighten the conflict a participant is experiencing. An example would be a parent's ambivalence regarding when to set firm limits with consequences and when to be more accepting of the child's behavior. The issue for a given parent might be needing to be seen by the child as a loving parent coupled with confusion over reasonable limit setting being punitive. Respect of the need for the participant to work through her concerns may prompt the leader to suggest that the participant bring up those concerns with her therapist.

Assumption about the participants are that they are often self-critical about their attempts at parenting, easily frustrated, and quick to underscore their ineptness. With this in mind, the leader needs to be very careful about the way in which homework assignments are presented, subsequently discussed, and in a sense evaluated. Otherwise the potential is there for the homework assignments to become one more arena of perceived failure by the participant. The leader's acceptance of the participants as individuals who vary in readiness to implement different parenting strategies in itself models an important parenting concept. What may appear to be small steps could be very big steps for a given individual. The person's comfort at being in the group may be enhanced by the perception that the leader appreciates the gains, however small, that each participant is making.

Pacing and the Coverage of Content

The curriculum outline described earlier is used as a guide. From parent group to parent group it will be necessary to alter the pacing in terms of content. The earlier described curriculum that covered the six sessions should be understood as a framework that can be modified as deemed appropriate by the instructor, There is that tendency on the part of these parents to begin commiserating and in that way potentially accentuating their feelings of helplessness. There is a role for the leader in tracking with the participants as they do that kind of sharing but then to shift the focus back to a content area. Some analysis of the "ain't it awful" commiserating can also help the parents to shift into a more positive problem solving mode.

Pacing and sensitivity to the participants' needs will be demonstrated by the group leader on a situation by situation basis. This means that at the end of the six sessions one group may have progressed farther than another group in terms of content covered. In some instances follow-up groups have been established. Follow-up sessions that could be more narrowly focused may be options at different times and depending on available agency resources.

Transference and Counter Transference Considerations

Given the neediness on the part of many of these parents related to their own problematic parenting experiences one can readily see how they might transfer to the leader certain attributions (Vannicelli, 1989). In some instances the leader is seen as the "good parent" who is kind, supportive and wise. In other instances the group leader might be seen as harsh, unfeeling, and demanding. Aside from what the realities might be of the group leader's personality, we can make the assumption that a trained group leader will be reasonably supportive, caring, and sensitive. The reaction to the group leader by the parents where they either aggrandize or demean the leader needs to be understood as possibly the bringing forward to the present of the participants' earlier parenting experiences. This can be dealt with in different ways, including some exploration of people's perceptions or probably in many instances more effectively by the leader continuing in a fairly kind and supportive way. Our experiences have been that as the leader stays in that supportive mode the parents who may have seen the leader in a negative light eventually soften their position and increase their awareness of how their own history has influenced their reactions.

Counter transference considerations are equally important and have been discussed in the literature (Vannicelli, 1989). The difficulties that individual parents experience can all pull from the group leader some subjective reactions. Regarding the complexities of family therapy some have argued the need for two therapists or some other arrangement such as the use of a one-way mirror. One can apply the same thinking to argue that perhaps, especially with larger groups, the parent education program being described could benefit from two leaders, possibly even a male and female. There is a real challenge for any group leader to maintain self-awareness and to relate with the participants in therapeutically helpful ways.

Developing Realistic Goals

It was earlier mentioned that the didactic framework for the program involved four areas, that of information giving, increasing self awareness, developing specific skills, and monitored practice. Each of these four areas lends itself to assessment of goal attainment on the part of participants. Given the time-limited nature of the program it would be unrealistic to expect major changes in these areas. It may be more realistic to examine perceptions and beliefs on the part of the participants about themselves and the parenting role.

Our own evaluations have been essentially in the form of discussion with the participants as to what they perceived as gains and areas of continuing concern. It appears that the program, because of its quasitherapeutic nature and intended sensitivity to the individual needs of participants, frequently serves the function of putting them more at ease in the parenting role. They see the role as less formidable and they feel more hopeful about being able to be at least a reasonable parent if not a "super parent." Given the frequent self-defeating dynamics of the participants, it may in fact be a very large gain for them to begin seeing themselves in a more adequate parenting role and to feeling more optimistic about being a positive and helpful influence in the lives of their children.

REFERENCES

Baumrind, D. (1989). Rearing competent children. In Damon, W. (Ed.), *Child development today and tomorrow* (pp. 349–378). San Francisco: Jossey-Bass.

Baumrind, D. (1991). The influence of parenting style on adolescence competence and substance use. *Journal of Early Adolescence, 11,* 56–95.

Beal, E. W., & Hochman, G. (1991). *Adult children of divorce: Breaking the cycle and finding fulfillment in love, marriage, and family.* New York: Delacorte Press.

Beavers, W. R., & Hampson, R. B. (1990). *Successful families: Assessment and intervention.* New York: Norton.

Becnel, B. C. (1991). *The co-dependent parent: Free yourself by freeing your child.* San Francisco: HarperCollins.

Chess, S., & Thomas, A. (1987). *Know your child: An authoratative guide for today's parents.* New York: Basic Books.

Collins, R. L., Leonard, K. E., & Searles, J. S. (1990). (Eds.). *Alcohol and the family: Research and clinical perspectives.* New York: Guilford.

Curran, D. (1983). *Traits of a healthy family.* Minneapolis, MN: Winston.

Craighead, L. W., Craighead, W. E., Kazdin, A. E., & Mahoney, M. J. (1994). *Cognitive and behavioral interventions: An empirical approach to mental health problems.* Boston: Allyn & Bacon.

DeFrain, J., & Stinnett, N. (1992). Building on the inherent strengths of families. *Topics in Family Psychology and Counseling, 1,* 15–26.

Dinkmeyer, D., & McKay, G. (1976). *Systematic training for effective parenting.* Circle Pines, MN: American Guidance Services.

Erikson, E. H. (1968). *Identity: Youth and crisis.* New York: Norton.

Gamson, B., Hornstein, H., & Borden, B. L. (1989). Adler-Dreikurs parent study group leadership training. In M. J. Fine (Ed.), *The second handbook on parent education: Contemporary perspectives* (pp. 279–302). New York: Academic Press.

Gladding, S. T. (1998). *Family therapy: History, theory, and practice* (2nd Ed.). Upper Saddle River, NJ: Prentice Hall.

Goldenberg, I., & Goldenberg, H. (1996). *Family therapy: An overview* (4th Ed.). Pacific Grove CA: Brooks/Cole.

Gordon, T. (1970). *P. E. T.: Parent effectiveness training.* New York: Wyden.

Gordon, T. (1980). Parent effectiveness training: A preventive program and its effects on families. In Fine, M. J. (Ed.), *Handbook on parent education* (pp. 101–121). New York: Academic Press.

Joyce, M. R. (1990). Rational-emotive parent consultation. *School Psychology Review, 19,* 304–314.

Mason, D. A. (1990). *Double duty: Parenting our kids while reparenting ourselves.* Minneapolis, MN: Compcare.

Meichenbaum, D. (1977). *Cognitive behavior modification: An integrative approach.* New York: Plenum.

Rolfe, R. C. (1990). *Adult children raising children.* Deerfield Beach, FL: Health Communications.

Steinglass, P. (1987). *The alcoholic family.* New York: Basic Books.

Stinnett, N., & DeFrain, J. (1989). The healthy family: Is it possible? In Fine, M. J. (Ed.), *The second handbook on parent education: Contemporary perspectives* (pp. 53–74). New York: Academic Press.

Vannicelli, M. (1989). *Group psychotherapy with adult children of alcoholics: Treatment techniques and countertransference considerations.* New York: Guilford.

Wassil-Grimm, C. (1990). *How to avoid your parents' mistakes when you raise your children.* New York: Simon & Shuster.

Windle, M., & Searles, J. S. (1990). (Eds.). *Children of alcoholics: Critical perspectives.* New York: Guilford.

CHAPTER 7

Supportive Family Training: Education and Support for the Parents of Persons with Serious Mental Illness

Sheila Le Gacy

The Family Support and Education Center,
Transitional Living Services, Syracuse, New York

Although the caregiving burden in all chronic illnesses has certain commonalties, persons who suffer from mental illness present unique burdens that call for specific interventions. In this chapter we describe one such intervention—Supportive Family Training (SFT)—a model of family education that has been helping parents of children and adults with neurobiological brain disorders for more than 20 years. SFT, an innovative 12-week curriculum that blends education, support, and advocacy training, was created by a family member/professional to assist parents to meet the challenges of caring for their loved ones and themselves.

There is a critical need for education and support for the millions of parents who provide care for their children with mental illness. Misunderstood, often feared, and still stigmatized, the most severe mental illnesses affect more than 10 million American adults and 7 million children and adolescents, causing inestimable suffering to these patients and their families. (Manderscheid, 1997). Today, there is a scientific consensus that the most serious and persistent "mental illnesses" are, in fact, *neurobiological brain disorders*, physical illnesses characterized by, or resulting from, malfunctions and/or malformations of the brain. The most common of these conditions are schizophrenia, schizo-affective disorder, bipolar and major depressive disorder, obsessive-compulsive disorder, and anxiety and panic disorder. These brain disorders are far more common than cancer, diabetes, heart disease, or arthritis. More hospital beds are occupied by people with these biologically based brain disorders than with any other disease (Peschel and Peschel, 1992). The National Institute of Mental Health (NIMH) estimates that one out of four families in the U.S. will have a loved one with a serious mental illness.

To appreciate the problems faced by parents with mentally ill offspring, we first provide some basic information about the serious and persistent mental illnesses, discuss the reaction of parents when these illnesses strike their children, and point out some important similarities and differences between caregiving in mental illness and in other chronic illnesses.

HOW COMMON IS MENTAL ILLNESS?

Mental illness is far more common than is generally known. "The prevalence of *serious mental illness* among Americans age 18 and over during a 12-month period (1997) is estimated to be 5.4%, or 10 million people. Of that group, almost 5.4 million people, are estimated to have *severe and persistent mental illness*" (News & Notes, 1997, p. 1216). When adults with any DSM-IV diagnosis within a 12-month period are included, the national prevalence rate for mental disorders is 28.9%, or 44.2 million people—and these figures do not include children with diagnosed serious mental illness (News & Notes, 1997, p. 1216).

As Secunda (1997) points out, the total number of people directly affected by mental illness is astronomical. Taking the most conservative statistical approach, if 26 million Americans (10% of the population) currently have some kind of incapacitating mental disorder, and, if each of those citizens has two parents, one sibling, and one child, that means that over 100 million Americans have mental illness in their immediate families—and that's without counting extended kin and partners.

In light of these statistics, it is impossible to overstate the need for effective education for caregiving parents. In 1982, it was estimated that, in the United States, 65% of psychiatric hospital patients were discharged to their families, and by 1987 about 35 to 40% of persons with severe and persistent mental illnesses lived with their families on an *ongoing* basis (Lefley, 1987). Currently, in Canada, approximately two thirds of persons with schizophrenia, about 80 thousand individuals—live at home with their families at any given time. In the U.S., more than one third of adult children with schizophrenia currently live with aging parents, and that number is likely to rise (Atkinson, 1994).

Ascher-Svanum's (1989) study notes that women are three times as likely as men to be the primary caregivers for their nonmarried, adult, mentally ill relatives. Her data suggest that the deinstitutionalization movement has, in effect, extended women's culturally prescribed nurturant role beyond their child-rearing years, that is, they are expected to manage and care for their mentally ill offspring and relatives for an indeterminate period, possibly throughout their lifetimes.

These statistics illustrate the accuracy of predictions made years ago when mental institutions began to empty their hospital beds without any community planning for follow-up care. Severe social consequences had been predicted for families taking their dysfunctional relatives into their homes, particularly for families having no caregiving skills, no training, and little or no help from the treatment system (Lefley, 1996). Unfortunately, given diminishing institutional and community resources, there is little likelihood that the trend toward the family becoming the patient's de facto caretaker will be reversed.

THE SCHIZOPHRENIAS AND THE SERIOUS AFFECTIVE (MOOD) DISORDERS

The schizophrenias and the serious affective disorders are typically chronic illnesses. Schizophrenia as a label applies to a group of related disorders; it is a syndrome rather than a single disease with a uniform cause and it manifests with different kinds of symptoms that appear in a variety of combinations and with a wide range of severity. The most common symptoms of this brain disease are hallucinations (hearing voices, seeing visions), delusions (false beliefs about commonly held views of reality), and bizarre thought patterns. These are called "positive" symptoms and they typically lead to psychiatric treatment and hospitalization. Often neglected are the "negative" symptoms of schizophrenia—social isolation and withdrawal, blunting of emotional expressiveness, poor communication skills, and decreased motivation and self-care. These symptoms are just as disabling as hallucinations and delusions (Gorman, 1996).

Affective (mood) disorders are not just "cases of the blues," but severe and persistent biological diseases. The two most common types of affective disorder are major depression (unipolar) and manic depression, or bipolar, illness. Major depression is marked by persistent depressive thoughts and moods, accompanied by physiological disturbances in sleep, appetite, and energy level. In bipolar illness, depressive episodes alternate intermittently with manic ones. Mania is marked initially by heightened energy and mood, sharpened and unusually creative thinking, irritability, and increased self-confidence. In full mania, these symptoms progress to grandiose delusions and psychotic, disruptive behavior. Bipolar disorders, in nearly all instances, are recurrent and chronic, with no promise that the afflicted person will "mature out of" the disease. Quite the contrary: if not treated, episodes of depression and mania may become longer and more frequent with time (Gorman, 1996). Suicide is a high risk in the schizophrenias (10%), but the rate is 30 times higher than the rest of the population for those suffering major mood disorders. In 1990 it was estimated that about 15,000 men and 3400 women committed suicide in the U.S. because of depression (Goleman, 1993).

Three fourths of persons with schizophrenia develop the disease between 16 and 25 years of age. The peak onset of manic depression is the same—in late adolescence and the early 20s (Gorman, 1996).

SIMILARITIES TO AND DIFFERENCES FROM OTHER CHRONIC ILLNESSES

Although the fundamental psychosocial factors requiring attention in severe mental disorders are, in most instances, identical to those affecting families dealing with any chronic illness, there are important differences. Unlike other illnesses, where one comes to terms with the facts of the illness, the process of stages of emotional response in parents is ongoing and cyclical: sometimes it starts all over again each time one's child has a relapse. The parents of persons with mental illness are on a "roller coaster ride" that has them "regularly cycling through hope and then despair" (Spaniol et al., 1992, p. 28). MacGregor (1992) quotes the poignant words of the mother of a son with manic depression: "*It's as though our son dies every two years*" (p. 6).

Limitations of Psychiatric Diagnoses

The diagnosis of a serious mental illness is made on the basis of clinical judgment, so diagnoses may differ from one professional to another—frustrating parents, and resulting in their loss of confidence in psychiatrists and other healthcare providers. Also, because of crossover symptoms, schizophrenia and the mood disorders are often mistaken for one another. At least 10% of people diagnosed with schizophrenia have their diagnosis changed over their lifetime (Stoll, Tohen, & Baldessarini, 1993). Furthermore, a major survey (1993) by the National Depression and Manic Depression Association (NDMDA) of persons with mood disorders found that 75% of those surveyed were first incorrectly diagnosed (News & Notes, 1993). The same survey found that it took an average of 10 years for individuals with manic depression to be properly diagnosed. Adding to the problem is the insensitivity of many professionals. In a recent article Bachrach (1997) notes that professionals continue to manifest a common lack of empathy with mentally ill patients and their families. In spite of clear indications that psychiatric and neurobiological disorders are synonymous, many clinicians are still operating from a conceptual framework that does not readily accept them as legitimate illnesses. Furthermore, in spite of overwhelming evidence to the contrary, families are still being pathologized because of their childrens' mental illness.

Substance Abuse

Mental illness and substance abuse are deeply intertwined problems. In fact, the mentally ill are almost twice as likely as other people to be alcoholics or on drugs (Butterfield, 1998). First of all, young adults with major mental disorders are "hypervulnerable—chemically, psychologically, and socially to the effects of even mild or recreational use of drugs and alcohol" (Brown, Ridgely, Pepper, Levine, & Ryglewicz, 1989). In addition, they have easy access to alcohol and other substances in the community which, in combination with inadequate patient education and social pressure has led many persons with mental illness to substance use and abuse, with the result that their symptoms have become exacerbated, and their progress in adapting to community living has been threatened (Bachrach, 1997).

Violence: Families at Risk

According to Monahan (1992), "the currently mentally disordered—those actively experiencing serious psychotic symptoms—are involved in violent behavior at rates several times those of nondisordered members of the general population" (p. 517). Furthermore, more than 85% of the violence committed by persons with mental illness was directed at family members or friends: only 14% of the attacks involved strangers (Butterfield, 1998). For example, research has identified single parents, especially single female parents, as vulnerable caregivers. "Mothers bear considerable responsibility for caring for relatives with mental illness and are at high risk of being the targets of repeated violence by those relatives" (Estroff et al., 1994). Although "these findings clearly indicate that public fears of violence on the street by discharged patients who are strangers to them are misdirected," (Butterfield, 1998, p. 14) they also illustrate a frightening and unpredictable problem with which many families of persons with mental illness have had to contend.

Stigma and Ignorance Surrounding Mental Illness

Unlike other chronic diseases, stigma still surrounds mental illness and it invariably leads to social isolation of the patient and family. "Despite continued efforts at public education and consciousness raising, and despite official mandates supporting their integration into society, persons with mental illness today remain basically unwanted in many neighborhoods" (Bachrach 1997, p. 282). The stigma that is attached to madness in our culture is especially severe, and carries with it a particularly heartless social judgment. Having a disordered or deranged mind is regarded as a mark of such shame that centuries of charity and good works have been unable to overcome the forces of ignorance, prejudice, and neglect. Stigmatization results in the marginalization and ostracism of the mentally ill and it even extends to their families and to the professionals who provide them with treatment (Fink & Tasman, 1992).

Unfortunately, many otherwise informed people do not believe mental illness exists as a legitimate illness. Whereas, mental retardation is accepted as biological, mind/body dualism still holds for the general public in respect to mental illness. In spite of energetic and ongoing efforts by NAMI and other advocacy groups to combat stigma, attitudes have not changed significantly. In a recent survey (News & Notes, 1995), 78% of respondents between the ages of 18 and 24 and 64% of those between the ages of 25 and 34 believed that people can prevent or bring themselves out of manic depression. The evidence that the serious psychiatric disorders are truly "no-fault" brain diseases has not been given credence in our culture.

THE NATURE OF THE CAREGIVING TASKS
IN SERIOUS MENTAL ILLNESS

Although a significant number of individuals with neurobiological brain disorders are able to live independently, the focus here is on functionally impaired children and adults who have ongoing needs for outpatient care and support. Offspring diagnosed with schizophrenia, major endogenous depression, bipolar disorder, disabling obsessive-compulsive disorder, and psychotic states are those most likely to be living at home under parental care. Even when mentally ill offspring live separately, however, family members give a great deal of themselves in terms of time, money, and social support. A recent study documented that 42% of these caregivers, by their own reports, make the majority of patient care and treatment decisions, and that the five care-giving activities most frequently cited are (1) providing emotional support, (2) managing finances and paperwork, (3) providing transportation or "company" for errands/appointments, (4) seeking information regarding patient's conditions and treatment, and (5) performing additional care-related tasks outside the homes. Fifty-eight percent of the respondents were involved in the selection of prescription medications for the patient, and 46% of the caregivers had requested that the physician prescribe new antipsychotic medications for the patient within the preceding 6 months (Consumer Health Sciences, 1998).

Two major goals of working with the parents of individuals with severe neurobiological brain disorders are to (1) realize the optimum potential of the patient through the best possible management and treatment of their disease and (2) to alleviate the suffering and burden on family members (World Schizophrenia Fellowship, 1998). As indicated previously, parents play a key role in the support system that is needed to sustain their ill offspring. Their ability to provide an emotionally supportive and predictable environment can be a key factor in the ability of the patient to achieve any significant level of independence. These demands, however, are not easy to meet. The presence of a mentally ill relative has profoundly disruptive effects on family life and severely strains the family's capacity to provide a rehabilitative environment. Studies show that caregivers experience substantial increases in family conflict, economic difficulties, as well as decreases in family communication and activities (Consumer Health Sciences, 1998). Hatfield (1994) has resorted to theories of coping and adaptation and to the literature on stress and behavior as tools for normalizing "the strong reactions of families . . . (as) something to be expected in the face of their devastating experiences" (p. 4). Unlike developmental defects evidenced at birth, in these brain disorders parents have no time to prepare. They are plunged into making decisions without an opportunity to digest the crisis. A more compelling point perhaps is the fact of having known their children for such a long period and then seeing them alter so dramatically. As a parent in a SFT class commented to this author: "It is as if you have to learn to love a stranger."

Emotional Reactions of Parents to the Diagnosis of Mental Illness

The reaction of parents who are confronted with severe mental illness is not unlike the reaction of parents to any other catastrophic illness. Families undergo periods of extreme disorientation, conflict, denial and fear. But there are differences. Lefley's (1987) comment, "watching the known personality decompensate is terrifying for the family, who can never be prepared for this experience," gives the feeling tone of this "existential crisis, devastating in its impact" (p. 47). Feelings of guilt, shame, anger, and ambivalence are typical. "In addition, because of the cognitive impairment and excessive neediness and self-absorption characteristic of these disorders, family members may experience little reward from interpersonal interactions" (Lefley, 1994, p. 92). Some parents report periods of deep depression, not unlike the intense sorrow experienced during mourning. A recent survey of 698 caregivers showed that 30% of those participating in the study suffered from depression: this rate is much higher than that in the general population (Consumer Health Sciences, 1998).

The impact of the diagnosis, itself terrifying, is reinforced by the stigma that surrounds mental illness. This double burden is often accompanied by the punishing reality of watching a son or daughter, often at the brink of promising young adulthood, undergo continuing, sequential personal losses—of competence, independence, friendships, and hopes. Indeed, the onset of mental illness precipitates a "lifetime of losses" (MacGregor, 1994, p. 7). For the parents themselves, these same losses are experienced as loss of their child's personality; loss of their child's role in the family; loss of the child's joy and pleasure in life; loss of potential, talents, and competence; loss of a hoped-for future; and, in some cases, actual loss of a child who wanders off to disappear among the homeless or who commits suicide.

Researchers have found higher levels of acute and ongoing grief in families with a chronically mentally ill child than in families whose child has died.

The families studied included children with chronic depression, bipolar disorder, schizophrenia, or a personality disorder (Atkinson, 1994, p. 3).

MacGregor (1994) notes that parents of persons with mental illness go through the same general phases of grief that parents travel through when they lose a child to death. Yet, whereas they experience a similar grief, their suffering is not generally recognized or validated by society. The sorrow experienced by the parents of individuals with mental illness has been aptly labeled "disenfranchised grief" because their loss is not "openly acknowledged, publicly mourned, or socially supported" (Doka, 1989, p. 4). As a result, healthy expression of parental grief in such instances is seriously inhibited, and problems, for parents and patient both, are exacerbated.

What is currently experienced by most parents of the mentally ill could be considered almost a worst-case scenario, which practically assures unacknowledged and disenfranchised grief (MacGregor, 1992, p.11).

EDUCATIONAL INTERVENTIONS FOR PARENTS OF THE MENTALLY ILL

SFT, as we discuss later, is one of several different approaches that has emerged since the early 1980s to help parents cope with a mentally ill child or adult. Family education evolved from psychoeducation, a more clinical approach that combines education with therapy. Both of these educational interventions represented a substantial break with the family-blaming eras of the 1950s and 1960s, when mental health professionals, for the most part, either rejected family members outright or ignored their requests for information and support. During those years, when psychoanalytic theory and family systems therapy were dominant, the patient's illness was believed to be serving some purpose within the dysfunctional family system and the family was advised to leave the therapist in charge of promoting change (Lefley, 1994, p. 89). For persons with severe mental illness, the goal of treatment was often to separate the psychiatric patient from what professionals considered to be a disturbed family system.

There was little change in attitudes toward families of the mentally ill until well into 1970. By the latter part of the decade, strong evidence for organic causes of mental illness began to emerge. With no solid evidence supporting the notion that the family was the causal factor in mental illness, there was no longer a legitimate basis for family blaming. By that time the deinstitutionalization movement that began in the late 1950s was well along. The psychiatric inpatient population had been reduced from 560,000 in-patients in 1955 to 193,360 by 1976—a decrease of two thirds in 2 decades (Marsh, 1992, p. 7).

The nation then was faced with the consequences of releasing patients to a community unprepared to give them the care they required. Because there were no institutional supports in place, the burden of care for these formerly institutionalized patients fell on families. This was the environment in which the earliest educational approaches to caregivers emerged, and when NAMI was formed. Families, in desperate need of help, began to advocate for improved services.

The Development of Psychoeducation and the Concept of "High Expressed Emotion" (EE)

The term psychoeducation has been broadly used to characterize a range of approaches to educating families. We use it here to describe approaches associated with the research construct of "high expressed emotion," defined as verbal criticism, hostility, and emotional overinvolvement. According to this theory, which has served as a theoretical framework for interventions with families in psychoeducational programs, families characterized by high expressed emotion (EE) contributed to the probability of relapse or exacerbation of symptoms in their relatives with schizophrenia. The goal of family intervention, then, was to reduce EE (Hatfield, 1994, p. 5)

Studies concentrating on the effect of high EE on relapse indicated that patients returning to a household characterized by conflict and tension had a greatly increased risk of relapse. Anderson, Reiss, & Hogarty's (1986) research showed that some patients with schizophrenia similarly relapsed when exposed to intensive rehabilitation programs, or even an enriched milieu. Looking at the data, they concluded that the evidence for an "environmental press" in schizophrenia was formidable (Anderson et al., 1986). It appears that people with schizophrenia are hypersensitive to their environments and have extraordinary difficulties in selecting relevant stimuli, directing and maintaining attention, recognizing and identifying stimuli, and integrating and using information appropriately (Hatfield, 1994, p. 5). These patients seem to possess a particular vulnerability to social stimuli such that severe or frequent stressful life events override the protective influence of medicine and result in a psychotic episode.

These data on schizophrenic vulnerability inspired Dr. Carol Anderson, the "mother" of psychoeducation, and her colleagues at the University of Pittsburgh to develop an innovative psychoeducational model in the late 1970s. Their goal was to prevent or delay relapse and rehospitalization by teaching parents about the illness, about dealing with symptoms, and about creating a healing environment. Basically this psychoeducational model presents schizophrenia as a medical illness that requires management, just like any other medical illness that a family and patient must learn to organize their lives around. Anderson and colleagues were able to show that a combined approach—educating families about schizophrenia and providing the ill person with medication and social skills training—resulted in the relapse rate falling to zero in the first year of its implementation (Anderson, Hogerty, & Reiss, 1980).

The educational and psychotherapeutic interventions inspired by Anderson targeted the well-being of the person with schizophrenia, specifically by teaching parents to change their behaviors to help their offspring avoid relapse. Although other models have since developed that are less clinical and more family focused than Anderson's (like SFT), which include working with the parents of persons with serious mood disorders, many of her major principles are still operative. To her credit, even in the family-blaming atmosphere in which she wrote, she strongly cautioned professionals to work with "the assumption of least pathology," i.e., do not look for family pathology—work with the healthy assets of the family.

The high EE construct, though useful in many ways, as demonstrated by Anderson's work, has been criticized as yet another way of blaming the family. McFarlane et al. (1993) have suggested that high expressed emotion should be more accurately described as "expressed exasperation." For example, a patient's behavior becomes annoying or strange and the family becomes agitated in response. Then the family becomes critical of the patient, resulting in the patient becoming stressed and subsequently relapsing. Understanding how this dynamic works can help families cope with exasperating behavior without becoming reactive and critical of the person manifesting the bizarre or simply difficult-to-live-with symptoms.

Le Gacy (1998) suggests that much of the "high EE" behavior manifested by some families, especially their critical comments, not only reflects an ignorance of the nature of their relatives' disorders but also serves as a defense against their own painful feelings, especially their feelings of grief. She believes that this aspect of the high expressed-emotion issue has not been sufficiently examined. Grief can be expressed in many different ways, she maintains. Sometimes it does not look like grief is typically expected to look; sometimes it may be expressed as anger, or as criticism.

From Psychoeducation to Family Education

Although it is true that psychoeducation has its roots in family therapy and has sought to combine the practice of education and therapy, an important distinction exists between educational and therapeutic models of family intervention. Psychoeducation explicitly begins with *patient* needs whereas the central focus of family education is the well-being of the *family* itself, seen as "worthy of education simply to make their own lives more manageable and satisfying"(Lefley, 1994, p. 91). If Anderson is the mother of psychoeducation, than Agnes Hatfield and Harriet Lefley share the credit for giving birth to family education. Both are family members who skillfully merged their professional expertise with their subjective experience of parenting children with serious mental illness. Their impressive contribution to the field has been responsible for changing the focus of educational interventions for parents into a "family friendly" approach. Although families have been tending to ill relatives for centuries, Hatfield and Lefley were among the first in the field of mental illness to develop a technology focusing on *the needs of caregivers as distinct from the needs of patients* (Lefley, 1994, p. 92). Hatfield maintains that educational approaches that view families' feelings of grief, loss, and irrational guilt as natural reactions can help families overcome them more readily than assuming they must be explored for their psychodynamic meanings. Furthermore, as Lefley (1994) points out, even though working with emotions is supposed to be the work of psychotherapy, "paradoxically . . . education that is family focused may deal with emotions more effectively than patient-focused therapeutic approaches aimed at lowering e.e." (p. 94).

Hatfield and Lefley maintain that education that validates the critical, hostile, or emotionally overinvolved responses of family members as normal responses to difficult behaviors serves as a basis for teaching families the harmful effects of this behavior without implying familial deficits. "Underlying this approach is the message that most families are *nonknowledgeable* rather than dysfunctional and that families are competent to change once they receive the necessary information" (Lefley, 1994, p. 94).

Family education is now one of the leading types of interventions used to help families cope with mental illness in their relatives. The rapid development of family education programs has occurred in the past decade for many reasons, some of the most obvious of which are that these programs are responsive to needs as families have identified them; they avoid pathologizing families; they are short-term and they do not tie up overburdened families in lengthy programs (Hatfield, 1994, p. 9).

Research on the relative efficacies of clinical psychoeducation programs and family-focused education is ongoing (Solomon, 1996). Current findings do indicate that models like SFT, which combine engagement, support and problem solving in addition to education, are superior to brief pyschoeducation alone (Dixon & Lehman, 1995; Solomon, 1996). These family-focused approaches also offer the critically important advantage of teaching advocacy, and of linking families to the ongoing support of advocacy groups like NAMI.

SFT: A FAMILY-FRIENDLY MODEL

Supportive Family Training (SFT) is a family-centered model, specifically designed to offer education, support, and advocacy to the parents of persons with mental illness. The primary goals of the program are to improve the parents' coping skills, and to alert them to the importance of self-care, as means of reducing their burden and enhancing their quality of life. SFT addresses these issues on the cognitive, emotional, and spiritual levels, drawing on a wide variety of techniques from adult education, peer counseling, stress reduction, meditation, yoga, bereavement work, and advocacy training.

SFT is based on a 600-page syllabus that includes detailed teaching instructions and copious handouts. At the beginning of each class, participants receive an outline of the information to be covered as well as related take-home material. Upon completion of the course, graduates are encouraged to join their local NAMI affiliate. In addition to parents, who make up the majority of most classes, the program may be attended by adult offspring, adult siblings, spouses, or concerned friends. It is recommended that no more than 10 patients be represented by their families in any one class. SFT requires an initial interview with prospective family members to take a history of their ill relatives, to discover how they have been dealing with their situations, and to seek out the kind of information they need most. The intake interview is a critical step in engaging families in the course. The program also encourages participation of a limited number of professional staff so that they can better grasp the realities of the parents' experience and the parents can better understand the perspectives of mental health professionals.

SFT is rooted in a *transpersonal* perspective that extends family education more deeply into emotional and spiritual realms than is present in conventional family education programs. The transpersonal ("beyond self" or "larger than self") approach seeks to free the energy of individuals who suffer by connecting them to the pain of the world. People are hungry for connection and meaning, and sometimes painful experiences, like the wrenching loss and grief experienced by the parents of people with mental illness, provide opportunities for making that connection. The ability of the SFT program to provide this connection is illustrated by the comments of a mental health professional whose daughter suffers from schizophrenia. She wrote in her evaluation at the end of the course: "This challenging curriculum goes beyond the more obvious and 'safe' topics we are usually exposed to and asks us to acknowledge and explore our pain. In this way, the classes are immensely restorative. Although it is not "therapeutic" as we know that term professionally, it accomplishes the same end; we feel met, understood, touched. Our hearts are less weary, our burdens lighter" (personal communication, 1990). Indeed, Le Gacy characterizes the SFT methodology as "*working through the heart.*" Because she believes that the most important and most difficult work for parents is dealing with their pain and their grief and their mourning for *their lost hopes, for what will not be*, she places a great deal of emphasis on working with suffering.

Although SFT concentrates on the needs of caregivers, its governing principle is to ease the burden for *all* members of the family and particularly for the relative with the psychiatric disorder. The SFT program facilitates changes that benefit the patient as well as his or her parents. Theories underlying this approach uniformly agree that (1) the ventilation of negative emotions tends to free psychic energy that might otherwise be channeled into counterproductive interactions with the patient; (2) grief work that builds upon the patient's strengths and assets helps to shift the family's emotional investment away from what has been lost to what can be gained; (3) reducing guilt diminishes the psychological pressure to overprotect and infantilize the ill person; (4) supportive groups help participants to feel accepted themselves and thus to accept their disabled relatives and to communicate an attitude of acceptance to them; and (5) the sense of safety that group members experience reduces their defensiveness, allowing them to become receptive to ideas about changing the way they relate to their relatives (Atwood, 1983, p. 192).

SFT: THE STRUCTURE OF THE TRAINING

The Educational Component of SFT

The educational component of Supportive Family Training (SFT) consists of providing caregivers with the latest research on the schizophrenias and the major mood disorders, instruction in coping and management skills, crisis intervention, communication techniques, practical problem solving, as well as information on community supports and rehabilitation. Parents are taught to recognize prodromal signs that may be pointing to a relapse so that they can take effective measures to avoid rehospitalization. Given the striking consistency in the prodromal symptoms that precede each episode, parents are taught to be aware of the specific symptoms that signal a recurrence of their offspring's illness.

In addition to receiving extensive information about the nature of the illnesses they are dealing with, parents are given strategies and terminology to make communication with mental health professionals more effective.

The Support Component: Stress Management and Self-Care

Many, if not most, parents are overwhelmed and seriously stressed by the multiple burdens they face as caregivers of children with mental illness. The stress may be constant or intermittent, depending on the stage of their offspring's illness, their own inner resources, their physical and emotional well-being, the availability of family and community supports, and their ability to live with uncertainty.

The supportive component of the training acknowledges the need for coping skills to counteract the stress of dealing with a relative with mental illness. Parents are urged first to become aware of their stress levels and what triggers their stress, and then to take action to deal with it. Depending on the individual, SFT recommends regular physical exercise, long walks, yoga, tai chi, guided imagery tapes, therapeutic massage, and meditation as ways to reduce stress. Meditation is presented as mental self-control that serves as a tool for reducing stress. Parents learn that anything done with focus, awareness, or mindfulness is a meditation, whether it is taking a walk, doing the dishes, or driving a car. The program also offers instructions in simple breathing techniques and relaxation exercises.

Because of the demands of caring for offspring with serious and persistent neurobiological brain disorders, many parents have severely neglected their own needs. Some of them have put their own lives on hold; some feel that it is selfish for them to even think of their own needs. This reaction is particularly true of mothers, and especially the cohort of women who became mothers before 1960 when maternal self-sacrifice was the order of the day. However, it is not uncommon for fathers, siblings, and adult children also to feel this way (Le Gacy, 1998).

If care giving becomes the central purpose of their life, to the neglect of their personal growth, relaxation, pleasure and health, then the odds of parents becoming physically ill and/or depressed are high. Parents need to understand that self-neglect leading to illness or depression ultimately adds to the burden on their loved ones. In other words, caregivers who do not care for themselves are not, in the long run, going to be helpful to anyone else. Parents who feel that it is selfish to think of their own needs are told that it is selfish of them *not* to take care of themselves. People who neglect themselves eventually become dependent on others and to let that happen knowingly is really a selfish act. Also, parents who neglect their own needs are poor role models for their ill offspring. It is essential to keep a balance in one's care giving. It all starts with the self (Le Gacy, 1998).

SFT's essential message to parents is that by attending to their own needs, they better serve the needs of their loved ones and the family as a whole. The importance of self-care is addressed from the very beginning of SFT, and is emphasized throughout the entire twelve weeks. In fact, working with this issue is given equal status with teaching about the causes and treatments of the schizophrenias and mood disorders.

Working with Guilt

Given its very common occurrence among parents, the SFT program places particular attention on guilt. From the onset of the course, parents are taught that they are *not* responsible for their family members being ill, but they *are* responsible for the way they respond to their illness. This is not an easy lesson to learn and, adding to the problem, some of the decisions parents are often forced to make can contribute to their guilt and ambivalence. There are times, for example, when parents may have to choose between making self-protective decisions and providing care for their ill relatives. Unfortunately, mutually beneficial solutions are not always possible (Lefley, 1994). There are frequently instances when what is good for the patient may not be good for the rest of the family or for individual members of the family (younger siblings, for instance, who may need to be protected). Lefley (1994) notes the many reports of siblings and children "being shortchanged as parents invest their efforts in literally saving the life of the one family member who was mentally ill" (p. 92). Obviously, each family needs to strike an appropriate balance.

Working with Grief

> Grief is a normal, healthy, spontaneous, and necessary response to loss. Moving through the process of grief and mourning toward some kind of resolution is hard, painful, and sometimes frightening (MacGregor, 1994, p. 164).

In Supportive Family Training, the grief issues discussed previously are brought out into the open by teachers who are encouraged to use examples from their own experience. In addition, hearing other family members share their emotional distress and talk about the issues with which they have struggled gives them what Spaniol and colleagues (Spaniol, Zipple & Lockwood, 1993, p. 30) describe as "genuine insight as well as a powerful incentive to work through" their own grief. In a very real sense, the group mourns together. The group process is very powerful and very necessary because, as MacGregor (1994) has noted, grieving can not be done in isolation—it is a social event. The success of bereavement groups indicates that families can learn to deal with grief and loss very effectively outside of a clinical context.

Lindemann's (1945) seminal work on the treatment of grief describes a successful short-term model for grief work. Grief is intense, but it does not have to go on forever. Lindemann was optimistic that, once persuaded to yield to the grief process, individuals could recover in a relatively short time. Supportive Family Training incorporates all the steps Lindemann considered necessary for individuals going through the grieving process, steps he maintained could be accomplished in eight to ten interviews:

> He will have to express his sorrow and sense of loss, find an acceptable formulation of his future relationship|s| . . . , verbalize his feelings of guilt, and find persons around him whom he can use as primers' for the acquisition of new patterns of conduct (v. 147).

The truth, as MacGregor (1994) wisely concludes, is that serious mental illness can represent a tragedy to a family, but it does not have to be an unending tragedy. Times of loss offer everyone the opportunity to deepen emotionally, to grow in maturity, to experience spiritual healing, and to connect with one another as human beings.

The Advocacy Component of SFT

Parents must learn to work more effectively with service providers if they are to obtain needed services for their offspring. SFT teaches parents ways to become more effective advocates for their offspring and for other families as well. As parents experience less self-blame and become more assertive, they often develop an increased interest in working more closely with knowledgeable and caring professionals. One way they can be particularly effective is by helping to train professionals to work with other families (Spaniol, Zipple, & Lockwood, 1992). SFT encourages this kind of involvement. In addition, as Spaniol et al. (1992) pointed out, professionals can benefit from family advocacy. Families can bring pressure to bear on the mental health system and its funding sources that professionals alone could never bring about.

In addition to teaching various kinds of advocacy strategies, the SFT program seeks to alleviate the social isolation and stigma that often attends the mentally ill and their families by connecting parents with NAMI, the nation's leading advocacy organization, and other supportive networks. The existence of local NAMI affiliates in most U.S. cities assures a continuation of contact and support for families after they "graduate" from Supportive Family Training.

The Teachers of SFT

Although it is possible for one person to teach SFT, what seems to work best is the partnership of family member and professional in a team-teaching model. If at all possible, at least one of the teachers should be the relative of a person with a serious mental illness. As Spaniol et al., (1993) have observed, "professionals can help families in many ways, but not with the kind of healing that one family member gives to another" (p. 30). Such a partnership has the added advantage of providing positive modeling for the participating family members, who are encouraged in the training to see themselves as equal members of the treatment team for their ill relatives.

SFT does not require its teachers to be mental health professionals, but it does demand certain basic teaching skills and a working knowledge of the major psychiatric disorders from a functional perspective. When emotional issues surface in the classes, teachers need to be comfortable offering guidance, rather than listening and reflecting back, as a therapist might. The families we deal with benefit more from practical advice, clear directions, help with the service system, and genuinely caring support at this time than they do from psychotherapy. Actually, the teacher's role in the program has much in common with the family consultant role described by Bernheim (1982). It is very directive work, given that, in most families we see, the capacity for adaptive decision making is often reduced by acute or chronic stress. Families are usually tired out and often depressed. Sometimes they want, and need, time out from decision making in which to regroup their defenses and their strength (Bernheim, 1982).

To help families access their feelings and speak out about painful issues, teachers need to be self-disclosing. Professional distancing is discouraged in the SFT model. In contrast, SFT professionals are encouraged to refer back to their own direct experience of pain, to stay in touch with their feelings, and to use their common sense. It is essential that they empathize with the chaos families experience when mental illness first strikes their loved ones and not to label their responses as "dysfunctional."

We have found that many mental health professionals who are seemingly suited for teaching families come with a clinical background that in some cases is a hindrance. Clinical training is not synonymous with effective teaching, which, in SFT, demands dropping the role of therapist and being open to learning from each family. It appears to be extremely difficult for some to embark on his kind of partnership with families and to leave their clinical training behind. As Spaniol et al. (1993) noted, "Most professionals have been taught about mental illness and some have been taught about families, but many professionals do not understand families who have experienced mental illness" (p. 28).

It is true that SFT's family member/teachers enjoy several important advantages over their clinically trained counterparts. They can share and confront in ways a professional lacking personal experience is discouraged from doing. When they speak from their own experience they are a catalyst for encouraging others to speak about painful issues. Furthermore, when they allow their vulnerability to show, and share their pain, they make it safe for the class members to do the same. However, the family member teacher is no better than a professional who has opened her heart, touched her own pain, and translated these experiences into the wisdom and compassion needed to help others (Le Gacy, 1998).

MEASURES OF EFFECTIVENESS

Many educational programs measure their effectiveness by testing for information retention. For us, the ability to retain factual information about brain dysfunction is not as important as retaining the focus on self-care that is emphasized throughout the course. Outcome studies of SFT have indicated that families feel that they have learned what they needed to know about the neurobiological brain disorders. However, more to the point, a recent evaluation of SFT measuring family satisfaction reported that 94% of the families completing the training felt increased confidence in their ability to deal with their relatives, 79% had improved their ability to take care of themselves, and 97% felt empowered by the experience of participating in the 12 week course (Horgan, 1995). Most important for us is the 97% left feeling empowered. Ultimately, the SFT training is about empowerment.

CONCLUSIONS

Although this paper has focused on meeting the needs of the families of persons with mental illness through an educational and supportive partnership, research has indicated that the ill relatives of these families clearly benefit from focused interventions such as SFT. "Since 1980, twenty-two controlled studies of psychoeducational family work show consistently strong outcomes for the mentally ill relative: major exacerbations of psychotic symptoms and admissions to hospitals are more than halved, social disability is reduced; with increased employment rates, burdens on caregivers are lowered and their health improved. Although there are small additional costs involved in the delivery of these strategies, they are dramatically offset by reductions in the need for crisis care, resulting in very high cost-effectiveness" (World Schizophrenia Fellowship, 1998, p. 6). One investigator concluded that "consistent evidence for the efficacy and feasibility of family intervention in schizophrenia has now demonstrated an effect, in medicated patients, equivalent to antipsychotic medication itself"(McFarlane, Lukens, & Link, 1995).

In spite of these impressive outcome studies, there is a continuing need to for education, support and outreach to the families of persons with serious mental illness (Dixon, Goldman, & Hirad, 1999). Although there have been impressive advances in genetics, pharmacology, and epidemiology, as well as innovations in psychotherapy and psychosocial rehabilitation, many individuals suffering from major neurobiological brain disorders continue to encounter severe obstacles to needed care (Bachrach, 1997). Until these barriers are removed, the burden of care will continue to fall on the family.

NOTE

Beyond the scope of this chapter is the subject of parenting by persons with serious mental illnesses. One result of deinstitutionalization has been increased sexual activity among patients and the accompanying rise in pregnancies, STDs, AIDs, etc. Several excellent parenting programs have been developed for this population, including day programs for psychiatrically ill mothers and their young children. As the numbers of pregnancies increase, mental health service providers continue to struggle to provide effective supports to the single parents and couples who try to keep their children.

Related to the rise in the pregnancy rate is the increasing involvement of grandparents, who in addition to providing care-giving for their adult offspring, are now being called upon to raise the children of their mentally ill offspring. Over 4 million children currently live in a household headed by a grandparent, and an increasing number of these grandparents are the parents of adults diagnosed with serious mental illness. The family burden continues . . .

REFERENCES

Anderson, C., Hogarty, G., & Reiss, D. (1980). Family treatment of adult schizophrenia patients: A psycho-educational approach. *Schizophrenia Bulletin, 6,* 490–505.

Anderson, C. M., Reiss, D. J., & Hogarty G. (1986). *Schizophrenia and the family.* New York: Guilford.

Ascher-Svanum, H. (1989). Caregivers of mentally ill adults: A women's agenda. *Hospital and Community Psychiatry, 40,* 843–845.

Atkinson, S. (1994). Chronic grief may affect parents of children with schizophrenia. *The Menninger Letter, 2,* 1–8.

Atwood, N. (1983). Supported group counseling for the relatives of schizophrenic patients. In W. McFarlane, (Ed.), *Family therapy in schizophrenia.* New York: Guilford.

Bachrach, L. (1997). Breaking down the barriers: Commentary on a conference theme. *Psychiatric Services, 48,* 3.

Bernheim, K. (1982). Supportive family counseling. *Schizophrenia Bulletin, 8,* 634–640.

Brown, V., Ridgely, S., Pepper, B., Levine, I., & Ryglewicz, H. (1989). The dual crisis:

Mental illness and substance abuse: present and future directions. *American Psychologist,* *44,* 565–569.

Butterfield, F. (1988). Studies of mental illness show links to violence. *New York Times.* *May 14,* A:14.

Consumer Health Sciences. (1998). Princeton, New Jersey: The Schizophrenia Caregiver Project. Brief summary of results.

Dixon, L., Goldman, H., & Hirad, A. (1999). State policy and funding of services to families of adults with serious and persistent mental illness. *Psychiatric Services, 50,* 551–553.

Dixon, L., & Lehman, A. (1995). Family interventions for schizophrenia. *Schizophrenia Bulletin, 21,* 631–643.

Doka, K. (1989). Disenfranchised grief. *Disenfranchised grief: Recognizing hidden sorrow.* In Doka, K. (Ed.), Lexington, MA: Lexington Books.

Estroff, S. E., Zimmer, C., Lachicotte,W., & Benoit, J. (1994). The influence of social networks and social support on violence by persons with serious mental illness. *Hospital and Community Psychiatry, 45,* 669–679.

Fink, P. J., & Tasman, A. (1992). *Stigma and mental illness.* Washington, DC: APA Press.

Goleman, D. (1993). Depression: Report on P. Greenberg study from journal of clinical psychiatry. *New York Times, Dec. 12.*

Gorman, J. M. (1996). *The new psychiatry.* New York: St. Martin's Press.

Hatfield, A. (1990). *Family education in mental illness.* New York: Guilford.

Hatfield, A. (1994). Family education: Theory and practice. In Hatfield, A. (Ed.), *Family interventions in mental illness.* San Francisco: Jossey-Bass.

Horgan, S. (1995). *Client satisfaction with the supportive family training program.* Syracuse, NY: Public Affairs Program, Maxwell School of Citizenship and Public Affairs, Syracuse University.

Lefley, H. (1987). The family's response to mental illness in a relative. In Hatfield, A. (Ed.), *Families of the mentally ill: Meeting the challenges.* San Francisco: Jossey-Bass.

Lefley, H. (1994). Interventions with families: What have we learned? In Hatfield, A. (Ed.), *Family interventions in mental illness.* San Francisco: Jossey-Bass.

Le Gacy, S. S. (1998). Working through the heart: A transpersonal approach to family support and education. *Psychiatric Rehabilitation Journal, 22,* 133–141.

Lindemann, E. (1945). Symptomatology and management of acute grief. *Archives of Neurology & Psychiatry, LIII,* 141–148.

MacGregor, P. (1992). Grief: The unrecognized parental response to mental illness in a child. Unpublished manuscript.

MacGregor, P. (1994). Grief, the unrecognized parental response to mental illness in a child. *Social Work, 39,* 160–166.

McFarlane, WR., Lukens E., & Link B. (1995). Multiple-family groups and psychoeducation in the treatment of schizophrenia. *Archives of General Psychiatry, 52,* 679–687.

McFarlane W., Dunne, E., Lukens, E., et al. (1993). From research to clinical practice: Dissemination of New York state's family psychoeducation project. *Hospital and Community Psychiatry, 44,* 265–269.

Manderscheid, R. (1997). Three prevalent estimates of adult mental illness. Federal statistics from the center for mental health services. *NAMI Advocate, July/August.*

Marsh, D. T. (1992). *Families and mental illness. New directions in professional practice.* New York: Praeger.

Monahan, J. (1992). Mental disorder and violent behavior. Perceptions and evidence. *American Psychologist, 4,* 511–521.

News & Notes (1993). National survey of NDMDA members finds long delay in diagnosis of manic-depressive illness. *Hospital & Community Psychiatry, 44,* 800–801.

News & Notes (1995). Americans' misperceptions about mental illness and manic-depression persist, new survey shows. *Psychiatric Services, 46,* p. 1204.

News & Notes (1997). New methodology for estimating prevalence of mental illness, finds 10 million adults affected. *Psychiatric Services, 48,* 1216.

Peschel, R. E., & Peschel, E. (1992). Neurobiological disorders in children and adolescents: A scientific approach. *Innovations & Research, 1,* 15–19.

Secunda, V. (1997). *When madness comes home. Help and hope for the children, siblings and partners of the mentally ill.* New York: Hyperion.

Solomon P. (1996). Moving from psychoeducation to family education for families of adults with serious mental illness. *Psychiatric Services, 47,* 1364–1370.

Spaniol, L., Zipple, A., & Lockwood, D. (1992). The role of the family In psychiatric rehabilitation. *Schizophrenia Bulletin, 18,* 341–348.

Spaniol, L, Zipple, A., & Lockwood, D. (1993). The role of the family In psychiatric rehabilitation. *Innovations & Research, 2,* 27–32.

Spaniol, L. (1987). Coping strategies of family caregivers. In Hatfield, A., & Lefley, H. (Eds.), *Families of the mentally ill: Coping and adaptation.* New York: Guilford, 208–222.

Stoll, A., Tohen, M., & Baldessarini, R. (1993). Shifts in diagnostic frequencies of schizophrenia and major affective disorders at six North American psychiatric hospitals, 1972–1988. *American Journal of Psychiatry, 150,* 1668–1673.

World Schizophrenia Fellowship Strategy Document: Families as partners in care (1998). Toronto, Ontario: World Schizophrenia Fellowship for Schizophrenia and Allied Disorders.

CHAPTER 8

Parent Education for Fathers

Stephen T. Sirridge

Department of Educational Psychology, Avila College, Kansas City, Missouri

There appears to be an essential contradiction in the evolving role of fathers. Many men seem tuned into their importance as nurturing and limit-setting figures, whereas others are oblivious, blinded by alcoholism, unemployment, and their own wounded psyches. Many men, looking back on their own barren relationships with their fathers, have taken the cue from child development specialists, religious leaders, and writers in the men's movement (Garbarino, 1993; Osherson, 1986; Kimball, 1988; Louv, 1994) to be more available to their children. Men are being asked to change their communication styles, methods of child management, and add more softness and tenderness to their child–parent interactions. Simultaneous with these changes have been charges that the pace of change is slow, and a large number of divorced, minority, and violent fathers have bypassed the new changes and remain as uninvolved, absent, and controlling as before. What is the truth about the newly emerging father? Is he the Promise Keepers/Million Man March male who apologizes for his past mistakes and promises a fundamental shift in attitude and behavior; or is he the man who leaves 40% of all children living without the physical presence of a father (80% in some communities)?

Many male authors (Osherson, 1992; Pittman, 1993; Kupers, 1993; Gurian, 1998) contend that males are part of a socialization process that

Handbook of Diversity in Parent Education

179

teaches competition and inhibition of caring and feelings. This training fuels the long pattern of patriarchal dominance and control that strangles the evolution of the family and community toward a greater level of equality and cooperation. Although it is difficult to gauge whether this entrenchment is abating, all sides of the debate are in unison when they speak of the consequences for children of male violence and family abandonment (Blankenhorn, 1995). Children grow up brutalized and fearful. Boys are indoctrinated with a model of fathering based on violence and control. Girls are taught to adapt and accommodate to husbands and fathers that abuse and dominate through coercion. Fathers who sexually abuse their children leave a nightmare of broken trust and devastation to their child's sense of self. Mean and critical fathers squash spontaneity and shatter self-confidence. Alcohol- and drug-abusing fathers build a climate of inconsistency and threat of harm. Uninvolved or self-absorbed fathers ignore their children's best efforts to be seen, heard, and praised. The bottom line seems to point to the fact that bad fathering leaves children with identity and confidence problems. For these children, trusting other people is hard, intimacy is threatening, alcohol and drug use a welcome antidote to personal pain, and fighting/violence preferable to negotiation and compromise.

We seem to be well aware of the negative consequences of father abuse and abandonment. Similarly, we seem to be able to catalog the failings of men which lead to their children's adjustment challenges. What we seem less sure of are the facets of fathering that facilitate growth and contentment in their children. What precisely do fathers bring to the parenting situation that provide, alongside the mother, a strong parental system? Do fathers and mothers provide the same characteristics, or do fathers infuse something special and unique in the child rearing process? What happens positively for boys and girls when an active male role model is present and available?

The next section of this chapter will take up the subject of a father's unique contribution to his role as a parent. Positive male virtues are identified, together with their impact on the healthy growth of children. The third section of this chapter will describe several specific parenting programs which are available for fathers, as well as a model program which this author believes can facilitate the re-education of fathers.

A FATHER'S LEGACY

Fathers can have a powerful influence on their children. They bring a unique influence from their core biological experience of maleness, as well as the social/cultural aspects of being male. A father's parental contributions include his physical playfulness and his capacity for warmth, attachment, and affirmation. A healthy mother–father team exchanges opportunities for each parent to express his/her hardness (limits) and softness (caring). Additionally, a father has an evolutionary history and many years of acculturation of being male which a female cannot duplicate (and likewise a woman and her femininity). Goldner (1995) states that we are born into a "symbolic and material world that is already gendered in every possible way, and it is impossible to overstate its effects on mind and culture. We can critique, disrupt, resist, and perhaps even transform maternal and paternal practice, but it will always read as male/female, because it will always be enacted and observed by a gendered subject" (p. 46). It is this eventual difference in male/female experience, which underlines the male's potential contributions to the growth of his children. The following legacies have emerged in the literature as discernible endowments that the father bestows on his children.

MASCULINE IDENTITY

A father transmits to his son (and in different form to his daughter) his experience of being male or masculine. Gurian (1998) states that a boy is hard-wired to move toward the world of men. The father models and invites identification with the "masculine" traits of "strength, virility, courage, tenacity and firmness" (Vogt & Sirridge, 1991, p. 7). Additionally, Gilligan (1982) states that male development includes identification through roles and positions. Self-esteem results from individual achievement, conceptualizing with a distinct and rational cognitive style, and ethics based on principles of justice.

In the past a masculine identity was a simpler template to pass onto offspring. The son followed in the footsteps of his father, learning a trade/profession, and marrying and raising children in the same style as his father. A daughter married someone like "good old dad," a solid breadwinner and pillar of the community. Re-inventing fatherhood in the 1990s means developing new roles that better reflect the needs of children in the modern era. A father needs to demonstrate loyalty and affection in his marriage and time involvement with his children. He must listen to the unique aspirations of his sons and daughters, affirming their distinct desires and goals. He must demonstrate to his son how to be a man of strength and nurturance who mixes fun, work, and connection to friends and extended family. A daughter uses a father to grow into her own industriousness, physicalness, and sexuality and internalizes an image of masculinity that will guide her life choices. "The roots of a woman's self-confidence lie in a little girl's knowledge that her father loves her for who she is and what she does. This early attention and positive reinforcement are linked to the grown woman's capacity for achievement and career success" (Osherson, 1992, p. 238).

THE PHYSICAL AND PLAYFUL FATHER

Children participate and borrow from their father a sense of protection, safety, security, and strength. It is comforting for children to feel like they belong to a powerful figure where they can be prized and protected. One source of this feeling of being cared about and secure comes from the limits and boundaries a father sets for his children. When children push on these limits, they are really pushing on their fathers to see if they will bend, break, or disappear (Vogt & Sirridge, 1991). Limits and consequence, along with physical play, are ways that children know that fathers are present and can be reliably counted upon. In fact, fathers who are play partners have kids that are more adept at reading emotional signals that others can recognize.

When fathers play with their children, they give them a chance to learn about their bodies and their emotions. They learn what it is like to be touched and feel the strength and warmth of a father's embrace. They learn how to manage their bodies in space and feel more confident, coordinated, and at ease with themselves.

A child must first experience the rhythm of father play and later incorporate the lessons of this play as a way to regulate emotions. When fathers abandon their children, they leave this teaching of emotions and limit setting to the mother, who would not choose to shoulder this responsibility alone. Children lose a certain forcefulness, dispassionateness, and strength when their father is not helping to play, protect, and supervise them. Girls and boys need to experience the force of a father in their lives. Children literally need to bump up against, push, and physically challenge him. This is a particular problem for boys who engage in more physical challenges and risk-taking behavior and need the firm hand of the father to set limits and levy consequences. Gurian (1998) states that it is men who must take the lead in teaching boys how to channel male energy. Fathers need to tutor boys in how to compete and to channel aggression effectively. Gurian (1998) suggests that this tutoring is a form of "paternal nurturing."

THE AFFIRMING AND IDEALIZED FATHER

Parents and children have built-in mechanisms to bond with each other. A father's tender love and fierce need to protect his children resonates with their need to be safe and nurtured. Optimally children are attached to two loving parents because there is a unique type of attunement and affirmation that each offers the child. Women offer a soft and delicate nurturance that is soothing to the child. A father offers novelty (a stimulus that is new and exciting) and a type of physicalness that children are equally sensitive and excited about. Each parent can perform either function; however, Gurian (1998) says that "paternal nurturing" is based on respect. If a boy does not act properly, a dad will withhold his respect and require his son to earn it back. Moms can find that kind of nurturing hard because they are attached to their sons differently.

When children and parents attach to one another, a bond develops at an emotional level. Fathers enhance ties between themselves and their children through consistently attuning their energy toward their children; smiling, playing, touching, and talking. Children need to be the center of a father's attention and have him respond to their accomplishments with joy and excitement. This celebrates their unique and individual qualities. The greatest gift a father gives to his children is a sense that they are good and valuable, and they can trust their natural way of being in the world. Loving attunement with children affirms their right to be themselves.

In the beginning children see fathers as perfect and innocently and wholeheartedly offer their loyalty. Children need to see fathers as uncompromisingly good and accomplished. "No matter how small or inadequate a father may feel, he is still larger-than-life to his young child. Our size, depth of voice, the fact that we work outside the home and seem 'heroic' or exciting to the child, all work to lead the young to want to wall us off, defeat us, get some emotional space from us. Even in today's world of working mother and work-at-home fathers, I suspect that most fathers have this heroically masculine, romantic aura for their children" (Osherson, 1992, p. 213).

Fathers are accorded a period of unquestioned worship and loyalty. These moments of perfection, however, are fleeting. Children eventually recognize a father's imperfections. Idealization is a natural process whereby children want to experience closeness with the father. Later, they need the opportunity to de-idealize and separate. An integrated, well-rounded view of the father will emerge from this cycle of adulation followed by devaluation.

THE GROUNDING AND LIMIT-SETTING FATHER

There is a "father hunger" (Pittman, 1993) that exists within children. This hunger is a yearning for a positive male influence. The hunger for a real, alive father does not diminish, and somehow each child must reckon with that fact sometime in his/her life. Many young men and women have not enjoyed the steady presence of a father in their lives. A father functions as an integral part of family rituals which celebrate important transitions for his children. A father acts as an authority or law in the family, and his physical force and power is a reminder to children that they must follow rules and respect other people. An able father sets up routines and guidelines and expects his children to learn values, competencies, and responsibilities. Ultimately, children must test this set of limits or guidelines and physically experience a father's reaction to his challenge. A potent father punctures the balloon of their grandiosity. Kohlreiser (1998) definitively states "that fathers must teach sons as children and adolescents how to deal with emotions, especially the emotions of grief and aggression. With all due respect, the mother is limited in her ability to do this because of the son's need for gender identification. Research consistently shows that young boys who have a secure male base—a healthy father/big brother attachment that stays with a child until age 20—are almost surely inoculated against violent and criminal behavior" (p. 7).

An adolescent culture without a male influence encourages kids to react defiantly to authority and supervision, and engage in risky and unlawful behavior. These kids leave school early, break laws, use drugs, and fail to take advantage of their educational opportunities. They believe they are entitled to whatever they want and fail to incorporate values which assist them in postponing gratification. A strong and interested father can soften a child's grandiosity and entitlement and preempt the development of behavior which is anti-authority and antisocial.

Children require a parent who can absorb their need to challenge (be angry, rejecting, and criticizing). Fathers are an excellent choice for children to test their power and strength. A man who is able to physically and emotionally handle his children's challenges, surrounds them with a boundary that lets them know where their rights and privileges begin and end. Children need to feel "impact" from their father, and this makes them feel real, vital, and alive.

EDUCATING FATHERS

Men have traditionally been a highly ambivalent subscriber/participant in counseling and psychoeducational activities (Palm and Palkovitz, 1988). Lack of interest, job/travel demands, and defensiveness about perceived parenting deficits are several factors that appear to derail fathers from active and full participation. This author's experience with men's/fathers groups is that the bulk of voluntary participation has occurred in a church community or an educational arena. A church or school community usually has a number of committed men who are motivated to come together and draw strength from sharing with each other. They are vested in the best interests of their children and increasing their own comfort and competence as fathers. More targeted male audiences or required participation also seem to be the norm. Gregg (1994) instituted a parenting program for single fathers, Mathews (1995) examined clinical issues central to understanding men who batter, and Murray and MacDonald (1996) proposed an early intervention model for working with fathers of special needs children. Additionally, Fagan and Stevenson (1995) helped implement a leader-led self-help program for African-American fathers whose children were enrolled in a Head Start programs. Last, Gabel and Johnson (1995) have instituted parenting programs for criminal, jailed, or imprisoned fathers. A commonality with all these programs is a concentration on a specified group of men (compared to a heterogeneous sample) in need of training or a group of men remanded for educational training as a part of rehabilitation plan.

GENERAL CONSIDERATIONS FOR WORKING WITH FATHERS

Palm and Palkovitz (1988) state that a father's needs, expectations, and perceptions of education for parenting need to be explored. They believe that parent educators for fathers need to be aware of the types of programs that are most effective at transforming fathers' motivation and interest into parenting skills and knowledge. "In general, the parent role appears to be less central to men's lives (Palm & Palkovitz, 1988, p. 369). Invariably fathers have less knowledge about child development. Men are less likely to have experience in taking care of children and have fewer supports available to assist them in becoming and feeling like competent caregivers.

Several authors (Levant, 1988, 1990; Moore, 1990; Gregg, 1994) have recommended that recruitment, group leadership, composition of participants, and activities be focused upon what will attract fathers and sustain involvement. The following is a list of recommendations that have emerged from the literature.

1. Define the group as psycho-educational, that is, groups need to be theme specific and intended to increase awareness of a particular problem or life event (e.g., birth of a new baby). Focus the group on development of new and better coping skills.

2. Groups need a diversity of formats. Include both experiential exercises as well as theme-oriented discussions, films, readings, and homework assignments. Men often require some immediate benefits of attending group sessions; therefore, including an informational component offers something tangible for fathers. Experiential exercises pull the group from being purely an intellectual exercise and highlights a "here-and-now" experience.

3. Keep the group's time limited (8 to 15 sessions).

4. Male leadership with parenting experience is more credible and tends to elicit fewer defensive reactions (as compared to female leader). Men often will not self-disclose with a woman, especially if it entails feelings of pain and shame. To a lesser extent (but still very important), groups of marginalized, minority men are best led by a group leader of the same racial background (Franklin, 1998). A same race leader can circumvent a level of group defensiveness and wariness and invite the men to be more open and honest with the impact of living in a racist/prejudicial society.

5. Plan possible activities/outings that include both children and fathers. Fathers often feel more comfortable while involved in specific activities. These activities can be a springboard for instructing fathers how to be involved with their children in a joint project, as men invariably want to completely take over projects, criticize children's efforts, or disengage.

6. Focus material on male strengths. Fathers are often reminded of their weaknesses/deficits and lack of information. These reminders spark feelings of incompetence and inferiority. Feelings of inferiority revive is-

sues of shame, leading to defensiveness or feigned lack of interest. A respectful approach strokes a father's choice to enroll in the course and investigate areas that they know they could use assistance. Palm and Palkovitz (1988) believe it is important to begin to identify some strengths that have been attributed to males such as playfulness, leadership, adventure, and independence.

7. Advertising a "parenting" class will not bring fathers to a class. If you want to target fathers, they must be specifically invited (i.e., fathers' group) because parenting to many men means mothers." Recruitment of men for fathering groups must be "intentional and deliberate" (Franklin, 1998).

8. Scheduling of group time periods should be carefully considered. Daytime groups can be organized to include shift workers and the unemployed. Evening and weekend options can be used for men with daytime work schedules.

9. With low-income, marginalized males, Franklin (1998) recommends a comfortable room at a location near the residences of attending fathers. Food should be available at every meeting (announce in advance that food will be available). He suggests that videos are an excellent teaching medium as many of these men are visual learners. Finding videos or film clips with role models that the fathers can identify with can be a powerful learning experience (e.g., Shaq folding/feeding a baby and talking about his father). Written material in the course should also be pitched at a sixth-grade level, with short phrases (bullets).

OPERATING PROGRAMS FOR FATHERS

Parenting programs aimed specifically for males are limited in number and scope. This section, however, discusses several current parenting projects which address the needs and concerns of fathers. First, a project from the Research Development Institute of Kansas City will be discussed which focuses upon parent training for incarcerated males. Second, a program implemented for training of fathers who are perpetrators of domestic violence will be discussed. Third, several types of parenting programs which operate from the National Center for Fathering will be surveyed. The National Center focuses its resources with minority and low income males. Last, the author will include a general model for a voluntary, time-limited father's group, with concluding remarks addressing the establishment of men's groups as a follow-up/extension of a parenting group.

INCARCERATED FATHERS

In 1992 the U.S. Department of Justice reported that there were approximately 690,000 fathers among the 1.23 million incarcerated men the United States. There are at least 1.5 million children of prisoners and at least 3.5 million children of offenders on probation or parole in the United States any given day (Gabel & Johnson, 1995). Most incarcerated fathers, for example, do not live with their children prior to arrest and do not have an ongoing relationship with their children's mother, yet most want contact with their children and a role in the children's lives (Gabel & Johnson, 1995). Unfortunately, most of these male inmates do not see their children, call, or correspond with them. Incarcerated fathers often feel powerless in the their role as parents, The finding of Gabel and Johnson's (1995) work strongly suggests that incarcerated men need to feel a sense of control over their activities as fathers. They suggest that in addition to more general services of education, drug treatment, and job training, incarcerated fathers have special needs in three areas.

1. Parental Empowerment. Inmate fathers need support of their pivotal role as a parent. This process begins with a realization of the negative impact of their own fatherless histories. Programs, then, need to consistently affirm a father's connection to his children and the positive benefits for him and his children.
2. Father–Child Separation. Inmate fathers need services which address pre-incarceration separations as well as those that support avenues for re-establishment of father–children contact.
3. Family Conflict. Incarcerated fathers need services directed toward the root causes of domestic conflict and interpersonal violence. Children, unfortunately, have likely been witness to or subjected to abusive treatment by fathers (Gabel, 1992). Anger management programs as well as services that assist prisoners achieve peaceful reunification are recommended.

Several agencies (PEP, 1988; Saul, 1992; Tilbor, 1993) throughout the country have implemented programs to meet the needs of incarcerated fathers. The PEP program in New York consisted of 16 2-hr workshops held once a week. The workshops included presentations of factual material, films, and other audio–visual materials, discussions, and participatory exercises such as role-plays. The fathering curriculum was made available to men who were fathers (or were expected to be fathers upon release) and whose release coincided with the completion of their sentences. They hoped to prepare the fathers to immediately practice the skills acquired in the program. The curriculum was diverse in its focus with modules ranging from anatomy arid physiology, male–female sexuality, life cycle, values clarification, self-esteem, and positive parenting. Graduation rates in the program were 80%, and word of mouth recommendations created a strong demand for the course.

Tilbor's (1993) Project H.I.P. was an 8-week module (young children and adolescent modules were developed separately) for incarcerated minimum/medium security inmates. The course content was structured with the usual topics of helping parents increase their children's self-esteem, how to set rules and logical consequences, and how to communicate feelings. A monthly father–child workshop combined free play and structured activities conducive to interacting with children. For some fathers (Tilbor, 1993) this was the first time (or the first in many years) that they had been alone with their children. Additionally, fathers who completed the 8-week sequence were eligible to participate in a support group. This group cemented the gains of the information segment and maintained the continuing involvement of fathers with longer sentences.

A research project in Kansas City (Johnson-Sharpe, 1997) has been implemented with 520 inmate parents. This project has targeted incarcerated mentally ill and/or substance abusing parents in order to decrease the future violence risk potential for their children. Sharpe-Johnson (1997) states that "previous research has identified several early childhood factors that are related to adult violence including (a) disrupted parental care and poor parenting practices and (b) family violence modeling and child abuse" (p. 2). Specifically, the purpose of this project was to provide inmate parents with training in parenting skills, child development, anger control, and conflict resolution. Mentally ill and/or substance abusing fathers were chosen due to the high rate of risk factors for later violence that is present for children of these parents.

Several interesting developments have occurred in the beginning phases of the teaching modules. First, the inmate groups were hungry for information concerning child development and communication skills. Modules were initially set up in a formal classroom format but were quickly changed to a round table in order to stimulate discussion and participation. Second, reestablishing communication between fathers and their children has proven to be especially important. Inmates were prompted to begin writing letters to their children (inmates were given stationary and stamps), and most group members sent letters 1 or 2 times per week. Letters talk about the fathers' life in prison, the father' inquiry into children's activities (eg.

school, sports) and the fact that the fathers are thinking about and caring about their sons/daughters. Preliminary follow-up has shown that the letter writing continues to be an activity that has been transferred following the termination of the parent training. Letter writing is a form of contact which traverses the distance/separation between father and child. Statistics from a study by Gabel and Johnson (1995) showed that only 55% of fathers had contact by phone, letter, or visit in the six months prior to the survey. One third of their sample had not had any contact with their children since entering prison. This cutoff is particularly disturbing as 70% of their sample had more than one child, 90% were fathers of children under 13 years of age, and two thirds of the sample had sentences greater than 20 years. "Men who are in prison do not give up their family aspirations or their parental concerns. Not unlike many other men separated from their children, however, they need help in understanding and fulfilling their family commitments and parental responsibilities" (Gabel & Johnson, 1995, p. 39). Programming such as the Violence Prevention Project in Kansas City are structured to offer skill building for fathers in how to talk to their children, use appropriate child management techniques, and effectively handling conflict. Particular emphasis has been placed on creating opportunities for child–father contact. Such contact reduces the fathers' isolation and worry about their children. Also, children benefit from knowing their fathers and experiencing their on-going interest/involvement in their lives.

PARENTING GROUPS FOR MEN WHO BATTER

Few programs focus on fathers who have been abusive toward a partner or a child, and little has been written about such efforts. Edward Gondolf of the Mid-Atlantic Addiction Training Institute has been studying the effectiveness of federally funded antibattering programs in four cities across the country (Peterson, 1998). His preliminary data showed that 60% of men did not physically assault their partners within a 30-month period after termination of their treatment programs. Roughly 70 to 80% of women living with a male batterer said they were better off and safer after the program. Unfortunately, 20 to 25% of the four city sample included females who were repeatedly beaten by their partners after termination of their 3 to 9-month program. Although these women claimed that things were worse because of their partners' mandated treatment, a clear majority indicated they were better off.

Mathews (1995) describes a model of parent training that was first implemented in 1987 where men receiving help in domestic abuse cases expressed an interest and a need to focus on their parenting. The Men's Parenting Program was "created with the intent of increasing a fathers' understanding of their children, confronting the fathers' violent behavior, increasing their understanding of how their violent behavior has affected their children, and providing an opportunity for these men to learn, develop, and practice their parenting skills" (Mathews, 1995, p. 108). This program meets 2½ hrs for 12 weeks. Each session has a structured set of group activities that combine written and verbal responses. Agendas are arrived at through two individual sessions with each participant (screening and assessment) and identification of popular topics during the group's introductory session. The overall agenda is determined by the counselors, taking into account the needs and the desired outcomes of the men. The Men's Parenting Program is based on the assumptions that violence is a learned behavior, a choice to gain power and control, and can be unlearned. The group philosophy mandates that all fathers are responsible for their behavior and that they all have the capacity to control their behavior. The program begins with attention toward the individual's motivation (level of resistance) for being in group, as most often fathers are court-ordered to complete the program. The issue of shame is invariably triggered through group discussion, shame regarding their own violence, as well as recalling intense feelings from their own experiences of witnessing violence. Consistent with other fathering programs, child development knowledge seems essential as men often do not know the difference between age-appropriate and undesirable behavior in children. Misinformation often leads to impulsive punishment, with the father gradually escalating his response. Similar to the inmate groups, hostilities were allowed to build up, leading to an explosion of violence. Particular attention is paid to teaching empathy ("What is in the best interest of the child?") and addressing the desire of fathers/perpetrators to make a commitment to violence-free parenting.

NATIONAL CENTER FOR FATHERING

The National Center for Fathering has selected low income/marginalized men as their focus for fathering programs. Intervention with the urban father is closely linked to the amelioration of a host of youth social problems including drug addition, gang activity, school dropout, and teen pregnancy. The Center has targeted three major areas in order to make contact with fathers. These areas are the faith community, school, and the courts. Programs have been established in several of the black churches who serve the African American male who attends services, noting that the men who attend church with their family have made a commitment to a set of values that affirm being involved with their children. The educational setting is the second area of program development. Elementary schools are identified, and fathers are invited to attend an assembly whereupon they are offered an opportunity to enroll in a ten week fathering group. A specific plea by the children to have their fathers (or father figures) has been important to the turnout for the assembly. On average 15 to 25% of the fathers who attend the assembly will agree to participate in the ten week program. The ten week program contains modules that address family of origin issues and teaching of specific communication and child management skills. The courts are the third area of emphasis. Direct referrals of fathers from family court for nonpayment of child support (over one thousand dollars in the rears) is one set of men mandated for group participation. Another group of fathers identified by the court with substance abuse and domestic violence problems are also required to participate in a fifteen week fathering program. The structure of this program is

5 weeks—family of origin work
7 weeks—parenting skills
3 weeks—relationship with the mother of their children

Family of origin work is essential because these urban fathers carry histories of deficient/absent parenting. Before new skills can be taught, each man must recognize the parenting model he internalized, and how that model has influenced the way he relates to his own children. Dr. Bernard Franklin (1998) of the National Center for Fathering states that "new wine (skills) must be placed in a new skin (internal frame). Family of origin work helps fathers unhook the past, and skill training prepares them for the future." The skills segment covers disciplining without physical punishment, how to listen and play with children, and instruction on tasks such as feeding/bathing/diapering infants and reading to children. The final segment facilitates the father group in communication with their current partner or the mother of their children. Fathers are instructed in ways to cooperate and problem solve as co-parents and how to avoid buttons which activate abusive behavior.

A MODEL FOR FATHERING PROGRAMS

Fathering programs are organized for a diverse population of fathers, for varied goals, and are sponsored by different agencies. Some groups are voluntary while others have court ordered participation. Some groups center around a specific problem\dilemma (e.g., single parenting, handicapped children), whereas other groups have participants who share circumstances in common (e.g., perpetrators of violence, prisoners). Although these variations require flexible planning by the group organizers, several general axioms will be helpful to keep in mind. The general level of resistance (and denial) of the group must be addressed early in the group's life. Feelings/attitudes about being in group are crucial to future engagement in the process. It is important, however, that some resistance will give way over the course of the program as men warm up to the tasks or find something of relevance or usefulness. Second, the organizing theme of the group must be addressed. For example, being a single, custodial father or the father of a handicapped child will carry certain implications that need to be made apparent and talked about. Discussion of the similarities that bind the group together in a common experience positively influences the unfolding of cohesion in the group. This author firmly believes that all fathering groups, regardless of whether it is strictly a skill-based group, need to address the role of males/fathers in the culture. These collective images enhance and detract from the sense of adequacy and self esteem of the participants. For example, African-American fathers inevitably face negative social images of being men who abandon families. These powerful male images unconsciously influence male behavior, and making them more overt raises awareness and thus the ability to take charge of them. Last, men in father groups inevitably talk about their own fathers. A place is mandatory in all curriculums to evaluate and share these childhood experiences. This discussion will give insight into the decisions men have made as to the type of father they will be and the degree of each man's success to be like/unlike his father.

In order to ensure a successful group experience leaders, need to assess the educational levels, resistance to participation, and motivation for change with regard to all training group members. The following guidelines will be helpful in setting a group structure.

Scheduling: Unless you have a captive audience (i.e., prison) there will be no time that will be optimal for all participants. Set the time, and invite men to make a commitment for attendance. Attendance is directly related to motivation and the priority placed on it. Length of sessions is typically 1½ to 2½ hours.

Duration: 8 to 12 weeks

Session Structure: Group check-in
                      Review readings/homework
                      Activity/teaching lesson
                      Discussion
                      Wrap-up

Leaders: Male co-leaders
Curriculum Topics: What does it mean to be a father in this culture?
What does it mean to be a man (black man, Latino man) in this society?
What is the impact of male power, control, and competition?
Family of origin work including relationships with father, mother, siblings, and extended family
How do you attend, listen, affirm, encourage and talk to your children?
Child development information (age appropriate behavior)
Child management strategies such as appropriate use of time-out and the use of logical and natural consequences
How to recognize, express, and manage feelings
How to play with and enjoy your children

MEN'S GROUP

As a sequel to a time limited parent group, a number of men may inquire into the availability of an ongoing men's group. This group may be open-ended, less structured, and enlarge the scope of topics to include male sexuality, exploring homophobia, spousal/partner relationships, friendships, work dilemmas, and in-depth family of origin exploration. Dougherty (1990), Osherson (1992), Real (1995), Kupers (1993), and Pollack & Levant (1998) have all written eloquently about the benefits of a men's group experience. A men's group can offer a healthy male experience that invites openness, sharing, and self-disclosure. Because many men feel isolated and belong to strictly work/activity groups, a group of men can provide a safe and secure environment for exploration of sensitive issues. Real (1995) calls his process of men's group work, "refathering," whereupon he attempts to undue "empathic reversal," which lies at the heart of understanding men in our society. Real (1995) says that "in such instances of abuse, the boy comes to shift his allegiance (identification) to the views and attitudes of the offender. He loses empathy with his own boyish needs, "feminine self" and adopts empathic attunement to those who hold that self in contempt. This is the loss of the boy's relational self" (p. 39). Refathering is a philosophy of treatment that attempts to re-establish the boy in the man, and accountability is re-asserted vis-à-vis the offender (whether that means the original offending caregiver, the offending messages from the culture at large, or the offensive parts of his grown-up self)" (Real, 1995, p. 40). He uses a variety of role play, family of origin work (letters, meeting with actual parents), and light trance regression work to relive and rework traumatic moments. Refathering is a slow, sometimes painful relearning of "how to take care of self"—how to bolster and cherish those inner voices that have been stilled, and how to listen to the needs of others.

SUMMARY

Historically, a father's role placed him in the position of being a peripheral figure, outside the emotional closeness shared between mother and children. Fathers who want to bridge that distance with their children find that their models for "fathering" are unhelpful. Often, fathers do not understand much about child development, and they lack the communication skills to talk with their children. Many men lack nurturing behavior and empathic attunement to the children's inner world. Fathers need parent education groups to assist them in questioning the kind of man/fathers they want to be and provide a set of rudimentary parenting skills. Model programs facilitate self-disclosure with other men. Group support invites an examination of their father–son wounds and reinforcement for experimenting with new styles of relating. Many father groups target specific populations, especially those males confronting challenges (single parenthood, handicapped children), men with histories of abuse and incarceration, and fathers from high-risk groups that have a history of family abandonment. These programs share in common the goals of motivating fathers to increase the amount and quality of their parenting. These groups are time limited and provide skill training in communication and child management strategies. Experiential exercises are combined with information to add a personalized, affective tone to the training (rather than purely an intellectual exercise).

Fathers are important to their children. Together with the mother, they form a glue that holds a family together and allows children to grow up with a sense of safety, security, and inner confidence. A good father aids his own confidence and success when he fulfills his responsibility as a parent.

> The role of the father is clear. As he invites and occasionally pushes his children into the world, he must arm them with the ability to take care of themselves. The challenge of the father is to teach his children to actively defend themselves and decipher safety from danger. The task of the father is to shield his children from the harshness of the world until they are ready to absorb it. And while his children are under that protection, they will need to grow in

their own strength, and develop their own capability to discern what is right. A father who makes a commitment to guide his children into the world gives his children an invaluable gift of potency, and in the process, takes his place with all the fathers from current and previous lifetimes who have done their duty. (Vogt and Sirridge, 1991, pp. 77–78)

REFERENCES

Blankenhorn, D. (1995). *Fatherless America*. New York: Basic Books.

Dougherty, P. (1990). A personal perspective on working with men in groups. In Moore, D. & Leafgren, F. (Eds.), *Men in conflict* (pp.168–182). Alexandria, Virginia: American Association for Counseling and Development.

Fagan, J., & Stevenson, H. (1995). Men as teachers: Self help program on parenting for African American men. *Social Work with Groups, 17*(4), 29–42.

Franklin, B. (1998). Personal communication.

Gabel, K. (1992). Children of incarcerated and criminal parents: Adjustment, behavior, and prognosis. *Bulletin of the American Academy of Psychiatry Law, 20*(1), 31–45.

Gabel, K., & Johnston D. (1995). *Children of incarcerated parents*. New York: Lexington Books.

Garabino, J. (1993). Reinventing fatherhood. *The Journal of Contemporary Human Services, 1,* 51–54.

Gilligan, C. (1982). *In a different voice*. Cambridge, MA: Harvard University Press.

Goldner, V. (1995). Boys will be men: A response to Terry Real's paper. In Weingarten, K. (Ed.), *Cultural response: Challenging beliefs about men, women, and therapy* (pp. 45–48). New York: Haworth Press.

Gregg, C. (1994). Group work with single fathers. *The Journal for Specialists in Group Work, 1,* 95–101.

Gurian, M. (1998). *A fine young man*. New York: Tarcher/Putnam.

Johnson-Sharpe, L. (1997). Violence prevention programs: Preventing violence in children of mentally ill, substance-abusing inmate parents. Unpublished manuscript.

Kimball, G. (1988). *50/50 parenting*. Lexington, MA: Lexington Books.

Kohlrieser, G. (1998). Violence begins when bonding ends. *The Script, 5*(23), 1–2.

Kupers, T. A. (1993). *Revisioning men's lives*. New York: Guilford Press.

Levant, R. F. (1988). Education for fatherhood. In Bronstein, P. & Cowan, C. P. (Eds.), *Fatherhood today: Men's changing role in the family*. New York: John Wiley & Sons.

Levant, R. F. (1990): Coping with the new father role. In Moore, D. & Leafgren, F. (Eds.), *Men in conflict* (pp. 81–94). Alexandria, VA: American Association for Counseling Development.

Louv, R. (1994). Remaking fatherhood. *Parents Magazine, 12,* 180–183.

MacKay, W. C. (1996). *The American father*. New York: Plenum Press.

May, R. (1990). Finding ourselves: Self-esteem, self-disclosure, and self-acceptance. In Moore, D. & Leafgren, F. (Eds.), *Men in conflict* (pp. 11–22). Alexandria, VA: American Association for Counseling and Development.

Mathews, D. J. (1995). Parenting groups for men who batter. In Pele, E., Jaffe, P. G., & Edelson, J. L. (Eds.), *Ending the cycle of violence*. Thousand Oaks, CA: Sage Publications.

Moore, D. (1990). Helping men become more emotionally expressive: A ten-week program. In Moore, D. & Leafgren, F. (Eds.), *Men in conflict* (pp. 183–200). Alexandria, VA: American Association for Counseling and Development.

Murray, J., & McDonald, L. (1996). Father involvement in early intervention programs: Effectiveness, obstacles, and considerations. *Developmental Disabilities Bulletin, 2*(24), 46–57.

Osherson, 5. (1986). *Finding our fathers.* New York: Free Press.

Osherson, S. (1992). *Wrestling with love.* New York: Faucett Columbine.

Palm, G. F., & Palkovitz, R. (1988). The challenge of working with new fathers: *Implementations for support providers.* In Palm, G. F. (Ed.), *Marriage and family review* (pp. 357–376). New York: Haworth Press.

Parents Education Program (PEP). (1988). Fathering: Parent education in prison. New York: Parent education program of planned parenthood.

Peterson, K. (1998). Programs help men unlearn violence. *USA Today, 7*(28), 10.

Pittman, F. (1993). *Man enough.* New York: G.P. Putnam & Sons.

Pollack, W. S., & Levant, R. F. (1998). *New psychotherapies for men.* New York: Wiley.

Real, T. (1995). Fathering our sons; refathering ourselves: Some thoughts on transforming masculine legacies. In Weingarten, K. (Ed.), *Cultural resistance: Challenging beliefs about men, women, and therapy* (pp. 27–63). New York: Haworth Press.

Saul, T. (1992). Breaking the intergenerational cycle of addiction. San Francisco, California: Prison MATCH program.

Tilbor, K. (1993). Prisoners as parents: Building parenting skills on the inside. Portland, Maine: National Child Welfare Resource Center for Management and Administration.

Vogt, G. M., & Sirridge, S. T. (1991). *Like son, like father.* New York: Plenum Press.

CHAPTER 9

Grandparents Raising Grandchildren

Oliver W. Edwards

Department of Educational Psychology, University of Florida, Gainesville, Florida

INTRODUCTION

With increasing frequency grandparents are serving as full-time surrogate parents to their grandchildren. The term "grandfamily" has been coined to identify families where children are raised by grandparents. "Surrograms" are the grandparents and "grandkin" are children in these families. Surrograms who raise their grandkin tend to experience elevated levels of stress that negatively impact their well-being. In addition, grandkin may develop problems with attachment and socialization, leading to poor psychological adjustment and school functioning. Professionals can help grandfamilies cope with the stress they experience and improve grandkin's school functioning by providing a home and school environment that fosters attachment and a strong social support network.

BACKGROUND

The phenomenon of grandchildren raised by their grandparents is hardly new (Burton, 1992; Doucette-Dudman & LaCure, 1996; Fuller-

Thomson, Minkler, & Driver, 1997; Strom & Strom, 1993), but not until recently have researchers begun to investigate what impact this altered family constellation has on grandchildren and their school functioning (Dubowltz & Sawyer, 1994; Edwards, 1998a, b, 1996a, b). Recent findings suggest both negative and positive conditions occur when grandparents raise their grandchildren (Edwards, 1998; Minkler & Roe, 1993; Poe, 1992; Sawyer & Dubowitz, 1994).

In many cases, grandparents must raise their grandchildren because of negative life events (Poe, 1992). While allowing grandchildren to remain part of their biological family and retain a connection to their family history, the altered family constellation can be quite stressful for both grandparents and grandchildren. Raising children for a second time is doubly difficult for grandparents who have not bargained on childrearing during what should be a time of peace and quiet.

Many grandparents believe they have no right to influence the rearing of their grandchildren when the children's parents are available (Cherlin & Furstenberg, 1986). This suggests that grandparents, unless explicitly supported by their children, neither want nor are expected to take an active role in the parenting of their minor grandchildren. Obliged to assume the surrogate parenting role, grandparents may experience adverse emotional and physical reactions.

Grandchildren are also under stress and may experience home and school problems as a result. The negative life events that are a precursor to grandchildren being raised by grandparents, along with the concomitant childhood trauma, and difficulty with attachment may cause grandchildren to have problems in the area of psychosocial functioning. This chapter will address the problems experienced by both grandparents and grandchildren involved in this altered family situation and will present potential solutions to help the family function more effectively.

A DIFFERENT FAMILY CIRCLE

Recently, there has been approximately a 40% increase in the number of grandparents who become surrogate parents to their school-age grandchildren (Strom & Strom, 1993). According to the American Association of Retired Persons, Grandparent Information Center (AARP–GIC), in 1995 nearly 4 million grandchildren lived in households headed by a grandparent. The numbers of children living with grandparents have increased by

6.2% since 1994 and 25.7% within a 5-year time span (AARP—GIC, 1997). It was reported by the AARP–GIC that most of these children live in homes where no biological parent is present.

The term coined to easily identify this modified family relationship is "grandfamilies." A grandfamily is a family where the grandparent(s) rather than the child's biological parents assume the role(s) of the primary caregiver(s) in the home (Edwards, 1998b, 1996a). The mother may remain in the home, but grants guardianship of the child to the grandparents or single grandparent, usually the grandmother. "Grandkin" are the children being raised by their grandparents, and the grandparents are called "surrogrands." Grandfamilies can be found among all religions, races, and socioeconomic classes (Edwards, 1998a, b; U.S. Census, 1990).

Surrogrands assume responsibility for their grandchildren due to the death of their children, their children's divorce, unemployment, and teenage premarital childbearing. Additionally, children are removed from parents' due to illegal drug use (Burton, 1992). Frequently, grandparents are the only close family members that express an interest in undertaking full-time parental responsibility for their needy grandchildren. Surrograds will choose to take in their grandchildren despite financial problems, adverse living conditions, and poor health for two primary reasons; (1) moral and religious values and (2) to prevent their grandchildren's entrance into a foster care system they do not regard positively (Edwards, 1998b; Burton, 1992).

NO ROUTINE ROLE

Grandparenthood is frequently viewed as a role without any definitive or "normal" characteristics because there are no explicit or set expectations. Although the dictionary defines grandparent as a parent of one's father or mother, there is more to being a grandparent than having a child who has a child.

One researcher suggested that in America it has been difficult for older adults to adapt to the grandparent role. This difficulty is thought to be a result of Americans' emphasis on individualism and narcissism as well as a certain lack of commitment to grandchildren (Johnson, 1983). Moreover, many grandparents may believe there is a lack of respect for the elderly and they may reduce the role they play in their grandchildren's lives because they do not wish to be rejected by their children or grandchildren.

Nonetheless, there is some satisfaction noted with respect to the grandparenting role. This satisfaction is usually seen as a result of the value afforded grandparents because of their financial, babysitting, safety valve, and stabilizing functions (Edwards, 1998b; Kivett, 1991).

Many grandparents perceive grandfamilies as God giving them a second chance to raise His children "right," because children are a blessing from the Lord (Burton, 1992; Poe, 1992). Although these grandparents may have good feelings about the surrogate parent role, they often find parenting difficult, succumbing to the problems inherent in caring for children. Clearly, raising children can be a difficult proposition even for the typical parent.

The relationship of grandparent to grandchild involves a family tie that is second only to the parent-child dyad (Kivett, 1991), but grandparents often adjust poorly when placed in the role of surrogate parents. Adjustment difficulties include illness, lack of desire, decreased energy level, and, conceivably, a hastening of the aging process. In fact, black grandparents who take on a surrogate parenting role were found to experience heightened stress that resulted in increased illness, depression, anxiety, alcoholism, and smoking (Burton, 1992). The heightened stress in turn diminishes surrogrands' energy for rearing their grandchildren. In addition, because grandparents are often more frail, sick, and older than the typical parent, they may have less energy to assist children with school work and related problems and issues. Surrogrands may have a more difficult time finding transportation to the school, preventing them from meeting with teachers and actively involving themselves in the child's education (Edwards, 1998b). All of these issues can foster a difficult school and educational experience for grandkin, particularly when the children also have to deal with the loss of their parents and, perhaps, other siblings.

When the nuclear family breaks down, the children often have a difficult time adjusting, and their behavior may become defiant or delinquent. Having to care for children with dysfunctional behaviors likely only serves to exacerbate surrogrands' physical and emotional problems. This can become a vicious cycle; the nuclear family breaks down and the children have problems as a result. Eventually they are sent to live with their grandparents, who, because they are past the typical parenting stage, along with illness, old age, and the grandchildren's difficult adjustment, have problems providing the appropriate care. Undoubtedly, any factor that significantly affects the home situation will tend to generalize to the school (Edwards, 1996a). Unless these issues are resolved, the net effect can result in great harm to grandchildren and their grandparents.

ADJUSTMENT ISSUES

The reorganization of families into grandfamilies significantly influences the adjustment of all family members. In cases where the grandchildren's biological parents die, there tends to be an easier adjustment process for all involved. The grandparents need not concern themselves about the grandchildren being removed by social services or that the children's biological parents will reappear and disrupt the parenting process. Once the grieving course has been completed, the grandfamily realizes that nothing anyone could have done would have changed the outcome and they are now a grandfamily forever. Often, greater support from family and friends and, perhaps, insurance money, is made available to the grandfamily (Poe, 1992).

Grandfamilies that emerge due to parental drug addiction, divorce, teenage premarital childbearing, and other such events customarily receive scarce emotional and instrumental support from family and friends (Burton, 1992). Moreover, the data suggest that attention-deficit hyperactive disorder, conduct or behavior disorder, learning problems, fetal alcohol syndrome, and conditions affect these grandchildren and reduce the effectiveness of parenting strategies (Doucette-Dudman & LaCure, 1996; Dubowitz & Sawyer 1994; Edwards, 1998; Sawyer & Dubowitz 1994). Consequently, surrogrands have to develop highly effective grandparenting skills if they wish their grandkin to flourish at home and in school (Edwards, 1998).

Biological parents who reside in the home, whether on a permanent or temporary basis, often provide little in the way of financial assistance to the grandfamily (Burton, 1992). Usually, surrogrands must provide the financial support not only for their grandchildren but also for their own children. Even when state agencies are involved in the removal of children from the homes of their parents, once the grandparents become legal guardians, they tend to receive, little, if any, social service assistance (Poe, 1992; Minkler, & Roe; 1993), all of which may exacerbate the problems experienced by surrogrands.

Grandparents must also often modify their living arrangement to accommodate their grandchildren. Grandparents who may have sold the family home upon retirement to move to smaller living quarters may need greater space for their grandchildren (Poe, 1992). Living in cramped quarters increases stress, but moving from neighborhoods that provided support can negatively impact the elderly, given the importance of neighborhood-based social relations (Brown & Harris, 1978).

GRANDPARENTS' EXPERIENCE

Surrogrands under the stress of new responsibilities of parenting, initially experience a great deal of concern and confusion. The process of adapting to the new demands and responsibilities follow a fairly predictable course: (1) concern for their own children, (2) fear about their ability adequately fill the role of surrogate parent, and (3) anger directed toward their children and grandchildren because of a sense of coercion. The final stages of adaptation may be either successful or unsuccessful. Successful adaptation results in a happy acceptance of the new role and subsequent enjoyment of the second-chance family. Unsuccessful adaptation results in conflict and contests of wills. In some cases, when stress reaches crises proportions, surrogrands renounce the role and give up their grandchildren to another family member or to the foster care system.

GRANDCHILDREN'S EXPERIENCE

Children who are removed from their nuclear families and enter grandfamilies experience a variety of emotions, including neglect, loss, rejection, anger, fear, acceptance, and, finally, either love or dejection (Edwards, 1998). These children generally have a history of acute and extensive hardship in the areas of cognitive, personality, and social functioning (Dubowitz & Sawyer, 1994; Sawyer & Dubowitz, 1994). Initially, because of perceived neglect by their parents, the children often feel abandoned. Once they realize their parents can no longer care for them and they are sent to live with grandparents, they begin to experience significant feelings of loss and perhaps rejection (Poe, 1992; Minkler & Roe, 1993; Doucette-Dudman & LaCure, 1996).

Grandkin fear they will never see their parents again. The sequence of emotions often proceed to anger directed at their parents for abandoning them, and at their grandparents for trying to take their parents' place. Although the grandkin often realize the sacrifice their grandparents make for them, they tend to have difficulty coping with the debilitating cycle of emotions (Poe, 1992; Minkler & Roe, 1993; Doucette-Dudman & LaCure, 1996).

In the ensuing period, when grandkin learn to accept that they have become permanent members of grandfamilies, they either develop strong feelings of love, or rejection, for their surrogrands. Feelings of love bind them to their grandparents, whom they try not to disappoint. Pervasive beliefs of abandonment lead to feelings of rejection, which is causal in grandkin having difficulty developing nurturing relationships and may drive a wide emotional wedge in the surrogrand–grandkin relationship (Poe, 1992; Minkler & Roe, 1993; Doucette-Dudman & LaCure, 1996). Regardless of which of these two emotions is most prevalent with grandkin, there tends to be conflict in the home.

In situations where natural parents are intermittently involved with the grandfamily, there is a blurring of the lines of authority. Boundary conflicts arise and the parents may oppose or diminish the parental influence of surrogrands (Poe, 1992). The grandkin also do not know how long they will have access to their parents and may become anxious and confused as to whom they should respond to as parent (Doucette-Dudman & LaCure, 1996). This adds to the grandkin's problems developing appropriate interpersonal relationships. With a lack of continuity within nuclear families, all children have a difficult time establishing strong egos and self-esteem that are crucial to proper psychosocial functioning. Furthermore, unless both grandparents and grandkin learn methods of coping with the stressors and the array of fluctuating emotions, grandkin will fail to function adequately at home and at school.

DEVELOPMENTAL FACTORS

Attachment theory provides important implications for the relationship between grandkin and surrogrands. It has long been recognized that the ability of children to function appropriately in the social world comes about as a product of close relationships experienced early in life (Hartup, 1989). Early vertical and horizontal relationships affect the development of children. Vertical attachments to primary caregivers begin during the early months of a child's life and establish an orientation towards others over the life span (Bowlby, 1973; Edwards, 1998; Hartup, 1989).

By contrast, horizontal relationships are usually formed with peers where their social judgment and understanding are comparable. Most often, these relationships are formed with individuals of similar ages and consist of reciprocal interchanges (Edwards, 1998; see also Hartup, 1989). The relationships that children form early in life serve as the basis for their later development with respect to cognitive, social, and emotional functioning. Research findings reveal that vertical and horizontal attachment relationships have predicted achievement in grades three through seven (Dubow, Tisak, Causey, Hryshko, Reid, 1991).

The data suggest that secure attachment and good social and school functioning are positively related. In all likelihood, securely attached children are more apt to develop and utilize problem solving skills. These children form such trust in their caregivers that they feel free to explore, assimilate, adapt, and learn from their environment (Hartup, 1989). Significantly, though, when disruptions in the attachment process occur, whether physical or emotional, it likely will disturb grandkin's ability to function in interpersonal relationships and in school (Edwards, 1998).

Another developmental theory that offers implications for children's social-emotional functioning is that of social support. A large corpus of research suggests social support acts as a buffer against stress and stress symptomatology (Antonucci, 1990; Hoffman, Ushpiz, & Levy-Shiff, 1988; Levitt, Guacci-Franco, & Levitt, 1994). Social support is defined as the amount of instrumental and emotional support made available to individuals from the people around them. Instrumental support refers to tangible help and emotional support refers to affective assistance. Because grandkin have difficulty establishing and maintaining appropriate social relationships, they may be more susceptible to the effects of stress (Edwards, in press, 1998). Individuals working with grandfamilies can assist them develop a social support system through the creation of vertical and horizontal relationships that will ease their stress.

SOLUTION-BASED INTERVENTION

Interventions with grandfamilies should include the familiar issues when working with dysfunctional families. These issues include vague expectations, boundary setting and clarification, inconsistent discipline, enmeshment issues, and poor communication.

More importantly, because attachment can be viewed as a developmental process that is open to remediation (Portello, 1993), interventions should help grandkin develop appropriate vertical and horizontal attachments. Further, interventions should help grandfamilies develop support networks to attenuate the stress and the associated emotional adjustment difficulties they may face. Interventions should also address issues and utilize resources cross-situationally, i.e., both in school and at home/community.

Given the importance of primary prevention, a proactive intervention approach is recommended for all grandkin at risk for school failure. Moreover, a case can be made for providing preventative intervention assistance even for grandkin who are considered to be currently functioning well.

Effective proactive intervention strategies demand several key ingredients to improve grandfamilies' functioning. These ingredients are peer and adult mentors, brief counseling, support groups, grandparent training, social support networks, and case management.

PEER PARTNERS

Peer partners are not peer counselors. They do not provide counseling or therapeutic assistance. Rather, they simply serve as friends and role models to grandkin in attempts to form a horizontal support dyad. Peer partners are classmates of grandkin who are asked to volunteer based on their teachers' recommendations. The criteria for peer partners are maturity, good academic skills, and good self-esteem. They should not be easily influenced to adopt the characteristics of the grandkin but should influence the grandkin to develop good school behavior. By acting as a role model, friend, and homework buddy, peer partners help grandkin adjust to the environment of the school (Edwards, 1998). Likewise, they form an appropriate horizontal relationship at the school. These peer partners should receive tangible and emotional support for the service they provide.

ADULT MENTORS

While in school, grandkin may also need adult staff assistance (e.g., counselor, support staff, paraprofessional, etc.) from someone other than their teacher who can nurture and affirm the child's worth. Grandkin's behavior and academic performance are positively regarded and reinforced by their adult mentors. The grandkin can spend time with the adult mentor on a regular basis to discuss school-related issues. The adult mentors function along the lines of a parent on the school grounds. The parent surrogate helps grandkin develop a proper vertical support relationship at the school. Peer and adult mentors at the school form a support network for the grandkin.

GRANDKIN GROUP COUNSELING

Brief counseling that address issues specific to grandkin is important in ensuring good school and social-emotional functioning. These issues are listed in Table 1.

TABLE 1   Issues That May Occur When Counseling Grandkin

1. Feelings of rejection
2. Feelings of loss
3. Feelings of hopelessness with respect to family reunification
4. Feelings of depression
5. Feelings of helplessness
6. Feelings of anger
7. Feelings of resentment
8. Feelings of vindictiveness
9. Feelings of fear regarding grandparents' death
10. Feelings of ambiguity

Grandkin are taught to cope with the noted feelings and to work through them for successful problem resolution. When intensive counseling issues arise that cannot be resolved at the school, referrals should be made. The process of vertical and horizontal support as well as brief counseling help grandkin develop a more trusting attitude toward adults and peers. Moreover, by ameliorating grandkin's problems there is an attendant reduction in the energy surrogrands must expend in the parenting process.

SUPPORT GROUPS

Support groups are means by which grandparents can find the encouragement and assistance they need. Support groups are designed to provide surrogrands a forum for grandparent-effectiveness training, meeting, sharing, commiserating, affirming, advising, and supporting each other. They, thus, begin to feel less isolated and hopeless.

Support group meetings and grandparent-effectiveness training allow surrogrands to learn they can utilize family members, friends, or members of their faith-based organization to help with homework, transportation, babysitting, and to serve as a general backup for the grandparents (Edwards, 1998). In addition, because a lack of supervision is highly correlated with behavioral problems (Larzelere & Patterson, 1990), surrogrands should be instructed on effective methods to supervise their grandchildren. When surrogrands cannot properly supervise their grandkin, they must attempt to access their support network for supervision assistance in order to reduce the possibility of their grandkin experiencing behavioral problems.

To secure good attendance at support group meetings, child care should be provided for grandkin and younger siblings. In addition, door prizes and refreshments tend to increase attendance. These reinforcers can be donations from the community groups. In that some grandparents may have difficulty with transportation, carpooling may be an effective means of securing high attendance. If attendance is not good, contacting a local religious or neighborhood facility to host the group meetings may be a method of increasing attendance. In most cases, starting a grandfamily support group requires more in the way of persistence than it does time.

CASE MANAGEMENT

Providing grandfamilies with a case manager who supervises the implementation of interventions and ensures all parties involved are aware of their timelines is essential to intervening with grandfamilies. Grandfamilies often do not participate in interventions as much as necessary to lead to successful problem resolution. Case managers are needed to work closely with surrogrands to encourage them, to provide frequent reminders of their appointments, reinforce obligations, and serve as family advocates. Surrogrands and grandkin also frequently need prompting and encouragement to attend brief counseling, grandparent effectiveness training, and support group meetings. Case managers also ensure that the peer partners and adult mentors maintain consistent and good relationships with the grandkin with whom they are paired.

Case managers should certify that counseling and support groups are scheduled appropriately and function as described. They may also make changes such as moving the meetings to neighborhood or church facilities. Case managers help grandfamilies establish a link between the school and community social service agencies that can assist. Finally, case managers may wish to utilize pre–post test designs to determine the effectiveness of the implemented interventions.

CONCLUSION

Significant numbers of grandparents have become the primary caregivers of their grandchildren. The emergence of grandfamilies is often a result of negative life events and childhood trauma. These circumstances can lead to the grandkin developing problems with attachment, psychosocial well-being, and academic functioning. Surrogrands also develop heightened level of stress. Providing a home and school environment that fosters attachment and strong social support networks can help grandfamilies cope with the stress and improve grandkin's psychosocial and academic functioning as well as surrograndu' emotional well-being.

REFERENCES

American Association of Retired Persons, Grandparent Information Center. (1997). Number of grandparent caregivers increases. *Parenting Grandchildren: A Voice For Grandparents* (p. 8), Summer. Washington, DC.

Antonucci, T. C. (1990). Social supports and social relationships. In R. H. Binstock & L. K. George (Eds.), *The handbook of aging and the social sciences* (3rd Ed.). (pp. 205–227). Orlando, FL: Academic.

Brown, G. I., & Harris, T. (1978). *Social origins of depression*. New York: Macmillan.

Burton, L. M. (1992). Black grandparents rearing children of drug-addicted parents: Stressors, outcomes, and social service needs. *The Gerontologist, 32,* 744–751.

Cherlin, A., & Furstenberg, F., Jr. (1986). *The new American grandparent*. New York: Basic.

Doucette-Dudman, D., & LaCure, J. R. (1996). *Raising our children's children*. Minneapolis: Fairview.

Dubow, E. F., Tisak, J., Causey, D., Hryshko, A., & Reid, G. (1991). A two-year longitudinal study of stressful life events, social support, and social problem solving skills: Contributions to children's behavioral and academic adjustment. *Child Development, 62,* 583–599.

Dubowitz, H., & Sawyer, R. (1994). School behavior of children in kinship care. *Child Abuse and Neglect, 18,* 899–911.

Edwards, O. W. (in press). Grandfamilies—grandchildren raised by grandparents: impact on students and school services. *Dissertation Abstracts International.*

Edwards, O. W. (1998). Helping grandkin—grandchildren raised by grandparents: Expanding psychology in the schools. *Psychology in The Schools, 35,* (2), 173–181.

Edwards, O. W. (1996a). *The Grandfamily Intervention Project.* Paper presented at the annual conference of the Florida Association of School Psychologists, Ft. Lauderdale, Florida.

Edwards, O. W. (1 996b). The grandfamily school support network. *NASP Communiqué, 25,* 16.

Fuller-Thomson, E., Minkler, M., & Driver, D. (1997). A profile of grandparents raising grandchildren in the United States. *The Gerontologist, 35,* 406–411.

Hartup, W. W. (1989). Social relationships and their developmental significance. *American Psychologist, 44,* 120–126.

Hoffman, S. A., Ushpiz, V., & Levy-Shiff, R. (1988). Social support and self-esteem in adolescence. *Journal of Youth and Adolescence, 17,* 307–316.

Johnson, C. L. (1983). A cultural analysis of the grandmother. *Research on Aging, 5,* 547–568.

Kivett, V. R. (1991). The grandparent-grandchild connection. *Marriage and Family Review, 16,* 267–290.

Larzelere, R. E., & Patterson, G. R. (1990). Parental management: Mediator of the effect of socioeconomic status on early delinquency. *Criminology, 28,* 301 –323.

Levitt, M. J., Guacci-Franco, N., & Levitt, J. L (1994). Social support and achievement in childhood and early adolescence: A multicultural study. *Journal of Applied Developmental Psychology, 15,* 207–222.

Minkler, M., & Roe, K. (1993). *Grandmother as caregivers.* Newbury Park, CA: Sage.

Poe, L. M. (1992). *Black grandparents as parents.* Berkeley, CA: Author.

Portello, J. Y. (1993). The mother-infant attachment process in adoptive families. *Canadian Journal of Counseling, 27,* 177–190.

Reid, J. B. (1993). Prevention of conduct disorder before and after school entry: Relating interventions to developmental findings. *Development and Psychopathology, 5,* 243–262

Sawyer, R., & Dubowitz, H. (1994). School performance of children in kinship care. *Child Abuse and Neglect, 18,* 587–597.

Strom, R. D., & Strom, S. K. (1993). Grandparents raising grandchildren: Goals and support groups. *Educational Gerontology, 19,* 705–715.

U.S. Bureau of the Census. (1990). *Marital status & living arrangements, (March, 1993)* pp. 20–478. Washington, DC: Government Printing Office.

CHAPTER 10

Parenting Emotionally Disturbed Children

Eric M. Vernberg and Anabella Pavon

Clinical Child Psychology Program, University of Kansas, Lawrence, Kansas

Parents and families of children and adolescents with significant emotional disturbances are thought to play important roles in the course of these disorders. Children with these disturbances also influence parents and families in important ways. Education is one potential tool for giving parents a greater recognition of the symptoms of emotional disturbances, and improved understanding of the etiology and course of specific disorders. This knowledge is important in enlisting parents' efforts to create as healthy environment as possible for their child, to select appropriate treatments, and to serve as effective advocates. Education also allows an opportunity to address feelings of guilt, blame, or responsibility that may make a difficult situation even more troublesome.

The line between overt behavior disorders and more internalized emotional disorders is often blurred in reality, with many clinically impaired children and adolescents meeting criteria for disorders from both general categories. Still, we focus here on parent education for commonly occurring internalized disorders, including anxiety disorders, e.g., obsessive-compulsive disorder (OCD), post-traumatic stress disorder (PTSD), fears, and phobias; mood disorders, e.g., depressive disorders, bipolar disorders;

and psychoses, e.g., schizophrenia, schizoaffective disorder. We review the types of parent education offered for families who have children with these disorders, and evaluate evidence on effectiveness of various approaches. A final section discusses priorities for program development and outcome research in this area.

PARENT EDUCATION AND ANXIETY DISORDERS

Anxiety disorders as a group occur for 5.7 to 17.7% of children aged 6 to 17 years old (Costello & Angold, 1995). The anxiety disorders occurring most frequently in childhood include specific phobias, generalized anxiety disorder, social phobia, separation anxiety disorder (SAD), selective mutism, OCD, and PTSD. The course of disorder and symptom severity varies between diagnostic categories and within individuals, yet consensus is emerging that childhood anxiety disorders increase the risk of developing anxiety disorders in adolescence or adulthood (Costello & Angold, 1995; Keller, Lavori, Wunder, Beardslee, Schwartz, & Roth, 1992). There is also evidence that appropriate psychological and biomedical interventions with anxiety-disordered children and adolescents produce significant symptom reduction and may reduce the risk of developing debilitating levels of anxiety later in life (Amaya-Jackson, March, & Mulle, 1998; Kendall & Southam-Gerow, 1996; March, Mulle, & Herbel, 1994).

It is worth noting that children and adolescents often report more symptoms of anxiety than do other sources, such as parents and teachers (Costello & Angold, 1995). Many symptoms of anxiety are difficult to observe or in some instances purposely hidden from observers. Even when symptoms are observed or reported, it is often difficult to judge their significance or need for treatment. Clearly, some episodes of anxiety are transitory and resolve without specific treatment. However, we are gaining an increasingly refined, empirically supported view of factors that predict the durability of anxiety symptoms and disorders (Keller et al, 1992; Kendall & Southam-Gerow, 1996; La Greca, Silverman, Vernberg, & Prinstein, 1996).

One goal for parent education is to increase awareness of symptoms of anxiety and the potential danger to children who develop an anxiety-ridden lens for viewing themselves and the world. A second, related goal is to help parents understand how and why their child's anxiety symptoms are occurring. This enhanced understanding may reduce parents' blaming of themselves or their child for the symptoms, while setting the stage for treatment. As with most psychiatric disorders, the etiology of anxiety disorders is diverse and our knowledge base is steadily evolving (see March, 1995, and Ollendick, King, & Yule, 1994, for comprehensive reviews of anxiety disorders in children). Biological factors are believed to contribute to the occurrence and severity of many instances of anxiety disorders, although social, behavioral, and cognitive factors also play a role in the course of all anxiety disorders. It is important to educate parents about the interplay between these multiple factors and to enlist parents' assistance in helping the child combat anxiety symptoms. Life disruptions, traumatic experiences, and other stressful events produce anxiety symptoms in many children and adolescents, and those with biological or cognitive vulnerabilities may be especially prone to increases in symptoms to the point of meeting criteria for an anxiety disorder. Modeling of anxious, fearful, or avoidant behavior by family members may play a role in some instances, as may inadvertent reinforcement of anxiety symptoms. Even in instances where anxiety disorders are believed to be primarily caused by biological factors (e.g., OCD, panic disorder), cognitive and behavioral interventions that directly target anxiety symptoms appear efficacious (March & Leonard, 1996; Ollendick & King, 1998). Too, pharmacological treatments for many childhood anxiety disorders have yet to be found effective in randomized clinical trials and have inherent problems in producing side effects. Medications seldom appear appropriate as the sole treatment for anxiety disorders in children and adolescents but are often viewed as potentially useful components of a broader intervention strategy (Bernstein, 1994; Kutcher, Reiter, & Gardner, 1995).

Programs and Resources

Most reports and descriptions of treatments for child and adolescent anxiety disorders provide general guidelines for parent involvement, including educational material. In the cognitive behavioral approach to treating generalized anxiety disorder, social phobia, and separation anxiety disorders developed by Kendall and colleagues, parents are asked at intake to focus on the present, rather than on issues of guilt or blame, and help their child learn more adaptive ways of coping with anxiety (Kendall & Gosch, 1994). After a few individual sessions with the child, the therapist meets with the parents to give information about the treatment program and enlist the parents' active support for the child. This often includes acting as a coach or model when the child is trying to cope with an anxiety-provoking situation.

Additional guidelines for working with parents of children with separation anxiety disorder are offered by Black (1995). He argues the greatest need for parents is support and reassurance that appropriate limit setting around the child's separation-related distress is the best course of action. Black notes that family dysfunction or psychopathology is a common cause of treatment failure, and should always be assessed and included as a focus of treatment when appropriate. Current research suggests a link between SAD in childhood and the later emergence of panic disorder or agoraphobia. Panic disorder and agoraphobia are thus far seldom diagnosed in prepubertal children, but childhood-onset SAD appears to increase the likelihood of developing either or both of these later. A childhood history of SAD indicates the need for vigilance toward symptoms of panic disorder and agoraphobia in adolescence and adulthood. Parents should also know that the efficacy of medications for treating SAD in prepubertal children is not firmly established (Black, 1995).

The cognitive-behavioral treatment for OCD developed by March and colleagues includes a review with parents and children of the current scientific understanding of OCD as an initial step in treatment (March et al., 1994; March & Mulle, 1995). This review articulates a neurobehavioral framework in which OCD symptoms are described as the product of a neurological problem, and emphasizes that these symptoms are not the result of lack of effort or self-control by the child (March et al., 1994). The parents are also told that their child will be taught how to "boss back" or "battle" these symptoms and will need both a "battle strategy" and "allies" in this struggle. To this end, parents may be asked to help their child tolerate exposure to a feared situation or stimulus, or to prompt their child to use coping strategies, taught by a therapist, in home and community settings.

A number of guidelines are available for parents whose children may show signs of PTSD following traumatic experiences. Some are offered in the form of parent "fact sheets" listing common signs of trauma-related distress in children and adolescents following natural and human-made disasters (American Red Cross, 1992; Federal Emergency Management Agency, 1989; National Organization for Victim Assistance, 1991). These fact sheets target the first few weeks after a traumatic event and emphasize children's increased needs for comfort and closeness with caretakers. Also noted is the value to children of resuming customary routines and roles as quickly as possible. Clinician-delivered treatment strategies typically involve reexposing the child, under safe conditions, to stimuli associated with the traumatic event (Vernberg & Vogel, 1993). Parents and other family members may play important roles by helping to rebuild a sense of safety and security, and also by encouraging children to resume normal activities despite the trauma. Several "parent workbooks" have been developed for specific traumatic events (Corder & Haizlip, n.d.; Storm, McDermott, & Finlayson, 1994). These are intended to provide a context for children and parents to revisit aspects of the traumatic experience through drawings, storytelling, or family activities. One of the only evaluations of the parent workbook approach found that parents liked this approach and thought it was helpful. However, children's symptoms of PTSD did not remit more quickly as a result of this parent-delivered intervention (McDermott, 1996).

Evidence of Effectiveness

Rigorous evaluations of the effectiveness of various approaches to parent education with anxiety-disordered children have yet to be conducted. There are many reasons to believe that parent involvement in the treatment of child and adolescent anxiety disorders is useful and often essential. Behavioral and cognitive-behavioral treatments for anxiety disorders emphasize the importance of modeling, the use of effective coping strategies, and reducing life disruptions and stress to manageable levels. Pharmacological treatments require a high level of cooperation from parents, and a clear understanding of the rationale for using medications, including limitations, side effects, and possible benefits, is essential. Education surrounding these issues may boost compliance with treatment regimens.

PARENT EDUCATION AND MOOD DISORDERS

Mood disorders are believed to affect 10 to 20% of adolescents and about 5% of prepubertal children (Reynolds & Johnston, 1994a). Major depressive disorder and dysthymic disorder are examples of unipolar mood disorders, or *depressive disorders,* because disturbances of mood primarily involve symptoms of depression (e.g., feelings of helplessness or hopelessness, depressed mood, lack of energy or low self-esteem). Mood disorders involving manic or hypomanic episodes (e.g., abnormally elevated, expansive, or irritable mood, inflated self esteem or grandiosity, or excessive activity level), often alternating with one or more depressive episodes, are known as *bipolar disorders* (e.g., bipolar disorder I and II, cyclothymia). A third group of mood disorders involves mood disruptions directly caused by a medical condition or chemical substance (e.g., side effect of pre-scribed medicine).

Depressive disorders are more common than bipolar disorders in children and adolescents, and clear-cut diagnoses of bipolar disorders in pre-pubertal children are rare (Poznanski & Mokros, 1994; Weller, Weller, & Fristad, 1995). In recent years, all of the mood disorders are being diag-nosed in children and adolescents more frequently, and there is likely to be continued refinement in diagnostic criteria and assessment procedures applied to juvenile-onset mood disorders (Birmaher et al., 1996a; Weller et al., 1995). The proportion of children diagnosed with mood disorders increases with age, with a relatively large increase during adolescence.

Several issues surrounding mood disorders deserve particular mention in relation to parent education. First, the systematic study of mood disor-ders in children and adolescents has increased dramatically over the past 2 decades, but many questions remain about diagnosis and treatment. There is debate about whether symptoms of depression and mania in ju-veniles represent general indicators distress, misery, or disturbance instead of early forms of specific disorders that are well-understood in adults (Carlson, 1995; Nurcombe, 1994). Diagnoses of disorders with a chron-ic, sometimes debilitating course, such as bipolar disorders, ought to be made cautiously. A significant proportion (50% or more in many studies) of children and adolescents who meet criteria for a mood disorder also meet criteria for one or more other disorders, most commonly anxiety disorders, conduct disorder, schizophrenia, and attention deficit hyperac-tivity disorder (Poznanski & Mokros, 1994). We are not yet able to predict very accurately which disorder is likely to predominate in adult-hood.

Second, similar to the anxiety disorders, many symptoms of mood dis-orders are internally experienced, and escape the notice of parents, teach-ers, and peers (Reynolds & Johnston, 1994a). Children and adolescents with chronic depressive symptoms may not be able to identify or report the fact that they are depressed because they are accustomed to the con-stant feelings of sadness or irritability. As a consequence, mood disorders may go untreated, leaving affected youth vulnerable to the numerous so-cial, behavioral, and academic difficulties wrought by depression. It is im-portant to increase parents' sensitivity to outward signs of internally expe-rienced distress in their children, and to emphasize the importance of tak-ing action earlier rather than later. These signs include avoidance of age-appropriate activities and challenges, frequent sadness or tearfulness, social withdrawal, negative statements about self, sleep or appetite problems, and irritability. In some instances, self-destructive behaviors and substance abuse may also signal mood disturbances (see Reynolds and Johnston, 1994b, for a comprehensive review of mood disorders in children and adolescents).

Although it is difficult to predict a life course of a specific mood disorder based on childhood symptoms, there is ample evidence that symptoms of mood disorders interfere with normal development and respond well to a number of treatment approaches (Birmaher et al., 1996b; Cicchetti, Rogosch, & Toth, 1994; Kaslow & Thompson, 1998). Psychological interventions, especially cognitive-behavioral approaches, appear effective at alleviating depressive symptoms in clinic samples (Kaslow & Thompson, 1998; Reinecke, Ryan, & DuBois, 1998). Some pharmacological treatments also appear useful in open trials and case reports, and double-blind studies are beginning to provide evidence that certain medications effective for adult mood disorders may also be helpful with child and adolescent populations (Birmaher et al., 1996a). Preventive or early interventions with children and adolescents who are at high risk for developing mood disorders (e.g., manifest subclinical levels of depressive symptoms, offspring of parents with mood disorders, experience significant loss or illness) appear quite promising for reducing risks for developing mood disorders (Kaslow & Thompson, 1998).

Third, symptoms of mood disorders are multidetermined, and single-cause explanations are seldom sufficient. Moreover, there is considerable variability in presentation, course, and response to treatment for youngsters who carry the same diagnostic label. The emergence and course of mood disorders may be influenced by psychosocial factors (e.g., stressful life experiences, loss, family dysfunction), social-cognitive factors (e.g., distortions in attributional style or cognitions, interpersonal skill deficits), and biological factors (e.g., genetical influences, illness or injury).

Programs and Resources

One of the only published studies of parent education for families of mood-disordered youngsters evaluated a 2-hr educational program for parents of hospitalized adolescents (Brent, Poling, McKain, & Baugher 1993). This program was designed to help parents recognize the symptoms and problems associated with mood disorders, describe possible causes and influences on the course of recovery, and encourage parents to be participants and advocates in their child's treatment (see Poling, 1989, for psychoeducational material used in the project). Additional areas of discussion included attitudes held by parents about their child's disorder, issues surrounding psychopharmacologic treatments, and the heightened likelihood of affective disorders in the parents of children with mood disorders. Brent and colleagues (1993) noted that the parents of depressed children often do not believe their child has a mood disorder or view symptoms as manipulative, leading to nonempathic responses to dysphoric emotions and behaviors. These responses may heighten the feelings of hopelessness and isolation often found in youngsters with mood disorders. A number of parents voiced concerns that their child may become addicted or dependent on psychoactive medications, and this education program provided information about drug treatments for depression, including how the drugs work, potential side effects, and limitations. Because parents with unrecognized, untreated mood disorders are more likely to offer an unsupportive or even chaotic family environment, the education program emphasized identification of mood disorders in parents and referral for appropriate treatment. Finally, the parents were given information about the frequently chronic, recurrent course of depression and the risk of suicidality during depressive episodes to help parents recognize a recurrence of symptoms.

A number of programs offer extensive intervention with parents and families of youth with depressed youth, and parent education is undoubtedly a component of these interventions. Stark, Rouse, and Kurowski (1994) argued that many parents with mood-disordered children engage in few recreational activities, rely on coercion and criticism as discipline strategies, and have difficulty expressing empathy. Inadvertent reinforcement of avoidant behavior by parents is also an area of concern (e.g., allowing a child to stay home from school because of depressive symptoms). These areas are targeted for change as part of treatment.

We found little research or resources on parent education regarding bipolar disorders in children and adolescents, perhaps because diagnosis of these disorders in youngsters is a relatively recent trend. There is a substantial literature on bipolar disorders in adults, but it is not yet clear how much of this applies to children and adolescents. Clearly, acute and prophylactic pharmacological treatments are important aspects of management of these disorders in adults, and a solid understanding by parents of the rationale, administration requirements and monitoring procedures seems essential when working with younger populations also. Many of the parent education issues identified in work with depressive disorders, such as increased vulnerability to stress, a recurrent course, and the likelihood of a higher rate of mood disorders among parents, apply in work with families of youngsters with bipolar disorders.

Evidence of Effectiveness

Scant evidence is available on the effects of parent education for children and adolescents with mood disorders. The study of a manualized psycho-educational program by Brent and colleagues (1993) found increased knowledge about several aspects of depressive disorders and a decrease in maladaptive beliefs about depression and its treatment. Parents also expressed satisfaction with the program and thought it useful. Evaluations of the effects of this and other forms of parent education on treatment compliance and course of disorder remain to be completed.

PARENT EDUCATION AND SCHIZOPHRENIA AND OTHER PSYCHOSES

Schizophrenia is rare in prepubertal children, but becomes more common during mid- to late adolescence, eventually affecting between 0.5 and 1% of individuals at some point in the lifespan (American Psychiatric Association, 1994). Psychotic symptoms include hallucinations, delusions, disorganized speech or behavior, and catatonia (American Psychiatric Association, 1994). Psychotic features may accompany a number of psychiatric disorders other than schizophrenia, including major depressive disorder, bipolar disorder II, and severe PTSD. Psychotic features are reported more commonly than full-blown schizophrenia in prepubertal children. Schizoaffective disorder presents a combination of the psychotic symptoms of schizophrenia and mood disruptions (both unipolar and bipolar depression). A variety of general medical conditions can also produce psychotic symptoms (e.g., acute infections, toxic substances). In addition to psychotic features, schizophrenia may include *negative* symptoms (restricted emotional expression, avolition, poverty of thought and speech) (American Psychiatric Association, 1994).

Although adolescence or adulthood is the most common age of onset for schizophrenia and other psychotic disorders, recent research has attempted to identify precursors of these disorders in children (e.g., Alaghband-Rad et al., 1998; Alaghband-Rad, Frasier, Giedd, Hamburger, &

Rapoport, 1997). This research indicates that very early onset schizophrenia (i.e., prior to adolescence) may be a more severe form, with more biological abnormalities and a more chronic course than late adolescent/early adult onset. There is often considerable diagnostic uncertainty in children showing psychotic-spectrum disturbances, and the term "multidimensionally impaired" has been suggested for instances when a diagnosis of schizophrenia is possible but not definite (Alaghband-Radetal., 1997).

Giving basic information about schizophrenia to parents is an important educational task, especially at the time of diagnosis. Parents of newly diagnosed adolescents are often extremely concerned about prognosis, treatment options, and causes of the disorder (Sheridan & Moore, 1991). A recent study of parents' adjustment years after the initial diagnosis in their offspring indicated persistent feelings of loss and grief regarding the disorder, and events at the time of first onset may continue to be a source of distress (Davis & Schultz, 1998). Support, both informational and emotional, from professionals and other parents, may be particularly useful during the difficult period following initial diagnosis (Sheridan & Moore, 1991).

A number of risk factors for developing schizophrenia are known, and many of these are biological in nature. However, family factors, and other social factors such as poverty and adversity appear to play a role in the onset and course of many instances of schizophrenia. Hostility, criticism, and intrusiveness by family members, referred to as *expressed emotion*, have repeatedly been found to complicate the course of recovery (Kavanaugh, 1992). Moreover, noncompliance with medication regimens is a second risk to recovery, and families are often important influences on medication usage, especially with younger patients living at home.

Recognition of the increased vulnerability to stressful events, including family conflict, seems a useful goal of parent education. Well-informed families may be able to reduce exposure to social stresses and help the adolescent cope more effectively with life challenges. Awareness of the biological underpinnings of schizophrenia and schizoaffective disorder may serve to reduce anger or blame about the disruption and distress accompanying these disorders. Parent support for medication use is often crucial, and it is important for parents to have well-developed strategies for encouraging and monitoring proper use of medications. These strategies also involve plans for dealing with medication noncompliance by adolescents.

Programs and Resources

Controlled studies indicate that parent education, offered as part of a more comprehensive family intervention, might reduce expressed emotion in families and prevent or delay relapse in the diagnosed individual (Hogarty et al., 1986; Leff, Kuipers, Berkowitz, & Sturgeon, 1985). These interventions use formal education about the disorder to encourage family members to become allies in treatment, to reduce anxiety and guilt, and give a greater sense of cognitive mastery (see Anderson, Reiss, & Hogarty, 1986, and Berkowitz, Eberlein-Fries, & Leff, 1984, for details of education components). Information on etiology, prognosis, medication management, treatment alternatives, and community resources form a common core for these education efforts.

Evidence of Effectiveness

Work with the relatives of schizophrenia patients, including parent education, seems important from the intervention studies conducted thus far (Leff et al., 1985; McClellan & Werry, 1994). Most of this research to date has focused on adults, rather than child or adolescent patients. One of the few published studies of parent education for adolescents with schizophrenia reported that the parents seemed to gain skills in managing their youngsters at home (Sheridan & Moore, 1991). This was not a controlled study but rather an initial attempt to demonstrate possible effects of parent education. Ironically, parents' factual knowledge about the disorder did not increase (in part because parents scored well on knowledge at pretest), and gains in managing adolescents were attributed to support received from other parents in the education group. Specific aspects of education content or delivery have not, to our knowledge, been formally evaluated for differential effectiveness in any published studies.

PRIORITIES FOR PROGRAM DEVELOPMENT AND RESEARCH

Education for parents of children and adolescents with anxiety, mood, or psychotic disorders undoubtedly takes many forms and is offered in a number of treatment contexts. We found descriptions of the types of information offered to parents with these various disorders, with the general intention of recruiting parents as allies in the treatment process by presenting an explanation for the symptoms, explaining treatment rationales, and giving guidelines for parents as helpers to their offspring. Relatively few parent education programs in this area appear to be manualized in terms of content or presentation format, and even fewer have been rigorously evaluated. From our review of this area, we offer several recommendations for program development and research.

Develop Empirically Supported Parent Education Materials

Research on the disorders discussed here has grown markedly in the recent years, and parents deserve up-to-date, empirically supported summaries of current knowledge on etiology, diagnosis, treatment, and prevention. Scientific and professional organizations increasingly are offering such summaries for professional audiences (e.g., Lonigan & Elbert, 1998; March & Leonard, 1996). Translation of these consensus statements into a format suitable for use in parent education is a logical next step. As access increases to information about a variety of health issues via electronic media, so does the risk of having inaccurate, misleading, or unsubstantiated claims about mental health disorders in children and adolescents passed off as scientifically supported knowledge. Parents, and those who work with parents, need ready access to the balanced, empirically supported views of leading researchers and clinicians. Some efforts are already being made in this direction. The American Psychological Association, the American Psychiatric Association, and the National Institute of Mental Health offer brochures or fact sheets for some disorders. Still, these thus far focus more on disorders in adults rather than children and adolescents. When child- or adolescent-onset psychiatric disorders are emphasized, externalized disorders are covered more often than the internalized disorders discussed here.

Evaluate the Effectiveness of Parent Education Efforts

In the cost-conscious climate surrounding mental health services delivery, it is critical to demonstrate that parent education yields benefits. Manualized, replicable parent education programs are a necessary step in providing this critical evidence. A few examples of manualized parent education programs are available (e.g., Brent et al., 1993; Dadds, Meard, & Rapee, 1992), but these have often been offered as part of a larger package of social interventions. Questions such as optimal format (e.g., group vs. individual, self-study vs. live presentation) or optimal candidates (e.g., education level of parents, parental psychopathology) for parent education need to be addressed. Even basic questions such as the amount of information retained or the level of understanding of education material seem to have received relatively little study.

Focus on Prevention and Early Identification

Anxiety and mood disorders in children and adolescents are identified and treated much less frequently than they occur. Recent evidence indicates that juveniles with anxiety, mood, or psychotic disorders respond well to several empirically supported treatments, and early treatment may prevent the development of more serious disturbances in the future. Life disruptions, traumatic experiences, and family disturbances all increase the likelihood of significant symptoms of anxiety, depression, or both. Family histories of some, but not all, of the disorders described here also convey increased risk. Greater attention to early signs of internalized disorders in childhood, along with information about effective treatment options or parent-directed efforts to help, could serve to increase utilization of existing services.

Research is needed on the types and sources of information on emotional disturbances that might appeal to parents of high-risk youngsters. Primary care providers, schools, public health officers, and media campaigns all offer possible mechanisms for information distribution. These options share common issues, but each also carries unique challenges that could be approached using scientific theory and methods.

Identify and Evaluate Naturally Occurring Strategies

A final, potentially useful research approach is to identify strategies used by families, or by children in relation to their families, to manage symptoms of mood disorders, anxiety, or psychoses. These strategies may be conceptualized as *coping assistance*, as they involve efforts by important people in a child's life to help cope with stressful circumstances, including internally-experienced distress (Thoits, 1986). For example, a study on how children cope with PTSD symptoms after a disaster indicated that elementary age youngsters rely heavily on parents for reestablishing normal roles and routines, and as a source of distraction when negative thoughts and feelings arise (Prinstein, La Greca, Vernberg, & Silverman, 1996). Activities involving emotional processing (controlled and repeated exposure to reminders of traumatic events) were more likely to come from friends than from parents, but were provided infrequently by any source. This type of research gives a view of how families try to help distressed children cope with internalizing problems and also identifies types of assistance that may be difficult for families to provide.

The usefulness of various coping assistance strategies can be evaluated by tracking changes over time in target symptoms or behaviors in relation to the use of strategies by parents or children. For example, a study of friendship formation in early adolescents identified four categories of strategies used by parents to help their children establish new friendships after relocation, a task made more difficult by social anxiety or depressive symptoms (Vernberg, Beery, Ewell, & Abwender, 1993). Strategies from the two categories requiring direct, active involvement by parents in the adolescent's social network (Enabled Proximity to Peers; Met Other Parents) predicted greater success in friendship formation using a prospective, longitudinal design. Strategies from the other two categories were more passive and did not involve active involvement in the adolescent's social network (Encouraged Activities, Talked to Adolescent). These strategies did not appear useful in terms of facilitating friendship formation. This line of inquiry identifies naturally occurring parental or family strategies that may be helpful to children facing social or emotional difficulties. These strategies could then be incorporated into parent education programs and evaluated using experimental or quasi-experimental designs.

REFERENCES

Alaghband-Rad, J., Frasier, J. A., Giedd, J. N., Hamburger, S. D., & Rapoport, J. L. (1997). Childhood-onset schizophrenia: Biological markers in relation to clinical characteristics. *American Journal of Psychiatry, 154,* 64–69.

Alaghband-Rad, J., Castellanos, F. X, Frasier, J. A., Gordon, C. T., Hamburger, S. D., Jacobsen, L. K., Kunna, S., Lanane, M., McKenna, K., Rapoport, J. L., Smith, A., Wiggs, E., & Zahn, T. P. (1998). "Multidimensionally impaired disorder": Is it a variant of very early-onset schizophrenia. *Journal of the American Academy of Child and Adolescent Psychiatry, 37,* 91–100.

Amaya-Jackson, L., March, J. S., Murray, M. C., & Schulte, A. (1998). Cognitive-behavioral psychotherapy for children and adolescents with posttraumatic stress disorder after a single-incident stressor. *Journal of the American Academy of Child and Adolescent Psychiatry, 37,* 585–594.

American Psychiatric Association (1994). *Diagnostic and statistical manual of mental disorders* (4th edition). Washington, DC: American Psychiatric Association

American Red Cross (1992). *Helping children cope with disaster* (ARC Publication No. 4499). Baltimore.

Anderson, C. M., Reiss, D. J., & Hogarty, G. E. (1986). *Schizophrenia in the family: A practitioner's guide to psychoeducation and management.* New York: Guilford Press.

Berkowitz, R., Eberlein-Fries, R., Kuipers, L., & Leff, J. (1984). Educating relatives about schizophrenia. *Schizophrenia Bulletin, 10,* 418–429.

Bernstein, G. A. (1994). Psychopharmacological interventions. In T. O. Ollendick, N. J. King, & Yule, W. (Eds.), *International handbook of phobic and anxiety disorders in children and adolescents* (pp. 439–451). New York: Plenum Press.

Birmaher, B., Ryan, N. D., Williamson, D. E., Brent, D. A., Kaufman, J., Dahl, R. E., Perel, J., & Nelson, B. N. (1996a). Childhood and adolescent depression: A review of the past 10 years. Part I. *Journal of the American Academy of Child and Adolescent Psychiatry, 35,* 1427–1439.

Birmaher, B., Ryan, N. D., Williamson, D. E., Brent, D. A., & Kaufman, J. (1996b). Childhood and adolescent depression: A review of the past 10 years. Part II. *Journal of the American Academy of Child and Adolescent Psychiatry, 35,* 1575–1583.

Black, B. (1995). Separation anxiety and panic disorder. In J. March (Ed.), *Anxiety Disorders in Children and Adolescents* (pp. 212–234). NY: Guilford.

Brent, D. A., Poling, K., McKain, B., & Baugher, M. (1993). A psychoeducational program for families of affectively ill children and adolescents. *Journal of the American Academy of Child and Adolescent Psychiatry, 32,* 770–774.

Carlson, G. A. (1995). Identifying prepubertal mania. *Journal of the American Academy of Child and Adolescent Psychiatry, 34,* 750–753.

Carlson, G. A. (1994). Adolescent bipolar disorder: Phenomenology and treatment implications. In W. M. Reynolds & H. F. Johnston (Eds.), *Handbook of Depression in Children and Adolescents* (pp. 41–60). New York: Plenum Press.

Corder, B. F., & Haizlip, T. (n.d.). *After the hurricane. A coloring book for children and their parents or helpers.* Raleigh, NC.

Costello, E. J, & Angold, A. (1995). Epidemiology. In J. March (Ed.), *Anxiety Disorders in Children and Adolescents* (pp. 109–124). New York: Guilford.

Dadds, M., Meard, P., & Rapee, R. (1992). The role of family interventions in the treatment of child anxiety disorders: Some preliminary findings. *Behaviour Change, 9,* 171–177.

Davis, D. J., & Schultz, C. L. (1998). Grief, parenting, and schizophrenia. *Social Science and Medicine, 46,* 369–380.

Federal Emergency Management Agency. (1989). *Coping with children's reactions to hurricanes and other disasters.* (FEMA Document 1989 0–941–901). Washington, DC: U.S. Government Printing Office.

Hogarty, G. E., Anderson, C. M., Reiss, D. J., Kornblith, S. J., Greenwald, D. P., Javna, C. D., & Madonia, M. J. (1986). Family psychoeducation, social skills training, and maintenance chemotherapy in the aftercare treatment of schizophrenia. (1986). *Archives of General Psychology, 43,* 633–642.

Kaslow, N. J., & Thompson, M. P. (1998). Applying the criteria for empirically-supported treatments to studies of psychosocial interventions for child and adolescent depression. *Journal of Clinical Child Psychology, 27*, 146–155.

Kavanagh, D. J. (1992). Recent developments in expressed emotion and schizophrenia. *British Journal of Psychiatry, 160*, 601–620.

Keller, M., Lavori, P., Wunder, J., Beardslee, W., Schwartz, C., & Roth, J. (1992). Chronic course of anxiety disorders in children and adolescents. *Journal of the American Academy of Child and Adolescent Psychiatry, 31*, 595–599.

Kendall, P. C., & Gosch, E. A. (1994). Cognitive-behavioral interventions. In T. O. Ollendick, N. J. King, & W. Yule (Eds.), *International handbook of phobic and anxiety disorders in children and adolescents* (pp. 415–438). New York: Plenum Press.

Kendall, P. C., & Southham-Gerow, M. A. (1996). Long-term follow-up of a cognitive-behavioral therapy for anxiety disordered youth. *Journal of Consulting and Clinical Psychology, 64*, 724–730.

La Greca, A. M., Silverman, W. K., Vernberg, E. M., & Prinstein, M. J. (1996). Symptoms of posttraumatic stress in children following Hurricane Andrew: A prospective study. *Journal of Consulting and Clinical Psychology, 64*, 712–723.

Leff, J., Kuipers, L., Berkowitz, R., & Sturgeon, D. (1985). A controlled trial of social intervention in the families of schizophrenic patients: Two-year follow-up. *British Journal of Psychiatry, 146*, 594–600.

Lonigan, C. J., & Elbert, J. C. (Eds.) (1998). Special issue on empirically supported psychosocial interventions for children. *Journal of Clinical Child Psychology, 27*, 137–232.

March, J. S. (Ed.). (1995). *Anxiety disorders in children and adolescents*. New York: Guilford Press.

March, J. S., & Leonard, H. L. (1996). Obsessive-compulsive disorder in children and adolescents: A review of the past 10 years. *Journal of the American Academy of Child and Adolescent Psychiatry, 34*, 1265–1273.

March, J. S., & Leonard, H. L. (1996). Obsessive-compulsive disorder in children and adolescents: A review of the past 10 years. *Journal of the American Academy of Child and Adolescent Psychiatry, 34*, 1265–1273.

March, J. S., & Mulle, K. (1995). Manualized cognitive-behavioral psychotherapy for obsessive-compulsive disorder in childhood: A preliminary single case study. *Journal of Anxiety Disorders, 9*, 175–184.

March, J. S., Mulle, K., & Herbel, B. (1994). Behavioral psychotherapy for children and adolescents with obsessive-compulsive disorder: An open trial of a new protocol driven treatment package. *Journal of the American Academy of Child and Adolescent Psychiatry, 33*, 333–341.

McDermott, B. (1996, August). The Sutherland Bushfire Trauma Project: A randomized controlled treatment trial. In E. M. Vernberg (Chair), *Evaluating post-disaster interventions with children*. Symposium conducted at the annual meeting of the American Psychological Association, Toronto, Canada.

McClellan, J. M., & Werry, J. S. (1994). Practice parameters for the assessment and treatment of children and adolescents with schizophrenia. *Journal of the American Academy of Child and Adolescent Psychiatry, 33*, 616–635.

National Organization for Victim Assistance. (1991). *Hurricane! Issues unique to hurricane disasters*. Washington, DC.

Nurcombe, B. (1994). The validity of the diagnosis of major depression in childhood and adolescence. In W. M. Reynolds & H. F. Johnston (Eds.), *Handbook of Depression in Children and Adolescents* (pp. 61–77). New York: Plenum Press.

Ollendick, T. H., & King, N. J. (1998). Empirically-supported treatment for children with phobic and anxiety disorders: Current status. *Journal of Clinical Child Psychology, 27,* 156–167.

Ollendick, T. O., King, N. J., & Yule, W. (Eds.). (1994). *International handbook of phobic and anxiety disorders in children and adolescents.* New York: Plenum Press.

Poling, K. (1989). *Living with depression: A survival manual for families.* Pittsburgh, PA: University of Pittsburgh, Western Psychiatric Institute and Clinic.

Poznanski, E. O., & Mokros, H. B. (1994). Phenomenology and epidemiology of mood disorders in children and adolescents. In W. M. Reynolds & H. F. Johnston (Eds.), *Handbook of Depression in Children and Adolescents.* (pp. 19–39). New York: Plenum Press.

Prinstein, M. J., La Greca, A. M., Vernberg, E. M., & Silverman, W. K. (1996). Children's coping assistance: How parents, teachers, and friends help children cope after a natural disaster. *Journal of Clinical Child Psychology, 25,* 463–475.

Reinecke, M. A., Ryan, N. E., & DuBois, D. L. (1998). Cognitive-behavioral therapy of depression and depressive symptoms during adolescence: A review and meta-analysis. *Journal of the American Academy of Child and Adolescent Psychiatry, 37,* 26–34.

Reynolds, W. M., & Johnston, H. F. (1994a). The nature and study of depression in children and adolescents. In W. M. Reynolds & H. F. Johnston (Eds.), *Handbook of depression in children and adolescents.* (pp. 3–18). New York: Plenum Press.

Reynolds, W. M., & Johnston, H. F. (Eds.). (1994b). *Handbook of depression in children and adolescents.* New York: Plenum Press.

Sheridan, A., Moore, L. M. (1991). Running groups for parents with schizophrenic adolescents: Initial experiences and plans for the future. *Journal of Adolescence, 14,* 1–16.

Stark, K. D., Rouse, L. W., & Kurowski, C. (1994a). Psychological treatment approaches for depression in children. In W. M. Reynolds & H. F. Johnston (Eds.), *Handbook of depression in children and adolescents.* (pp. 275–308). New York: Plenum Press.

Storm, V., McDermott, B., & Finlayson, D. (1994). *The Bushfire and me.* Newtown, Australia: VBD Publications.

Thoits, P. A. (1986). Social support as coping assistance. *Journal of Consulting and Clinical Psychology, 54,* 416–423.

Vernberg, E. M., Beery, S. H., Abwender, D. A. & Ewell, K. K. (1993). Parents' use of friendship facilitation strategies and the formation of new friendships in early adolescence: A prospective study. *Journal of Family Psychology, 7,* 250–263.

Vernberg, E. M., & Vogel, J. (1993). Interventions with children following disasters. *Journal of Clinical Child Psychology, 22,* 485–498.

Weller, E. B., Weller, R. A., & Fristad, M. A. (1995). Bipolar disorder in children: Misdiagnosis, underdiagnosis, and future directions. *Journal of the American Academy of Child and Adolescent Psychiatry, 34,* 709–713.

CHAPTER 11

Parenting Children with Learning Disabilities

Paula E. Lancaster

Center for Research on Learning, University of Kansas, Lawrence Kansas

I remember the first time I realized that I might have a learning disability. I was visiting with my brothers and sisters over the holidays. We were sharing stories from Christmases past, birthdays, and other special events. It was a very enjoyable visit. The problem was that I couldn't recall a single event. I know I was there for all of these days, and when my brothers or sisters would start a telling a story, I had a vague recollection. I just couldn't recall a story on my own. At that moment I also realized why Dennis, my son, struggles so much in school. He seems to be experiencing the same problems that I have.

The topics of parenting and parent involvement as areas of study have a long history (Simpson, 1996; Turnbull & Turnbull, 1997). Given the diversity within families today and the increasing prevalence of children diagnosed with learning disabilities (LD), educators need to gain an understanding of the issues that parents and families of children with LD face (Dyson, 1996). Each child with LD exhibits some unique characteristics and learning needs. That uniqueness is also apparent in families. Although the scenarios provided throughout the chapter depict common issues raised by parents of children with LD, each family will have its own individual characteristics, strengths, and needs.

Handbook of Diversity in Parent Education

An LD manifests itself in a range of difficulties in academic subject areas and secondary problems in social, emotional, and metacognitive domains (Mercer, 1997). Generally, individuals with LD achieve average scores on intelligence tests and below-average scores on at least one achievement test. When this discrepancy between perceived ability and achievement is large, classification is likely to occur (Ysseldyke, Algozzine, & Thurlow, 1991). Research has shown that apart from their academic difficulties, children with LD have been found to have lower self-concept, lower peer acceptance rates (Vaughn, Elbaum, & Schumm, 1996), and lower engagement rates on academic tasks (McIntosh, Vaughn, Schumm, Haager, & Lee, 1993) than their nondisabled peers.

The invisible nature of LD is problematic for the both individual and family members. Parents, family members, and educators often react to the unexplainable lack of success experienced by many students with LD by assuming them to be underachieving or unmotivated. These assumptions sometimes lead to a level of intolerance toward the child in school and often to heightened stress in the family (O'Hara & Levy, 1984). Parents often experience difficulties in the years prior to identification of the LD and during the school years as they struggle with the education system. As children with LD struggle to make the transitions to new grade levels and adult living, so too do parents and family members struggle to offer the right amount of support. Parents and family members may express concerns about the socialization of their child with peers and siblings as well as the general management of their home.

Unlike other disabilities that are apparent from birth or early infancy, the invisible nature of LD referred to above often delays identification by the school system and subsequently the supports and services that come with the identification. The very definition of an LD is such that a child must experience considerable failure before a diagnosis is made. Thus, parents, family members, and especially the child often suffer through years of unexplainable failures and frustrations. Family members often react to this frustration by placing or accepting unnecessary blame (Atkins, 1991) and spending an inordinate amount of time on academic remediation to the detriment of family socialization and relationship building (Dyson, 1996). For example, Dyson (1996), in a study of the experiences of families of children with LD related to parental stress, family functioning, and sibling self-concept, found that parents with at least one child with LD exhibited significantly more indicators of stress than parents of one or more nondisabled child. Qualitative data were also collected through open-ended home interviews. Sixty-three percent of families reported problems resulting from the excessive amount of time and energy expended on the child with LD and his or her parent's continuing difficulty with accepting their child's disability. Identification of a LD can lead to responses such as shattered expectations, guilt, anger, and parental conflict (Mercer, 1997). When a child is finally referred for special education services, school personnel such as the general education teacher, special education teacher, guidance counselor, or social worker are often the primary contacts for the parents.

The following section provides descriptions of different approaches to parent and family involvement that educators may take. The remainder of this chapter addresses ways educators can build supportive partnerships with parents and families and is organized based on stages through which parents and their children with LD will progress including referral and assessment, placement and the educational process, and transitions. Remaining sections address opportunities for educators to support parents and families as they deal with the social and organizational skills of their children with LD and additional home and family issues.

APPROACHES TO PARENT AND FAMILY INVOLVEMENT

Historically, parent education and family involvement have been viewed from different perspectives. Kellaghan, Sloane, Alverez, and Bloom (1993) provide an analysis of three approaches: deficit, difference, and empowenment. Each will be discussed below. Also, a framework is described that educators should consider when working with parents and families that acknowledges unique characteristics, strengths, and needs that families possess. In order to make the most of opportunities to support and collaborate with parents and families, an understanding of the family as a system and an empowering approach is needed.

Deficit and Difference Approaches

In the 1950s through the 1970s service providers utilized a *deficit* approach when working with parents and families. Through this approach, families experiencing challenging circumstances such as poverty, poor health, or joblessness were thought to be deficient in some way and in need of professional care in order to be repaired. Services were prescriptive in nature and often based on what seemed to work for the majority culture. The *difference* approach, beginning in the mid-1970s and prevalent in many of today's programs, acknowledges the cultural and economic differences inherent in individual families and attempts to help families adjust to the majority culture while maintaining their identity. For example, parents speaking languages other than that spoken by the majority culture might be encouraged to enroll in English language courses or taught methods for supporting their children's use of English in the home and at school. As well intentioned as these suggestions are, they may not consider the parents' available time and energy or the presence of extended family in the home that may or may not speak English. Although the difference approach is an improvement over the deficit approach, differences are still the main focus and viewed as in need of remediation, and the vast strengths and unique insights families bring to the educational table are rarely acknowledged. The empowerment approach attempts to do just that.

The Empowerment Approach

In the context of parent and family involvement, empowerment refers to mutual collaboration toward a shared goal.

> The empowerment approach, in which the concepts of power and control are central is based on the idea that people's circumstances can be changed by people themselves. It aims to help parents gain control over their own lives to become more effective advocates for themselves and for their children in interacting with social agencies and institutions, and to engage more actively in the education of their children, by direct involvement or by obtaining resources (Kelleghan, Sloane, Alvarez, & Bloom, 1993, pp. 93–94).

Turnbull and Turnbull (1997) suggest that mutual empowerment (i.e., empowerment of oneself and others) should be the goal for professionals supporting families. This goal suggests a change in perspective on the part of the professional to one of supporter, collaborator, or partner, as opposed to one of merely service provider.

Thus, when collaborating with parents and families of children with LD, an equal partnership is developed over time. The mutual goal of the partnership is to provide a sound education for the child along with support to all those involved. Just as parents should be able to count on educators for support and guidance in educational decision making, so too, should educators be able to count on parents for expertise on the nature, characteristics, and experiences of the child. Within the empowerment framework described by Turnbull and Turnbull (1997), families and educators each have particular responsibilities or factors to consider. Through collaboration, these factors are brought together to increase the likelihood that all collaborators will reach their goals.

For example, the Turnbulls (1997) point out that families need to possess motivation, knowledge, and skills. Educators can help to increase parent motivation for involvement in the education of their children by including families in the Individualized Education Plan (IEP) process in a meaningful way and contacting families to seek advice and share positive events. They can help to increase knowledge about and skills for educational involvement by sharing information, communicating consistently, and creating true partnerships between the schools and the home. Educators, on the other hand, are responsible for providing opportunities for partnerships and establishing reliable alliances. Reliable allies can be depended on to provide ". . . nonjudgmental, unconditional, and ever-available support. They probably make you feel better about yourself, provide support and information to you within the context of a personal relationship, and therefore strengthen your belief in yourself" (Turnbull & Turnbull, 1997, p. 30). Some opportunities for partnerships are created when educators communicate regularly, meet families' basic needs, and help to extend learning in the home and community. Some of the ways educators can create reliable alliances include knowing themselves, knowing families, communicating positively, and envisioning great expectations (Turnbull & Turnbull, 1997).

Mutual empowerment does not occur because families want it to or because families and educators use the term loosely in conversation. Simpson (1996) suggests that successful communication and collaboration require development of competencies for interacting and a personal philosophy that values communication and interaction. He asserts that "individuals who expect to adequately serve the needs of parents and families must possess a genuine interest in people and willingness to invest time and energy seeking solutions to needs and problems" (p. 28). In order for educators to effectively serve the best interests of children, parents, and families who may come from distinctively different cultures and backgrounds than their own, educators should begin to understand their own values first. Therefore, educators need to evaluate their interest level, their level of dedication, and their ability to listen effectively.

With an understanding of their own values and a desire to engage in communication and collaboration, educators are better prepared to attend to and collaborate with parents and families. Attending meetings and being available is essential yet collaboration is not limited to physical presence at a meeting or in a classroom. Being available can also mean being a good listener and making an effort to fully understand the family's needs and desires. When educators truly listen and react to what they have heard instead of a preconceived notion of what is best for each family, trust and rapport can be established more easily, and mutual empowerment can occur. Finally, Simpson notes that "sensitivity to the demands and stresses commonly experienced by families of exceptional children and youth will aid educators in keeping educational matters in proper perspective and in assisting families with the numerous noneducational issues with which they must contend" (p. 31). Andrews and Lupart (1993) add support by reminding educators that, "When communicating with parents, the two most critical points for teachers to keep in mind are to be a *good listener* and to *avoid making judgments or blaming parents*" (p. 251).

Family Systems Framework

Becoming familiar with a framework such as the Family Systems Framework described by Turnbull and Turnbull (1997, chap. 6) will help educators to understand the issues facing each family. This framework considers the family as a system. At the center of the framework are the family interactions that include the marital, extended family, parental, and sibling relationships that vary along continuums of cohesiveness and adaptability and change as individuals move through developmental stages and transitions. The family's functioning is impacted by inputs such as the characteristics of the family, personal characteristics of the members, and special challenges along with outputs such as affection, self-esteem, economics, socialization, recreation, education, and daily care. The framework makes clear the point that "Simply understanding the child does not mean that you will understand the family, yet understanding the family is necessary to understanding the child" (Turnbull & Turnbull, 1997, p. 97).

The framework facilitates a broader approach to thinking about and working with families. Most educators communicate primarily with the child and his or her parents. Occasionally, a teacher may come to know a sibling in the school, but this is rarely the case. Thus, the picture of the family the educator has is very limited and may not provide an opportunity to get to know the unique strengths, interests, and needs each family possesses. By taking the time to see the larger picture, energy and time will ultimately be saved as strengths and interests are tapped and energy is focused on real, not assumed, issues and needs. The next sections address various opportunities for supporting families, parents and children with LD throughout the stages of the schooling experience and suggestions for building collaborative partnerships. Examples of how to take an empowering approach and draw from a family systems framework are included.

SUPPORTING PARENTS AND FAMILIES THROUGH THE SPECIAL EDUCATION PROCESS

> I wish I could understand exactly what it is that prevents Trey from learning as fast as other kids. Believe me, this child loved school when he first started. In kindergarten he was always so excited when he came home. He would show us his work and talk about the day. This excitement stopped as he got older. By the time he was in fourth grade, he was making up illnesses so that he could stay home. I don't know why he doesn't read well. We worked with him just as much as we did with his sister. For some reason he just doesn't seem to get it. He gets so frustrated too. I can tell he really wants to read, and do well in school, but for some reason his hard work doesn't pay off.

> I've always been involved in the schools. I was a room mother, have sold my share of raffle tickets, and have yet to miss a parent-teacher conference. When we found out that Maria had a learning disability, I attended all of those meetings too, but I really didn't understand much of what they were saying. They used a lot of terms that I didn't understand, read off a bunch of test scores, and asked me to sign some papers. They all acted like they knew what was best, and that my role was to just agree. I had to go to other parents to learn about what was going on with Maria's education.

Although students may have experienced academic difficulties from the beginning of the school career, a diagnosis rarely occurs before the third grade, and frequently later that this. Thus, all students with LD, their parents, and family members will at some point in time encounter similar stages in a process. The following section offers suggestions on how to support parents and families through the referral and assessment process, the placement and educational process, and the transition process.

Referral and Assessment

The first experience parents or family members may have with the special education system is during the initial referral and assessment process. For parents of children with LD this is often the culmination of months and sometimes years of frustration. Many have spent a considerable amount of time and sometimes money worrying about their child's progress, speculating about the reasons for failures, and placing blame on themselves or others. Smith (1998) states that some parents react to a diagnosis by becoming overindulgent, others by becoming distant and removed. Parents may experience a wide range of emotions including anger, inadequacy, and guilt. In reaction, Smith (1998) recommends that educators attend to parents' feelings, exercise patience through the emotional crisis, and remain available for support.

The challenges for parents and family members may not end just because the source of the difficulties is found. Parents in Dyson's (1996) study expressed dissatisfaction with the initial delayed diagnosis. During this process parents often feel their opinions or thoughts are of little concern and they perceive a lack of control over the entire system (Winters, 1993). Harry, Allen, and McLaughlin (1995) completed a 3-year investigation of the participation of African-American parents in special education programs. Utilizing interview and observational data, the authors found that the absence of meaningful communication throughout the assessment and placement process was the cause of much stress and confusion for the parents. Thus, this is a crucial time period for educators to engage in communication in order to form positive, trusting relationships with parents and family members.

The first step is to listen to and acknowledge the issues parents and family members raise. Vaughn, Bos, and Schumm (1997) list elements necessary for effective listening. These include listening for the real content and the underlying feelings in the message, restating content and reflecting feelings, and allowing the speaker an opportunity to confirm or correct your restatement. Referring back to the empowerment framework, educators can help prevent dissatisfaction with the referral and assessment process and alienation from the system by sharing knowledge of parents' rights in terms that avoid educational jargon. Along with some possible negative feelings toward the process, parents will have many questions including but not limited to the following: What is a learning disability? Exactly what is wrong with my child? What can we do? How did this happen? What can we expect the future to bring? Addressing questions and concerns through telephone conversations or meetings can also help parents alleviate stress as well as provide the educator with an opportunity to become familiar with the family prior to placement. By establishing a partnership early on, the likelihood that goals established by each participant will be reached is increased.

Answers to questions around the nature of LD need to be provided in clear, understandable terms. Parents need to understand that much is not known about the cause of LD and that there is no need to place blame on themselves or others for their child's diagnosis. In her practical book for parents, Stevens (1980) suggests a simple way to answer questions regarding what an LD is. She recommends describing four points that all professionals agree are true for individuals with LD including (1) the fact that individuals with LD do not learn satisfactorily from standard or traditional methods of instruction, (2) the basic cause of failure to learn is not a lack of normal intelligence, (3) the basic cause is not psychological in nature, and (4) the basic cause is not a physical disability, although one can be present.

Parents also need to understand the many options for degrees of involvement they have as they prepare to assist their child. As noted by Kavale, Forness, and Bender (1988), "Family time is precious, and extra time is rare, particularly today when over half of the nation's children live in homes where both parents are employed" (p. 229). Parents who are able to participate can do so at various levels. Although many experts in the field of parent involvement have described different levels of involvement, Epstein and Dauber (1989), citing earlier work, provide five types of parent involvement present in various school programs. The first level includes supporting parents as they meet basic obligations to their children such as developing parenting skills, caring for their health and safety, and ". . . building *positive home conditions* that support school learning and behavior across all school years" (p. 2). For parents of children with LD, this level may include support with behavior management plans, providing structure and support for homework, focusing on strengths, building persistence for task completion, and preventing the learning disability from becoming the central focus of the family. The next level involves basic obligations of the school such as communicating with parents in terms of student progress and conduct. Included in this level are the possible tasks of conveniently scheduling the IEP meeting so that parents are able to attend, creating and/or completing daily or weekly progress reports, and coordinating meetings or conversations with other educational personnel. The third level centers on the parent's involvement at school as a volunteer, a tutor, but also ". . . refers to parents who come to school to support student performances, sports, or other events" (p. 2). Participation at this and the next level should be based on an understanding of the family as a system and on what is best for all members. At the fourth level, schools support parent involvement in providing various learning activities in the home. This level includes providing information on helping students with homework, participating in decisions about educational placements, and insuring student success at each grade level. The last level addresses supporting parents as they become involved in governance and advocacy programs such as the PTA or advisory councils. At this level, educators can lend support by directing parents to local parent groups and state and national organizations. As always it is important to not overburden already stressed families. While some families may find participation in any of these groups helpful, others may simply not have the time, energy, or desire.

Parents may participate at any level at any given time, moving in and out of levels as time and energy permits. According to Wissbrun and Eckart (1992), parents typically weigh the following five factors before committing to any level or type of involvement: "(1) need/issue and degree of concern, (2) knowledge of the need/issue or a willingness to learn about it, (3) risk involved in becoming active, (4) amount of flexibility of time to devote to school participation, and (5) degree of commitment to make a difference" (p. 125). The key to any successful parent and family involvement is having a supported program in place. Dietz (1997) suggests having a board-approved policy in place that uses language that welcomes all families and encourages any level of involvement, having strongly committed leadership along with staff parents and students, designing a clear and complete program with well-defined roles, and including a needs assessment, goals statement, prioritization of activities, strategy development, implementation plans, and evaluation tools as part of the plan as ways to insure success.

Parents may want to wait until a placement is made to decide on the level of involvement that they wish to pursue. They can support their child during the referral and assessment stage by discussing what an LD is and how the assessment process will demonstrate the strengths the child possesses as well as any weaknesses. Parents can also discuss how the assistance students receive will help them to be more successful in school. Gaining information through available literature and the experiences of other parents is a good place to start. With this in mind, educators should provide informative literature to the parents and guide them toward formal associations or informal local groups wherein they may learn about what to expect from parents experienced in the process.

When communicating with parents about any of these questions, concerns, or issues, educators should consider the following as options:

- Send a letter home or invite parents to the school in order to explain the assessment process in understandable terms.
- Follow-up with a call to answer any questions.
- Avoid any educational jargon in correspondence.
- Invite parents to meet with assessment personnel prior to placement meetings.
- Introduce parents and family members to other parents or invite them to attend group meetings.
- Share with parents important information regarding learning disabilities and disability advocacy groups.
- Take time to listen to the parents and view all communications as opportunities to learn about the family.

Placement and the Educational Process

Deciding on and securing the most appropriate direct services for their children are among parents' most pressing needs (Simpson, 1996). Parents will also have many questions prior to making a decision regarding placement. These questions might include the following. What placement is best for my child? Will he always be enrolled in special education programs? How will I know if she is learning? How can I best support him at home? Can she participate in extra-curricular activities? Will he be able to socialize with other students besides those also in special education? The choices they make about the kind and amount of support they provide will depend on the strengths, interests and needs of their family. Before making any choices, they should consider their entire family and factors including available time and energy, hobbies and interests of siblings, and available support from extended family members.

Again, avoiding educational jargon is important. Rather than simply listing the placement options, educators need to explain what happens in the resource room or provide examples of what consultations might look like and what accommodations might include. The concept of inclusion should be explained and operationalized for the particular school setting. Parents may not be familiar with terms such as least restrictive environment, appropriate education, and due process or the differences between direct and indirect support. This would also be a good time to discuss the IEP as a collaboratively designed plan subject to all participants' input and requiring agreement by all parties in order to be accepted. It should be explained that parents and family members as well as the child are essential members of the IEP development team, and they should also know that the annual review of the IEP is *not* the only time that discussions should occur or changes could be made. Meetings to discuss progress toward the goals on the IEP can be held on a more regular basis or as needed depending on the specific needs of the child and the family. Harry (1992) suggests the parents be responsible for providing progress reports from home and school at IEP meetings as a way to increase involvement and reach a shared understanding.

Once placement occurs, regular communication is essential. By referring back to the family systems framework educators can begin to capitalize on the individual strengths of the family. For example, some family members may be better at communicating progress to educators while others may have a gift for helping the child to understand outside events. One member of the family may excel in organization and meeting preparation, whereas another may have a knack for keeping the atmosphere pleasant and congenial. Educators can also gain a better understanding of the needs of the family and address those in a personal way. If a partnership has already been established, educators may be aware of the level of involvement at which families are willing and able to participate. Due to extenuating circumstances in their lives, some family members may choose not to or be unable to participate in the education of their child to the extent educators expect. They may be working two or more jobs or dealing with health issues of either another member of the family or their own. Also, some families may be able to rely more heavily on extended family members while others may need support outside the family. Whatever the issues, educators need to realize that lack of participation is frequently not indicative of a lack of support or interest.

For parents and family members who are willing and able to become extensively involved in educating their children, tutoring at home is an option. Controlled studies on the effects of parents as tutors do exist and are worthy of mention. For example, in a study completed by Duvall, Delquadri, Elliott, and Hall (1992), parents were trained in a tutoring technique to help improve the reading skills of their elementary-aged children with LD. Researchers found that parental tutoring led to a substantial increase in correct answers on comprehension questions as well as moderate to significant increases on standardized achievement tests. Thurston and Dasta (1990) completed a similar study that also yielded positive results. Researchers found increased comprehension scores on teacher-made instruments and increased scores on a standardized test of reading comprehension. Although questions remain about the long-term effects of parent tutoring programs, if parents and children desire to participate in a home tutoring program available research lends support.

Facilitating the tutoring process requires considerable collaboration and communication from both sides. In the studies mentioned above, parents completed training sessions on tutoring techniques and record keeping. The sessions required the cooperation of the family in order for a quiet space to be available at a consistent time in the day. Possessing a knowledge of the family as a system will help educators to determine whether this level of involvement is appropriate for any family.

Acting as a tutor or teacher is not the only way parents and family members can support their children with LD. Mercer (1997) provides three categories of home-based services and activities including parent observations of their children, home management, and parents as teachers. Parents can lend support in a number of ways including discussing the school day, contacting teachers regularly to report or discuss progress, engaging their children in educational activities, and teaching their child strong advocacy and decision-making skills. Advantages to home-based parent and family interventions include

- Strong relationships between the child and primary caregiver can be built.
- Parent and family members have opportunities to work individually with the child.
- Interventions can begin early in the child's life.
- Parents experience increases in self-confidence and motivation to pursue education or job training.
- Parents become better advocates.
- Treatment will continue, or generalize, without the program.
- Other children in the household will benefit. (Kelleghan, Sloane, Alverez, & Bloom (1993).

Some disadvantages to home-based parent and family interventions include

- Time commitment may cause additional stress in the family.
- The work may interfere with the child–parent relationship.
- Time spent with one child is time taken away from siblings.
- Very little research has been done measuring the long-term effects of home-based interventions.

Regardless of the level of parent and family involvement, when communicating with parents about any of these questions, concerns, or issues, educators should consider the following as options:

- Invite parents to visit the special education setting and view any materials used.
- Provide additional literature that accurately and clearly describes available services.
- Assure parents and family members that their participation and their child's participation in IEP meetings is not only requested but desired and essential to providing their child with the best possible education.
- Explain to parents the pros and cons of various levels of involvement in their child's education.
- Accept parents' and family members' level of participation at any given time as their very best.
- Facilitate parent group meetings in order to better understand issues surrounding education, curriculum, and home support.
- Hold realistically high expectation for children and families.
- Avoid any educational jargon in correspondence.
- Take time to listen to the parents and view all communications as opportunities to learn about the family.

As children progress through school, placements may change annually. Along with these changes will come changes in the needs of the individual with LD and his or her parents and family. The next section address supporting parents and families during these frequent times of transition.

Transition Process

Anxiety about the future is often high in families where one or more child has a disability (Kavale, Forness, & Bender, 1988). Parents and families of children with LD can also lend support during time of transition. Transitions occur when students move from home to school, one grade level to another (e.g., the third grade to the fourth), one school level to another (e.g., elementary to middle), teacher to teacher within a grade level, and from the educational system to employment or postsecondary education. Based on data that show post secondary outcomes for individuals with disabilities such as employment, participation in secondary education, independent living, and adult adjustment to be significantly lower than those experienced by nondisabled individuals (Blackorby & Wagner, 1996), the field of special education has begun to examine closely the transition process. Throughout this examination, educators have been attempting to identify the components of the transition process that lead to success.

Although most of the work in the area of transition focuses on the transition from secondary education to postsecondary education or work (Halpern, 1993; Johnson & Rusch, 1993; Rojewski, 1992; Okolo & Sitlington, 1988), many educators view transitions more broadly (Blalock & Patton, 1996; Ropetto & Correa, 1996; Syzmanski, 1994). Syzmanski (1994) suggests that, because transitions occur across the span of a lifetime, they should be planned for throughout the school career. She states that transition planning should include a longitudinal focus with families as partners. Parental support for this perspective is apparent in an analysis of testimony from public hearings sponsored by the National Council on Disability. In their qualitative analysis of transcripts from the hearings, Lattin and Tronsdal (1994) found two major themes arising from the testimony with one theme woven throughout the topic of transition. The first theme was the stated belief that transition planning and services should span across a person's entire life. The second theme addressed changes that needed to be made in the process while the overriding theme was one of collaboration.

Halpern, Yovanoff, Dora, and Benz (1995) examined the predictive power of various variables in relation to students pursuing post-secondary education including whether parents were satisfied with the instruction their child received, parents' perception that their student no longer needed help, and whether the parent and student had similar expectations for the student's participation in post-secondary education. Six variables, including parent satisfaction with instruction and parent perception that student no longer needed help, were found to be predictive of student participation in post-secondary education. Much follow-up is needed; however, based on these findings, that parents possess valuable insights into what constitutes good instruction for their children as well as the competency level of their children is obvious. Thus their input in the transition process should be valued.

Although research in this field needs to continue, results from the studies described do indicate a desire and need to involve parents and families in the transition process. Similar to parental involvement in the educational process, involvement in the transition process will vary depending on the availability of the parents and the needs of the child. As transition planning places a focus on the future, parents and family members may have questions about the possibilities the future may hold. These questions may center on the appropriateness of career goals, the likelihood of attending college or other postsecondary options, readiness for independent living, and the general adult experiences of individuals with learning disabilities.

Once again, the empowerment approach can be used to guide this discussion. Parents and family members will need information about the transition process and also on the postsecondary options available to their children. Because of the high variability of skills and intellectual ability between individuals with LD, appropriate postsecondary options vary tremendously (Dunn, 1996). Thus, the transition planning process should include an assessment of the student's present level of functioning across academic areas but also include assessment of independent living and social skills. Results from this assessment must be useful to the parents and family members, the student, and educators in determining the student's needs, preferences, and interests (Clark, 1996). Through the sharing of this information along with information gleaned from conversations at home, sound decisions can be made. Utilizing the family systems approach will help to narrow the range of post-secondary options to ones that best fit the unique challenges and characteristics of the family.

Given the large numbers of transitions students must make, families of children with LD and educators might consider beginning this process long before the IDEA mandated age of 14. Blalock and Patton (1996) offer common themes heard throughout a recent transition symposium. These themes include the acknowledgment that (1) student participation is crucial, (2) efforts should be made to get families involved in the transition process, (3) transition efforts should start early, (4) transition planning must be sensitive to cultural factors, and (5) transition planning must be comprehensive. When communicating with parents about any of these questions, concerns, or issues, educators should consider the following as options:

- Assure parents and family members that their participation and their child's participation in transition planning meetings is not only requested but desired and essential to providing their child with the best possible education.
- Share with parents literature on adult outcomes.
- Complete transition assessments and share the results in understandable terms.

- Encourage parents to hold their child with disabilities responsible for the same household chores and employment responsibilities that his or her siblings completed.
- Encourage parents, family members, and children to dream about and plan for the future
- Begin instruction on self-advocacy as early as possible.
- Hold realistically high expectations for children and families.
- Share information about colleges with programs specifically designed for individuals with learning disabilities as well as vocational and occupational training programs.
- Avoid any educational jargon in correspondence.
- Take time to listen to the parents and view all communications as opportunities to learn about the family.

The next section addresses supporting parents and family members as they help their children with LD overcome difficulties with social and organization skills, and as they deal with complications that may arise in the home environment.

SUPPORTING PARENTS AND FAMILIES IN THE HOME ENVIRONMENT

> What I would like more than anything is for Anthony to have some friends his own age. I know he's a little immature, but I just think that if kids would take the time to get to know him, they might like him. He's always sort of heard his own drummer. Although I think this makes him interesting, his peers probably think he is weird. He just has a difficult time communicating with people he doesn't know very well. He's a genuinely nice kid though.

> We have five children in our family, and they are all in school right now. For the most part, our kids like school. They do well. The problem is that Jennifer wants to do just as well as her brothers and sisters. I want her to succeed too, but helping her takes so much time. Finishing assignments and studying for tests takes her twice as long as it does for her older sisters. She resents this, but her sisters do, too. Time spent helping Jennifer is time that we could be spending on recreation or attending to the many other things going on in our household I've missed many volleyball and softball games staying home to help Jennifer. Her sisters remind me of this often.

All students who are identified as having LD share some common ground. Their identification likely stemmed from repeated, unexplainable failure in one or more academic area. At some point in time, they will have gone through the referral and assessment stages, will be eligible for placement in a special education program, and will encounter many transitions throughout their school career. In most cases the similarities end there. For example, not all students with disabilities demonstrate deficits in the same academic area, respond well to the same instructional programs, or share the same strengths. Many, however, do have difficulties in the areas of social and organizational skills, and many families struggle with the pressure of maintaining a balance between helping their child with LD and attending to the needs of the rest of the family.

Enhancing the Development of Social and Organizational Skills

As was mentioned earlier, individuals with LD have been found to have lower self-concept, lower peer acceptance rates (Vaughn, Elbaum, & Schumm, 1996), and lower engagement rates on academic tasks (McIntosh, Vaughn, Schumm, Haager, & Lee, 1993) than their nondisabled peers. Lower self-concept is often the cause of the unexplained failures experienced prior to identification. Multiple failures may prove traumatic for many students and result in a total loss of confidence and inability to take academic risks. Scanlon (1996) lists three factors to which poor social skills in the classroom may be linked: limited opportunity to learn, negative academic and social self-concept, and social isolation. Recognizing that not all students with LD demonstrate poor social skills, Scanlon provides a range of possibilities related to social skill functioning. This range includes no social skills problems, poor constructive communication skills in such areas as asking questions, offering opinions, and judging social roles and negative consequences such as being ignored by others, judged to be less desirable, and making inappropriate social decisions.

Educators can help parents grapple with this problem by evaluating the extent to which the social behavior is problematic and recommending interventions or counseling as needed. Involving parents in the assessment of social skills through direct observations and completion of checklists will help to develop awareness and focus attention on specific, problematic behaviors. Strategies do exist for teaching social skills to children with learning disabilities. Many, but not all, have a parent involvement component. (See Scanlon, 1996 for a recent review.)

Children with LD often lack organizational skills. Teachers may choose o teach strategies for helping children to organize themselves and their assignments. Many middle and high schools issue daily planners for students to use to record important assignments, tests, and events. The Quality Quest Planner (Hughes, Ruhl, Rademacher, Schumaker, & Deshier, 1995) can help students keep track of assignments on a monthly basis, plan weekly schedules to accomplish all of their goals, and track their grades. The Quality Quest Planner was designed to help students not only be well organized but to be able to complete assignments appropriately. To this end, the Assignment Completion Strategy has been developed to help students complete and turn in high quality assignments (Hughes, Ruhl, Deshler, & Schumaker, 1995). Parents can become actively involved in the use of a planner such as the Quality Quest Planner and the learning of a strategy such as the Assignment Completion Strategy by systematically checking the planner for use and discussing the effectiveness of the strategy with their children. As the planner should go to and from school every day, it can also serve as a source of communication between home and school. In schools that do not issue planners, educators should secure one or recommend to parents that they purchase one for their child and assist them in setting up a plan for its use.

Parents can also help improve the organization skills of their children by providing a neat, well-lighted place for studying that is free of distraction. Having designated times for studying wherein all of the children do homework and parents are available for assistance demonstrates that homework is a valued, normal part of the day. Asking students to bring home a daily or weekly assignment sheet that parents check and sign will not only help children stay organized but it will also serve as another possible communication device to inform parents about the work being completed and the progress of their children.

Enhancing the Home Environment

Kavale, Forness, and Bender (1988) point out that parents and other family members need to exercise caution in not letting the LD become the ultimate focus of the family. Although time spent on academic remediation in the home may produce immediate gains in school, the long-term effects of the time taken from other siblings and family activities must by considered. Kavale, Forness, and Bender (1988) state that siblings can serve as social and emotional models and in this role can help to further the development of the child with disabilities; however, in their discussion of parent and sibling interventions they go on to offer possible effects felt by siblings of children with LD. These effects range from pressures to succeed and over-achieving to feelings of neglect, guilt, and a reluctance to show their true abilities. The authors further state that, "Within the life cycle perspective, the potential problems faced by siblings of the LD child are a consideration of anxiety reactions to parental concerns, and role distortions occurring as a result of the increased attention to the LD child" (p. 225). With this in mind, educators need to support parents in exercising great care to insure the emotional well-being of their nondisabled children. Some families will handle this situation with relative ease and will be able to balance the needs of all siblings, whereas others may need professional assistance. In situations that may require family counseling, an understanding of the family as a system will help educators to know if counseling is desired and possible.

SUMMARY

Although many educators may view collaborating with parents and families of children with LD as a burden to be avoided as much as possible and tolerated when avoidance is impossible this view isn't necessary. What is needed is a goal of mutual empowerment reached through collaborative partnerships in which all parties benefit. When educators take an empowering approach and begin to view families as systems with many strengths and interests mutual goals are more likely to be met. Educators can apply the empowerment approach and a family systems framework as parents, families, and children work through various stages including referral and assessment, placement in the educational process, and through various times of transition. Finally, educators can lend support in dealing with social and organizational skills as well as issues that may arise in the home. The collaborative partnerships that are built will benefit all parties involved especially the children.

REFERENCES

Andrews, J. & Luport, J. (1993). *The inclusive classroom: Educating exceptional children.* Scarborough, Ontario: Nelson Canada.

Atkins, S. P. (1991). Siblings of learning disabled children: Are they special too? *Child and Adolescent Social Work Journal, 8,* 525–533.

Blalock, G. & Patton, J. R. (1996). Transition and students with learning disabilities: Creating sound futures. *Journal of Learning Disabilities, 29*(1), 7–16.

Blackorby, J., & Wagner, M. (1996). Longitudinal postschool outcomes of youth with disabilities: Findings from the National Longitudinal Transition study. *Exceptional Children, 62,* 399–413.

Clark, G. M. (1996).Transition planning assessment for secondary-level students with learning disabilities. *Journal of Learning Disabilities, 29*(1), 79–92.

Dietz, M. J. (1997). *School, family, and community: Techniques and models for successful collaboration.* Gaithersburg, MD: Aspen Publishers, Inc.

Dunn, C. (1996). A status report on transition planning for individuals with learning disabilities. *Journal of Learning Disabilities, 29*(1), 17–30.

Duvall, S. F., Delquadri, J. C., Elliott, M., & Hall, R. V. (1992). Parent-tutoring procedures: Experimental analysis and validation of generalization in oral reading across passages, settings, and time. *Journal of Behavioral Education, 2*(3), 281–303.

Dyson, L. L. (1996). The experiences of families of children with learning disabilities: Parental stress, family functioning, and sibling self-concept. *Journal of Learning Disabilities, 29*(3), 280–286.

Epstein, J. L. (1991). Effects on student achievement of teachers' practices of parental involvement. *Advances in Teaching Language Research* (5), 261–276. Greenwich, CT: JAI Press.

Epstein, J. L. & Dauber, S. L. (1989). *Teachers attitudes and practices of parent involvement in inner-city elementary and middle schools.* Johns Hopkins University: The Center for Research on Elementary and Middle Schools. Supported by OERI grant number OERI-G-90006.

Halpern, A. S. (1993). Quality of life as a conceptual framework for evaluating transition outcomes, *Exceptional Children, 59*(6), 486–498.

Halpern, A. S., Yovanoff, P., Dora, B., & Benz, M. R. (1995). Predicting participation in postsecondary education for school learners with disabilities, *Exceptional Children, 62*(2), 151–164.

Harry, B. (1992). Restructuring the participation of African-American parents in special education. *Exceptional Children, 59*(21), 123–131.

Harry, B., Allen, N., & McLaughlin, M. (1995, April). Communication versus compliance: African American parents involvement in special education. *Exceptional Children, 61*(4), 364–377.

Hughes, Ruhl, Deshler, & Schumaker, (1995). *The Assignment Completion Strategy.* Lawrence, KS: Edge Enterprises.

Hughes, Ruhl, Rademacher, & Schumaker, (1995). *The Quality Quest Planner.* Lawrence, KS: Edge Enterprises.

Kavale, K. A., Forness, S. R., & Bender, M. (1988). *Handbook of learning disabilities volume II: Methods and interventions.* Boston: Little, Brown, & Co.

Johnson, J. R. & Rusch, F. R. (1993). Secondary special education and transition services: Identification and recommendations for future research and demonstration. *Career Development for Exceptional Individuals, 16*(1), 1–18.

Kellaghan, T., Sloane, K., Alvarez, B., & Bloom, B. S. (1993). *The home environment and schooling: Promoting parental involvement in the education of children.* San Francisco: Jossey-Bass Publishers.

Lattin, D. L. & Tronsdal, T. (1994). Transition services: IDEA testimony analysis. University of Kansas, Unpublished manuscript.

McIntosh, R., Vaughn, S., Schumm, J. S., Hanger, D., & Lee, O. (1993). Observations of students with learning disabilities in general education classrooms. *Exceptional Children, 60*(3), 249–261.

Mercer, C. D. (1997). *Students with Learning Disabilities* (5th ed.). New York: Prentice Hall.

O'Hara, D. M. & Levy, J. M. (1984). Family adaptation to learning disability: A framework for understanding and treatment. *Learning Disabilities: An Interdisciplinary Journal,* *3*(6), 63–77.

Okolo, C. M. & Sittington, P. (1988). The role of special education in LD adolescents' transition from school to work. *Learning Disability Quarterly, 9,* 141–155.

Rojewski, J. W. (1992). Key components of model transition services for students with learning disabilities. *Learning Disabilities Quarterly, 15*(2), 135–150.

Ropetto, J. B. & Correa, V. I. (1996). Expanding views on transition. *Exceptional Children, 62*(2), 551–563.

Scanlon, D. (1996). Social skills strategy instruction, In *Teaching adolescents with learning disabilities: Strategies and methods* (2nd ed.). D. D. Deshler, E. S. Ellis, & B. K. Lenz (Eds.), Denver: Love Publishing.

Schumaker, J. B. & Hazel, J. Stephen. (1984). Social skills assessment and training for the learning disabled: Who's on first and what's on second? Part 1. *Journal of Learning Disabilities, 17*(7), 422–431.

Schumaker, J. B., Pederson, C. S., Hazel, J. Stephen, & Meyen, E. L. (1983). Social skills curricula for mildly handicapped adolescents: A review. *Focus on Exceptional Children, 16*(4), 1–16.

Simpson, R. L. (1996). *Working with parents and families of exceptional children and youth: Techniques for successful conferencing and collaboration,* (3rd ed.) Austin, TX: PRO-ED, Inc.

Simpson, R. L. & Kamps, D. W. (1996). Parental involvement in Exceptional children in today's schools, (3rd ed.) E. Meyen (Ed.). Denver: Love Publishing Co.

Smith, C. R. (1998). *Learning Disabilities: the interaction of learner, task, and setting.* (4th ed,) Boston: Allyn & Bacon.

Stevens, S. H. (1980). *The learning-disabled child: Ways that parents can help.* Winston-Salem, N.C.: John F. Blair, Publisher.

Syzmanski. E. M. (1994). Transition: Life-span and life space considerations for empowerment. *Exceptional Children, 60*(5), 402–410.

Thurston, L. P. & Dasta, K. (1990). An analysis of in-home parent tutoring procedures: Effects on children's academic behavior at home and in school and on parent's tutoring behaviors. *Remedial and Special Education, 11*(4), 41–52.

Turnbull, A. P. & Turnbull, H. R. (1997). Families, professionals, and exceptionality: A special partnership, Third Edition. Columbus, OH: Merrill.

Vaughn, S., Bos, C. S. & Schumm, J. S. (1997). Teaching mainstreamed diverse, and at-risk students in the general education classroom. Boston: Allyn & Bacon.

Vaughn, S., Elbaum, B. E. & Schumm, J. S. (1996). The effects of inclusion on the social functioning of students with learning disabilities. *Journal of Learning Disabilities, 29*(6), 598–608.

Wissbrun, D. & Eckart, J. A. (1992). Hierarchy of parental involvement in schools. In *Education and the family,* L. Kaplan (Ed.), Boston: Allyn & Bacon.

Winters, W. G. (1993). *African American mothers and urban schools: The power of participation.* New York: Lexington Books.

Ysseldyke, J. E., Algozzine, B., & Thurlow, M. L. (1991). *Critical issues in special education* (2nd ed.). Boston: Houghton Mifflin Company.

CHAPTER 12

Parenting Children with Brain Injury

William J. Warzak

Department of Pediatrics, Munroe-Meyer Institute for Genetics and Rehabilitation,
University of Nebraska Medical Center, Omaha, Nebraska

Cynthia M. Anderson

Department of Psychology, West Virginia University, Morgantown, West Virginia

Children with brain injuries comprise a unique subset of children with special needs. The child-rearing issues that confront the parents of these children can be perplexing and often are more complex than those encountered by the parents of other special needs children. For example, brain injuries are typically acquired, often occur suddenly, and require parents to rapidly adapt to changing circumstances. Further, a brain-injured child's neuropsychological profile may be scattered, with unusual patterns of cognitive and behavioral functioning. The considerable variability often evident during recovery can render behavior difficult to predict, and unforeseen and uncommon complications may stress parents already overwhelmed by the parenting requirements incumbent in raising a child.

This chapter addresses these issues from the perspective of parent training. Parents are perhaps the most important influence in the lives of children and training parents to shape and maintain a child's adaptive behavior has a long and fruitful history. To provide a context for training parents of brain-injured children, we begin with a brief review of the nature of brain injuries and the cognitive and behavioral sequelae that often result from them. Next, methods of parent training are reviewed. Contributions to the empirical parenting literature relevant to special populations and the parenting of children with traumatic brain injury (TBI), in particular, are addressed. Based on this literature, we provide a summary of behavioral principles and procedures that may be effective in parenting children and youth with brain injury. We conclude the chapter with a discussion of two difficult issues often faced by families of children with brain injury: re-integrating a child into his or her social environment (e.g., school, community) and learning to adapt to living with a child who often is markedly different than he or she was pre-injury.

BRAIN INJURY AND ITS SEQUELAE

Brain injury is a leading cause of mortality and morbidity among children and adolescents (Brandstater, Bontke, Cobble, & Horn, 1991). It is esti-mated that 1 out of every 25 children will experience some form of a head trauma by the time they graduate from high school and that as many as 8 to 20% of all special education students have sustained a TBI that predates their eligibility for special education services (Savage, 1991). Even minor head injuries that involve no loss of consciousness may result in impaired attention, memory, and emotional control (Binder, 1986; Levin, Benton, & Grossman, 1982) or may exacerbate pre-existing cognitive deficits (Dean, 1985). In addition, because a child's injury may interrupt normal neurological development, deficits may not be immediately apparent at the time of injury (Rutter, Chadwick, & Shaffer, 1983). Indeed, the full extent of a child's injury may not be apparent for several years depending upon a number of factors including its location and severity, the age of the child at the time of injury, and whether the injury was the result of closed head trauma or a penetrating wound.

Depth and duration of coma and duration of posttraumatic amnesia (PTA) are among the best indicators of an injury's severity and likely course (Alexander, 1984; Levin, Benton, & Grossman, 1982; McGuire & Rothenberg, 1986). Based upon these and other factors, TBI may be de-scribed as mild, moderate, or severe, with differing levels of residual im-pairment. For example, children with severe injuries may experience chronic speech and language impairment, significant deficits in attention and concentration, memory, reasoning, and impulse control. Motor im-pairment and behavioral and affective disturbance are common (Mitiguy, Thompson, & Wasco, 1990). Children who present with this level of impairment will not be able to function independently and may require much day-to-day care.

Moderate injuries result in less severe impairment, but even patients who make a relatively good recovery frequently complain of persistent headaches, memory deficits, and difficulties with activities of daily living, including interacting with friends and family (Rimmel, Giordani, Barth, Boll, & Jane, 1981). Many moderately and severely injured children recover some previously learned cognitive abilities, with most of these gains seen in the first year post-injury (Jaffe, Polissar, Fay, & Lao, 1995; Koskiniemi, Kyykka, Nybo, & Jarho, 1995). Subsequently, adaptive living skills may continue to improve, whereas intellectual, neurocognitive, and academic functioning tend to plateau. Performance levels often remain substantially below that of their pre-injury status and below that of uninjured peers (Jaffe et al., 1995).

Mild brain injury (e.g., minimal cerebral bruising, swelling, or tissue strain) accounts for approximately 80% of all closed head injuries (Kraus, Black, Hessol, Ley, Rokaw, Sullivan, Bowers, Knowlton, & Marshall, 1984), with an annual incidence of approximately 250,000 potential concussive injuries occurring in high school contact sports alone (Cantu, 1988; LeBlanc, 1994). Up to 50% of patients who sustain mild head injuries report symptoms months later (Rimmel et al., 1981; Rutherford, 1989), with headaches and impaired memory continuing as long as one year post-injury (Evans, Evans, & Sharp, 1994). Even subtle residual deficits may have considerable impact on social, familial, and academic functioning (Eisenberg, 1989; Levin, Benton, & Grossman, 1982; Rosenthal, 1983). Forty-five percent of families surveyed by Hu and colleagues (Hu, Wesson, Kenney, Chipman, & Spence, 1993) reported that their lives had not returned to normal 6 months post-concussion, with 23% continuing to report disrupted family functioning up to 1 year post-injury. Behavioral changes may be misinterpreted by parents and school staff as lack of motivation, noncompliance, or defiance. Because behavior may be affected by injury as well as by concurrent developmental and environmental factors, it may be difficult to determine the controlling variables for any particular behavior (Warzak, Allan, Ford, & Stefans, 1995).

For example, frontal lobe syndrome may present as behavioral excesses that are maintained not only by defective contingencies of reinforcement but also are exacerbated by defective self-monitoring, self-regulation, and difficulty responding to changing environmental circumstances (i.e., difficulty learning from experience; Warzak, Evans & Ford, 1992). Similarly, some children, particularly those with right hemisphere injuries, may not read social cues accurately and may demonstrate a lack of social awareness, also resulting in inappropriate social behavior at home and elsewhere (Borod & Koff, 1990). That is, these children may possess appropriate social behavior, but have difficulty interpreting social cues that dictate when such behavior should be emitted. In both of these examples, a confluence of developmental, behavioral, and neuropsychological factors may obscure a clear etiology for behavioral dysfunction and make relevant parenting decisions difficult.

PARENT TRAINING

Parenting a child with a brain injury presents special challenges. Problem behavior may be less amenable to previously effective parenting strategies given the child's current neuropsychological status and behavioral repertoire. For example, the simple verbal delivery of requests or commands may no longer be sufficient if the child's ability to respond to auditory stimuli, understand spoken language or retain commands over time has deteriorated. Also, stimuli, events, and conditions that previously served to reinforce or punish behavior may no longer be effective because of changes in cognitive functioning (e.g., changes in perceptual, sensory, or motor functioning).

Nevertheless, parents of children with brain injury may benefit from strategies with proven effectiveness across a wide variety of children and problem behaviors. Although brain injuries may affect behavior targeted for intervention and the particular procedures used in treatment, the behavioral principles that underlie those procedures have great generality and may be used to guide treatment (cf. Honig and Staddon, 1977; Leitenberg, 1976; Warzak and Kilbourn 1990). In that regard, behavioral parent training, grounded in the principles of behavioral psychology, is increasingly recognized as one of the most effective methods available for managing the behavior of children and youth. This approach typically involves teaching parents specific ways of interacting with their children, thereby fostering the development of an adaptive and appropriate repertoire, that is, the focus is on changing the behavior of the parent to effect changes in the child's behavior.

Although behavioral parent training is widely used, no research has evaluated the efficacy of structured parent training programs for parents of children with brain injuries, perhaps reflecting the diverse nature of brain injuries and their sequelae. Such diversity may preclude development of structured parent training programs, but it is possible to extrapolate from other programs and adapt procedures to the needs of children with brain injuries. In this section we briefly review approaches to parent training that have been effective for unimpaired children as well as for children impaired by other sorts of developmental delays. Next we extract common features of these programs and extend them to children with brain injury.

Parent Training for Typically Developed Children

Behavioral parent training strategies for unimpaired children have burgeoned in recent years. Clinic-based therapies, parenting books, videos, and CD-ROMS have become widely available. The efficacy of clinic-based behavioral parent training, in particular, has been demonstrated in many studies. For example, studies have shown that clinic-based parent training programs result in improved parental behavior management skills and concomitant decreases in child problem behaviors (e.g., Eyberg & Robinson, 1982; Webster-Stratton, 1985). Additionally, parents report that child adjustment improved and they feel better able to manage their child's behavior following behavioral parent training (Patterson & Fleischman, 1979; Webster-Stratton, 1985; Webster-Stratton, Hollinsworth, & Kolpacoff, 1989). Research also has demonstrated that treatment gains are maintained after treatment ends (Forehand, Rogers, McMahon, Wells, & Griest, 1981; Long, Forehand, Wierson, & Morgan, 1994; Patterson & Fleischman, 1979; Webster-Stratton, 1984).

Clinic-based parent training typically involves weekly meetings between a therapist, child, and his or her parents. The focus is on parent–child interaction and parents are taught specific behavior management strategies. For example, parents may be taught how to give effective instructions, make effective transitions, or minimize distractions and how to deliver consequences (e.g., selective ignoring, timeout, contingent removal of a privilege) following challenging behavior. Similar strategies may be used to facilitate the acquisition of desirable target behaviors. Reinforcing desirable behavior when it occurs increases the frequency of that behavior and correspondingly decreases the time available for problem behavior. In addition, reinforcing desirable behavior makes other strategies, such as time-out, more effective by ensuring contrast between reinforcement and its absence.

An example of a clinic-based behavioral parent training package is

Parent–Child Interaction Therapy (PCIT) developed by Hembree-Kigin and McNeil (1995). Like most behavioral parent training programs, PCIT is a multicomponent parent-training package. Parents are first taught specific "relationship enhancement" skills such as using labeled praise (e.g., "I like the way you are sitting quietly" and descriptive statements (e.g., "You put the red block on the top"). When parents are able to use these skills effectively, they are taught "discipline" skills designed to increase their child's compliance and decrease problem behavior. Parents are taught how to give instructions and use time-out through therapist instruction, modeling, behavioral rehearsal, and role play. Supervised interactions with their children, in session, are used to ensure skill acquisition. During directed parent-child practice, therapists provide parents with feedback via an in-ear listening device (i.e., "bug in the ear") that allows the therapist to talk to the parent without disrupting the interaction. Parents are given homework assignments to practice new skills between sessions.

Parenting "self-help" books offer an alternative to clinic-based services. Biblio therapy may be useful for parents who want to improve their parenting skills but are unwilling or unable to attend clinic sessions. Most behavioral parent training books are designed to provide parents with specific child management strategies that have demonstrated efficacy. Frequently used behavioral parent training books include *Little People* (Christophersen, 1988), *SOS! Help for Parents: A Practical Guide for Handling Common Everyday Behavior Problems* (*SOS*; Clark, 1996), and *Families: Applications of Social Learning to Family Life* (Patterson, 1975), a classic programmed learning guide to parenting. All begin by providing a behavioral framework within which parents can understand their child's behavior; illustrating that any behavior that continues to occur, whether it is appropriate or inappropriate, is somehow maintained by environmental consequences. These books provide parents with specific strategies to increase appropriate behavior (e.g., rewarding good behavior, helping a child practice good behavior) and decrease inappropriate behavior (e.g., ignoring, time-out, removal of privileges). As with most clinic-based therapies, behavioral parent training books typically provide parents with well-proven behavioral strategies in a format that is easily used and understood.

Parent Training for Children with Brain Injury

Parenting a child with a brain injury requires a sensitivity to the uncommon needs of these children and a need to integrate varied sources of evaluative data into one cohesive management program. In our view, parent training for children with brain injury requires more than off-the-shelf protocols to facilitate acquisition of adaptive behavior or to manage problem behavior. Instead, parents may benefit most from learning problem-solving approaches and how to generalize those approaches to a variety of target behaviors. Such a strategy would provide parents with the skills to solve both now and in the future.

Brain-injured children present with unique characteristics that necessitate a specialized approach to behavior management encompassing both environmental and brain-behavior variables. Efforts to tailor parenting strategies to match the specific needs of these children may require extensive preliminary assessment that includes both a neuropsychological and behavioral evaluation prior to intervention. We next present recommendations for evaluation and treatment that are extrapolated both from current work with children with brain injuries as well as from relevant research with unimpaired children and children with developmental disabilities. Our aim is to provide caregivers with the skills they need to promote the acquisition of adaptive behavior, as well as identify, quantify, and manage a variety of challenging behavior. Given the unique nature of the brain-injured child, we believe a grounding in these fundamentals will result in the most effective "parent-training" for this very special population.

Neuropsychological Evaluation

A neuropsychological evaluation of a child with TBI may be needed to determine basic brain-behavior integrity. A comprehensive neuropsychological assessment examines brain-behavior relationships through tests that assess specific domains of brain functioning, especially those sensitive to impairment as a function of brain damage. A typical evaluation requires approximately 4 to 6 hr of testing, depending upon the presenting problem and the assessment methods selected. Neuropsychological assessment may determine current levels of functioning in critical brain-behavior relationships such as attention, memory, perceptual-motor skills, etc., and may assist in identification of salient stimuli and potential child responsiveness to discriminative stimuli and ostensibly reinforcing consequences.

Behavioral Assessment and Treatment Strategies

Having taken note of neuropsychological factors that affect their child's behavior, parents must consider the environmental factors that influence everyday functioning. Recognition of these provides the fundamental keys to parenting children, regardless of their cognitive status. Prior to initiating a treatment plan for a child with problematic behavior, behavioral objectives must be developed for both parent and child. For the parent, knowledge of behavioral fundamentals must be imparted; for the child, behavioral objectives must be selected and defined. Optimally, target behavior will be defined sufficiently to permit quantification. Our initial emphasis is on parenting tasks that facilitate the acquisition of new behavioral competencies and the reliable performance of skills present in the child's repertoire. Next, we focus on strategies to decrease problematic behavior. Finally, we delineate strategies to assist parents in re-integrating their child into his or her social and academic environment.

Skill Acquisition

Following a brain injury, a child may need to relearn skills that previously were in his or her repertoire. For example, a child may no longer be able to dress himself or independently walk to the school bus stop. The first step in the development and maintenance of a new skill is to complete a task analysis by dissecting the skill into component behavioral objectives. If, for example, the goal is to teach the child to bathe independently, component steps might involve gathering bathing supplies, turning on the water, checking the temperature, adjusting the temperature as necessary, removing clothing, getting in the tub, etc. The behavior required to meet each objective should be operationally defined to permit accurate measurement of performance and to facilitate the delivery of appropriate consequences contingent upon the child's behavior. For example, the step, "washing hair" could be defined as wetting the hair, taking the lid off the shampoo bottle, pouring shampoo into the hand, and rubbing it on the head for 15 sec, rinsing for 30 sec, etc. The response requirements of each task should be carefully considered to ensure that they remain within the range of the child's current behavioral competency. Special consideration should be given to the child's current limitations, both cognitive and motoric, that arise as a function of brain injury. The child may be less coordinated, motorically slower, less responsive to previously effective preinjury cues and consequences. For example, the child may be able to remove his or her clothes but may initially need assistance in checking the temperature of the water. As the child progresses the level of assistance required to successfully complete each step should be gradually decreased.

Parents should keep in mind that many children will clearly recall their pre-injury abilities and be fully aware of recently acquired limitations. The child may respond emotionally to situations previously mastered but now beyond their capability. Therefore, extrinsic incentives may be needed to shape, increase, and maintain newly acquired skills. Although the child may have bathed independently and without extrinsic rewards pre-injury, it may now be necessary to use incentives (e.g., points redeemable for various rewards, stickers, snacks) to motivate the child to complete various steps of the bathing routine.

The selection of consequences used to motivate a child's performance needs to be carefully considered. Unlike unimpaired children, the child with a brain injury may have experienced physical or neuropsychological changes that render him or her unable to perceive or respond to previously effective consequences. Potential reinforcers may be identified through discussion with the child, completion of reinforcer survey schedules (e.g., Cautela & Kastenbaum, 1967; Clement & Richard, 1976; Elliot, 1993), and by observing a child's daily preferred activities. Potential reinforcers also can be determined by conducting a choice assessment, during which the child is systematically presented with and allowed to briefly interact with a variety of stimuli and the child's response to each is recorded (Pace, Ivancic, Edwards, Iwata, & Page, 1985; Piazza, Fisher, Hagopian, Bowman, & Toole, 1996). Those that evoke the most interest (as measured by reaching for the object, looking at it, etc.) are selected as potential rewards. Once potentially reinforcing stimuli, events, or conditions have been identified, they can be used to reinforce more appropriate behavior by allowing the child access to them after a desirable behavior has occurred. For example, if parents would like their child to say "hello" when greeting someone, parents could provide the child with a preferred item (e.g., their attention via eye contact, verbal praise, a parental touch) following the child's saying "hello" in an appropriate context.

It is important to note that stimuli that function as reinforcers vary widely depending on a child's age and level of functioning, as well as individual preferences. If one item is used too often, the child may satiate (lose interest in obtaining the reward), and the item will no longer function to motivate behavior. Thus, a variety of items should be used to shape and maintain targeted behavior. One strategy that often works well is to write the names of rewards on index cards or slips of paper and place several slips in a "grab bag" from which the child draws a slip when he or she earns a reward. This ensures that a variety of reinforcers will be used. Similarly, items can be listed on a reinforcer menu, with selections from the menu contingent upon the occurrence of the target behavior.

Finally, although many tangible items such as snacks, small trinkets, or television time may function as rewards, parents may want to ensure that intangible rewards, such as parental attention are paired with the presentation of these consequences as well being used as consequences in their own right. In the former case, a verbal "thank you" or other form of verbal praise should accompany the extrinsic consequence.

Addressing Problem Behavior

Some children with acquired brain injury exhibit significant challenging behavior. Moderate to severe injuries tend to provoke higher rates of intense and aggressive behavior during early stages of recovery, but these often will resolve while the child is still an inpatient; and therefore, they may not be the focus of parent training, per se. Mild injuries typically present with less severe behavior problems, and in some cases parents may not need ongoing formal consultation. Rather, parents may consult one of the previously mentioned parenting books for suggestions. If behavior problems are more severe or persistent, however, a more focused approach may be required. In such cases, a functional assessment should be conducted to guide treatment. Based on the results of the functional assessment, a comprehensive treatment plan can be developed. A comprehensive treatment plan for challenging behaviors typically includes three key components: (1) ecological changes, (2) skill building, and (3) structured differential consequences provided contingent upon the occurrence of challenging behavior and appropriate behavior (see O'Neil et al., 1997 for detailed information on conducting a functional assessment and developing a comprehensive behavior support plan).

Conducting a Functional Assessment

When working with children who exhibit challenging behavior it often is useful to conduct a pretreatment functional assessment. Using specific techniques, such as interviews and direct observation, it is possible to identify environmental events that trigger (i.e., antecedents) and maintain (i.e., consequences) problem behavior. To illustrate: a child's challenging behavior may be triggered by such events as the presentation of tasks (e.g., requests to clean a room) or removal of preferred activities (e.g., putting toys away at bed time). Additionally, the behavior may be maintained by such events as attention from others (e.g., parental attention), access to preferred toys or activities (e.g., being allowed to continue playing), or escape or avoidance of some unpleasant activity (e.g., cleaning the room). Once the environmental variables related to challenging behavior are identified, treatment involves altering those variables in some way. For example, if a child's tantrums appear to be maintained by parental attention, one possible treatment might be to ignore tantrum behavior or to isolate the child from parental attention (i.e., time-out). The child could be taught a more appropriate means of gaining attention, such as raising his hand or saying, "Excuse me," or "Play with me." In contrast, if the behavior is maintained by escape or avoidance contingencies, an appropriate treatment might involve not allowing the child to avoid tasks when challenging behavior occurs. Rather, he or she might be permitted to take brief breaks in routine for appropriately saying "Stop," or "Break please."

A variety of direct and indirect functional assessment methodologies have been developed and can be adapted for parental use. Indirect functional assessment methodologies involve gathering information about the target behaviors and the environmental variables that are associated with it without observing the child. One example is the Functional Analysis Interview (FAI; O'Neill et al., 1997). The FAI provides a structured format to gather information about (1) the topography (i.e., description), frequency, and intensity of the behavior(s) of interest; (2) antecedent events, setting events, and establishing operations; and (3) consequences maintaining behavior. The interview allows also for the assessment of a variety of adaptive behaviors, including communication and daily living skills, and it may assist in the identification of potential reinforcers to motivate behavior change.

Direct methods of functional assessment involve observing an individual's behavior in typical environments (e.g., home, school). Typically, such an assessment involves recording each occurrence of the target behavior as well as antecedent and consequent events. Repeated collection of such data over time (e.g., over 1 or 2 weeks) allows parents to identify functional relations between a behavior and environmental antecedents and consequences. One example of a descriptive analysis is the A-B-C (antecedent-behavior-consequence) analysis chart (Sulzer-Azaroff & Mayer, 1977). This chart provides a format for parents to record what happened just before and just after challenging behavior occurs over a prespecified period of time. A sample A-B-C observation form is included in Table 1. Using this form, parents or professionals record the date of the observation and target behavior(s) being evaluated.

When a target behavior occurs, the time of the behavior and the situation in which the behavior occurred is recorded. This involves identifying

TABLE 1 Functional Assessment Observation Form

Target Behaviors:
1. _____ defined as: _____
2. _____ defined as: _____
3. _____ defined as: _____

		ANTECEDENT			BEHAVIOR	CONSEQUENCE	
Date	Time	What is the location?	Who is present?	What is occurring?	Behavior	Who acted?	What did they do?

who was present, the location and what was occurring (e.g., mom asked the child to clean up, the child was playing alone). Also, what happened following the behavior would be noted in terms of who responded and specifically what they did (e.g., mother prompted the child to move, sister moved away from the child). Once several instances of a behavior have been observed, it is possible to look for patterns of behavior. For example, challenging behavior may occur most often when the child is asked to do something (e.g., take out the trash, clean his room), and typical consequences might be that the task is removed or delayed (e.g., the child is sent to time-out, thus avoiding completing the task for several minutes or that the task is completed by the parent). Conversely, disruptive behavior may occur in response to "don't" commands or when the child is denied requests.

Developing a Comprehensive Treatment Plan

The first step in developing a plan to reduce challenging behavior often involves making ecological changes. Ecological changes are environmental changes implemented before the problem behavior occurs, with the goal of making challenging behavior less likely to occur. Such changes should be made based on the results of the functional assessment. For example, many individuals with moderate to severe injury, or acute mild injuries have difficulty coping with complex social stimuli (Alexander, 1984; Goethe & Levin, 1984; Lezak, 1989). If challenging behavior often occurs when the child is in large, noisy groups, efforts could be made to minimize the amount of time the child spends in such settings, or to allow the individual to leave the situation when needed. Similarly, the functional assessment may reveal that problems are more likely to occur at the end of the child's school day. Fatigue is a frequent complaint during recovery from a head injury (Warzak et al., 1995) and research suggests that a schedule that allows for daily structured rest time may be valuable in reducing incidents of problem behavior as well as facilitating performance in school and elsewhere (Cohen, 1991).

The second component of a comprehensive treatment plan is teaching the child new skills (or helping him or her re-acquire old ones) that meet the same function as the challenging behavior. For example, if the child is teasing peers to get their attention, the child could be taught new and more appropriate ways to obtain peer attention. Table 2 delineates examples of skills that could be taught depending on the function of the challenging behavior. Importantly, when the child is learning the new skill, it is critical that the desired consequence be provided whenever the child

TABLE 2   Treatment Options Matched to the Function of Challenging Behavior

If the function is:	New skills to teach:	Consequences for appropriate behavior	Consequences for challenging behavior
Positive reinforcement (obtain adult attention)	Adult attention seeking skills such as • Hand raising • Saying "Hello" (or some other verbalization matched to the child's functioning level) • Using adaptive communication (e.g., touch talker, computer, buzzer)	• Provide brief instances (5 to 10 seconds) of adult attention when the child is not exhibiting the challenging behavior, for example, when the child is sitting quietly, completing work, or playing nicely with peers • Provide the child with 10 to 15 minutes (or more) of "special time" every day, during which the child and an adult spend the time engaging in an activity the child enjoys, such as going for a walk or playing with a toy	• Timeout in a chair or in another location where adult attention is unavailable (the goal of timeout is to remove access to attention and other reinforcing items) • Extinction (do not provide attention when the challenging behavior occurs) • Adults in timeout: move away from the child when challenging behavior occurs
Positive reinforcement (peer attention seeking)	Consider a social skills program focusing on skills such as • Initiating conversations • Sharing • Turn taking • Conflict resolution • Provide the child with opportunities to interact with peers in structured, supervised situations, such as scouting, extracurricular activities, or sports	• If in a classroom, have children spend several minutes each day pointing out one positive thing that every other child did • Provide the child with feedback when you observe him or her interacting appropriately with peers	• Timeout in a chair or another location where peer attention is unavailable • Teach peers to ignore challenging behavior

(continues)

TABLE 2 (*continued*)

If the function is:	New skills to teach:	Consequences for appropriate behavior	Consequences for challenging behavior
Negative reinforcement Escape or avoid work	• Teach the child more appropriate ways to take a break such as asking to use the restroom, or saying "may I take a break, please?" • Ensure that the child is able to emit the responses necessary to successfully complete the task	• Allow the child to take brief breaks when he or she is working well. Try to provide breaks (or the opportunity to request a break) before challenging behavior occurs • Provide breaks when the child has successfully completed a task	• Extinction (do not allow the child to escape or avoid the task when challenging behavior occurs) • Use a "job jar" through which the child is required to complete an extra job (such as dusting or sweeping the floor) when challenging behavior occurs • Assign extra work contingent on challenging behavior • Remove privileges until the task is completed (e.g., no television, no going outside)

emits the target response. For example, if the child is being taught to say "May I have a break please" to request a break from work, the child should initially be given a break whenever he or she emits that response. Although parents may worry that the child will emit the desired response overly frequently (e.g., always requesting a break, and never completing any assignments), a significant amount of research has demonstrated that, if consequences are provided consistently, over time the rates of the alternative behavior will decrease to an acceptable level (Bird, Dores, Moniz, & Robinson, 1989). If the rates of the request remain high, a fading procedure can be implemented through which the child learns that, when he or she emits the target response, the desired consequence will generally (but not always) follow. For example, parents could initially provide attention every time their child requested it. They could then begin to provide attention for the first request their child made after 2 min had past since the last request, then 5 minutes, etc. Alternatively, a stimulus control procedure could be implemented to teach the child when communication would and would not be effective. For example, a red circle could be placed on the child's desk during times the child is required to work on tasks without requesting breaks. During times that requests for breaks will be honored, a green circle could be on the desk. (Detailed information on developing and implementing a communication-based intervention is available in Durand's book, (1990) *Severe Behavior Problems: A Functional Communication Training Approach* or a book by Carr and colleagues (1994), *Communication-based Intervention for Problem Behavior: A User's Guide for Producing Positive Change.*)

The final component of a comprehensive treatment plan involves identifying consequences for both challenging and appropriate behavior. Again, consequences should be identified based on the results of the functional assessment. For example, if the functional assessment suggests that challenging behavior is maintained by adult attention, it is important that such attention not be provided contingent upon the occurrence of challenging behavior. Also, the child should receive frequent adult attention, when he or she behaves appropriately (see Table 2). Some children may benefit from the use of additional reinforcers, such as access to preferred activities or items contingent on exhibition of appropriate behavior. Such items could be withdrawn temporarily if the child exhibits problem behavior. Strategies for determining such reinforcers were delineated in the section focusing on teaching new skills.

RE-INTEGRATING A CHILD AND DEALING WITH FAMILIAL CONCERNS

Thus far we have addressed strategies for skill building and for dealing with behavioral excesses and deficits that may arise following a head injury. These strategies are likely to be useful when a child exhibits either traditional skills deficits or challenging behavior post-injury. However, there are additional issues that merit inclusion within the context of parenting children who are brain injured. Parents commonly report significant concerns in two other areas: ensuring that their child participates in "typical" activities to the greatest extent possible and adapting to life with a brain-injured child. Although such topics do not typically arise within the parent training context, they are relevant because failure to properly address them may result in increased familial distress and the development of challenging behavior. For example, if a child with a brain injury is not provided with strategies that allow him or her to interact with peers in meaningful ways, the child may begin to exhibit problem behavior as a means of coping with feelings of loneliness and isolation or in an attempt to recruit peer attention. In this section we briefly review problems that may be faced and suggest strategies to address these problems.

Following a brain injury, many children feel isolated from peers and may not be able to participate in activities in which they were previously involved. Adolescents in particular, may have difficulty coping with limitations imposed by their injuries. Driving, dating, and general independence of functioning may be postponed indefinitely, functionally isolating the adolescent (Warzak et al., 1995). Parent training in such cases is not limited to simply providing consequences contingent upon the occurrence or nonoccurrence of target behaviors. Parents must be taught the importance of fostering their child's social contacts, perhaps by encouraging or arranging activities for them and ensuring that they have the appropriate repertoire to engage in those activities. Finally, parents must work to assist their child's return to effective peer interaction. The issue of social reintegration is an important one for this population because many children with acquired brain injuries demonstrate difficulty interacting with others. Poor monitoring of social cues and difficulty to self-correct and self-regulate behavior complicates these situations (Borod & Koff, 1990; Hopewell, Burke, Weslowski, & Zawlocki, 1990), and these limitations may lead to other dysfunctional behavior that then becomes a target for parental intervention in the traditional sense.

Some children with brain injury may present with specific social skills deficits, whereas others may have adequate skills but have difficulty reading social cues and behaving correctly in context. To the extent that a child's social repertoire is impaired, he or she may experience difficulty maintaining old friendships and be limited in the ability to develop new ones. Behavior that once served to encourage the presence of peers (e.g., telling contextually appropriate jokes, conversational reciprocity) may no longer be present and new behaviors may appear that are inappropriate, thus discouraging social contact by others.

Children with skills deficits should be provided training to teach them the specific social skills they are lacking and to provide an opportunity to practice newly learned skills. For example, a common complaint among those with brain injuries is difficulty following the flow of a conversation and contributing to it. This is especially the case in "busy" social situations with multiple sources of distraction (e.g., classroom situations, cafeteria settings, on the school bus) where screening out extraneous stimuli is made difficult due to brain injury. This may result in low levels of participation or non sequiturs that may make others uncomfortable. Parents might assist by teaching their child how to stand in relation to peers so as to minimize distractions or to request of their peers that they move a conversation to a location with fewer distractions. Practicing making these requests with parents allows the skill to be initially taught and reinforced at home. First the parent models the appropriate behavior, and then the child practices in the presence of the parent, who provides supportive feedback and reinforces approximations to the desired end result. Then the child practices with another child or some other confederate (e.g., peers, brothers, sisters) who has been instructed to reinforce the correct response (for example, by saying, "Sure, that would be fine," and then changing position or location to minimize distractions). Eventually such programmed consequences may be removed as the response likely will be maintained by more natural consequences—such as positive peer interaction in the extra-therapeutic environment.

Rehabilitation and educational efforts that occur in school could be reinforced by school staff as well as parents via a home-school note, a means of providing frequent feedback to the child during the course of the academic day and a quantifiable summary of the child's behavior to his or her parents. Parents then present appropriate consequences, contingent upon the nature of the daily report, thus extending their influence from the home to school. A sample home-school note is depicted in the Appendix. For this child, the target behaviors are "Being prepared when class begins," which is defined as having appropriate books and a pencil on the desk, being in his or her seat when the bell rings, and "participating in class," defined as raising his hand and asking two relevant questions or making two relevant points in each class. It is important that the target behaviors are defined in objective and measurable terms so that the child, teachers, and parents all are aware of expectations. At the end of each class, the teacher records a "plus" or a "minus" to indicate that the child met the behavioral expectations. When the child returns home, if he has more "pluses" than "minuses" he earns a special after-school snack. If not, the child does not get a snack.

Re-integration efforts could further be facilitated by developing a "team" of individuals who work with the child and who have expertise in relevant areas. Such an approach may be especially useful with a child who is significantly compromised post-injury. To illustrate, a team for a child with multiple needs might include the child, the child's parents, regular and special education teachers, the school psychologist, an occupational therapist, a physical therapist, a speech therapist, and the school principal. Together the team could develop goals (such as reductions in challenging behavior, increased participation in extracurricular activities) for the child and then identify the steps needed to achieve those goals. For example, the team might address the goal of increased participation in extracurricular activities by having the speech therapist work with the child on clear articulation (so as to decrease the likelihood the child would be teased by peers) while the occupational therapist might help the child develop skills needed to participate in an activity. Finally, the school psychologist might meet with children currently participating in the activity and discuss the challenges currently faced by the child with the brain injury.

In addition to helping a child participate in academic and community life, parents of children with significant brain injury must learn to adapt to a child who may be different from the person they knew pre-injury, perhaps with significant limitations, a different social repertoire, and affective and behavioral deficits (Cooley & Singer, 1991; Warzak et al., 1995). Families may benefit from the guidance of a professional who is familiar with the sequelae of brain injury, including cognitive, behavioral, and emotional consequences. Such a professional may provide realistic expectations to parents and child and may contribute coping strategies to family members over and above traditional parent training and behavior management.

Parents also may experience financial difficulties, behavioral problems in siblings, and marital tensions not present prior to their child's injury (Wade, Drotar, Taylor, & Stancin, 1995). These changes place significant burdens on parents and can greatly impede coordinated effective parenting efforts. The degree of a family's stress post-injury varies from family to family depending upon the family's pre-morbid cohesiveness, family attitudes about illness and responsibilities, and financial and social support (Lezak, 1988; Leaf, 1993). Directing parents to their state's Brain Injury Association or to community behavioral health agencies that can provide respite and other services for parents of children with special needs, is often as important to the success of the parent training process as the training of traditional parent training skills themselves.

SUMMARY AND CONCLUSIONS

Children with traumatic brain injury often present with a myriad of complex difficulties. Recent years have seen an increased understanding of the cognitive and psychosocial implications of these injuries (e.g., Barry & O'Leary, 1989; Lezak, 1988; Warzak, Evans, & Ford, 1992), and day-to-day obstacles that confront pediatric patients and family members have been empirically identified, thus furthering our understanding of CNS dysfunction and its sequelae (Asarnow, Satz, Light, Lewis, & Neuman, 1991; Warzak et al., 1995; Warzak & Kilburn, 1990). It is clear that children who have experienced a brain injury may exhibit a variety of behavioral excesses and deficits, which may or may not be functionally related to the injury itself. As a result, parents of these children are faced with many difficulties including understanding the nature of their child's injury and then determining whether the injury has resulted in loss of skills or increases in difficult behavior. If behavioral changes are present, parents must develop and implement a plan to increase skills and/or decrease problem behavior.

Although children with traumatic brain injury may present significant challenges to their families, strategies are increasingly becoming available to assist parents in working with their children to foster independence and success in a variety of environments. In this chapter we delineated a variety of strategies to assist parents in meeting these goals. First, we provided a brief review of the nature of brain injury and its affects. Next, we reviewed issues relating to parenting a child with a brain injury. Although parents of children with less severe injuries or mild problem behavior may benefit from strategies shown to be effective with typically developed children, we noted that parents of children with more severe deficits may benefit from learning general problem-solving approaches. Thus, we focused extensively on strategies to increase functional skills, motivate children, and develop a comprehensive plan to address problem behavior. The chapter concluded with a discussion of strategies that may be useful in re-integrating a child into school, home, and community following an injury. Such re-integration is critical to enhancing the quality of life of both the child and the family and is the ultimate goal of parent training.

REFERENCES

Alexander, M. P. (1984). Neurobehavioral consequences of closed head injury. *Neurology and Neurosurgery: Update series, 5*(20).
Asarnow, R. F., Satz, P., Light, R., Lewis, R., & Neuman, E. (1991). Behavior problems and adaptive functioning in children with mild and severe closed head injury. *Pediatric Psychology, 16,* 543–555.

Barry, P., & O'Leary, J. (1989). Roles of the psychologist on a traumatic brain injury rehabilitation team. *Rehabilitation Psychology, 34*(2), 83–90.

Binder, L. M. (1986). Persisting symptoms after mild head injury: A review of the postconcussive syndrome. *Journal of Clinical and Experimental Neuropsychology, 8*(4), 323–346.

Bird, F., Dores, P. A., Moniz, D., & Robinson, J. (1989). Reducing severe agressive and self-injurious behavior with functional communication training. *American Journal of Mental Retardation, 94*(1), 37–48.

Borod, J. C., & Koff, E. (1990). Lateralization for facial emotional behavior: A methodological perspective. *International Journal of Psychology, 25,* 157–177.

Brandstater, M. E., Bontke, C. F., Cobble, N. D., & Horn, L. J. (1991). Rehabilitation in brain disorders: Specific disorders. *Archives of Physical Medicine and Rehabilitation, 72,* S332–S340.

Cantu, R. C. (1988). When to return to contact sports after a cerebral concussion. *Sport Medicine Digest, 10,* 1–2

Carr, E. D., Levin, L., McConnachie, G., Carlson, J. I., Kemp, D. C., & Smith, C. E. (1994). *Communication-based intervention for problem behavior: A user's guide for producing positive change.* Baltimore, MD: Brookes Publishers.

Cautela, J. R., & Kastenbaum, R. (1967) A reinforcement survey schedule for use in therapy, training, and research. *Psychological Reports, 20,* 1115–1130.

Christopherson, E. R. (1988). *Little people.* Kansas City, MO: Westport Publishers.

Clark, L. (1996). *SOS! Help for parents: A guide for handling common everyday behavior problems.* Parents Press: Bowling Green, KY.

Clement, P. W., & Richard, R. C. (1976). Identifying reinforcers for children: A children's reinforcement survey. In E.J. Mash, & L.G. Terdal (Eds.), *Behavior therapy assessment: Diagnosis, design, and evaluation.* New York: Springer.

Cohen, S. B. (1991). Adapting educational programs for students with head injuries. *Journal of Head Trauma Rehabilitation, 6*(1), 47–55.

Cooley, E. & Singer, G. (1991). On serving students with head injuries: Are we reinventing a wheel that doesn't roll? *Journal of Head Trauma Rehabilitation, 6*(1), 47–55.

Dean, R.S. (1985). Foundation and rationale for neuropsychological bases of individual differences. In L. Hartledge & K. Telzrow (Eds.), *Neuropsychology of individual differences* (pp. 7–39). New York: Plenum.

Durand, V. M. (1990). *Severe behavior problems: A functional communication training approach.* New York: Guilford Press.

Eisenberg, M. G. (1989). Introduction: Special issue on traumatic brain injury rehabilitation. *Rehabilitation Psychology, 14*(2), 67.

Elliot, S. (1993). *Preferred behavioral inventory and intervention planner.* Madison, WI: University of Wisconsin Press.

Evans, R. W., Evans, R. I., & Sharp, M. J. (1994). The physician survey on the post-concussion and whiplash syndromes. *Headache, 34,* 268–274.

Eyberg, S. M., & Robinson, E. A. (1982). Parent child interaction training: Effects on family functioning. *Journal of Clinical Child Psychology, 11,* 130–137.

Forehand. R., Rogers, T., McMahon, R. J., Wells, K. C., & Griest, D. L. (1981). Teaching parents to modify child behavior problems: an examination of some follow-up data. *Journal of Pediatric Psychology, 6*(3), 313–322.

Goethe, K. E., & Levin, H. S. (1984). Behavioral manifestations during the early and long-term stages of recovery after closed head injury. *Psychiatric Annals, 14,* 540–546.

Hembree-Kigan, T. L., & McNeil, C. B. (1995). *Parent-child interaction therapy.* New York: Plenum.

Honig, W. K., & Staddon, J. E. R. (1977). *Handbook of operant behavior.* Englewood Cliffs, NJ: Prentice-Hall.

Hopewell, C. A., Burke, W. H., Weslowski, M., Zawlocki, R. (1990). Behavioral learning therapies for the traumatically brain-injured patient. In R. L. Wood & I. Fussey (Eds.), *Brain damage behavior & cognition: Cognitive rehabilitation in perspective.* (pp. 229–245). New York: Taylor & Francis.

Hu, X., Wesson, D. E., Kenney, B. D., Chipman, M. L., & Spence, L. J. (1993). Risk factors for extended disruption of family function after severe injury to a child. *CMAJ, 149*(4), 421–427.

Jaffe, K. M., Polissar, N. L., Fay, G. C., & Liao, S. (1995). Recovery trends over three years following pediatric traumatic brain injury. *Archives of Physical Medicine and Rehabilitation, 76,* 17–26.

Koskiniemi, M., Kyykka, T., Nybo, T., & Jarho, L. (1995). Long-term outcome after severe brain injury in preschoolers is worse than expected. *Archives of Pediatric and Adolescent Medicine, 149,* 249–254.

Kraus, J. F., Black, M. A., Hessol, N., Ley, P., Rokaw, W., Sullivan, C., Bowers, S., Knowlton, S., & Marsghall, L. (1984). The incidence of acute brain injury and serious impairment in a defined population. *American Journal of Epidemiology, 119,* 186–201.

Leaf, L.E. (1993). Traumatic Brain Injury: Affecting family recovery. *Brain Injury, 7*(6), 543–546.

LeBlanc, K. E. (1994). Concussions in sport: Guidelines for return to competition. *American Family Physician, 50,* 801–806.

Leitenberg, H. (1976). *Handbook of behavior modification and behavior therapy.* Englewood Cliffs, NJ: Prentice-Hall.

Levin, H. S., Benton, A. L., & Grossman, R. G. (1982). *Neurobehavioral consequences of closed head injury.* New York: Oxford University Press.

Lezak, M. D. (1988). Brain damage is a family affair. *Journal of Clinical and Experimental Neuropsychology, 10,* 111–123.

Lezak, M. D. (1988). The walking wounded of head injury: When subtle deficits can be disabling. *Trends in Rehabilitation, 3,* 4–9.

Long, P., Forehand, R., Wierson, M., & Morgan, A. (1994). Does parent training with young noncompliant children have long term effects? *Behaviour Research and Therapy, 32*(1), 10 1–107.

McGuire, T. L., & Rothenberg, M. B. (1986). Behavioral and psychosocial sequelae of pediatric head injury. *The Journal of Head Trauma Rehabilitation, 1*(4), 1–6.

Mitiguy, J. S., Thompson, G., & Wasco, J. (1990). *Understanding brain injury: Acute hospitalization.* Lynn, MA: New Medico Head Injury System.

O'Neill, R. E., Horner, R. H., Albin, R. W., Sprague, J. R., Storey, K., & Newton, J. S. (1997). *Functional assessment and program development for problem behavior: A practical handbook* (2nd ed.). New York: Brooks/Cole.

Pace, G. P., Ivancic, M. T., Edwards, G. I., Iwata, B. A., & Page, T. J. (1985). Assessment of stimulus preference and reinforcer value with profoundly retarded individuals. *Journal of Applied Behavior Analysis, 18,* 249–255.

Patterson, G. R. (1975). *Families: Applications of social learning to family life.* Research Press: Champagn, IL.

Patterson, G. R., & Fleischman, M. J. (1979). Maintenance of treatment effects: Some considerations concerning family systems and follow-up data. *Behavior Therapy, 10,* 168–185.

Piazza, C. C., Fisher, W. W., Hagopian, L. P., Bowman, L. G., & Toole, L. (1996). Using a choice assessment to predict reinforcer effectiveness. *Journal of Applied Behavior Analysis, 29*(1), 1–9.

Rimmel, R. W., Giordani, B., Barth, J. T., Boll, T. J., & Jane, J. A. (1981). Disability caused by minor head injury. *Neurosurgery, 9,* 221–228.

Rosenthal, M. (1983). Behavioral sequelae. In M. Rosenthal, E. R. Griffith, M. R. Bond, & J. D. Miller (Eds.), *Rehabilitation of the head injured adult* (pp. 197–208). Philadelphia: Davis.

Rutherford, W. H. (1989). In H. S. Levin, H. M. Eisenberg, & A. L. Benton (Eds.), *Mild head injury.* New York: Oxford University Press.

Rutter, M.. Chadwick, O., Shaffer, D. (1983). Head injury. In M. Rutter (Ed.), *Developmental Neuropsychiatry,* New York: Guilford.

Savage, R. C. (1991). Identification, classification, and placement issues for students with traumatic brain injuries. *Journal of Head Trauma Rehabilitation, 6*(1), 1–9.

Sulzer-Azaroff, B., & Mayer, G.R. (1977) *Applying behavior-analysis procedures with children and youth.* New York: Holt, Rinehart and Winston.

Wade, S., Drotar, D., Taylor, H. G., & Stancin, T. (1995). Assessing the effects of traumatic brain injury on family functioning: Conceptual and methodological issues. *Journal of Pediatric Psychology, 20*(6), 737–752.

Warzak, W. J., Evans, J., & Ford, L. (1992). Working with the traumatically brain injured patient: Implications for rehabilitation. *Journal of Comprehensive Mental Health Care, 2,* 115–130.

Warzak, W. J., & Kilburn, J. (1990). Behavioral approaches to activities of daily living. In D. E. Tupper & K. D. Cicerone (Eds). *The neuropsychology of everyday life. Vol. 1: Assessment and basic competencies* (pp. 285–305). New York, NY., Martinus Nijhoff.

Warzak, W. J., Allan, T. M., Ford, L. A., & Stefans, V. C. (1995). Common Obstacles to the Daily Functioning of Pediatric Traumatically Brain Injured Patients: Perceptions of Caregivers and Psychologists. *Children's Health Care, 24*(1), 133–141.

Webster-Stratton, C. (1984). Randomized trial of two parent-training programs for families with conduct-disordered children. *Journal of Consulting and Clinical Psychology, 52,* 666–678.

Webster-Stratton, C., Hollinsworth, T., & Kolpacoff, M. (1989). The long-term effectiveness and clinical significance of three cost-effective training programs for families with conduct-problem children. *Journal of Consulting and Clinical Psychology, 57*(4), 550–553.

APPENDIX: SAMPLE HOME-SCHOOL NOTE
BEN'S HOME-SCHOOL NOTE

Target Behaviors

1. *Prepared when class begins:* If Ben has the appropriate books and a pencil on his desk and is in his seat when the bell rings he receives a "plus."

2. *Participating in class:* If Ben raises hand and asks two relevant questions or makes two relevant comments, he receives a "plus."

Instructions

At the end of each class, Ben will walk to his teacher's desk and retrieve the note. If he received a "plus" his teacher will praise him and review briefly what he did to earn the "plus."

Date: _____ / _____ / _____

Behavior	English	Science	Social Studies	Spelling	Gym	Math
Prepared when class began						
Participated in class						

Comments: _____
_____
_____
_____

Parenting Chronically Ill Children

Steven W. Lee

Department of Psychology and Research in Education, University of Kansas, Lawrence, Kansas

Thomas P. Guck

Creighton Family Health Care, Creighton University School of Medicine, Omaha, Nebraska

INTRODUCTION

This chapter emphasizes the diversity and specificity of problems faced by the parents and families of chronically ill children. Both medical and psychosocial models have influenced attempts directed toward understanding and treating psychosocial problems in chronically ill children. The dialectical tension between these models has resulted in new model formulations that seek to explain the complexity of coping with chronic illness in the developing child. These new models are presented in this chapter.

The second half of the chapter defines parent education and summarizes the extant literature on educational programs for parents of chronically ill children. The context-specific nature of the effects of chronic illness is emphasized and a strong argument is made for using collaborative consultation, problem solving, and functional behavior analysis for the development of context-specific parent education programs.

DEFINITION AND CLASSIFICATION OF CHRONIC HEALTH CONDITIONS IN CHILDREN

Early definitions and classification of chronic illnesses in children were made almost exclusively on the basis of disease-specific biomedical factors.

Handbook of Diversity in Parent Education
277

The biomedical definition and classification approach continues today and emphasizes the categorical differences among disorders. From this perspective, a genetic component such as a chromosomal disorder or other genetic defect affecting other biological process is determined to be the cause of the childhood disease (Perrin & MacLean, 1988). The biomedical approach to childhood illness has led to many advances in the recognition and treatment of what once were considered life-threatening conditions. Even today this approach has led to the identification of 200 genes that cause hereditary disease, while new genes are isolated at a rate of one per month (Singer & Berg, 1997).

As the treatment of chronically ill children continues to evolve, dissatisfaction with a purely biomedical view of the conditions has emerged. Psychosocial factors such as developmental, structural, and functional manifestations of the conditions are seen as very important. Although these new and important dimensions can be used for definition and classification, they too are often grouped into categories according to bodily systems (Thompson & Gustafson, 1996). For example, the National Center for Health Statistics classification scheme includes eight impairment categories such as impairment of vision, hearing, speech, special senses, intelligence, and extremity loss. Also included are 14 disease and injury categories such as infections, neoplasms, endocrine, metabolic, and blood disorders and diseases of the respiratory, digestive, and musculoskeletal systems (Newacheck et al., 1986). A more recent review provides a compilation of 96 rare and common health-related disorders in childhood and adolescents (Phelps, 1998). This compilation is a disease-specific categorical approach that also provides information on the behavioral, educational, social-emotional, medical, and neuropsychological consequences of each disorder. Phelps' (1998) review also provides psycho-educational implications for intervention.

Although the condition-specific or categorical approach has proven useful among biomedical researchers and clinicians, professionals and policy makers interested in psychological and social correlates of chronic conditions in childhood have experienced dissatisfaction with a purely biomedical approach (Perrin, et al., 1993). Some of the difficulties encountered with the categorical approach include (1) the study of the psychosocial implications of each of the many diseases separately, likely does not justify the cost and effort; (2) only easy to classify conditions that occur with at least moderate frequencies are studied, whereas rare and difficult-to-define conditions are often not addressed; (3) condition-specific approaches compromise generalizability and comparability among research efforts, leading to unnecessary competition among specific condition researchers for resources and among parents for services; (4) fair and equitable health policies are difficult to establish using the categorical approach; and (5) many conditions involve more than one biological system in their etiology, characteristic symptom presentation, and management.

Because of these difficulties, some researchers have moved away from definitions and classifications of chronic childhood conditions based on a categorical approach. Instead, they have opted for a noncategorical approach with a focus on the commonalities across illness conditions facing children and their families. The noncategorical approach to classification assumes that, regardless of the specific disease, children with chronic conditions and their families face common life experiences that are based on generic dimensions of their conditions (Stein & Jessop, 1982). In one of the more thorough discussions of issues involved in the definition and classification of chronic health conditions, Perrin et al. (1993) outlined a number of generic noncategorical dimensions for describing a child with a chronic health condition. These dimensions include (a) duration; (b) age of onset; (c) limitations of age-appropriate activities; (d) visibility; (e) expected survival; (f) mobility; (g) physiologic functioning; (h) cognition; (i) emotional/social functioning; (j) sensory functioning; (k) communication; (l) course (stable vs. progressive); and (m) uncertainty (episodic vs. predictable)

The categorical approach focuses on the presence of particular conditions and has fostered biomedical advances and the provision of treatment regimens that have improved the lives of children with chronic conditions. The noncategorical approach emphasizes the impact of illness conditions on children and their families and recognizes common challenges and needs of children with chronic illness and their families, which have implications for program development and public policy considerations (Thompson & Gustafson, 1996).

Historically the definition and classification of childhood chronic conditions have been determined by positions taken on two critical issues, biomedical versus psychosocial model and categorical versus noncategorical approach. More recently there appears to be some consensus emerging that an either-or approach to definition and classification is not necessary. For example, Perrin et al. (1993) argued that different applications require different definition decisions. They proposed that a definition of chronic illness should be comprehensive, generic, and flexible and argued for a two-level approach they believed satisfied these criteria. The first level involves duration of the condition as the only decisive criterion. Perrin et al.

(1993) recommend that a condition be considered chronic if it has lasted or is expected to last more than 3 months. They recommend that the second level of the definition of chronic illness take into account the impact of a condition on the child. The authors provided the following example of how definition decisions can affect the epidemiology of chronic conditions. A report of the National Health Interview Survey indicated that 31% of children younger than 18 were classified with a chronic condition using the first level criterion set at 3 months duration (Newacheck & Taylor, 1992). When the second level based on function was included in the definition, the prevalence dropped to 5.3% of children (Adams & Benson, 1990). When the definition was further restricted to children who were unable to conduct their major activity, the prevalence of chronic illness dropped to 0.6% (Adams & Benson, 1990).

Following their review of definition and classification issues with chronically ill children, Thompson and Gustafson (1996) supported the view of Pless and Perrin (1985) that a partial or modified categorical approach has merit for research, clinical practice, and policy formation. They advocated that both illness-specific and generic processes are of importance to adaptation of children and families to chronic illness. Furthermore, it is premature for the field to solely adopt a categorical or noncategorical approach.

Another perspective on the debate between biomedical versus psychosocial and categorical versus noncategorical views of the definition and classification of childhood conditions is that both approaches are necessary for the advancement of the field. From a dialectical perspective, it is the constant tension between opposing views that leads to greater understanding. Introduced by the ancient Greek philosophers, dialectics have influenced almost every social and natural science field during the past century (Kuhn, 1970). Dialectics assumes that reality is not static but is comprised of opposing forces ("thesis" and "antithesis"), out of whose integration ("synthesis") evolves a new set of opposing forces (Linehan, 1993). Therefore, neither of the original positions can be regarded as "absolutely true." The synthesis, however, always suggests a new antithesis and thus acts as a new thesis. Truth, therefore, is neither absolute nor relative; rather, it evolves, develops, and is constructed over time. It is the tension between the thesis and antithesis forces within each system (biomedical and psychosocial and categorical and noncategorical) that produces new understandings of childhood chronic illness. From a dialectical perspective, the definition and classification of childhood chronic conditions will continue to evolve and receive further clarification.

The dialectical perspective can also increase understanding of the evolution of theoretical models of chronic illness in children. The tension between biomedical and psychosocial factors has been especially influential in the development of integrated models of childhood chronic illness. In addition, the synthesis between child (thesis) and family-systems (antithesis) views have greatly influenced model development.

PSYCHOSOCIAL MODELS OF CHRONIC ILLNESS IN CHILDREN

The purpose of this section is to briefly describe some of the more influential psychosocial models that integrate the many factors correlated with chronic illness in children. Early research examining relationships among childhood chronic illness factors emphasized child-centered biomedical issues. When psychosocial factors were examined, the studies emphasized the psychopathological differences between chronically ill children and their healthy counterparts (Kazak, 1989). It wasn't until the 1970s that psychosocial models of childhood illness began to view these conditions as stressors requiring "normal" adaptation (Pless & Pinkerton, 1975). More recent research is characterized by a focus on family systems and social-ecological factors associated with chronic illness (Kazak, 1989). In addition, families with chronically ill children are seen as essentially "normal" families coping with a demanding, distressing, and potentially long-term series of stressors (Kazak et al., 1995).

Biomedical, child-focused models will not be presented here. However, their influence is still present and creates an undercurrent of tension in a dialectical sense with the psychosocial, family-focused models that will be presented. Four psychosocial models of childhood chronic illness are presented that progressively incorporate the evolving role of parenting. A common feature of psychosocial models is that chronic illness is viewed as a potential stressor. Therefore, the general stress and coping model of Lazarus & Folkman (1984), which has been very influential in the development of the psychosocial models of childhood illness is presented first.

Perhaps the most influential model of stress over the past 3 decades is the work of Lazarus and Folkman (1984). They argued that, when confronted with an event, a primary appraisal is made to determine whether the event is irrelevant, benign, or harmful. An event is considered a stressor if it is appraised as threatening, harmful, or challenging. Simultaneously, the secondary appraisal is initiated to assess the adequacy of one's coping ability and resources to meet the harm, threat, or challenge of the event. According to Lazarus and Folkman (1984), the subjective experience of stress is ultimately a balance between primary and secondary appraisals. When harm and threat are high, and coping ability is low, substantial stress is felt. When coping ability is high, stress is minimal.

Many environmental, behavioral, physiological, and cognitive coping responses have been studied. Some researchers have suggested that people have coping styles or habitual ways of responding to stress. Flexible coping styles, in which one's approach to coping with stressful situations are tailored to the situation and changeable across settings appear to be quite effective (Lester et al., 1994). Parents and families with a chronically ill child are required to make primary and secondary appraisals of a potentially stressful event based on multiple factors including those outlined above by Perrin et al. (1993). Different appraisals of the same medical or illness event could account for some of the discrepant findings regarding parenting of chronically ill children.

Lazarus and Folkman's (1984) research has been the cornerstone for several models of childhood chronic illness. Pless and Pinkerton (1975) presented the first comprehensive model that viewed chronic illness as a stressor. Their work introduced several important concepts that have served as a basis for therapeutic intervention and foundation for subsequent models. Pless and Pinkerton (1975) viewed adjustment as being determined by the individual's multiple transactions with his or her environment. A related conceptual premise suggests adjustment changes over time and at any given time psychological functioning reflects the cumulative product of earlier transactions. As a result, early childhood functioning is predictive of later functioning, therefore, early intervention is important. Pless and Pinkerton (1975) also emphasized self-concept and coping strategies as major determinants of one's response to the stress of chronic illness. Self-concept and coping style are thought to be determined by multiple factors including the child's intrinsic attributes (i.e. temperament, personality, and intelligence), which are influenced by genetic, family, and social processes.

A second model called the disability-stress-coping model (Wallander & Varni, 1992) builds on some of Pless and Pinkerton's (1975) concepts by expanding both child adjustment outcomes and the factors that contribute to the outcomes. Child adjustment or adaptation is viewed multidimensionally and includes consideration of mental health, social functioning, and physical health, which are organized into a risk-and-resistance framework. The primary risk factor for adjustment problems is stress, which is thought to emanate from the physical condition (e.g., disease/disability parameters), as well as environmental circumstances (e.g., functional limitations). In addition, general stress factors may have a more profound impact on children with an illness condition than their healthy counterparts (Wallander & Thompson, 1998). Three types of resistance factors hypothesized to influence adjustment include intrapersonal, stress processing, and social ecological factors. Intrapersonal factors involve relatively stable factors such as temperament, competence, effectance motivation, and problem-solving ability. Stress processing factors include cognitive appraisal and coping behaviors. Social ecological factors include family resources, such as the family's characteristic mode of perceiving and interacting with the social world as well as practical resources available to deal with acute and chronic problems and issues (Wallander et al., 1989).

The third stress and coping model is called the transactional stress and coping model, developed by Thompson and colleagues (Thompson, et al., 1993; Thompson et al., 1992). This model incorporates both the stress and coping theory of Lazarus and Folkman (1984) and ecological-systems theory (Bronfrenbrenner, 1979). In the transactional stress and coping model, chronic illness is seen as a potential stressor to which the child and family system must adapt. Similar to Lazarus and Folkman's (1984) stress model, the illness-outcome relationship is hypothesized to be a function of the transactions among biomedical, developmental, and psychosocial processes. However, the new and unique contribution of this model is the focus on child and family adaptational processes. These child and family adaptational processes are hypothesized to further influence the psychological adjustment of children and their mothers, beyond the contributions of biomedical and demographic parameters (Wallander & Thompson, 1998). This model does not address the role of fathers; however, the focus on the mother's adjustment recognizes the significance of parenting in the adaptation to childhood chronic illness.

The fourth model of adaptation to chronic childhood illness integrates family-systems theory and social ecology (Kazak, 1989; Kazak, Segal-Andrews, & Johnson, 1998). The family-systems social-ecological model proposes that social support buffers or reduces stress, and that the family is a child's primary support system. Kazak (1989), drawing from systems theory, proposes that a problem in any member of a family has an effect on all other members, and changes in any member of the system affect all others.

A chronic illness in a child is therefore not contained within the child but has ramifications for all members of the family system. Changes resulting from a childhood illness may result in discomfort that elicits homeo-static processes as the family system attempts to develop a sense of stability. The homeostatic processes employed by family systems as they adjust to chronic illness can be adaptive or maladaptive. From a family systems per-spective, interventions that address these homeostatic patterns may be more effective than interventions focused on a particular individual within the system.

The social-ecological portion of this model is based on the framework provided by Bronfrenbrenner (1979). Social ecology is defined as the study of the relation between the developing human being and the set-tings and contexts in which the person is actively involved. In the model, the child is at the center of a series of concentric circles, which represent settings that have bidirectional influences on the child. The concentric circles further away from the child represent societal values and culture, whereas whose closer to the child indicate settings of a smaller scale, such as parents and family.

From a family-systems social-ecological perspective, assessment and intervention for a chronically ill child requires an analysis of the child within the context of his or her social networks. An especially important component of this analysis is the child's relationship with his or her parents.

This portion of the chapter has reviewed some of the models that have been developed integrating the variables considered important in the treatment of childhood chronic illness. The presentation has demonstrated that parenting has become a progressively more important element in models of chronic illness with children. In the next section, the role of parenting and the efficacy of parenting programs with chronically ill chil-dren are reviewed.

RESEARCH ON PARENTING CHRONICALLY ILL CHILDREN

The research on parenting chronically ill children is in its infancy. Scholars in this area are still striving to understand the phenomena of chronic health conditions and its impact on the child and family (Drotar, 1997). Research to date on the adjustment of parent and families of children with chronic health conditions may be summarized into three global areas. The first area includes studies attempting to understand the phenomena of child chronic illness and its effects on parents and family (Heller, Rafman, Zuagulis, & Pless, 1985; Lavigne, Nolan, & McLone, 1988; Wallander,

Varni, Babani, Banis, & Wilcox, 1989). The second domain of studies recognizes the emotional toll that parenting a chronically ill child can have on a family. These investigations have focused on reducing maladjustment and bolstering coping skills in parents and other family members (Powers, Blount, Bachanas, Cotter, & Swan, 1993; Kupst, Schulman, Henig, Maurer, Morgan, & Fochtman, 1982; Kupst & Schulman, 1988; Satin, LaGreca, Zigo, & Skyler, 1989). Last, a small core of studies has researched the effectiveness of traditional parent education programs. It is these studies that are the focus of this chapter. However, first let's examine what we mean by "traditional parent education programs."

Parent Education Defined

It should be recognized that from a broad perspective parent education could be construed as an indirect service (Gutkin & Curtis, 1999) aimed at giving information to parents. In this context, information regarding personal coping strategies for fathers or mothers, support groups, family therapy, etc. could fall under the purview of parent education. However, the foregoing discussion will concentrate on a more narrow and traditional view of parent education as defined below.

Parent education programs are designed to help parents (1) understand the nature and impact of their child's disorder, (2) train the parent(s) in techniques to assist their child to cope with the disorder, (3) manage or change the behavior of their child, (4) help the child to progress socially, emotionally and academically, and (5) assist the parents in coping with the disorder. Traditional parent education programs have the following elements: (1) specific foci (e.g., children with a specific disorder or problem), (2) formalized written manual or material, (3) utilize step-by-step procedures to enhance treatment integrity, and (4) demonstrated research effectiveness.

Parent Education Programs for Parents of Chronically Ill Children

It appears from the literature that all attempts to explain, assess, or treat chronically ill children and their families must take into account specific factors related to the illness itself (e.g., severity, life threat, acute versus chronic elements), adaptation and adjustment to the illness (e.g., parent and child coping mechanisms), premorbid factors (e.g., parental communication), and age of the child to name a few (Thompson & Gustafson, 1996). The heterogeneity of this population hinders the effort to develop a general parent education program gleaned from an explanatory model to be used with all parents of chronically ill children.

The literature in this area focuses on diagnosis and context-specific factors in parenting. In an effort to emulate the literature, we will eliminate the term "parent education for chronically ill children" in favor of "educating parents of children with specific medical disorders."

Status of Educating Parents of Children with Specific Medical Disorders

Diversity within the population of chronically ill children have led parent educators and researchers to create and evaluate parent education programs that are specific to problems faced by chronically ill children and their families. To our knowledge, global parent education programs have not been developed, evaluated, and reported in the relevant psychological or educational literature (Kazak, 1997; Drotar, 1997). Instead the literature on parent education in this area focuses on coping skills and adjustment to the medical procedures such as surgery or injections. Parent education programs such as those developed for defiant (Barkley, 1997) or ADHD children (Wodrich, 1994) that meet the above-mentioned definition will be presented as exemplars for the types of parent interventions that have been researched in this area.

Powers, Blount, Bachanas, Cotter, and Swan (1993) trained parents to coach their child through painful injections required as treatment for their leukemia. The parents in this study were trained to help their child cope with the injections through distraction activities, breathing, and counting strategies. Less child distress and improved coping skills were evident after implementation of the parent education program.

The effects of a family oriented group intervention program for Satin, LaGreca, Zigo and Skyler (1989) studied children with insulin-dependent diabetes mellitus. A 6-week support and family education training session was conducted and focused on discussion of feelings related to the disorder, problem-solving, managing dietary restrictions, and included simulation exercises for measuring glucose levels, following a meal plan and exercise regime, and administration of daily injections. Adolescents in the group-family intervention with parent simulation of diabetes showed improved glycemic control.

Zastowny, Kirschenbaum, and Meng (1986) evaluated the effects of two different training programs with parents of children scheduled for surgery. In addition to a control group, parents in the anxiety-reduction group were trained to identify and manage stress responses through relaxation and positive cognitions. Parents in the coping skills group were trained in stress-inoculation techniques including specific ways to prepare and handle stressors. The results showed that the parents trained in coping skills helped their children to adapt better to surgery than the other two groups under study. In addition, the children in the coping skills group showed the fewest behavior problems before and after hospitalization.

Pinto and Hollandsworth (1989) evaluated a parent education program that was employed to prepare pediatric patients for surgery with a goal of reducing anxiety and fear. In addition, a cost-benefit analysis was performed comparing the average hospital costs for each patient (i.e., length of stay, additional procedures, medicine) and the expense of the two treatment procedures (parent or child narrated videotape or presurgery with coping narrative) and a no-treatment control group. These investigators found that children in both videotape conditions exhibited fewer symptoms of anxiety than the control group, but no significant differences were observed between the two treatment groups on the anxiety measures. The cost–benefit analysis demonstrated that surgery preparation intervention was more effective in reducing medical costs.

The studies summarized here point away from general approaches to parent education and toward the context dependent nature of the effects of chronic illness (Shriver, 1998) on the family, school, peers, and, of course, the child. Accordingly, Lee (1991), Lee and Guck (2000), Shriver (1998), and McMahon, Lambros, and Sylvia (1998) have argued convincingly for a framework for working with parents that incorporates collaborative consultation, problem solving and functional analysis to aid in the development of parenting approaches that are specific to the needs of their ill child and the ecological context of the situation. This "framework" emphasizes *process* expertise and *content* expertise (Lee, 1991) in working with parents of chronically ill children. Process expertise refers to the skills in interacting with others as well as methods for solving problems and developing specific, ecologically valid interventions that could be implemented by parents. Content expertise includes specific knowledge of the disorder in question and the known effects of the disorder on people close to or in the situation. Defined in this way, process skills provide a framework for developing effective interventions (Shriver, 1998) based on proven methods and drawing upon the content expertise of everyone involved, and especially the parent of the ill child. In the following section of this chapter, we will coalesce well-researched process approaches into a multi-element program for developing specific, ecologically valid interventions for the chronically ill child and his or her family.

PARENT INTERVENTION: CONSULTATION, PROBLEM-SOLVING, AND FUNCTIONAL BEHAVIOR ANALYSIS

The multi-element intervention approach proposed here features techniques designed to incorporate behavioral technology and problem solving into a consultative framework. Each element of the program will be presented separately below but the helping professional should work toward merging these elements into a seamless intervention approach for developing ecologically valid and specific interventions.

Collaborative Consultation

Numerous scholars point to consultation as an important and needed human service intervention (Brown, Pryzwansky, & Shulte, 1995; Zins & Heron, 1996; Randolph & Mitchell, 1995; O'Hearn & Gatz, 1996). The psychologist working within a consultative framework may serve more children in a shorter time by imparting psychological techniques to parents who can work with their child. From a preventive standpoint, parents may gain skills that will enable them to work with their ill child (or the siblings) in more effective ways in the future.

Numerous theoretical models of consultation have been developed in medicine, psychiatry, psychology, and education for working on behalf of troubled or ill children. These models include mental health consultation (Caplan, 1970, 1974; Caplan & Caplan, 1993), behavioral consultation (Bergan & Kratochwill, 1977), a client-centered consultative model (Burns & Cromer, 1978), collaborative team model (Roberts & Wright, 1982), and the ecobehavioral model of consultation (Gutkin & Curtis, 1999). The model proposed here entitled collaborative consultation emphasizes the close contact with parents in problem identification, data collection, problem analysis, and intervention planning implementation. This is not a new model but follows the theory and techniques of ecobehavioral consultation. A description of the consultation model is described in brief below.

Consultation is an indirect service focusing on the development of a collaborative relationship between consultant (mental health professional) and the parent for the purpose of assisting the parent in problem solving and implementing interventions on behalf of their child. The collaborative-consultation service delivery model focuses primarily on the parent and the daily interaction of the parent with the child and other important persons in the child's life. In collaborative consultation the referral may come from the parent or other professionals. The consultant typically interviews the parent about the problem(s). It is the parent's view of the problem(s) that is deemed ecologically valid and is the focus of subsequent data collection and intervention. The consultant may interview the ill child directly or use surveys or questionnaires as information-gathering approaches. Subsequent data collection may include direct observation of the parent–child interaction or information obtained via behavior-rating scales. Clearly defined behavioral data should be collected for a baseline against which progress may be judged. The collaborative consultation process is a verbal exchange between the parent and the consultant following a problem solving format (Lee, 1991). Finally, solutions generated through problem solving are designed for the specific problem(s) at hand to be implemented within the ecology of the family environment. These solutions are implemented by the parent and evaluated for effectiveness against the baseline data.

The collaborative consultation process features mutually agreed upon goals and interventions that maximize parent ownership for the goals and interventions and increases the likelihood of adherence. The collaborative process may include other important people by examining their role in shaping the environment for the ill child. There is open and ongoing communication between the consultant and the parent(s), which allows integration of new information regarding the illness, child, and/or family. The collaborative-consultant views the parent as competent, and the relationship involves joint responsibility for intervention or change. Finally, the collaborative-consultative model uses familiar terminology in that the problems as depicted by the parent are the focus of the consultative effort.

Problem Solving

Although collaborative consultation emphasizes techniques for developing effective interventions, problem solving provides the structure for parental interactions. The problem solving process used in conjunction with collaborative consultation and functional behavior assessment has both intervention and preventive goals. The primary goal is to develop effective interventions to be implemented by the parent. A secondary goal is to teach the parent(s) a process for solving problems that they may use in the future. Table 1 shows the basic problem-solving format. Although effective use of the process will yield targeted interventions, to reach the secondary goal the clinician must make the problem-solving process overt. This can be done in a variety of ways, including (1) describing the process and/or using a visual aid or handout that shows the process, (2) make overt process statements, and (3) modeling.

Establish an Optimal Problem-Solving Set

Heppner (1978) suggests that a problem-solving set "is an inferred predisposition that influences a client to behave in a certain manner" (p. 367). This "inferred predisposition" for problem solving includes attitudinal and emotional factors such as (1) emotional rationality, (2) an acknowledgement that problems regularly occur and it is possible to cope with them, (3) a sense of environmental control, (4) the ability to identify and label difficult problems, and (5) a tendency to be reflective and not avoid the problem. The consultant may work toward establishing the optimal problem-solving set by modeling emotional rationality and calmness (Kampwirth, 1999). Other techniques discussed by Heppner (1978) designed to induce optimal problem solving include the use of rational emotive techniques to reduce irrationality and substitute realistic/adaptive cognitions.

TABLE 1   Problem-Solving Process

Step	Step Name
1	Establish an optimal problem solving set
2	Problem identification
3	Problem analysis
4	Solution development
5	Solution implementation and follow-up

Active reinforcement of parental thoughts or behaviors directed toward confronting rather than avoiding the problem as well as using self-monitoring techniques designed to increase awareness of their reactions to problematic situations are useful techniques for establishing an optimal problem-solving set.

Problem Identification

Clarifying the nature of and prioritization of the problem(s) may be the most important stage of problem solving. Accurate identification of key problems is influenced by many factors including trust of the consultant, emotional clouding of the problem(s), outside forces impinging on the problem, lack of goals, and an inability of the consultee to articulate the problem(s). These aggravating factors may be mitigated with patience and the use of good communication skills (Kampwirth, 1999). Clear, accurate, and empathic communications will enhance trust in the consultant and reduce emotionality surrounding the problem (Friend & Cook, 1992).

Data collection or assessment is essential to the process of problem identification. Assessment is defined as any information collected that may be fruitfully used in the identification or analysis of the problem(s) at hand. This broad definition includes the use of interviews, observations, test results, and medical, psychological, or educational records. Shriver (1998) provides a thorough discussion of data collection techniques in teaching parenting skills. From an ecological viewpoint (Gutkin, 1999), information should be collected from parents and other involved adults, the child, and the environment. Information collected during consultation catalyzes action and clarifies the nature and extent of the problem(s). Ongoing data collection related to the problem can be used in subsequent stages for the analysis of influences on the problem and solution development.

Finally, the process of problem solving regulated by the consultant can add significantly to problem delineation. The consultant should initially seek to uncover all of the problems of concern to the consultee. With the help of the consultant these can then be prioritized by the consultee with the end result a concrete behavioral definition of the highest priority problem. Realistic goals can then be developed based on the current frequency, duration, and/or intensity of the problem.

Problem Analysis

This phase involves the use of information collected in subsequent stages for the development of hypotheses factors maintaining the problem(s)

(Shriver, 1998). Interviews, observations, and archival data generate a discussion of possible antecedents and consequences that maintain the problem behavior or situation. Hypotheses formed from this dialogue drive the selection of possible solutions.

Solution Development

This stage includes both the elaboration of possible solutions but also the selection of interventions to be implemented. The development of solutions is based on the analysis of the problem. The hypotheses formed in the previous stage regarding the problem serve as the platform for brainstorming. Brainstorming in this context is the generation of possible intervention ideas from both the consultant and the parent(s) without immediate critique. Quantity of possible solutions is desired and creativity is promoted (Friend & Cook, 1992). For some parents, an incubation period may be helpful prior to brainstorming to consider the information and hypotheses developed to that point (Heppner, 1978).

Given the nature of consultation as an indirect service, it is assumed that the parent will be responsible for implementing the selected intervention. Therefore, several important factors should be considered when selecting the intervention such as (1) complexity of the intervention (Gutkin & Curtis, 1999), (2) parent ownership for the intervention (Reimers, Wacker, & Koeppl, 1987), (3) knowledge base of the parent, (4) ecology of the situation (Gutkin, 1993), (5) available resources (e.g., time, money, assistance), and (6) parent's beliefs about behavior change. These factors influence the likelihood that the intervention will be implemented with integrity and should be carefully considered when developing interventions. Many of the concerns listed above may be managed through the initiation of structured parent training sessions (Shriver, 1998; Ehrhardt, Barnett, Lentz, Stollar, & Reifin, 1996).

Solution Implementation and Follow-Up

With a specifically developed intervention ready for implementation by a trained parent the focus turns to two important issues: (1) treatment fidelity and (2) the evaluation of intervention effectiveness. Treatment fidelity is defined as "the extent to which the treatment conditions as implemented conform to the . . . specifications for the treatment" (Borg & Gall, 1983, p. 648). Many techniques may be used to enhance treatment fidelity including written treatment protocols, audio/video taping of intervention implementation, and direct observation techniques. Regular follow-up sessions with parents will assist in detecting problems in treatment fidelity and their causes.

The evaluation of intervention effectiveness may be evaluated by monitoring the target behavior or problem and comparing frequency, duration or intensity of occurrence against established short- or long-term goals. Ongoing monitoring of the behavior both before and after the implementation of the intervention yields preliminary information on the effects of the intervention. Although this information is not definitive, it may lead parents to hope that an effective intervention program may be found.

Functional Behavior Analysis (FBA)

Functional analysis of human behavior began in the late 1960s as principles of applied behavior analysis were applied to social problems (Martens, Witt, Daly, & Vollmer, 1999). The initial application of FBA was to children with disabilities but more recently it has been applied to all children (Skiba, Waldron, Bahamonde, & Michalek, 1998). FBA enhances understanding of the context of behavior and assists in generating hypotheses regarding the environmental factors that are maintaining the behavior of interest (Skiba et al., 1998).

FBA, when used in conjunction with collaborative consultation and structured problem solving, provides a powerful process of creating ecologically valid and individualized interventions for chronically ill children and their families. FBA is a set of assessment strategies designed to identify antecedent events and consequences to the target behavior or problem. FBA also includes the implementation of trial interventions based upon the analysis of influencing factors (Broussard & Northrup, 1995). The effectiveness of interventions based on FBA provides support for the hypotheses about the problem. In this way, confirmation of diagnostic decisions about the case may be made (Macmann & Barnett, 1999; Broussard & Northrup, 1995; Daly, Witt, Martens, & Dool, 1997).

A typical FBA also uses a problem solving format. In problem identification, the clinician may use interviews, checklists, and observations in an effort to generate possible hypotheses about the stimulus and consequent variables that are maintaining the problem behavior. The unique aspect of FBA includes the identification and implementation of ongoing progress monitoring of the problem behavior, the use of mini-experiments (i.e., ABA, ABAB), and brief treatment probes (Broussard & Northrup, 1995) to support or refute the hypothesis about the behavior. In this way, intervention decisions are based on a thorough analysis of behavior and actual trial interventions that greatly increase the possibility for effective treatment.

CONCLUSIONS

It is recognized that parent education programs for those with chronically ill children must take into account the multitude of factors that influence the problem(s) such as the severity of the disorder, functional level of the child, premorbid family functioning, to name a few. These factors weigh heavily into the behavioral, academic, social, and medical problems faced by these families. Indeed the heterogeneous problems faced by families with chronically ill children necessitate a process for developing parent interventions or educational programs rather than expecting canned programs to be effective for all.

The process proposed here includes a collaborative consultation approach using problem-solving and functional behavior analysis for the purpose of developing specific and ecologically valid intervention programs. The emphasis on baseline and ongoing data collection, goal setting, and follow-up places a premium in data-based decision making. Clinical practice of this sort sets the stage for action research by clinicians thus adding to our knowledge of effective interventions (Johnson, Stoner, & Green, 1996).

REFERENCES

Adams, P. F., & Benson, V. (1990). Current estimates from the National Health Interview Survey, 1989. *Vital Health Statistics, 176*(10). National Center for Health Statistics, U.S. Department of Health and Human Services.

Barkley, R. A. (1997). *Defiant children: A clinician's manual for assessment and parent training.* New York: Guilford.

Bergan, J. R., & Kratchowill, T. R. (1977). *Behavioral consultation and therapy.* New York: Plenum.

Borg, W. R., & Gall, M. D. (1983). *Educational research: An introduction* (4th Ed.) New York: Longman.

Bronfenbrenner, U. (1979). *The ecology of human development.* Cambridge MA: Harvard University Press.

Broussard, C. D., & Northrup, J. (1995). An approach to functional assessment and analysis of disruptive behavior in regular education classrooms. *School Psychology Quarterly, 10,* 151–164.

Brown, D., Pryzwansky, W. B., & Schulte, A. C. (1995). *Psychological consultation: Introduction to theory and practice* (3rd ed.). Boston: Allyn & Bacon.

Burns, B. J., & Cromer, W. W. (1978). The evolving role of the psychologist in primary health care practitioner training for mental health services. *Journal of Clinical Child Psychology, 7,* 8–12.

Caplan, G. (1970). *Theory and practice of mental health consultation.* Boston: Allyn & Bacon.

Caplan, G. (1974). *Support systems and community mental health.* New York: Behavioral Publications.

Caplan, G., & Caplan, R. B. (1993). *Mental health consultation and collaboration.* San Francisco: Jossey-Bass.

Daly, E. J., Witt, J. C., Martens, B. K., & Dool, E. J. (1997). A model for conducting a functional analysis of academic performance problems. *School Psychology Review, 26,* 554–574.

Drotar, D. (1997). Relating parent and family functioning to the psychological adjustment of children with chronic health conditions: What have we learned? What do we need to know? *Journal of Pediatric Psychology, 22,* 149–165.

Ehrhardt, K. E., Barnett, D. W., Lentz, F. E., Stollar, S. A., & Reifin, L. H. (1996). Innovative methodology in ecological consultation: Use of scripts to promote treatment acceptability and integrity *School Psychology Quarterly, 11,* 149–168.

Friend, M., & Cook, L. (1992). *Interactions: Collaboration skills for school professionals.* New York: Longman.

Gutkin, T. B. (1993). Moving from behavioral to ecobehavioral consultation: What's in a name? *Journal of Educational and Psychological Consultation, 4,* 95–99.

Gutkin, T. B., & Curtis, M. J. (1999). School-based consultation theory and practice: The art and science of indirect service delivery. In C. R. Reynolds & T. B. Gutkin (eds.). *The handbook of school psychology* (3rd ed.) (pp. 598–637). New York: Wiley.

Heppner, P. P. (1978). A review of the problem-solving literature and its relationship to the counseling process. *Journal of Counseling Psychology, 25,* 366–375.

Johnson, T. C., Stoner, G., & Green, S. K. (1996). Demonstrating the experimenting society model with classwide behavior management interventions. *School Psychology Review, 25,* 199–213.

Kampwirth, T. J. (1999). *Collaborative consultation in the schools: Effective practices for students with learning and behavior problems.* Upper Saddle River, New Jersey: Merrill.

Kazak, A. B. (1989). Families of chronically ill children: A systems and social ecological model of adaptation and challenge. *Journal of Consulting and Clinical Psychology, 57,* 25–30.

Kazak, A. E., (1997). A contextual family/systems approach to pediatric psychology: Introduction to the special issue. *Journal of Pediatric Psychology, 22,* 141–148.

Kazak, A. E., Boyer, B., Brophy, P., Johnson, K., Scher, C., Covelman, K., & Scott, S. (1995). Parental perceptions of procedure-related distress and family adaptation in childhood leukemia. *Children's Health Care, 24,* 143–158.

Kazak, A. B., Segal-Andrews, A. M., & Johnson, K. (1998). Pediatric psychology research and practice: A family/systems approach. In M. C. Roberts (Ed.), *Handbook of pediatric psychology.* New York: Guilford Press.

Kuhn, T. S. (1970). *The structure of scientific revolutions.* (2nd ed.). Chicago: University of Chicago Press.

Kupst, M. J., Schulman, J. L., Henig, G., Maurer, H., Morgan, E., & Fochtman, D. (1982). Family coping with leukemia: A one year after diagnosis. *Journal of Pediatric Psychology, 7,* 157–174.

Kupst, M. J., & Schulman, J. L. (1988). Long-term coping with pediatric leukemia: A six-year follow-up study. *Journal of Pediatric Psychology, 13,* 7–23.

Lavigne, J. V., Nolan, P., & McLone, P. G. (1988). Temperament, coping, and psychological adjustment in young children with myelomeningocele. *Journal of Pediatric Psychology, 13,* 363–378.

Lazarus, R. S., & Folkman, S. (1984). *Stress, appraisal, and coping.* New York: Springer.

Lee, S. W. (1991). The family with a chronically ill child. In M. J. Fine (Ed.), *Collaboration with parents of exceptional children.* (pp. 201–218). Brandon, VT: Clinical Psychology Publishing Company.

Lee, S. W., & Guck, T. P. (2000) The family with a chronically ill child. In M. J. Fine & R. L. Simpson (Eds.). *Collaboration with parents and families of children and youth with exceptionalities.* Austin, Texas: Pro-Ed.

Lester, N., Smart, L., & Baum, A. (1994). Measuring coping flexibility. *Psychology and Health, 9,* 409–424.

Linehan, M. M. (1993). *Cognitive-behavioral treatment of borderline personality disorder.* New York: Guilford Press.

Macmann, G. M., & Barnett, D. W. (1999). Diagnostic decision making in school psychology: Understanding and coping with uncertainty. In C. R. Reynolds & T. B. Gutkin (Eds.), *The handbook of school psychology* (3rd ed.) (pp. 519–548). New York: Wiley.

Martens, B. K., Witt, J. C., Daly, E. J., & Vollmer, T. R. (1999). Behavior analysis: Theory and practice in educational settings. In C. R. Reynolds & T. B. Gutkin (Eds.), *The handbook of school psychology* (3rd ed.) (pp. 638–663). New York: Wiley.

McMahon, C. M., Lambros, K. M., & Sylvia, J. A. (1998). Chronic illness in childhood: A hypothesis-testing approach. In Watson & Gresham (Eds.) *Handbook of child behavior therapy.* (pp. 311–333) New York: Plenum.

Newacheck, P. W., Budetti, P. P., & Halfon, N. (1986). Trends in activity-limiting chronic conditions among children. *American Journal of Public Health, 76,* 178–184.

Newacheck, P. W., & Taylor, W. R. (1992). Childhood chronic illness: Prevalence, severity, and impact. *American Journal of Public Health, 82,* 364–371.

O'Hearn, T. C., & Gatz, M. (1996). The educational pyramid: A model for community intervention. *Applied and Preventive Psychology, 5,* 127–134.

Perrin, J. M., & MacLean, W. E. (1988). Biomedical and psychosocial dimensions of chronic childhood illness. In P. Karoly (Ed.), *Handbook of child health assessment: biopsychosocial perspectives.* New York: John Wiley & Sons.

Perrin, E. C., Newacheck, P., Pless, I. B., Drotar, D., Gortmaker, S. L., Leventhal, J., Perrin, J. M., Stein, R. E. K., Walker, D. K., & Weitzman, M. (1993). Issues involved in the definition and classification of chronic health conditions. *Pediatrics, 91,* 787–793.

Phelps, L. (Ed.) (1998). *Health-related disorders in childhood and adolescents.* Washington, DC: American Psychological Association.

Pinto, R. P., & Hollandsworth, J. G. (1989). Using videotape to prepare children psychologically for surgery: Influence of parents and costs versus benefits of providing preparation services. *Health Psychology, 8,* 79–95.

Pless, I. B., & Perrin, J. M. (1985). Issues common to a variety of illnesses. In N. Hobbs & J. M. Perrin (Eds.), *Issues in the care of children with chronic illness.* San Francisco, CA: Jossey-Bass.

Pless, I. B. & Pinkerton, P. (1975). *Chronic childhood disorders: promoting Patterns of adjustment.* London, England: Henry Kimpton Publishers.

Powers, S. W., Blount, R. L., Bachanas, P. J., Cotter, M. W., & Swan, S. C. (1993).

Helping preschool leukemia patients and their parents cope during injections. *Journal of Pediatric Psychology, 18,* 681–695.

Randolph, D. L., & Mitchell, M. M. (1995). A survey of consultation articles in key counseling journals, 1967–1991. *Journal of Educational and Psychological Consultation, 6,* 83–94.

Reimers, T. M., Wacker, D. P., & Koeppl, G. (1987). Acceptability of behavioral treatments: A review of the literature. *School Psychology Review, 16,* 212–227.

Roberts, M. C., & Wright, L. (1982). The role of the pediatric psychologist as consultant to pediatricians. In J. Tuma (Ed.), *Handbook for the practice of pediatric psychology.* (pp. 251–289). New York: Wiley.

Satin, W., LaGreca, A. M., Zigo, M. A., & Skyler, J. S. (1989). Diabetes in adolescence: Effects of multifamily group intervention and parent simulation of diabetes. *Journal of Pediatric Psychology, 14,* 259–275.

Shriver, M. D. (1998). Teaching parenting skills. In Watson & Gresham (Eds.) *Handbook of child behavior therapy.* (pp. 165–182) New York: Plenum.

Singer, M., & Berg, P. (Eds). (1997). *Exploring genetic mechanisms.* Sausalito CA: University Science Books.

Skiba, R., Waldron, N., Bahamonde, C., & Michalek, D. (1998, May). A four-step model for functional behavior assessment. *Communique, 28,* 24–26.

Stein, R. E. K., & Jessop, D. J. (1982) A non-categorical approach to chronic childhood illness. *Public Health Report, 97,* 355–359.

Thompson, R. J., Gil, K. M., Burbach, D. J., Keith, B., & Kinney, T. R. (1993). The role of child and maternal processes in the psychological adjustment of children with sickle cell disease. *Journal of Consulting and Clinical Psychology, 61,* 468–474.

Thompson, R. J., & Gustafson, K. E. (1996). *Adaptation to chronic childhood illness.* Washington, DC: American Psychological Association.

Thompson, R. J., Gustafson, K. E. Hamlett, K. W., & Spock, A. (1992). Psychological adjustment of children with cystic fibrosis: The role of child cognitive processes and maternal adjustment. *Journal of Pediatric Psychology. 17,* 741–755.

Wallander, J. L., & Thompson, R. J. (1998). Psychological adjustment of children with chronic physical conditions. In M. C. Roberts (Ed.), *Handbook of Pediatric Psychology.* New York: Guilford Press.

Wallander, J. L., & Varni, J. W. (1992). Adjustment in children with chronic physical disorders: Programmatic research on a disability-stress-coping model. In A. M. LaGreca, L. J. Siegel, J. L. Wallander, & C. E. Walker (Eds.), *Stress and coping in child health.* New York: Guilford Press.

Wallander, J. L., Varni, J. W., Babani, L. V., Banis, H. T., & Wilcox, K. T. (1989). Family resources as resistance factors for psychological maladjustment in chronically ill and handicapped children. *Journal of Pediatric Psychology, 14,* 157–173.

Wodrich, D. L. (1994). *Attention Deficit Hyperactivity Disorder: What every Parent wants to know.* Baltimore: Brookes.

Zastowny, T. R., Kirschenbaum, D. S., & Meng, A. L., (1986). Coping skills training for children: Effects on distress before, during, and after hospitalization for surgery. *Health Psychology, 5,* 231–247.

Zins, J. E., & Heron, T. E. (Eds.). (1996). Current practices, unresolved issues, and future directions in consultation. *Remedial and Special Education, 17*(6).

CHAPTER 14

Education Programs for Parents and Families of Children and Youth with Developmental Disabilities

Earle Knowlton

Department of Special Education, University of Kansas, Lawrence, Kansas

Douglas Mulanax

Lawrence Public Schools, Lawrence, Kansas

INTRODUCTION

Since the U.S. Congress enacted the *Education for All Handicapped Children Act of 1975* (P.L. 94-142), and with it the requirement that parents of children and youth with disabilities participate in the appropriate education of their daughters and sons, considerable efforts have been expended to support parental participation. Traditionally, this support has taken three forms: (1) to involve parents in educational decision making, (2) to present them with information regarding the processes, procedures, and outcomes of special education and rehabilitation, and (3) to provide them with skills to perform specific tasks that augment the services professionals are providing. Efforts to engender parental participation in the education of students with developmental disabilities have evolved from piecemeal, narrowly focused programs that the literature of the 1970s and early 1980s reports to widescale family systems approaches currently in vogue.

In this chapter, we will review parent education models, programs, and their effectiveness data and draw conclusions about the current state of practice with respect to the education of parents and families of children

Handbook of Diversity in Parent Education
Copyright © 2001 by Academic Press. All rights of reproduction in any form reserved.

and youth with developmental disabilities. We first attempt to clarify selected terminology. We then proceed to discuss the various models and programs followed by some concluding remarks concerning current practices and future needs.

RELATED TERMINOLOGY

Perusal of the relevant literature reveals limited clarification on the part of authors of terms related to the thrust of parent programs, e.g., parent training. Moreover, anyone familiar with the literature of the disability field will recognize the confusion created by the proliferation of acronyms and the convolution of terminology usage here as well. For the purpose of this chapter, we clarify the following terms.

Parental Participation

In the strict sense, parental participation is a legal term used in conjunction with federal and state statutes pertaining to the requirement of a free, appropriate public education for children and youth with disabilities. Schools were first required by P.L. 94-142 (the *Individuals with Disabilities Education Act Amendments of 1997*, hereafter will be referred to as the 1997 IDEA Amendments) to engage parents in the development and implementation of their daughters' and sons' Individualized Education Programs and to inform them clearly of their rights to appeal and/or refuse the services contained therein. This requirement set the stage for a host of parent education efforts that functioned to equip parents with pertinent information (information sharing) with parents or to teach them specific skills (skill building).

Information Sharing

For parents of children and youth with developmental disabilities, information sharing refers to the goal of transmitting information and knowledge rather than specific attitudes, skills, and/or behaviors to parents. Upon P.L. 94-142's passage in 1975, schools began as required to provide parents with written information concerning their rights; however, it was parent advocacy groups such as the ARC (formerly, the Association for

Retarded Citizens and, initially, the Association for Retarded Children) that provided educational programs for parents. These programs systematically reviewed P.L. 94-142's features, resulting in increased knowledge of the law on the part of parents who took part in such programs.

Skill Building

In contrast to information sharing, skill building focuses on teaching parents specific skills and/or training parents in new patterns of behavior. Behavioral programs are the most common among these sorts of training efforts, that is, those programs that are based in techniques of operant conditioning (e.g., applied behavioral analysis), wherein a parent is trained to define, observe, and record her or his child's desired and undesired behaviors, and attempt to increase the former while decreasing the latter. Training of this type requires the parent to learn, practice, and refine specific attitudes, skills, and behaviors.

Developmental Disabilities

Frequently, the usage of "developmental disabilities" is as an umbrella term, covering developmental delays with reference to young children, mental retardation with reference to school-age children and youth, and, nominally, developmental disabilities with reference to those at or beyond majority age (usually 15). The term often includes congenital conditions such as autism, severe/multiple disabilities, cerebral palsy, and other physical disabilities but not mental or physical conditions for which onset is adventitious, such as traumatic brain injury. Developmental disabilities as a term is also employed, without regard to age, as a synonym for mental retardation by those authors who view the latter term as stigmatizing and pejorative.

THE EVOLUTION OF PROGRAMS FOR PARENTS OF CHILDREN AND YOUTH WITH DEVELOPMENTAL DISABILITIES

As discussed in the introduction to this book, parent programs are not new; indeed nearly 30 years ago, Gordon (1971) published *Parent Effective-*

ness Training and, earlier, Ginott (1965) published the first of his trilogy, *Between Parent and Child*. The popular literature, as characterized by these examples, as well as similar-era publications in the professional literature (e.g., Auerbach, 1968), point to a period in which widespread interest in parent education began to be reflected in both the popular and professional literature.

Descriptions of programs for parents of children and youth with developmental disabilities similarly are not new, and the chronology of their dissemination roughly parallels those programs geared to parents of normally developing children. Though, as mentioned above, significant promulgation of these programs and, later, systems models, occurred on the heels of P.L. 94-142, sporadic publications can be traced back to the early and mid-1960s (cf. Appell, Williams, & Fishell, 1964; Patterson & Gullion, 1968).

An early comprehensive literature review of programs for parents of children and youth with disabilities was conducted by Clements and Alexander (1975). Its publication in October of that year preceded P.L. 94-142's enactment by 1 month. Accordingly, the authors, perhaps unwittingly but certainly significantly, provided a glimpse at practices that were in place up to the point at which children and youth with disabilities in the U.S. were accorded the right to an appropriate education and their parents, the right to participate therein.

Pre-P.L. 94-142 Practices

Clements and Alexander (1975) observed that, prior to the 1960s when special education began its rapid expansion, parental involvement was essentially nonexistent. Only when serious abuses of the civil rights of children and youth with disabilities, particularly developmental disabilities and learning disabilities, came to light did the political action of various parent advocacy groups emerge (e.g., the aforementioned ARC, and the Association for Children with Learning Disabilities). The work of these advocacy groups, and their literal education and training of parents who affiliated with them, were major factors in the various state special education statutes that were enacted in the 1970s, the class action litigation of the 1960s and early 1970s, and the eventual passage of P.L. 94-142.

Prior to the emphasis on political action by parents just prior to P.L. 94-142's enactment, parent programs of the 1960s and 1970s were of three types: (1) behavioral, (2) psychological insight, and (3) experiential (Clements & Alexander, 1975).

Behavioral Programs

These programs by and large were oriented toward skill building, i.e., teaching parents specific skills with which to modify their daughters' and sons' academic and social behaviors. Parents were taught to define and chart target behaviors as well as specific techniques to reinforce, maintain, extinguish, or punish these behaviors. Chief among the programs popular during this era were those that focused on discipline and the management of disruptive behavior (cf. Madsen & Madsen, 1972; Patterson & Gullion, 1968).

Psychological Insight Programs

Given the supplementation of published materials of this type with face-to-face instruction, these programs were primarily educational, seeking to achieve in parents an understanding of the nature of the developmental disability and its impact on learning, development, behavior, and vocational aptitude. Stewart's (1974) *Counseling Parents of Exceptional Children* was a popular example of this type of parent education approach.

Experiential Programs

Similar to behavioral programs, this approach sought to train parents in specific interaction patterns with their children through instruction that featured guided experience. Unlike the behavioral category, however, the grounding of programs of this type was not limited to operant principles, nor were the objectives of the training limited to the modification of children's academic and social behavior. Instead, many experiential programs attempted to train parents to enhance various aspects of development (e.g., language, motor) that otherwise would have been impeded by the disability. Jordan's (1971) special issue of the journal, Exceptional Children, was devoted to this approach to parent education.

Post-P.L. 94-142 Trends

The number of programs to train parents of children and youth with developmental disabilities accelerated in the decade following P.L. 94-142's passage. Most of these programs were funded by the U.S. Office of Special Education (formerly, the Bureau of Education for the Handicapped) and focused on the home as the site of the training. The majority were behavioral in their approach (Elksnin & Elksnin, 1991).

In 1983, and again in 1986, The *Education for All Handicapped Children Act* was amended.[1] The 1983 Amendments specified how the collaborative process between and among schools and adult service agencies should proceed with respect to the school-to-adult-life transition all students with disabilities must make. The 1986 Amendments similarly clarified the collaborative process between and among agencies responsible for early childhood special education. The 1986 Amendments also required public schools to provide children from ages 3 to 4 a free, appropriate public education, enacting an "ages certain" under the law as 3 through 21 (Turnbull,, 1993).

Taken together these two amendments in a span of 3 years opened the door to parent education efforts that focused not only on school-aged children and youth with disabilities, but also on preschoolers and youth in transition to adult life. By the mid–1980s, there began the evolution of parent programs that were less discrete with regard to information and skill building objectives and foci and more systemic with particular attention to family systems and the impact on them by the child or youth with a developmental disability (e.g., Turnbull, Brotherson, & Summers, 1985).

EFFECTIVENESS OF PARENT PROGRAMS IN THE 1980s AND 1990s

Clearly, the availability of federal monies, authorized by P.L. 94-142 and its subsequent amendments, and the demand for outcome accountability by consumers and the research community stimulated not only the promulgation of parent programs in the 1980s and 1990s but also empirical documentation of their effectiveness. With reference to developmental

---

[1]The *Education for All Handicapped Children Act* has been amended numerous times since 1975. In addition to the amendments enhancing the processes of transition from school to adult life and early childhood special education, the most significant amendments occurred in 1990 and 1997. In 1990, the classifications of autism and traumatic brain injury became reimbursable and the Act was renamed the *Individuals with Disabilities Education Act* (IDEA). The 1997 *IDEA Amendments*, addressed selected disciplinary procedures, earmarked the general education curriculum as the reference point for instructional adaptations and accommodations, added classroom teachers to placement and planning team compositions, and revised the classification and reimbursement system.

disabilities, the work of Baker (1988, 1989) perhaps best attests to this dual thrust of program development and evaluation.

Baker (1989) advanced 11 criteria with which to evaluate skill-building programs for parents of children and youth with developmental disabilities. For ease of presentation, we group these criteria in terms of (1) parental perception criteria and (2) consequential criteria.

Perception Criteria

Five of the criteria directly or indirectly address parental perceptions and satisfaction. The first, social validity, asks if parents view as worthwhile the programs goals and methods. The next three criteria, enrollment, completion, and participation, focus on whether parents involve themselves in training opportunities, complete the program, and do what they are asked to do, respectively. The fifth criterion addresses parents' overall satisfaction with the program.

Consequential Criteria

These six criteria reflect program outcomes. The criterion of proficiency addresses parental learning, whereas the next three criteria, child gains, maintenance of gains, and maintenance of teaching, respectively, refer to the degree to which the child behaves as the program intended, maintains that behavior, and whether parents maintain the skills they learned during the program. The final two criteria, benefits and advocacy, focus on changes in attitudes of the parents and the nature of parental advocacy for their children's education, respectively.

Baker's own program, "Parents as Teachers" has been extensively evaluated and is perhaps the flagship training program for parents of preschool and school-age children and youth with developmental disabilities (Baker, 1989; Baker, Landen, & Kashima, 1991). Its qualities include its longitudinality (over 25 years) and its data (demographics and outcomes for hundreds of families). Parents as Teachers is a behaviorally based program intended to enhance the development of children, ages 3 to 13, by increasing their parents' skills in the application of applied behavior analysis. Specific disabilities of the children include autism, cerebral palsy, congenital brain damage, and mental retardation. Training spans 10 weeks with three assessment probes interspersed, one at the beginning, one at the midpoint, and one at the program's conclusion. Content focuses on self-help skills, behavior management, and the generalization of trained skills to natural settings.

Demographic, perception, and consequential data for 341 families, trained between 1972 and the late 1980s were taken from samples in Boston and Los Angeles of families of mixed ethnicity and socioeconomic status (Baker, 1989). Of import were the program's consequential data, which demonstrated significant pre- to post-increases in participants' teaching skills and, concomitantly, significant gain scores in their children's self-help skills and appropriate social behavior (Baker, 1989).

The literature reveals a smattering of efforts at information sharing and skill building for parents at scales smaller than that reflected in Baker's (1989) work; these efforts are reviewed below.

Volenski (1995) developed the Parent Education and Guidance Program, an 8-month effort consisting of bimonthly meetings designed to educate parents about the nature of their son's or daughter's developmental disability, and ways in which the public school system could assist them in gathering information pertinent to the needs of their children. Parental self-awareness was a secondary objective of the program. The program featured discussions concerning the acceptance of the child and her or his disability, parent–child and parent–parent communication skills, and parental "burn out."

Volenski (1995) administered a preprogram questionnaire to 80 participants. Questions centered on what parents knew about their son's or daughter's disability, their views regarding the responsiveness of the public schools, and their predictions for their son or daughter insofar as the future is concerned. Preprogram results indicated that parents felt isolated and did not know of resources for help and guidance. In addition, parents wanted to educate themselves and be effective when working with their children. At the completion of the program, it was reported that the stress parents experienced several months earlier had diminished, and anxiety in the areas of parent–child communication and school-home communication had been reduced.

Heritage, Rogers, and West (1994) created a program that provided formal and informal support to parents of children with Down syndrome who indicated that overwhelming feelings of stress, changes in lifestyle, and continued concern for siblings were their most important concerns. Formal networks of informational support included community services such as schools, health professionals, and support groups consisting of other parents. The informal network consisted of immediate family and friends. The dual existence of both formal and informal support networks proved to be most helpful and influential.

One of the most useful formal supports reported by parents was the opportunity to share feelings and experiences with other parents of children with Down syndrome (Heritage, Rogers, & West, 1994). Parents reported that they benefited from opportunities to compare and contrast situations and circumstances with other parents. Parents reported that they were more empowered as they interacted with professionals and more compassionate toward spouses and other family members. With respect to informal support, mothers listed their spouses as the most important support persons. They suggested that when support is given by the spouse, they were more confident in their ability to care for their child, and they were more likely to assume an attitude of acceptance of her or his disability. Conversely, when the spouse did not share a commitment in the child's development, the mother tended to feel unprepared and overwhelmed.

Schafer, Bell, and Spalding (1987) observed that many professionals underestimate the amount of valuable information that parents can supply to professionals. Moreover, the authors noted that parents of young children with developmental delays often overestimate the child's level of development. On the basis of these observations, the authors trained parents to assess the developmental progress of their sons and daughters over an extended period of time. As a result of the training, parents began to assess their child's behavior and progress more accurately during and after the training and their tendency toward overestimation was reduced.

Lantzy and Gable (1989) developed a training program to enhance collaborative behavior management efforts between parents and teachers of preschool children with developmental delays. Participating parents were given two 1-hr training sessions that covered basic principles of behavior analysis. Once problem behaviors were targeted, parents were taught how and when to praise their child contingently. Parental training included role playing, selection of intervention strategies, and verbal praise and correction procedures. Parents were also coached regarding how to decrease undesirable behaviors through extinction, interruption, and redirection. The results suggested that, when parents are trained to carry out behavioral procedures at home in a manner that is consistent with the use of these procedures in the school setting, appropriate social behavior was increased and unacceptable behavior was decreased.

FAMILY SYSTEMS APPROACHES TO EDUCATION AND TRAINING

Concerns in regard to the effects of family ecology on both the amenability of parents to information sharing and skill building programs and the ultimate benefits of such programs on their children led practitioners to begin by the early to mid-1980s to apply concepts pertinent to family systems theory (Bricker, 1986). Minuchin (1974), for example, theorized that at least four systems operate in an interdependent manner for any one family: parent–child, parent–parent, child–child (if there are siblings), and family–extrafamily (extended family, friends, and neighbors). Researchers and practitioners interested in the implications of family systems for parents of children and youth with developmental disabilities began to advance models and programs that, by the 1990s, had become the principal approach to information sharing and skill building programs.

Family systems approaches[2] to educating parents of children and youth with developmental disabilities generally have targeted two crucial transition periods in the lives of these individuals and their families: the transition from early childhood to K–12 schooling and the transition from school to adult life and work (cf. Able-Boone, Sandall, Loughry, & Frederick, 1990; Knowlton, Turnbull, Backus, & Turnbull, 1986). Either transition brings with it exceeding concern and stress on the part of families. The overriding aim of information provision and skill building efforts in these areas is to affect outcomes that will enable the child or young adult and her or his family to achieve these transitions successfully. Below we examine family systems approaches in early childhood-to-school and school-to-adult living transitions, respectively.

The Transition from Early Childhood to K–12 Schooling

Unlike disabilities that manifest in relation to classroom academic demands, e.g., learning disabilities, most developmental disabilities are evident during the early childhood years if not at birth (Battshaw, 1997). Thus, parents often find themselves requiring information and skills as their child progresses through infancy, toddlerhood, and the preschool

---

[2]Several synonymous terms describing this approach appear in the literature. They include family-focused, family-centered, family-friendly, and family-directed (Bailey et al., 1998).

years. Issues emerging during this period that require information through a family systems approach include accurate diagnostic interpretations, coping with stigma, and forming realistic expectations for the child (Turnbull & Turnbull, 1997) as well as the skills necessary to adapt to the daily and episodic demands that having a child with developmental disabilities can produce (Gallimore, Weisner, Bernheimer, Guthrie, & Nihira, 1993). Family systems approaches are grounded in the assumption that effective early intervention includes provisions of support, in the form of information and skills, to the child's parents, siblings, and other involved family members (Dunst, 1985). Although evaluation research with respect to child-centered outcomes of early intervention is evident in the literature, surprisingly little data exist to document the effectiveness of family systems approaches in terms of outcomes for parents, siblings, and other family members (Bailey et al., 1998).

Bailey and colleagues (Bailey et al., 1998) recently proposed a framework for assessing such outcomes. This framework consists of a series of evaluative questions that center on family perceptions of early intervention and the transition to K–12 schooling and questions that incorporate indices of impact that services have had on the child and her or his family. Perception-oriented questions ask if the family sees intervention services as making a difference in the life of the child and in the life of the family. The authors appropriately point out that such questions, although potentially useful, are perhaps necessary but insufficient for evaluative purposes because parents and other family members often have no standard against which early intervention services can be judged (Bailey et al., 1998).

Impact-oriented questions proposed by Bailey et al. (1998) center on changes in parents' and family members' levels of competence with respect a variety of issues a child with developmental disabilities presents. Five areas of impact are targeted. The first relates to parent–child interactions and whether services have improved the nature of these interactions and thus enhanced the child's development. The second area of impact concerns improved working relationships with professional service providers; often termed "empowerment," the question in regard to this area of impact is whether the family has gathered the knowledge and skills necessary to achieve a better sense of control over their lives currently and in the future. Third, the framework of Bailey et al. (1998) focuses on the strength of the family's support system. Supports are informal and consist mainly of networks of extended family members, friends, and persons of various professional and nonprofessional roles in the community (e.g., social worker, pediatric nurse, bus driver) who the family can count on to assist as necessary.

The final two impact areas target expectations for the future and eventual lifestyle quality. Turnbull and Turnbull (1997) aptly observed that the nature of the relationship among family members and professionals shapes the view, especially on the part of parents, of the child's future and of the potential for an adequate if not optimal quality of life. These two areas of impact represent the bellwether of any evaluation of a family systems approach because they focus on the ultimate functioning of the child, despite her or his young age. Too often, services for young children with developmental disabilities and their families are myopic, inordinately mired in the present without regard to the long-term information and skills necessary for maximum independence and the highest possible quality of life (Knowlton, 1998).

The Transition from School to Adult Life and Work

Like the transition to K–12 schooling for young children with developmental disabilities, the transition from K–12 schooling to adult life and work places challenging demands on parents (Knowlton et al., 1986). Despite their legal right to informed participation in this transition process, parents and family members have experienced a lack of pertinent information and difficulty adapting to the adult status of their sons and daughters or family members with developmental disabilities (Brotherson et al., 1988; Ferguson, Ferguson, & Jones, 1988; McDonnell, Wilcox, Boles, & Bellamy, 1985; McNair & Rusch, 1991). If one were to accept the argument that future planning is desirable for families of young children with developmental disabilities, one would agree that it is crucial for the successful transition to adult living. Moreover, the historic lack of attention to future planning by service providers led to the stipulation in the *IDEA Amendments of 1997* that an individualized transition plan must be in place for all students with disabilities no later than age 14.

Thus, there continues to be a need for effective familywide services and programs that can assist in this transition. Well over two dozen follow-up studies, conducted from the mid-1980s through the 1990s, have demonstrated that youth with developmental disabilities consistently (1) experience significantly higher unemployment rates in contrast to youth without disabilities, (2) tend toward solitary and sedentary lifestyles, and (3) live with their parents or caregivers at significantly higher rates than do their nondisabled peers (cf. Hasazi et al., 1985; Wagner, Blackorby, Cameto, & Newman, 1994).

One of the more significant and pertinent findings that emerged from these studies is the correlation between long-term, meaningful employment for youth with developmental disabilities and the existence and utility of a "self-friend-family network" (Hasazi et al., 1985, p. 232). When a nurtured, perpetual system of support existed among the family and members of the community, the odds were higher that the youth with developmental disabilities would find and maintain employment and experience a satisfactory quality of life. As suggested by Bailey et al. (1998) with respect to early intervention programs for families and by Heritage, Rogers, and West (1994) with reference to parental acceptance of their child's disability, skills and information that enable the development and maintenance of informal support networks appear to affect in a positive manner the transition from school to adult life and work for youth with developmental disabilities.

Turnbull, Turnbull, Bronicki, Summers, and Roeder–Gordon (1989) produced perhaps the most comprehensive compendium of transition-related information for parents and families of youth with developmental disabilities. The compendium assists families with information regarding financial planning, government benefits, community services, and advocacy. The information, supplemented with examples of its applications in vignettes, is sequenced in a manner that smoothes the shift, as viewed from the parental perspective, from the public school context to the more complex and ambiguous context of the adult service system—a shift that will produce significant stress for parents and other family members (Brotherson et al., 1988). Moreover, Turnbull et al. (1989) provide families with useful guidelines for selecting appropriate options (e.g., majority status versus consent) as the important decision-making junctures of this transition period present themselves.

CONCLUDING REMARKS

As mentioned at the outset of this chapter, parents' participation in the education of children and youth with developmental disabilities is a right accorded to them by federal law. In this chapter, we have attempted to demonstrate that programs designed to share relevant information with parents and to teach them skills to work effectively with their children have evolved through the years from discrete programs dedicated to specific aims and outcomes to more comprehensive, family-systems approaches. Data regarding the effectiveness of the more discrete programs suggest that they generally have achieved what they have intended. With regard to family-systems approaches, there appear to be more data indicative of needs on the part of parents and family members than there are data that clearly delineate positive outcomes of these approaches.

Clearly, the presence of a legal mandate for parental participation has not only been sustained by the numerous amendments to P.L. 94-142 in the past quarter century, it has been fortified by those amendments. Owing in no small part to the continuing need to involve not only parents but also siblings and other family members in educational planning and programming decisions throughout the lifespan of persons with developmental disabilities, family systems approaches have come to the fore.

There is no reason to suspect that these approaches will attenuate in number and kind. Unfortunately, however, it is currently difficult to ascertain exactly how effective family-systems approaches are in terms of increased awareness and use of pertinent information, and increased skill levels on the part of parents and families. Until such information is reported, family-systems approaches will lack a database sufficient for judgments as to their effectiveness. In the meantime, perceptions of their appropriateness and the promise of their effectiveness will perpetuate their popularity with practitioners and families.

REFERENCES

Abel-Boone, H., Sandall, S., Loughry, A., & Frederick, L. (1990). An informed, family-centered approach to Public Law 99-457: Parental views. *Topics in Early Childhood Special Education, 10,* 100–111.

Appell, M., Williams, C., & Fishell, L. (1964). Changes in attitudes of parents of retarded children. *American Journal of Mental Deficiency, 68,* 807–812.

Auerbach, B. (1968). *Parents learn through discussion: Principles and practices of parent group education.* New York: John Wiley & Sons.

Bailey, D., McWilliam, R., Darkes, L. A., Hebbeler, K., Simeonsson, R., Spiker, D., & Wagner, M. (1998). Family outcomes in early intervention: A framework for program evaluation and efficacy research. *Exceptional Children, 64,* 313–328.

Baker, B. (1988). Evaluating parent training. *Irish Journal of Psychology, 9,* 324–345.

Baker, B. (1989). *Parent training and developmental disabilities.* Washington, DC: American Association on Mental Retardation.

Baker, B., Landen, S., & Kashima, K. (1991). Effects of parent training on families of children with mental retardation: Increased burden or generalized benefit? *American Journal on Mental Retardation, 96,* 127–136.

Batshaw, M. (1997). *Children with disabilities* (4th Ed.). Baltimore: Paul Brookes.

Bricker, D. (1986). *Early education of at-risk and handicapped infants, toddlers, and preschool children.* Glenview, IL: Scott, Foresman & Co.

Brotherson, M. J., Turnbull, A., Bronicki, G., Houghton, J., Roeder-Gordon, C., Summers, J., & Turnbull, H. R. (1988). Transition into adulthood: Parental planning for sons and daughters with disabilities. *Education and Training in Mental Retardation, 23,* 165–173.

Clements, J. E., & Alexander, R. (1975). Parent training: Bringing it all back home. *Focus on Exceptional Children, 7*(5), 1–12.

Dunst, C. (1985). Rethinking early intervention. *Analysis and Intervention in Developmental Disabilities, 5,* 165–201.

Elksnin, L. & Elksnin, N. (1991). Helping parents solve problems at home and school through parent training. *Intervention in School and Clinic, 26,* 230–233, 245.

Ferguson, P., Ferguson, D., & Jones, D. (1988). Generations of hope: Parental perspectives on the transitions of their children with severe retardation from school to adult life. *Journal of the Association for Persons with Severe Handicaps, 13,* 177–187.

Gallimore, R., Weisner, T., Bernheimer, L., Guthrie, D., & Nihira, K. 1993). Family responses to young children with developmental delays: Accommodation activity in ecological and cultural context. *American Journal on Mental Retardation, 98,* 185–206.

Ginott, H. (1965). *Between parent and child.* New York: Avon Books.

Gordon, T. (1971). *Parent effectiveness training: The "no-lose" program for raising responsible children.* New York: Peter W. Hyden.

Hasazi, S. B., Gordon, L., Roe, C. A., Hull, M., Finck, K., & Salembier, G. (1985). Statewide follow-up on post high school employment and residential status of students labeled "mentally retarded." *Education and Training of the Mentally Retarded, 20,* 222–234.

Heritage, J., Rogers, H., & West, W. (1994). Effects of support on the attitude of the primary care giver of a child with Down syndrome. Unpublished document, Middle Tennessee State University.

Jordan, J. (Ed.) (1971). The exceptional child's early years [Special Issue]. *Exceptional Children, 37*(9).

Knowlton, H. E. (1998). Considerations in the design of personalized curricular supports for students with developmental disabilities. *Education and Training in Mental Retardation and Developmental Disabilities, 33,* 95–107.

Knowlton, H. E., Turnbull, A., Backus, L., & Turnbull, H. R. (1986). Letting go: Consent and the "yes, but . . ." problem in transition. In B. Ludlow, A. Turnbull, & R. Luckasson (Eds.), *Transitions to adult life for people with mental retardation: Principles and practices* (pp. 45–66). Baltimore: Paul Brookes.

Lantzy, T. J., & Gable, R. (1989, September). *Effects of parent training on the behavior problems in the home of preschool handicapped children.* Paper presented at the 67th Annual Convention of the Council for Exceptional Children, Chicago, IL.

Madsen, C. K., & Madsen, C. H. (1972). *Parents, children, discipline: A positive approach.* Boston: Allyn & Bacon.

McDonnell, J., Wilcox, B., Boles, S., & Bellamy, G. T. (1985). Transition issues facing youth with severe disabilities: Parents' perspective. *Journal of the Association for Persons with Severe Handicaps, 10,* 61–65.

McNair, J., & Rusch, F. (1991). Parent involvement in transition programs. *Mental Retardation, 29,* 93–101.

Minuchin, S. (1974). *Families and family therapy.* Cambridge, MA: Harvard Press.

Patterson, G., & Gullion, M. (1968). *Living with children: New methods for parents and teachers*. Champaign IL: Research Press.

Schafer, S., Bell, P., & Spalding, J. (1987). Parental vs. professional assessment of developmentally delayed children after periods of parent training. *Journal of the Division for Early Childhood, 12*, 47–55.

Stewart, J. (1974). *Counseling parents of exceptional children: Principles, problems, and procedures*. New York: MSS Information Corporation.

Turnbull, H. R., III (1993). *Free appropriate education: The law and children with disabilities* (4th Ed.). Denver: Love Publishing.

Turnbull, A., & Turnbull, H. R. (1997). *Families, professionals, and exceptionality: A special partnership* (3rd Ed.). Upper Saddle River, NJ: Prentice Hall.

Turnbull, A., Brotherson, M. J., & Summers, J. (1985). The impact of deinstitutionalization on families: A family systems approach. In R. H. Bruininks (Ed.), *Living and learning in the least restrictive environment* (pp. 115–152). Baltimore: Paul Brookes.

Turnbull, H. R., Turnbull, A., Bronicki, G., Summers, J., & Roeder-Gordon, C. (1989). *Disability and the family: A guide to decisions for adulthood*. Baltimore: Paul Brookes.

Volenski, L. (1995). Building school support systems for parents of handicapped children: The parent education and guidance program. *Psychology in the Schools, 32*, 124–129.

Wagner, M., Blackorby, J., Cameto, R., & Newman, L. (1994). *What makes a difference? Influences on postschool outcomes of youth with disabilities*. Menlo Park, CA: SRI International.

CHAPTER 15

Educating Parents to be Advocates for their Children

Michelle L. Moriarty

Department of Psychology and Research in Education, University of Kansas, Lawrence Kansas

Marvin J. Fine

Department of Psychology and Research in Education, University of Kansas, Lawrence Kansas

This chapter addresses the importance of parents serving as advocates for their children especially in regard to their children's educational needs. Because parents find themselves in contact with their children's teachers most frequently in the context of parent–teacher conferences, this chapter describes the specific content and process components of an educational program for parents addressing the issues and skills relating to child advocacy. The authors have utilized the components individually and in total in their work with parent groups. The information easily lends itself to single sessions with parents who are experiencing a specific problem, or a comprehensive multisession program for agencies providing parent training. What follows is an explanation and justification for an advocacy role and a description of the various program components of the conference and the rationale for their inclusion.

INTRODUCTION

In the current context of American society it is a peculiar irony that, whereas social commentators, politicians and pundits articulate a "children first" agenda, the needs of our nation's children are often last in line. Regardless of the issue, economics, education, health care, or mental health services, children in this country are woefully underserved. Based on reports from the Children's Defense Fund it is estimated that 20% of children in the United States are poor. Every day, 100,000 children are homeless, every 26 sec a child runs away from home and each day 105 babies die before reaching their first birthday. Yearly, 300,000 children are in foster care, 500,000 more reside in juvenile detention facilities, many of which are grossly overcrowded and understaffed, and there are almost 3 million reported cases of child abuse (Soler, 1992).

Thankfully, most children have parents or guardians to look after them, to ensure their basic needs are being met, and to protect them from exploitation and harm. The role of provider and protector generally comes naturally to parents along with the wish to offer one's children opportunities and benefits never realized by oneself.

With the low priority often placed on services for children as a group, even less emphasis on providing services for children on an individual basis, and ever-shrinking resources for programs tied to the welfare of children, it has become apparent that parental responsibilities must be more far reaching than that of protector and provider. Given the various institutions in which children find themselves, it is becoming essential for parents to place themselves in the role of advocates for their children as well. However, as the role of parents must expand to encompass these additional responsibilities, parents are receiving less support to accomplish the task (Amidei, 1993).

This lack of support for parents is not a new phenomenon. Society is quick to blame parents when things go wrong in the lives of children. Historically, "parent-bashing," especially in relation to mothers, has been prevalent and is still a popular activity today. So-called experts and "family values" proponents are quick to lay blame and shame on parents for the high divorce rate, sending their children to day care, allowing their children to watch too much television, and for feeding them junk food (Keniston, 1979). However, while blaming parents for not rising to their responsibilities, society offers no real solutions to assist parents in this task. Parents are unquestionably the most important people in children's lives. If the lives of children are to be improved efforts should be aimed at improving the lives of parents. Society must not criticize the way that parents raise their children when resources and support necessary for them to do a good job is scarce. Rather than being criticized, parents need help to become effective at the most important job they will ever undertake, caring and advocating for their children.

Although most parents are willing to include advocacy on the list of responsibilities to their children, when faced with the possibility of exercising that role many are ill-prepared to do so. It is in the best interest of children to teach their parents to be competent advocates for them. To do this, parents must learn skills associated with tactful and assertive communication, negotiation, problem solving, and conflict management. Additionally, parents need to be knowledgeable with respect to what issues lend themselves to the advocacy role in dealing with matters involving their children.

PARENT ADVOCACY AND CHILDREN'S EDUCATION

In order to provide a framework for the discussion of parental advocacy we refer to the most common institution in which children and by default, their parents, are involved and for which the role of advocate is particularly well suited, the educational arena. Although both parents and teachers are responsible for the education and socialization of children, many times the relationship between the two is fraught with uncertainty, misunderstanding, distrust, and, often, outright animosity. At times it appears that the school and home represent two "worlds apart" (Lightfoot, 1978). Although teachers, by virtue of their academic course work and continuing professional training generally are prepared to deal with the assortment of problems and difficulties that parents may present, even the most educated parents are often at a disadvantage because they are unfamiliar with educational jargon, school politics, and curriculum. They may know something is wrong at school but not have a clear idea of how to approach the teacher, leaving the child in limbo and the problem unsolved. Parents who are savvy with respect to such matters can become a powerful ally with their child in their educational pursuit (Greene, 1998).

The advocacy role can be understood in three connected dimensions. The first is the parents' acceptance of the idea that they must be ready to actively represent the interests of their children. The second dimension is an awareness by parents of the content or what is actually involved in the advocacy role. The third dimension is both understanding and becoming skilled in the process of advocating for their children in various situations.

In terms of the *content* of parent training in the advocacy role, parents need to be aware of what an advocate is and how a parent functions in this role. Further, parents need an explanation of why children need advocates and why parents are the logical choice to fill this role. Even more important, parents must be convinced that they can be successful in advocating for their children. Parents need an awareness of the barriers that prevent them from functioning as effective advocates and strategies to overcome these barriers. Finally, parents need an understanding of the issues and problems that require the advocacy role in matters pertaining to their children.

Although content skills focus on information and facts necessary to accomplish a task as well as domain specific and background knowledge, *process* skills are yet another matter. Perhaps the more critical of the two, process skills include the "how to" of the task. These can be categorized as the communication or interpersonal skills necessary to work successfully with other people around an issue of mutual interest and concern. Process skills include tactful communication, assertiveness, active listening, conflict management, and negotiation. An effective framework for coherently organizing the process of advocacy has been presented by Fine (1992). He developed a conflict-resolution model of parent–teacher conferences that is targeted primarily at teachers. The goal of the model is to promote the resolution of difficulties and the building of a collaborative parent–teacher partnership. Another way of conceptualizing content and process skills is to view them as the art and science of a particular activity. Although science refers to the underlying knowledge and facts about the activity, art refers to the personal skills necessary to get the job done. To be an effective advocate, both content and process skills or the art and science of the job are necessary (Idol, 1990).

A parent with training in both content and process skills represents a formidable force to be dealt with when discussing the welfare of children and making decisions that have a substantial influence on their lives. The agency that presents such training to parents provides a unique and worthwhile service to children, parents, and the community by empowering parents and giving them a sense of efficacy in dealing with professionals around issues involving their children. The program described in this chapter focuses on both content and process skills and a format that is uniquely suited to the parent teacher conference, identified by a majority of parents as one of the most effective and preferred methods of communicating with the schools (Cattermole & Robinson, 1985).

There are those who might cringe at the thought of parents armed with the knowledge and skills necessary to require school personnel to explain policies, procedures, and decisions and being subjected to probing questions by those same parents. There is a large body of literature that describes the ramifications of this unfortunate but often prevailing attitude on the part of schools toward parents (Lareau & Benson, 1984; Fine, 1990). There is an equally large body of research that points to the many and varied benefits of parental involvement at all levels of education (Christenson & Cleary, 1990; Iverson, Brownlee & Walberg, 1981; Walberg, 1984). If educators wish to reap these well-documented benefits, it is necessary to level the playing field and allow parents to take their rightful place as full partners and collaborators in the education of their children.

WHAT IS AN ADVOCATE?

A child advocate is a person who works on behalf of a child to address issues relating to the child's welfare. Advocates can work alone or in a group, advocating for an individual child or groups of children. Advocates must know what the child needs, what resources are available to meet those needs, and how to obtain them. This may represent an obstacle for parents who may not be well versed in pinpointing the specific educational needs of their children. Even though such parents are involved with their children and invested in their academic success, parents are often unfamiliar with curricular requirements, school policies, and the options available for assisting their children. Information and education for parents is the foundation of the advocacy role.

Advocates for children can operate on three levels. On a *personal* level an advocate works on behalf of an individual child or a group of children. *Private* advocacy concerns advocacy for children in the private sector; *public* advocacy involves group advocacy for children with respect to political issues, legislation at the state or national level, advocacy for children involved in the court system, or addressing causes in the public sector (Goffin and Lombardi, 1988). Although parents are certainly qualified to advocate for children at all levels, our focus is on advocacy at the personal level, involving one's own child or children. Once the skills are attained they are easily transferable to the wider arena of advocacy in the private or public sector (Fernandez, 1980).

In examining the interactions of parents and their children, parents already serve a myriad of advocacy roles for their children. Maintaining a home, securing food, clothing, and access to medical care for one's children are basic aspects of that role. Supporting a child's educational efforts by enrolling them in school, ensuring good attendance, supervising homework, and providing the means to participate in extracurricular activities is another aspect of that role. Emotional support of children, discipline, protecting their self-esteem and well-being, familiarizing oneself with the child's friends, and providing a secure base from which the children will be launched into the world rounds out the role for parents. Although these responsibilities often seem overwhelming, in general parents do a creditable job of fulfilling these roles.

However, life today is more complicated than ever. The road through childhood and adolescence is more difficult and challenging with many more problems along the way. If being a child is more challenging it follows that a parent's job becomes tougher as well. In addition to their many basic responsibilities parents must be able to determine how to help their offspring navigate their path to adulthood in an increasingly unstable world and secure the information and resources necessary to do so. Additionally, parents need to be able to use that information to be able to speak skillfully on behalf of their children with other adults who are involved with their children such as teachers and other school personnel. Parents are the people who know their children best and who are a constant presence in the lives of their children. These factors make parents uniquely suited to the advocacy role (Rotter, Robinson, & Fey, 1987; Williams, 1985).

WHY CHILDREN NEED ADVOCATES

Margolis and Salkind (1996) cite five reasons that illustrate why children need advocates. First, children have little or no political power as a group or on an individual basis. Issues that concern children usually receive little notice until those issues become a factor that influences adults. For example, until "the adult voting community" required child care due to the increasing numbers of parents in the workforce, legislation concerning day care was not politically popular (p. 109).

Second, in terms of economics, children do not have the means to be significant paying consumers of goods and services. This is not to say that most child-related industries and businesses neglect to appeal to the wants and needs of children through marketing strategies. However, these institutions and agencies target the adults who are in charge of financial decision making and who make the ultimate choices in what their children will acquire.

Third, children are physically and psychologically immature, which makes it difficult for them to demonstrate their needs or articulate their concerns. Our society looks to adults to provide for the needs of children as they see fit, although sometimes matters other than what is best for the children prevail.

Fourth, children are cognitively immature as well and not always aware of the consequences of their actions and decisions nor how their behavior might affect the future. Finally, because children are excluded, largely due to the reasons cited above, from the planning and execution of services designated to help them, they have little influence on such services and are generally the passive recipients of those efforts.

Although the previous explanation details why children need advocates in general, there are more specific reasons that pertain to the need for advocacy in the educational realm. American education proposes to serve the masses while still addressing the needs of individuals. In practice, however, instruction, curriculum, activities, and resources are designed and aimed at the "average" student. For children who are far outside the mainstream population, individualized educational programming is mandated by special education legislation. Children who are not being reached through the traditional curriculum with teaching methods aimed at those average students but who do not qualify for special education often fall through the cracks. These students, frequently labeled as slow learners, underachievers, or children at risk, represent a growing population in need of a voice to assist them in reaching their potential and their educational goals. Teachers are often too busy to fill that role or are reluctant to do so (McCraven, 1976; Finders & Lewis, 1994).

Students entering public schools are becoming more diverse in terms of racial, ethnic, and cultural backgrounds and are presenting with a wide range of both strengths and challenges. Family structures are changing as well with the traditional two-parent biological intact family giving way to single-parent families, grandparents raising grandchildren, and children living with extended family or in foster care situations. As the line between regular and special education becomes less clear responsibilities of educators will increase. Teachers must teach in situations with fewer resources and more students with widely varied social and economic backgrounds. In this environment the need for child advocacy in the school becomes glaringly apparent.

In our culture and in the culture of American schools, independence and self-reliance is a major theme. When problems occur at school the blame is usually placed on the parents. If parents do not display the appropriate level of concern and support as determined by school personnel, the parents are often characterized as uneducated in regard to what the school is trying to accomplish and uninterested in their child's progress. This view is essentially based on a deficit model illustrating that schools don't believe such parents are capable of helping their children in school (Finders & Lewis, 1994). Without question this view of parents affects children. If students cannot benefit from instruction and parents are seen as uninvolved or uncooperative, struggling students are without a voice to communicate their needs. Without services or someone interested in the success of these children the result is often failure (Moats & Lyon, 1993).

Funding for public schools is based on local property taxes. This system of school financing ensures that public education will replicate the culture of "haves and have-nots" that is becoming prevalent in our society. Students in affluent areas will continue to have access to resources that students in poor areas can only dream of. Parent advocacy on behalf of students in less well-financed school districts may represent the only means for such students to obtain the resources they need and deserve. Parents who are "in the know" with respect to such resources stand a much greater chance of obtaining them for their children.

Although many adults are charged with caring for the needs and interests of children such as doctors, nurses, mental health professionals, and teachers, it is parents who have a unique biological and deeply emotional tie to their children. It is this connection that makes parents especially well-suited to the advocacy role. Through their sustained nurturance of their offspring, parents are uniquely "tuned-in" to the moods, temperament, needs and abilities of their children as well as their potential. Time deepens the bond and the knowledge and as children mature parents have the desire to continually provide an environment and situations that will enhance and support their children in their plans and dreams. It follows that, when children experience difficulties or obstacles in their path, it is the parents, already deeply invested in the well-being of their children, who will come to the child's aid in whatever avenue necessary to address the problem and provide guidance toward a solution. Because parental motivation already exists it makes sense to prepare the parent to speak and work on behalf of the child on issues of importance to their development, especially in an area that is crucial to the child's future as is their education.

BARRIERS THAT KEEP PARENTS FROM ACTING AS ADVOCATES FOR THEIR CHILDREN

Although parents are well suited to the advocacy role and as the chief proponents of their children's welfare, the likely candidates to fill that role, why does it seem that so many children are being shortchanged by the educational system? More often than not the lack of effective child advocacy on the part of parents can be explained by a variety of obstacles and barriers to their participation.

One of the largest hurdles that must be overcome is the lack of knowledge with respect to parental rights in education. Harkening back to the saying "God helps those who help themselves," many parents are clueless to whether they even have rights much less as to what they actually are and under what circumstances they apply. If one is going to be able to truly "help oneself," a basic requirement is to be aware that there is such help available and to know how to gain access to that assistance.

Another barrier to effective intervention by parents is the limit on time, energy and other resources. As life becomes more complicated and families face the challenges of meeting personal, career and social obligations, many parents have neither the time or energy to squeeze one more responsibility on their "to do" list.

Finally, some parents may eschew the advocacy role due to temperamental or personality characteristics that prevent them from dealing with bureaucracies efficiently. Many parents are uncomfortable within the culture of the school where the emphasis is often on mainstream, middle class values. Other parents avoid school involvement because of their own negative experiences as students. Parents who are insecure about their interpersonal skills or who are from diverse cultural or ethnic backgrounds may be reluctant to interact with teachers whom they feel are ignorant or disapproving of their language, customs, and approach to child-rearing (Mayer, 1994).

Breaking through these barriers requires a commitment on the part of both parents and educators. School personnel should be sensitive to the population they serve. An awareness and understanding of the cultural and economic diversity among students and families assists the school in planning activities and dealing with students and parents fairly. Educators need to be cognizant of the financial and time constraints on the parents of their students. It is the responsibility of the school to create a warm, supportive, and welcoming environment for the parents of the students they serve (Wise, 1988). One way of illustrating commitment to collaboration with parents is for the school to offer educational programs and support to help parents help their children.

Parents have a responsibility to keep in touch with their children's teachers and other school personnel. Parents should be persistent when interacting with teachers and understand that information sharing and collaborating will generally clear up any misunderstandings that arise. If parents feel uncomfortable in certain situations they must be mature enough to address the problem or obtain advice from someone who can assist them in their dealings with the school. Again, it is the ultimate responsibility of the school to make parents aware of how they can best help their children. Further, the school must support parental efforts in that direction.

ISSUES AND PROBLEMS THAT CAN BE ADDRESSED THROUGH THE ROLE OF CHILD ADVOCATE

When parents are trained in the role of child advocacy there are a variety of circumstances and settings in which these skills can be applied. Because the focus of this chapter has been child advocacy in the school arena, we will limit our discussion of the issues to that area, specifically to the issue of parent–teacher conferences.

When a child enters school a new set of responsibilities confront the parent. The most important responsibility parents must face is to make sure their child is getting the most from his or her educational experience. Parents must do this by keeping in contact with the child's teacher on a regular basis to prevent possible problems and addressing any concerns immediately. Parents must not be afraid to question teachers, counselors, principals, or district personnel about policies or procedures they feel are unfair or are counterproductive to the educational pursuits of their children. Parents have the right and duty to seek clarification of the school calendar and to have explained to them why their children have so many days off or why their child seems to have a substitute teacher so often. Grading policies, standardized testing, and placement in special programs is another area well-suited to advocacy on the part of parents. Parents must be made aware of what is going on in their child's classroom and in the school and should be prepared to ask questions and seek answers to their concerns (Keogh, 1997).

Additionally there are specific concerns that are unique to each child that require advocacy. Children who are having difficulties in certain academic subjects, who have personality conflicts with teachers or other school personnel, or who are having problems with other students may need an advocate to work to see the situation rectified. Students who are having personal problems outside of school may also need an advocate to explain the situation to school personnel in an effort to lessen the stress on the student. Parents who are able to advocate successfully for their children in these situations are able to ensure that their children will be gaining the best from their educational experience. Although information can be obtained through letters and phone calls, there is no substitute for the face-to-face meeting of parent and teacher to discuss mutual concerns. What follows is a six-stage plan for structuring such meetings to ensure that both sides can communicate their ideas in an atmosphere of confidence and collaboration (Fine, 1992).

THE PARENT–TEACHER CONFERENCE: A COLLABORATIVE PROBLEM-SOLVING MODEL

Whereas one image of an advocate is that of a confrontive and highly assertive person, the dynamics of advocacy can be incorporated into a collaborative orientation. The parent should be appropriately assertive as needed but also able to view the teacher as a potential partner who can ultimately share in advocating on behalf of the child. There may indeed be occasions where a parent believes the appropriate course of action is to "go over" the teacher and deal with administrators or the school board or even initiate legal action. Before pursuing such an adversarial position face-to-face attempts to work effectively with the teacher and other educational personnel should occur.

A video-based program illustrating a model of collaborative parent–teacher conferencing (Fine, 1991) has been used fairly extensively in teacher preparation and in-service programs. The video and workbook (Fine, 1992) lend themselves to relatively brief, (i.e., a 2-hr workshop) or more extensive training experiences, (i.e., two to four separate sessions). The program has also been used with a combined group of parents and teachers as a means of increasing empathy and communication between the two groups.

More recently a video program has been developed specifically for parents (Moriarty, 1998). The format involves parents in the video sharing their concerns with a consultant who answers their questions and addresses their concerns. Then the video is stopped and the leader and parents in the training group pursue a line of discussion or role-playing in line with what has been suggested in the video. As with the original video for teachers, this video for parents stresses the potentially collaborative nature of parent–teacher conferences and the benefits that can be realized when such a partnership is established. The intent of the conference is for parent and teacher to openly explore areas of concern, to reach reasonable consensus, and to develop a coordinated plan of action.

What follows is a description of the six-step conferencing model. These steps follow a basic problem-solving format with an emphasis on effective listening and communication skills. The value orientation of the program is that of parents and teachers building a working partnership that is sensitive and responsive to the needs of children. Professionals interested in supporting parents in an advocacy role may want to consider incorporating the parent–teacher conference model into a series of presentations or workshops with parents. The needs and availability of the parents will help to direct the most useful training format in terms of time and scheduling.

STAGE ONE—GETTING STARTED

This, the beginning stage of the conference process sets the tone for the entire interaction. and, quite likely, all future interactions. Collaboration suggests that both parties share concern and responsibility, that each views the other as possessing something important to contribute and that the members see themselves as partners on the same "team." The main purpose of this initial stage is to orient the participants to a solution focus, to create open and shared communication and to develop a "we-ness" to the situation.

This is accomplished through tactful communication, which is described as the "ability to recognize the delicacy of a situation and then to say the most considerate or appropriate thing" (Gabor, 1994, p. 15). Strategies such as taking time to think before speaking, apologizing quickly when making a mistake, and approaching the conference in a cooperative rather than competitive manner are all ways of engaging in tactful communication. Additionally, a parent who approaches the conference with positive expectations, such as the belief that the teacher is committed to the child's success, the teacher is truly concerned about the child and that the teacher welcomes parent involvement assists in setting a collaborative tone for the conference. Specific techniques such as "door openers" and "I statements" (Gordon, 1970) can be of assistance in beginning the discussion around the issue of concern. Although the focus of Gordon's communication techniques is parent–child communication, these skills are readily adapted to adult–adult interaction.

STAGE TWO—SHARING INFORMATION

The main purpose of this stage is to bring information to the surface in terms of background information, identifying major and minor issues, and discovering perceptions and to obtain clarification on confusing points. The most important strategies necessary for success at this stage are listening skills. Although there is a distinction between hearing and listening, many people use the words interchangeably. However, there is a definite distinction. Hearing describes the sensory process that enables auditory stimuli to be detected and received by the ears and transmitted to the brain. Listening is a more complex perceptual process involving organizing and interpreting those auditory sensations (Drakeford, 1967). Active listening (Gordon, 1970) is a crucial skill to be utilized by anyone attempting to clarify issues and understand another person's point of view. Listening effectively is often a tough task for many people, especially in emotion-laden situations, as is often the case when parents are called to school to discuss issues involving their children.

Parents can enhance their effectiveness as advocates for their children through development of good listening techniques. Listening skills can be divided into three subsets of skills that when practiced yield an effective listener. Considering that listening takes up a major portion of people's time and that it is estimated that 75% of oral communication is ignored, these skills are a vital part of a parent's repertoire when advocating on behalf of their children. These skills are attending, following, and reflecting (Stewart, 1986).

Attending refers to offering physical attention to another. A person who is attending to someone positions their body in a way that leaves no question as to their focus. Their posture, such as facing the speaker directly and openly, and maintaining a suitable distance from the person are all important attending behaviors. Likewise, maintaining eye contact and movement of the body so as to orient oneself to the speaker and insisting on a distraction-free environment are also components of attending behavior.

Following skills relate to one of the most important jobs of a listener, which is to keep quiet long enough to determine how the speaker feels about the situation. Frequently, listeners interrupt or ask so many questions that the speaker finds it impossible to concentrate on the message that he or she wants to get across. Following skills are opening statements, verbal encouragements, open-ended questioning, and quiet attention.

Opening statements refer to short statements that are nonthreatening invitations to talk. These are appropriate to use at the beginning of a conversation when the listener/observer senses that the person may be reluctant to start a discussion even though they appear to need to talk. Verbal encouragements are intended to allow the speaker to continue while demonstrating that the listener is still part of the conversation. Statements such as, "Really?" or "Hmmm," combined with an appropriate facial expression indicates the listener is still "with" the speaker.

Open-ended questions allow the speaker to make his or her feelings known without being constricted by the nature of the listener's closed questions which call for a specific response. It is important to limit even open-ended questions as much as possible to allow the speaker time to complete the message.

Finally, one of the most important listening skills is quiet attention. If the listener is quiet and attentive, the speaker is free to communicate the message, organizing his or her thoughts without worrying that he or she will be interrupted with comments, questions, or observations by the listener. The speaker can be certain of having adequate time to explain and elaborate and the listener will be able to obtain the whole story. This is not to say that the listener should never question or verbally respond, only that he/she should be judicious in doing so.

Reflecting skills, or active listening, refer to the activities of paraphrasing, reflecting feelings and meanings, and summarizing (Gordon, 1970; DeVito, 1990). Listening reflectively allows the listener to communicate understanding of what the speaker has said. This facilitates successful communication by ensuring that the listener has been truly listening and allows the speaker to determine if the message has been delivered correctly. Reflective listening is feedback that allows the speaker to continue with the message or backtrack to clarify confusing points (Hartley, 1993).

All of these skills can be taught to parents as a pathway to more effective communication between them and their children's teachers. An added benefit of educating parents in effective listening is that these skills are essential for successful communication with their children and others and may serve to improve relationships in those areas as well.

STAGE THREE—FINDING AGREEMENTS

The third stage is an opportunity arrive at some mutualization of perceptions in regard to the issues and concerns that necessitated the conference in the first place. The challenge at this stage is an obvious one; agreement about what the specific concerns are may be difficult to achieve given that both the parent and teacher may have somewhat of a different view of the problem, even if they have been successful in its identification. It is at this point in the conference when conflict is most likely to arise and why it is important for parents to be skilled in conflict management and in assertive communication as these two strategies provide a pathway for maneuvering successfully through this stage

Conflict Management

Verderber and Verderber (1989) describe four types of conflict. Pseudo conflict is false conflict that seems to be real. This occurs when people believe that two goals cannot be achieved simultaneously when in reality they can. Content conflict is conflict that concerns that accuracy of a message and can take several forms. This conflict may be over a fact, over an interpretation of a fact or an inference drawn from a fact or series of facts. Content conflict may also arise over the definition of something or a choice among goals, actions or means of arriving at those goals. Value conflicts are differences of opinion about views of life in general. In ego conflicts the people involved see winning or losing the conflict as a measure of their knowledge or expertise, their image, or self-worth. In this type of conflict the real reason for the conflict actually becomes less important than the egos of the people involved.

Conflict resolution and negotiation skills are usually successful at dealing with the first two types of conflict. However, conflicts that involve value systems or egos are the most difficult to manage.

An awareness of how different people handle conflict is necessary for learning how to effectively deal with the types of conflicts described above. One way to deal with conflict is to simply withdraw, either physically or psychologically, or both. Although this does not solve the conflict it may be necessary to create some "space" between the conflicting persons so as to calm down enough to deal with the conflict more responsibly. Surrender is another way of dealing with conflict. Although this may work on issues where the person who is surrendering isn't totally invested, many times this type of conflict management approach results in resentment and a wish to "get even" next time. Aggression is a coercive form of getting one's own way. Aggression can be physical or psychological. The negative effect of this type of conflict management is obvious and does not require explanation here.

Persuasion is an attempt to make the other person in a conflict situation see things "your way." Again, although this may work when the persuader is especially skilled in persuasive argument, this approach also may lead to resentment or anger on the part of the person being persuaded. Finally, the most adaptive and healthy way to deal with conflict is through discussion and negotiation.

Constructive conflict management consists of recognizing the signs of conflict, focusing on specific topics, keeping an open mind, and acting in a spirit of cooperation rather than competition (Verderber & Verderber, 1989).

Parents who understand the nature of conflict as well as how to manage conflict are in a better position to deal with concerns surrounding their child, especially when they and their child's teacher fail to see eye to eye on issues concerning the child.

Assertive Communication

Assertiveness refers to the process of understanding one's own thoughts and feelings, needs and wants and being comfortable expressing those things in appropriate ways in relationships with others (McFarland, 1986). Assertive communication allows individuals to take responsibility for their feelings and make them known to others in ways that protect one's own rights and dignity and preserves the rights and dignity of others as well.

Most people have learned to make their feelings known through means other than assertive communication. Many resort to aggression, which allows a person to have their own way at the expense of another person's rights. Some use a passive style of relating that denies the worth of their own wishes while allowing the wishes of others to prevail. A third maladaptive way of communicating wants and needs is through passive aggressive communication. On the surface passive aggression seems like compliance or agreement but undermines successful communication through being less than honest. Comments such as "I meant to do what you asked," or "I forgot," are possible clues to the passive aggressive communicator. In the aggressive or passive form of communication someone becomes the winner and someone the loser. In passive–aggressive communication it can be argued that neither person accomplishes anything. All of these styles of relating dash any hopes of an equitable solution and possibly damage any future hopes for successful collaboration.

Parents who are skilled in assertive communication are able to work with teachers from a position of confidence in themselves and respect for teachers that enhances the possibility of a desirable outcome for all.

STAGE FOUR—EXPLORING ALTERNATIVES

The purpose of this stage is to identify viable options and related resources, to examine the implications of those options, and to arrive at a consensus between the parent and teacher. Assuming that a reasonable mutualization of concern has been agreed upon the parent and teacher are now in a situation where they can consider possible options and must consider and listen to each other's contributions. The concepts of empowerment, mentioned earlier as a way for parents to view themselves as a successful advocate for their child are illustrated in this stage of the process due to the way in which this stage represents the opportunity for parent and teacher to think together, consider alternatives, and to learn from one another. A willingness to review and brainstorm possible options can be more personally educative than being intellectually constrained by the idea that there is a definite right or wrong way to accomplish something.

This stage is a good time to consider the complexity of the options suggested. Anything that will be enacted involves action on the part of the teacher and parent and leads to certain outcomes or consequences for the child as well as the parents. For example, if the parent agrees to keep a record of time spent by the child on homework, this option would require the parent to plan and implement the record keeping and the parent to take responsibility to see that the records were delivered to the teacher. The question becomes, does the parent have the time to institute such a program? Is the parent able to handle the ramifications of being the record keeper of an activity that has historically been problematic for the child? Is it possible that there is a less complicated method of achieving the goal given the demands on the parent's time and energy? These are necessary questions to ask to determine the viability of the various options. Often, the most theoretically desirable option may not be the most feasible due to logistical or personal considerations on the part of the parent or teacher.

Negotiation is required when people are attempting to establish an effective plan or offer solutions to problems but have different ideas about how to structure the plan or to solve the problem (Wheeler & Janis, 1980). Many people fail to engage in negotiation even though it often provides a pathway for people with differing agendas to arrive at a solution that is acceptable to all parties.

In industrial settings it is a recognized fact that those in power must make some sort of allowances for negotiating with subordinates even though the powerful have the ability to impose their will on workers. Without negotiations the subordinates have the power to sabotage the goals of those in charge by performing substandard work or through other, more detrimental means (Wheeler & Janis, 1980).

This scenario is easily played out in the educational arena as well. Teachers or parents who feel the need to impose their "view of the world" on the other may in fact find a resentful parent or teacher undermining their efforts. In such cases it is the student who is the loser.

Negotiation is accomplished in three steps. Step 1 involves airing of conflicting claims and ideas. It is important that discussion during this step be issue oriented and not personal, where the parties reflect on the insensitivity of each other. Step 2 involves realistically looking at issues to determine areas of agreement, offering both sides a chance to see things from the other's point of view. Step 3 involves choosing a solution to the problem and seeking a fair agreement. It is important to stress that utilization of the previously mentioned skills of assertiveness, active listening, conflict management and tactful communication makes successful negotiation more likely. Proficiency in all of these skills makes negotiation possible and increases the likelihood of a positive outcome for the child at the center of the problem.

STAGE FIVE—MAKING A PLAN

After discussing possible options and negotiation, the parent and teacher are able to arrive at some agreement as to a particular course of action. The agreement may be that they have not yet arrived at a solution and they may make plans to meet at another time. However, when an actual plan is implemented it should include specifics in relation to who is responsible for what tasks and in what manner those tasks will be accomplished. It is of great importance to have all parties agree on what the next steps will be, including when they will meet again and how future communication will occur. Many parent–teacher conferences that have been successful up to this point fail to successfully address the problem because no follow-up or clarification of responsibility is defined.

Even with a specific and clear plan that appears to be agreeable to all parties in the actual application of the plan other problems or difficulties may arise. In this case it is essential that there be a system of follow-up and tracking and that pathways for continued communication be built into the plan.

At this point it is also necessary to summarize the ground that has been covered during the conference. This process assists in highlighting what the parties have shared and explored and illustrates the way in which parent and teacher have worked collaboratively to formulate a plan of action.

STAGE SIX—FOLLOW UP

The purpose of the sixth and final stage of the parent–teacher conference process is to evaluate the plan being proposed, to address any new issues, and to decide how to proceed from that point. Whether the follow-up is in the form of another conference or even a telephone conversation, the first five stages previously discussed come to bear on this stage. Specifically, one begins the follow-up stage with opening statements and inquiries, similar to the first stage. This would be followed by processing of what may have occurred, mutualization and understanding, and then proposing of a continued direction for the parent and teacher. Again, a review of options would be considered with a decision made to continue the existing plan, to modify it in some way, or to terminate the plan.

As previously discussed, even with careful navigation of each successive stage and a well-thought-out program there is always the possibility of unexpected elements. If this has occurred and the plan was not implemented as agreed upon, it is necessary to view this happening in terms of the fact that "things happen." Being able to "go back to the drawing board" is mutually reinforcing for both parent and teacher as each supports the other in a collaborative, solution-focused process.

The evaluation stage is an extremely important one in terms of maintaining the collaborative spirit between home and school and encourages both parties to continue their commitment and involvement in whatever program has been established. It is necessary to draw appropriate closure and reduce ambiguity, uncertainty, and confusion regarding the conference process.

CONCLUSION

As indicated, the content and process skills described in this chapter represent basic components of a parent-education program on child advocacy. Any or all of the components can be used with small or large groups of parents or individual parents. The information can be imparted through a formal parent-training program complete with a leader, discussion, practice, and feedback or can be prepared in written form as a resource for parents. Regardless of the form, the material described represents a major step toward empowering parents and offering them an additional pathway for securing what is best for their children.

Although school-based professionals may be especially sensitive to the importance of parents advocating in the educational arena, any person involved in promoting parent education through community-based programming can incorporate the elements of advocacy that will assist parents in their dealings with teachers. Instead of treating each other as adversaries, the emphasis here has been on parents working toward collaborative relationships with their children's teachers.

REFERENCES

Amidei, N. (1993). Child advocacy; Let's get the job done. *Dissent, 40:2,* 213–220.

Berger, E. (1995). *Parents as partners in education: Families and schools working together.* Upper Saddle River, NJ: Prentice Hall.

Cattermole, J., & Robinson, N. (1985). Effective home-school communication: from the parent's perspective. *Phi Delta Kappan, 40,* 48–50.

Christensen, S., & Cleary, M. (1990). Consultation and the parent-educator partnership. *Journal of Educational and Psychological Consultation, 1*(3), 219–241.

Christensen, S., & Conoley, J. (Eds.). (1992). *Home school collaboration: Enhancing children's academic and social competence.* Silver Spring, MD: National Association of School Psychology.

DeVito, J. (1990). *Messages: Building interpersonal communication skills.* New York: Harper & Row.

Drakeford, J. (1967). *The awesome power of the listening ear.* Waco, TX: Word.

Eisler, R., & Fredrikson, L. (1980). *Perfecting social skills: A guide to interpersonal behavior development.* New York: Plenum.

Fernandez., H. (1980). *The child advocacy handbook.* New York: Pilgrim Press.

Finders, M., & Lewis, C. (1994). Why some parents don't come to school. *Educational Leadership,* 50–54.

Fine, M. (1990). Facilitating home-school relationships: A family oriented approach to collaborative consultation. *Journal of Educational and Psychological Consultation, 1*(2), 169–187.

Fine, M. (1992). *Parent-teacher conferences: Resolving conflicts.* Topeka, KS: Menninger Foundation.

Fine, M. (1991). *Parent-teacher conferences: Resolving conflict* [Videotape]. (Available from Menninger Foundation, Topeka, KS 66601).

Friedman, R. M., Duchnowski, A. J, & Henderson, E. L. (Eds.) (1989). *Advocacy on behalf of children with serious emotional problems.* Springfield, IL: Charles C. Thomas.

Gabor, D. (1994). *Speaking your mind in 101 difficult situations.* New York: Simon & Schuster.

Goffin, S., & Lombardi, J. (1988). *Speaking out: Early childhood advocacy.* Washington, DC: National Association for the Education of Young Children.

Gordon, T. (1970). *P.E.T.; Parent effectiveness training: The tested new way to raise responsible children.* New York: Plume Books.

Greene, L. (1998). *Finding help when your child is struggling in school.* New York: Golden Books.

Hartley, P. (1993). *Interpersonal communication.* Routledge: London.

Idol, L. (1990). The scientific art of classroom consultation. *Journal of Educational and Psychological Consultation, 1*(1), 3–22.

Iverson, B., Brownlee, G., & Wahlberg, H. (1981). Parent–teacher contacts and student learning. *Journal of Educational Research, 74,* 394–396.

Keniston, K. (1979). Children and families; our society's future. *The Journal of Home Economics, 71,* 14–16.

Keogh, J. (1996). *Getting the best education for your child: A parent's checklist.* New York: Fawcett-Columbine.

Lareau, A., & Benson, C. (1984). The economics of home-school relationships: A cautionary note. *Phi Delta Kappan,* 401–404.

Lightfoot, S. (1978). *Worlds apart: Relationships between families and schools.* New York: Basic Books.

Margolis, L., & Salkind, N. (1996). Parents as advocates for their children. *Journal for a Just and Caring Education, 2:2,* 103–120.

Mayer, J. (1994). From rage to reform: What parents say about advocacy. *Exceptional Parent, 24*(5), 49–51.

McCraven, C. (1976). *An advocacy manual for parents of handicapped children.* Los Angeles, CA: The Institute For Child Advocacy.

McFarland, R. (1986). *Coping through assertiveness.* New York: Rosen.

Moats, L. C., & Lyon, G. R. (1993). Learning disabilities in the United States: Advocacy, science, and the future of the field. *Journal of Learning Disabilities, 26*(5), 282–294.

Moriarty, M. (1998). *Parent-teacher conferencing skills: a guide for parents.* [Videotape]. (Available from Johnson County Community College, 12345 College Boulevard, Overland Park, KS 66210.)

Rotter, J., Robinson, E., & Fey, M. (1987). *Parent-teacher conferencing.* National Education Association.

Soler, M. (1992). Advancing child advocacy: A blueprint for the '90s. *Children's Legal Rights Journal, 13*(2), 2–7.

Stewart, J. (1986). *Bridges, not walls: A book about interpersonal communication.* New York: Random House.

Verderber. R., & Verderber, K. (1989). *Interact: Using interpersonal communication skills.* Belmont, CA: Wadsworth.

Walberg, H. (1984). Families as partners in educational productivity. *Phi Delta Kappan,.* 397–400.

Wheeler, D., & Janis, I. (1980). *A practical guide for decision-making.* New York: Free Press.

Williams, D. (1985). *Handbook for involving parents in education.* Atlanta, GA: Humanics, Ltd.

Wise, P. (1988). *Better parent conferences: a manual for school psychologists.* National Association of School Psychologists.

Yoneshige, D. (1983). *Advocacy skills: Applied to integration and access of special education children in full learning environments.* ERIC Document Reproduction Service No. ED 256–129. Honolulu Department of Special Education, Hawaii University, Honolulu, HA.

CHAPTER 16

Managing Crisis:
Intervention Skills for Parents

K. C. Lazzara

Department of Psychology and Research in Education, University of Kansas, Lawrence, Kansas

Scott Poland

Cypress-Fairbanks Independent School District, Houston, Texas

Our society generally views childhood as an innocent care-free time for children, void of overwhelming responsibilities and worries. However, the implication that children are shielded from the emotional and psychological effects of traumatic events is tragically misunderstood. Although their suffering is commonly overlooked or underestimated, children are just as susceptible to horrific traumas and personal crises as adults (Johnson, 1998). As a community, perhaps we've fallen short of providing effective, adequate, accessible resources for children and their families. Children and adolescents are demonstrating their need not only by a lack of academic success but through their increasingly violent and self-destructive behavior.

Parents' and teachers' best attempts to provide a nurturing, enriching environment for children is no guarantee against the natural process of development. Unfortunately, children are exposed to the same tragic events that drastically affect the lives of the adults around them (Danzy, 1989; Ray, 1989). They become terminally ill, involved in accidents, and are victims to crime and natural disasters. Childhood offers no protection against the pain from the death of a loved one. Disturbing events in their own families, in their neighborhoods, in their schools, in the lives of their

Handbook of Diversity in Parent Education

friends, or in the world may leave children feeling confused, vulnerable, and frightened. Parents and teachers attempt to raise their self-esteem and self-concepts yet witness their reckless and self-destructive behaviors as a means of relief (Johnson, 1998). Under severe circumstances, children and adolescents escape the tragedy in their lives by running away—or even more tragically—suicide.

What happens to a family in crisis? How can mental health professionals, teachers, and parents help a child in crisis? Most families will face a major crisis at some time, and the way in which the family responds can determine how their children perform and function in the school environment (Ray, 1989; Steele & Raider, 1991). What behaviors should teachers look for in the classroom? How should school personnel respond to a child who is considering suicide? When should a parent or teacher refer a child for professional help? With such a broad range of potential crises that children may experience, these questions must be addressed in order to determine a child's needs and intervene effectively. The aim of this chapter is to answer these questions for parents, teachers, counselors, psychologists, and others who provide services to children. Johnson (1998) suggests that the answers to these and many related issues prove valuable for the professional and parent when called upon to

- Identify crisis situations
- Recognize who is and who is not affected
- Formulate options
- Intervene appropriately
- Monitor post-crisis recovery
- Determine when and how to follow-up

Understanding the family system involves viewing the structure and dynamics of interrelatedness among members beyond the positions and responses of individuals (Lattanzi-Licht, 1996; Steele & Raider, 1991). "A family crisis is not necessarily a particular event, but rather a family's perception of an event as being dangerous or threatening, something they do not, cannot, or have not succeeded in resolving, removing, avoiding, or controlling. Understanding this helps to explain why two families react so differently to the same event" (Steele & Raider, 1991, p. 7). Crises put great stress on family members, often interrupting routines and causing abrupt changes in everyday life. More specifically, communication patterns, roles, and expectations for each other's behavior and flexibility in tolerating individual needs are just some of the affected dimensions of the system (Lattanzi-Licht, 1996). When working with families, the goal of crisis intervention is to prevent self-defeating or self-destructive behaviors and to replace them with adaptive coping skills that can reduce anxiety and enhance the family's ability to successfully navigate through the period of crisis, or at least return them to their level of functioning prior to the crisis state (Steele & Raider, 1991).

On a continuum of health and well-being, there are many elements that distinguish family functioning. Knapp (1986) has summarized characteristics of families that can mediate or exaggerate the distress. In labeling them "integrated" or "isolated" families, Knapp (1986) provides a type of family structure for each extreme.

CHARACTERISTICS OF INTEGRATED FAMILIES

- Better prepared and equipped to handle stress
- Open channels of communication and cooperation
- Family-based response to stress
- Trusting of other people
- Warm interrelationships with each other
- Confidence in themselves and others
- Free interactions with the larger social system
- More personal, family, and external resources

These family characteristics identify strengths in preventing crisis as well as effectively coping with the crisis upon occurrence. On the opposite extreme, the "isolated" families are limited in their abilities to respond effectively to crisis.

CHARACTERISTICS OF ISOLATED FAMILIES

- Individual rather than family viewpoint
- Devastated by the crisis of a death
- Sense of isolation
- Little or no support available
- Operate as a closed system
- Minimal social contacts within and outside the family
- Limited resources to draw on

This construct of polarities outlines family characteristics that can identify areas of vulnerability in children and adolescents. Most families operate between these two extremes of "integrated" and "isolated" families, and their foundation of beliefs and resources are the key determinants of effective crisis response. In addition to these polarities, Lattanzi-Licht (1996) suggests four characteristics that well-functioning families include (1) members believe that the family is a safe, accepting, loving group where open expression is encouraged, (2) negotiation is the central element in communication and problem solving, (3) flexible coping styles are used within the family, and (4) the family functions as a unit and as individuals with well-defined boundaries.

Mental health professionals and school personnel working with children and their families need to have overall awareness of the types and frequencies of childhood crisis. More specifically, the means in which adolescent crises are both a product of prior childhood traumas in addition to compounding present crisis must be understood (Johnson, 1998). To provide comprehensive review of all the research currently available is beyond the scope and intent of this chapter, but a directive approach rather than exhaustive is presented.

The many crises and experiences that affect children and their families are varied. For purposes of review in this chapter they are classified into four groups: school-related difficulties, child maltreatment, suicide and bereavement, and school crisis teams. An investigation of the crises and reactions within each group is presented, and implications for parents and school personnel are offered. Finally, two informational handouts are provided in the Appendices, which outline additional strategies and intervention skills for parents and educators.

SCHOOL-RELATED DIFFICULTIES

Crises consist of emotional turmoil paired with maladaptive behavioral response, upon which a student may act in unpredictable, perhaps violent and destructive ways. Consequently, the student's typical means of coping break down and no longer suffice (Slaikeu, 1984), and their maladaptive behavior can range from truancy and verbal abuse to violent physical assaults with and without weapons (Ray, 1989). As the most severely underrated problems within the current educational system, peer conflict and peer victimization are significant—particularly involving assault of same-sex peers (Ray, 1989; Sommer, 1988; Stephens, 1997). Peer conflict refers to a broad spectrum of behaviors that can range from low-level harassment to bullying, gang confrontations, and aggravated physical assault. The conflict may involve one-on-one harassment, the ganging up of several against one, or violent confrontations between cliques or groups (Sommer, 1988).

Bullying, a pervasive form of victimization, can be defined as when one or more individuals engages in overt, aggressive, hostile, violent, hurtful, and persistent behavior that is intentionally designed to injure and/or create fear and distress in one or more persons who appear defenseless, thus giving the bully a sense of satisfaction. According to Olweus (1993), for bullying to have occurred, there must be an imbalance of power or dominance. Consequently, the victim is defenseless and ultimately feeling helpless. Beane (1998) suggests that, although peer victimization is a complex problem without a simple solution, its complexity should not discourage school personnel and parents from developing strategies designed to provide a safe arid caring learning environment.

Shaw (1992) identifies three areas of influence seen as playing a role in the development of personality and behavioral patterns, including delinquency. These influences are home and family, peer group and community, and psychological and biological factors. To address these spheres, effective intervention must reach all three areas. Appendix B of this chapter provides ways in which parents can teach their children to avoid becoming victims of delinquency. The following strategies identified and developed by Bean (1998) focus on changing policies and procedures as well as the attitudes and behavior of school personnel, peers, parents, and the students. All of the strategies and rationale cannot be discussed in this chapter; however, the following is a sampling of the strategies. The goal of these strategies is to create an environment where adults and children model the importance of discipline, responsibility, acceptance of differences, support, respect, and zero tolerance of peer victimization.

System-Centered Strategies

1. Protect children through adequate supervision.
2. Develop and utilize formats for reporting and tracking efforts (reporting box, helpline).
3. Implement strategies that add structure to less structured activities (recess, lunchtime).
4. Establish a community-wide parent education program through interagency cooperation that addresses behavior that often contributes to the problem of peer abuse and rejection.
5. Establish a peer mediation program.

Family-Centered Strategies

1. Parents should be discouraged from trying to rescue the child by attempting a quick solution.
2. Parents should respond immediately by recording the facts without interrogating their child.
3. Parents should assure their child that they will help solve this problem in an appropriate way.
4. Parents should ensure that their child apologizes and make amends for the behavior.
5. Encourage parents to be observant of their children and to reward nonviolent behavior.

Child-Centered Strategies

1. Help the rejected child to develop social awareness and social skills that have value.
2. Arrange for new students to meet some classmates prior to the first day of school.
3. Teach children to have positive expectations regarding their own social acceptance.
4. Teach children to control their anger through refraining and other techniques.
5. Teach children to emphasize similarities between themselves and their peers.

Comprehensive and collaborative approaches must be designed and implemented to support the safety all schoolchildren (Poland, 1997; Quinn & McDougal, 1998; Sommer, 1988; Stephens, 1997). The success of school intervention strategies will be contingent upon the dominant presence of several key factors:

- Reduce the presence of guns, weapons, gangs, drugs, and nonstudents on campus.
- Establish clear behavior standards while enforcing rules fairly and consistently.
- Provide adequate adult presence, surveillance, supervision, and involvement.
- Establish a school climate with outstanding leadership and extensive community involvement.

- Develop cooperative relations between schools and all agencies that serve young people.
- Believe that the school can make the difference.
- Foster cooperation and interdependence.

Appendix B of this chapter provides additional suggestions to aid parents in preventing violent behavior in their children. In order to facilitate communication between the school and the family, Christenson, Hirsch, and Hurley (1997) recommend that school personnel maintain positive, trusting relationships with parents; intervene early to identify the factors that predict antisocial outcomes; and adopt health promotion strategies that build competence in children and families. These researchers additionally provide five broad-based actions for the consideration of school professionals who work with families of aggressive children and adolescents:

1. Develop a system to educate school personnel and families about ways to promote academic, social, and behavioral competence in students.
2. Provide supportive opportunities for parents so that they can assist their children's or adolescent's development and competence.
3. Home-school communication strategies that reach all families must be developed and maintained. These include (1) maintaining a positive orientation for communication, rather than a deficit based and (2) focusing communication on the progress of the students.
4. Attrition rates and the reasons for attrition must be considered in designing programs for families of aggressive children.
5. Provide workshops on strategies for communicating with families; conflict resolution and structured problem solving; and ways of handling angry parents.

CHILD MALTREATMENT

The term maltreatment is chosen here because it includes both acts of commission upon the child, in addition to acts of omission. Thus, maltreatment refers to physical, emotional and sexual abuse, and parental neglect (Germain, 1988). School personnel routinely make referrals to authorities when they observe alarming behaviors in the school setting. Because children attend school daily and engage in many interactions with peers, symptomatic behavior frequently manifests in the classroom. School personnel can provide the best source of information about the child's progress, gauging academic performance, behavioral responses, and interactions with peers and adults (Gil & Johnson, 1993; Ingraham, 1988; Johnson, 1998).

Teachers come into frequent contact with children who are physically, sexually, or emotionally abused. The tragic lasting effects of abuse are created by the repeated pattern of destructive behavior that expresses to a child that they are worthless, unwanted, unloved, or only of value in meeting another's needs (Bonner, Kaufman, Harbeck, & Brassard, 1992; Lystad, 1989). If teachers are alert to the signs and symptoms of abuse, they can take the first steps in helping children. Teachers can provide several valuable services to their students that ultimately serve educational goals and must be prepared to deal with both the educational and emotional capabilities of the student (Hillman & Solek-Tefft, 1988; Johnson, 1998; Ray, 1989). Germain (1988) and Besharov (1990) provide some behavioral and physical disorders that are commonly associated with child maltreatment:

- Failure to thrive or even less extreme deficits in growth or development
- Habit disorders (head banging, sucking, biting, rocking)
- Conduct disorders (antisocial or destructive behavior)
- Neurotic traits (sleep disorders, speech disorders, inhibition of play)
- Psychoneurotic reactions (hysteria, obsession, compulsion, phobias, hypochondria)
- Behavior extremes (excessive compliance and passivity, overly aggressive and demanding)
- Overly adaptive behavior (inappropriately adult or inappropriately infantile)
- Developmental lags (physical, cognitive, emotional)
- Sudden and severe drops in school performance, emotional appearance, general functioning
- Suicidal ideation or actual suicide attempts

It is important to emphasize that these conditions may exhibit any one of a number of organic or environmental causes besides maltreatment. Sandoval (1988) indicates that one of the most important ways to intervene with a child who has been maltreated is to seek legal intervention. Professional education programs and school districts should sensitize all child-serving professionals to the effects of child abuse and should instruct them in the procedures of filing a report. In addition, programs should outline the interrelated responsibilities of child protective agencies, law enforcement agencies, the courts, and community human service agencies. The following is a list of basic topics Besharov (1990) offers to be covered in any program of professional education:

- Persons who must report
- Liability for failing to report
- Sources of information
- How to handle emergencies
- Respecting parental rights
- Persons who may report
- Definitions of child abuse and neglect
- Indicators of child abuse and neglect
- Preserving evidence
- Reporting procedures

Prendergast (1996) suggests that the primary reason children fail to verbally ask for help lies in the adults not communicating that they are accessible, accepting, and nonjudgmental toward the abused child. He emphasizes that this communication must begin in early childhood and include the following conditions:

- Availability and accessibility
- Belief in the child and the assurance that the child will not be punished
- Assurance that the child will have a voice
- Assurance of continued love and support for the child

Appendix B of this chapter provides suggestions for parents that include giving children consistent love and attention, supervision guidelines, and appropriate adult modeling behaviors. In addition, Prendergast (1996) offers the following traits lacking in parents of children who are vulnerable to victimization:

- Lack of physical contact and supervision
- Failing to assure the child/adolescent of care and love
- Lack of defective value teaching
- Lack of concrete value teaching
- Teaching or modeling that sex equals love
- Lack of credibility between parents and their children
- Teaching blind obedience
- Parental denial

SUICIDE AND BEREAVEMENT

Although crises can unite families in strength and love, the death of a child places overwhelming strain on the family (Jones, 1997; Stahlman, 1996). When providing intervention to children, an important consideration is the degree to which children are capable of experiencing grief and mourning in response to the death of a family member (Stahlman, 1996; Wilson, 1988). Parents can help their children by knowing how children grieve and allowing them to own and express their feelings (O'Toole, 1996). Parents must be aware that children may feel guilty, confused, or unable to cope with the loss. In addition, children desperately need a parent to openly communicate that they are not the cause of the family's sorrow nor are they responsible for restoring happiness in the family.

Parents may hold back from recovering from the loss of their child out of their own guilt. Denial, sadness, anger, fear, guilt, longing, and other emotions associated with grieving also apply in the case of suicidal deaths (Poland, 1989; Rando, 1984; Stahlman, 1996). However, grieving for people who killed themselves can be especially difficult because of the disgrace attached to suicide. Family members may feel ashamed to tell people how the person died (Coulliard, 1991; Jones, 1997).

Those mourning someone who committed suicide probably will spend a lot of time wondering why (Jones, 1997). They might ask, "Why didn't I see this coming?" "What could I have done to stop it?" Survivors might start to remember "clues" the person indicated through their behavior or what they may have said. To successfully mourn a suicide death, parents, teachers, and students need to resolve their overwhelming sense of guilt (Cassini & Rogers, 1996; Coulliard, 1991; Rando, 1984).

Unfortunately, survivors may never understand why loved ones killed themselves. Depression is consistently associated with the suicide of a child, adolescent, or adult (Patros & Shamoo, 1989; Poland, 1989; Range, 1996). However, though depression and suicidal ideation may overlap, they are distinguishable. One reason for the overlap between depression and suicide is that both contain an overall sense of hopelessness (McEvoy & McEvoy, 1994; Range, 1996). Jones (1997) suggests that mourning a suicide death will be easier for those who understand depression. They can get help from a psychologist, counselor, therapist, or grief support group.

In the midst of a crisis, suicide may present no unusual identifying background characteristics. The crisis, which may be typically diagnosed

as a reactive depression, follows sudden traumatic incidents and is characterized by dramatic behavioral change, hostility, and signs of confusion
and disorganization (Johnson, 1998; Range, 1996; Coulliard, 1991). In
addition to family members and friends, school personnel should be alert-
ed for physical and emotional signs of depression in children. Poland
(1989) provides some major symptoms of depression and warning signs of
the suicidal child:

- Withdrawal from friends and activities
- Changes in sleeping and eating habits
- Preoccupation with death
- Concentration problems
- Giving away prized possessions
- Emotional or rebellious outbursts
- Uncharacteristic low self-esteem
- Loss of joy in life and a bleak outlook for the future
- Risk-taking or reckless behavior
- Increased somatic complaints
- Frequent mood changes
- Making out a will or list of final wishes
- Decreased attention to physical appearance
- Lack of confidence in abilities and decision making

Despite the importance of involving schools in suicide prevention,
McEvoy & McEvoy (1994) suggest that educators often suffer from the
propensity of training that focuses on what personnel should and should
not do and that personnel continue to be uninformed about procedures
for identifying, referring, and following up on those students experiencing
a crisis. Not only do school personnel need to recognize the warning signs
of suicide but they must be able to respond to the verbal and behavioral
cues of students who are suicidal. Poland (1997) recommends seven points
to which personnel can respond to help students in crisis:

1. Try to remain calm, and seek collaboration with a colleague.
2. Gather information and approach the student as if he or she were
   planning a trip.
3. Ask specific questions about the suicidal plan and the frequency of
   suicidal thoughts.
4. Emphasize that there are alternatives and that the student is not the
   first to feel this way.

5. Refrain from making deals to keep the student's suicidal thoughts a secret, and explain the ethical responsibility to notify the student's parents.
6. Have the student sign a no-suicide contract and provide the student with the phone number of the local crisis hotline.
7. Supervise the student until parents have assumed responsibility.

In addition to warning signs for school personnel, Johnson and Maile (1987) have suggested the following guidelines for parents of the child who is suicidal:

1. Be patient with the child.
2. Take threats and gestures seriously.
3. Show them love, acceptance, and tolerance, and seek out the help that they need.
4. Keep communication going and avoid isolation.
5. Offer help with no strings attached.

Together these points target an appropriate, immediate reaction to be elicited by parents and school personnel (see Appendix A for additional steps for parents following a trauma).

Educators and parents must recognize the seriousness of the crisis and the crucial importance of a quick response. In addition to warning signs and appropriate immediate response, it is important to identify goals that educators should consider when developing in-service training sessions on suicide prevention (Miller & DuPaul, 1996; Poland, 1989). Concerning potential topics to be provided to school personnel, Poland (1989) recommends the following:

1. To give school personnel knowledge about the warning signs of suicide
2. To eliminate the misperceptions about suicide
3. To provide accurate information about the incidence of youth suicide and causation factors
4. To clarify the school system's procedures and identify community resources
5. To empower personnel with the knowledge that they can make a difference and save a life
6. To clarify the personnel's role in suicide intervention
7. To clarify confidentiality issues: staff must not keep secrets about suicidal behavior

Several different strategies have been identified by teachers and counselors as useful in intervening upon the death of a student. Many school systems include various death education units in their regular curriculum to facilitate discussion about suicide, loss, the dying process, and working through grief. Complementary to these prevention strategies are various interventions that may be implemented following the death of a child (Davis, 1988; Wilson, 1988). Many strategies utilized in the classroom require that the adults leading the activities be knowledgeable in the area of bereavement, have strong facilitation skills, and be comfortable discussing death, suicide, and grief (O'Toole, 1996; Toray & Oltjenbruns, 1996; Worden, 1996).

The immediate goal of classroom intervention is to limit the emotions within appropriate expression in order to provide means of acknowledging these feelings so that anxiety may be kept to a tolerable level (Klingman 1993). With regards to implementing crisis-related activities, Johnson (1998) suggests that the decision on how to address the crisis should take several factors into consideration:

• The group or class would benefit from a structured process.
• Students are feeling isolated and need assistance in sharing about the incident.
• Discussion would benefit from impetus, direction, context, and leadership.
• Activities are chosen with consideration toward student sensitivities and needs.

Johnson (1998) further states that most activities—art, writing, or enactment and simulation—can be modified to change their impact. The impact of activities can be softened when prompts involve individual rather than group activity.

• Require cognitive rather than affective responses.
• Encourage general rather than specific responses.
• Invite universal rather than personal or individual responses.
• Involve principles or lessons learned rather than relating experiences.
• Involve problem solving rather than dwelling upon the impact of the crisis.
• Require global impressions rather than sensory images.
• Involve writing rather than sensory images.
• Involve art rather than enactment or simulation activities.

Just as it is important for intervention in the classroom setting, it is also critical for teachers and parents to know when to seek professional help.

With regards to identifying children for professional evaluation, Worden (1996) indicates that the focus should not be on the mere presence or absence of a symptom or behavior but on its duration and degree to which psychological defense mechanisms are successful in protecting the child from anxiety (Koocher & Gudas, 1992). The goals of therapeutic intervention should include (1) the safe expression of feelings, (2) relief of painful symptoms and post-traumatic behaviors, (3) corrections of any misunderstandings and self-blame, (4) restoration of hope for the future, and (5) establishing a renewed sense of trust in oneself and the world (see Appendix A for complete parent handout on trauma and children). The following red-flag behaviors are offered (Cassini & Rogers, 1996; Koocher & Gudas. 1992; Worden, 1996). If any of the following behaviors continue for several months, a professional evaluation may be warranted.

- If the child has persisting difficulty talking about the deceased parent
- If aggressive behavior persists or takes form of property destruction or self-injurious behavior
- If symptoms of anxiety persist (such as clinging to surviving parent or exhibits school phobia)
- If the child exhibits prolonged bodily distress or develops psychosomatic problems
- If the child demonstrates marked social withdrawal, particularly previously outgoing children
- Persistent self-blame or guilt along with an overall sense of unworthiness
- If the child is using drugs or alcohol to cope with stress

After the death of a child, life will never be the same again for a family, and as with any other death it is possible for families to heal and again enjoy living. Worden (1996) identifies four tasks for grieving families:

1. To share acknowledgment of the reality of death
2. To share experience of the pain of grief
3. To reorganize the family system
4. To redirect the family's relationships and goals

In order to address these tasks, Coulliard (1991) and Jones (1997) offers the following recommendations:

1. Survivors should include friends and family in mourning rituals. Grandparents, siblings, aunts, uncles, baby-sitters, schoolmates, and neighbors need to express their grief, too.

2. Grieving families need someone who can temporarily assume the daily adult responsibilities, so the surviving parents can have time to grieve while knowing that their surviving children are being provided for.

3. Grieving families need information about the grief process as well as resources they can continue to utilize as needed.

4. Parents should pay extra attention to their surviving children. It should be emphasized that their parents don't blame them for the family's sadness.

5. Survivors should accept their emotions. Grieving parents recover "one day at a time."

6. Parents should acknowledge and accept feelings of guilt. No parent is perfect and almost all grieving parents feel like they failed their child. Unresolved guilt and blame can destroy individuals, marriages, and families.

7. Grieving families need people around them who are comfortable talking about the loss, who acknowledge their pain rather than try to limit it.

8. Grieving families need someone whom they can displace their anger, pain, and frustration, who understands these reactions and does not take them personally, and who remains available as a friend when the family is able to let them be there for them.

SCHOOL CRISIS RESPONSE TEAMS

Several professional areas that specialize in working with students in crisis situations become familiar with the literature about crisis response. Within the school setting, it is essential that school psychologists and other school personnel develop the skills necessary to implement crisis intervention services (Poland, Pitcher & Lazarus, 1995; Steele, 1992). The value of developing such crisis teams lies in their unique ability to immediately convene and assist the school in being able to respond to student and staff needs while reinforcing standard operation of the school (McEvoy & McEvoy, 1994; Johnson, 1998; Klingman, 1993). The supportive climate of the school is increased, and the school is once again recognized as a secure place that ensures the safety of students. As these teams generate new effective strategies and approaches, they will add to the response options of school personnel, mental health professionals, and community agencies.

Just as there are building and district school crisis response teams, there

352 Managing Crisis: Intervention Skills for Parents

are also nationally recognized teams that provide emergency intervention upon a major occurrence. The National Organization for Victim Assistance (NOVA) is a private, nonprofit membership organization guided by four purposes: national advocacy, providing direct crisis services to victims, serving as an educational resources to victim assistance and allied professionals, and promoting better communication among its membership (NOVA, 1997). NOVA has developed a model that can be implemented by school psychologists that includes team roles, ground rules, timing and logistics, and procedures and processes (Poland et al., 1995). Poland (1997) emphasizes three points for schools to follow when developing crisis teams:

1. Staff members must review the crisis situations that have already occurred, with an emphasis on how the event could have either been prevented or managed more effectively.
2. Each school or district must examine its own resources and circumstances and make a plan that fits its particular functions and needs.
3. School crisis planning must be based on a theoretical model that includes primary, secondary, and tertiary levels of intervention.

In addition, Poland (1997) cites key principles outlined by the National Institute of Mental Health to guide schools in their capabilities to serve students and their families in crisis:

- School mental health workers are encouraged to seek out children who need their help.
- Children need to be provided with opportunities and permission to express a range of emotions. The most common reactions that children have to a crisis are fear of future bad events, regression in behavior, and difficulty in sleeping.
- Parents need to be provided with information about childhood reactions to crisis and need to be given specific suggestions about how to assist their child. This can often be accomplished by conducting a meeting with parents as quickly as possible.

Because of the limited time school personnel have to be successful in intervening in a potential suicide or other crisis situation, their approach should be able to utilize quickly (Steele, 1992). A successful crisis intervention team is the product of both policies and procedures that document and support an effective, efficient intervention model program. A school crisis team does not supplement the need for other mental health services but rather engages personnel to immediately assist in relieving the suffering of children and to refer for appropriate follow-up services as warranted.

CONCLUSION

Children and adolescents yearn for loving attention, acceptance and meaningful interactions with their families, teachers, and peers. In the absence of these quality relationships, growing up can be painful, isolating and even permanently disabling. As parents become increasingly distant and inaccessible, children face maltreatment and are forced to adopt compensatory roles in order to survive. Witnessed in our homes and schoolyards, children of all ages react to fear, rejection, and abuse by engaging in aggressive and rebellious behavior, running away, turning to drug abuse, and joining gangs. Often these children become severely depressed, withdrawn from family and peers, and tragically take their own lives. It is vital that we continue to identify the effects of crises upon the dynamics of family functioning, as well as continue to develop methods in which professionals can assist families in helping themselves.

School districts, urban and rural, operate under numerous policies and procedures that govern and identify the various functions within the district. Certainly all school districts face the challenge of maintaining a budget. Moreover, school personnel have a primary role and responsibility to educate children. However, when school districts become systems based on exception, they begin to lose their focus and perhaps their mission to serve the desperate needs of children and adolescents. The strategies outlined in this chapter can assist schools in discouraging victimization, identifying students who are suicidal, and ultimately foster a positive, healthy school climate. With national intervention teams such as NOVA and the competent personnel serving local school crisis response teams, these resources demonstrate the school's capabilities to provide immediate, efficient intervention to children and adolescents.

ADDITIONAL RESOURCES

National Organization for
  Victims Assistance
1757 Park Road, NW
Washington, DC 20010
1-800-TRY-NOVA

American Association of Suicidology
Suite 310
4201 Connecticut Ave., NW
Washington, DC 20008
202–237–2280

REFERENCES

American Psychological Association, American Academy of Pediatrics. (1996). *Raising children to resist violence. What you can do.* [Brochure]. Washington, DC.

Beane, A. (1998). The trauma of peer victimization. In T. W. Miller (Eds.), *Children of trauma: Stressful life events and their effects on children and adolescents* (pp. 205–218). Madison, CT: International Universities Press.

Besharov., D. J. (1990). *Recognizing child abuse: A guide for the concerned.* New York: The Free Press.

Bonner, B. L., Kaufman, K. L., Harbeck, C., & Brassard, M. R. (1992). Child maltreatment. In C. E. Walker & M. C. Roberts (Eds.) *Handbook of clinical child psychology* (2nd ed., pp. 967–1008). New York: Wiley.

Cassini, K. K. & Rogers, J. L. (1996). *Death and the classroom: A teachers guide to assist grieving students.* Cincinnati, OH: Griefwork of Cincinnati.

Christenson, S. L., Hirsch, J. A., & Hurley, C. M. (1997). Families with aggressive children and adolescents. In A. P. Goldstein & J. C. Conoley (Eds.), *School violence intervention: A Practical handbook* (pp. 325–365). New York; Guilford.

Coulliard, J. (1991). Grief: Family related issues. In S. N. Elliott & J. C. Witt (Eds.), *Working with families in crisis: School-based intervention* (pp. 117–144). New York: Guilford.

Danzy, E. S. (1989). Crisis intervention: A response to the mental health needs of children and youth. In W. P. Fowler & J. L. Greenstone (Eds.), *Crisis intervention compendium* (pp. 107–110). Littleton, MA: Copley.

Davis, J. M. (1988). Suicide and the schools: Intervention and prevention. In J. Sandoval (Ed.), *Crisis counseling, intervention, and prevention in the schools* (pp. 187–203). Hillsdale, NJ: Erlbaum.

Germain, R. B. (1988). Maltreatment of children. In J. Sandoval (Ed.), *Crisis counseling, intervention, and prevention in the schools* (pp. 73–91). Hillsdale, NJ: Erlbaum.

Gil, E. G., & Johnson, T. C. (1993). *Sexualized children: Assessment and treatment of children who molest.* New York: Launch Press.

Hillman, D., & Solek-Tefft, J. (1988). *Spiders and flies: Help for parents and teachers of sexually abused children.* New York: Lexington Books.

Ingraham, C. L. (1988). School-related crisis. In J. Sandoval (Ed.), *Crisis counseling, intervention, and prevention in the schools* (pp. 35–49). Hillsdale, NJ: Erlbaum.

Johnson, K. (1998). *Trauma in the lives of children: Crisis and stress management techniques for counselors, teachers, and other professionals.* Alameda, CA: Hunter House.

Johnson, S., & Maile, L. (1987). *Suicide and the schools.* Springfield, IL: Charles C. Thomas.

Jones, C. (1997). *R.I.P.: The complete book of death and dying.* New York: HarperCollins.

Klingman, A. (1993). School-based intervention following a disaster. In C. F. Saylor (Ed.) *Children and disasters.* New York: Plenum Press.

Knapp, R. J. (1986). *Beyond endurance: When a child dies.* New York: Schocken Books.

Koocher, G. P., & Gudas, L. J. (1992). Grief and loss in childhood. In Walker & Roberts (Eds.) *Handbook of clinical child psychology.* (2nd ed., pp. 1025–1034). New York: Wiley.

Lattanzi-Licht, M. (1996). Helping families with adolescents cope with loss. In C. A. Corr & D. E. Balk (Eds.) *Handbook of adolescent death and bereavement* (pp. 219–234). New York, NY: Springer.

Lazarus, P. J. (1996). *Trauma and children: A parent handout for helping children heal.* [brochure]. Washington, DC: National Association of School Psychologists.

Lystad, M. H. (1989). Family violence: A mental health perspective. In W. R. Fowler & J. L. Greenstone (Eds.), *Crisis intervention compendium* (pp. 122–131). Littleton, MA: Copley.

McEvoy, M. L., McEvoy, A. W. (1994). *Preventing youth suicide. A handbook for educators and human service professionals.* Holmes Beach, FL: Learning Publications.

Miller, D. N., & DuPaul, G. J. (1996). School-based prevention of adolescent suicide: Issues, obstacles, and recommendations for practice. *Journal of Emotional and Behavioral Disorders, 4,* 221–230.

National Organization for Victim Assistance. (1997). *Community crisis response team manual* (2nd ed.). Washington, DC.

Olweus, D. (1993). *Bullying at school: What we know and what we can do.* Cambridge, MA: Blackwell.

O'Toole, D. (1996). *Growing through grief A K-12 Curriculum to help young people through all kinds of loss.* Burnsville, NC: Mountain Rainbow.

Patros, P. G., & Shamoo, T. K. (1989). *Depression and suicide in children and adolescents.* Boston: Allyn and Bacon.

Poland, S. (1989). *Suicide intervention in the schools.* New York: Guilford.

Poland, S. (1997). School crisis teams. In A. P. Goldstein & J. C. Conoley (Eds.) *School violence intervention: A practical handbook* (pp. 127–159). New York: Guilford.

Poland, S., Pitcher, G., & Lazarus, P. J. (1995) Best practices in crisis intervention. In A. Thomas & J. Grimes (Eds.) *Best practices in school psychology—III* (pp. 445–458). Washington, DC: National Association of School Psychologists.

Prendergast, W. E. (1996). *Sexual abuse of children and adolescents: A preventive guide for parents, teachers, and counselors.* New York: Continuum.

Quinn, K. P., & McDougal, J. L. (1998). A mile wide and a mile deep: Comprehensive interventions for children and youth with emotional and behavioral disorders and their families. *School Psychology Review, 27,* 191–203.

Rando, T. A. (1984). *Grief, dying, and death: Clinical interventions for caregivers.* Champaign, IL: Research Press.

Range, L. M. (1996). Suicide and life-threatening behavior in childhood. In C. A. Corr & D. M. Corr (Eds.) *Handbook of childhood death and bereavement* (pp. 71–88). New York: Springer.

Ray, B. M. (1989). The teacher's role in crisis intervention. In W. R. Fowler & J. L. Greenstone (Eds.), *Crisis intervention compendium* (pp. 84–88). Littleton, MA: Copley.

Sandoval, J. (1988). *Crisis counseling, intervention, and prevention in the schools.* Hillsdale, New Jersey, Erlbaum.

Shaw, W. J. (1992). Delinquency and criminal behavior. In C. E. Walker & M. C. Roberts (Eds.) *Handbook of clinical child psychology* (2nd ed., pp.695–724). New York: Wiley.

Slaikeu, K. A. (1984). *Crisis intervention: A handbook for practice and research.* Boston: Allyn and Bacon.

Sommer, B. (1988). Peer conflicts. In J. Sandoval (Ed.), *Crisis counseling, intervention, and prevention in the schools* (pp. 167–186). Hillsdale, NJ: Erlbaum.

Stahlman, S. D. (1996). Children and the death of a sibling. In C. A. Corr & D. M. Corr (Eds.) *Handbook of childhood death and bereavement* (pp. 149–164). New York: Springer.

Steele, W. (1992). *Preventing self-destruction: A manual for school crisis response teams.* Holmes Beach, FL: Learning Publications.

Steele, W., & Raider, M. (1991). Family crisis facing schools. In S. N. Elliott & J. C. Witt (Eds.), *Working with families in crisis: School-based intervention* (pp. 3–15). New York: Guilford.

Stephens, R. D. (1997). National trends in school violence: Statistics and prevention strategies. In A. P. Goldstein & J. C. Conoley (Eds.), *School violence intervention: A practical handbook* (pp. 72–90). New York: Guilford.

Toray, T., & Oltjenbruns, K. A. (1996). Children's friendships and the death of a friend. In C. A. Corr & D. M. Corr (Eds.). *Handbook of childhood death and bereavement* (pp. 165–178). New York: Springer.

Worden, J. W. (1996). *Children and grief: When a parent dies.* New York: Guilford.

Worden, J. W. (1982). *Grief counseling and grief therapy: A handbook for the mental health practitioner.* New York: Springer.

Wilson, P. (1988). Helping children cope with death. In J. Sandoval (Ed.), *Crisis counseling, intervention, and prevention in the schools* (pp. 131–149). Hillsdale, NJ: Erlbaum.

APPENDIX A: TRAUMA AND CHILDREN: A PARENT HANDOUT FOR HELPING CHILDREN HEAL[1]

Background

Every parent at one time has worried about harm befalling their children. When trauma to children occurs, the territory of everyday life becomes frightening and unfamiliar not only for children but parents as well. Parents may find themselves overcome with anxiety and fear. Trauma may send a shockwave to the system and parents may respond with a wide range of feelings. These feelings may include a sense of disbelief, helplessness, isolation, despair, or horror. Parents may try to make sense out of a senseless act. Who can prepare for their children being physically or sexually assaulted, kidnaped, mugged, robbed, or involved in a severe automobile accident? Who can prepare for children being diagnosed with a life threatening illness or experiencing a natural or man-made disaster?

Traumas typically occur suddenly, often leaving children little or no time to prepare physically or emotionally. Traumas are unpredictable and outside what is to be expected in children's lives. During a trauma, children experience intense fear, horror or helplessness. Typical methods of coping no longer work. Following trauma, children require extra support and need to learn new coping strategies.

Parents can be instrumental in their children's recovery. Therefore, helping children recover from a trauma is a family matter. Parents need to

[1]From Lazarus, P. J. (1996). National Association of School Psychologists. With permission.

take the lead and model positive coping. Yet parents themselves may require extra information, support, and resources to assist their children. Some first steps that parents can take are to understand the impact and symptoms of trauma and how to help in the aftermath. This handout provides this information.

The Impact of Trauma

Trauma can change the way children view their world. Assumptions about safety and security are now challenged. Children's reactions will depend upon the severity of the trauma, their personality makeup, their characteristic coping style and the availability of support. It is common for children to regress both behaviorally and academically following a trauma. A constructive way to view the situation is that they are normal children in an abnormal circumstance.

It is natural for children to first experience some sort of *denial*. For example, children may insist upon returning to a house that has been destroyed. *Fears, worries, or nightmares* are common following a trauma. *Sleep disturbances or eating difficulties* may happen. Also children may begin to *regress emotionally* or act younger than their chronological age. They also may become more *clinging, unhappy, and needy of parental attention and comfort*. Feelings of *irritability, anger, sadness, or guilt* may often emerge. *Somatic complaints* such as headaches, stomachaches, or sweating are not unusual. Some *loss of interest in school and poor concentration* are some other common reactions.

Symptoms Associated with Post-Traumatic Stress Disorder

Following a trauma children may experience some of the symptoms of post-traumatic stress disorder (PTSD). The main symptoms are as follows:
    Reexperiencing of the trauma during play or dreams. For example, children may

- Repeatedly act out what happened when playing with toys
- Have many distressing dreams about the trauma
- Be distressed when exposed to events that resemble the trauma or at the anniversary of the trauma
- Act or feel as if the trauma is happening again

Avoidance of reminders of the trauma and general numbness to all emotional topics. For example, children may

- Avoid all activities that remind them of the trauma
- Withdraw from other people
- Have difficulty feeling positive emotions

Increased "arousal" symptoms. For example, children may

- Have difficulty falling or staying asleep
- Be irritable or quick to anger
- Have difficulty concentrating
- Startle more easily

What Can I Do as a Parent Following a Trauma?

- *Establish a sense of safety and security.* It is essential that children feel protected, safe and secure in the aftermath of a trauma. Ensure that all basic needs are met, including love, care, and physical closeness. Spend extra time to let children know that someone will nurture and protect them. Children will need a lot of comforting and reassurance.
- *Listen actively to your children.* Seek first to understand before trying to be understood. Parents may underestimate the extent of the trauma experienced by their children. It is often not as important what you say, but that you listen with empathy and patience. In some instances your children may be reluctant to initiate conversations about trauma. If so, it may be helpful to ask them what they think other children felt or thought about the event. Also, it may be easier for children to tell what happened (e.g., what they saw, heard, smelled, physically felt) before they can discuss their feelings about the trauma. In other instances, children will want to tell their parents the story of the trauma over and over. Retelling is part of the healing process. Children need to tell their stories and have their parents listen, again and again to each and every agonizing detail.
- *Help your children express all their emotions.* It is important to talk to your children about the tragedy—to address the suddenness and irrationality of the disaster. Reenactment and play about the trauma should be encouraged. It is helpful to ensure that children have time to paint, draw or write about the event. Provide toys that may enable children to work through the trauma. Examples may include such items as a toy fire engine,

ambulances, fire extinguisher, doctor kit, etc. for a girl injured in a fire. imagining alternate endings to the disaster may help empower your children and allow them to feel less helpless in the aftermath of a tragedy.

• *Validate your childrens' feelings.* Help children understand that following a trauma all feelings are acceptable. Children will probably experience a myriad of feelings which could include shame, rage, anger, sadness, guilt, pain, isolation, loneliness, and fear. Help your children understand that what they are experiencing is normal and to be expected.

• *Allow your children the opportunity to regress as necessary.* This is important so that they may "emotionally regroup." For example, your children may request to sleep in your bed with the lights on or you may need to drive your children to school. Previously developed skills may seem to disappear or deteriorate. Bed wetting or thumb sucking may occur. Aggression and anger may emerge in a previously non-aggressive child. Be patient and tolerant and never ridicule. Remember that most regression following a trauma is temporary.

• *Help children clear up misconceptions.* Help correct misunderstandings regarding the cause or nature of the trauma, especially those that relate to inappropriate guilt, shame, embarrassment or fear. (Examples may be "I should have been able to save my brother from the car wreck." "God struck my sister dead because God was angry at her." "My father died of cancer and I will catch it from him.")

• *Educate yourself about trauma and crisis.* The more you know about trauma, the more empowered you may feel. To help educate yourself, consider setting up a conference with the school psychologist or mental health professional in your school. A good place to start is by reading the text listed below under "Resource for Parents."

• *Help predict and prepare.* If your children need to go to a funeral or deal with surgery, carefully explain what will happen each step of the way. Allow your children to ask all kinds of questions. If they need to appear in court, explain what they will see, hear, do, etc.

• *Arrange support for yourself and your family as necessary.* Consult with your clergy, rabbi, physician and friends as necessary. You may need extra emotional, religious, medical, and/or psychological support. If possible take appropriate time for recreational or pleasurable experiences with your children to establish a sense of normalcy and continuity.

• *Communicate with the school and staff about what occurred.* Most teachers will be understanding and helpful if they know that children had a traumatic experience. Teachers may be able to provide additional support both educationally and emotionally. They can also provide information to doctors or therapists or alert you to troublesome behaviors they observe.

• *Affirm that your children are capable of coping and healing in the aftermath of a trauma.* Plant "emotional seeds" that express confidence in your children's ability to heal. Remember the messages that you give your children have incredible power.

• *Seek professional assistance for your children and family as necessary.* When seeking help, make sure the professional has experience with children and has treated crisis and trauma. Feel free to discuss with the therapist all your concerns and all aspects of treatment. If your children are experiencing the symptoms of PTSD, then therapy may be warranted.

What Can I Say as a Parent Following a Trauma?

• Sometimes knowing exactly what to say is difficult. However, your emotional expression of love and concern is more important than words. Just saying "this is very hard for us" can lead to emotional relief and understanding.

• Always be honest with your children about what has happened and what may occur. Remember that following a trauma, children may lose a sense of trust about the safety and security of the world. Therefore, honesty is essential so your children can maintain a sense of trust.

• Respect your children's fears. Children cannot be helped by trying to argue them out of their fears by appeals to bravery or reason. What is most helpful is an approach that says "I know you are feeling frightened of _____ now." This can be followed by an offer of assistance and support by saying, "Let's see what we can do to make this less scary for you."

• Make sure that your children know that you are aware of the seriousness of the situation. Allow your children to cry. Saying to your children "Don't cry, everything will be fine" denies the seriousness of the situation.

• Try to recognize your children's feelings and put them into words. For example, if a child's close friend died in an automobile accident, you might say to your child "You are sad and angry that your friend was killed. I know that you must miss him very much." Or if a child feels overwhelmed by fears in the aftermath of a hurricane, you may say, "I know that you are frightened, but we have a plan to protect us if another hurricane occurs."

What Should I Do if I Believe My Child may be Suffering from PTSD?

Consult with your local school psychologist or contact a mental health professional who has experience in this area such as a psychiatrist, psychologist or mental health counselor. Your school psychologist or pediatrician may direct you to the appropriate resources,

What Type of Therapy is Recommended for Traumatized Children?

A variety of methods may be used depending on the orientation of a particular therapist. Very different approaches to the same problem can be equally effective when undertaken by an insightful and skilled professional. Approaches may include individual, group or family therapy. Therapists often use play, art, and drama methods in their treatment as well as "cognitive-behavioral" approaches, which help children reinterpret events and feelings in a more positive way, or in some cases they might use clinical hypnosis. As part of the therapy experience, children will be guided to reprocess the trauma in a safe and supportive environment in some instances medication may be used to control severe anxiety, depression, or sleeplessness. However, medication should not be used as a substitute for psychotherapy for traumatized children.

If I Seek Therapeutic Services for My Children, What will be the Goals of Therapy?

The goals of therapy with traumatized children should include:

- Gaining a sense of mastery and control over one's life
- The safe expression and release of feelings
- Relief of painful symptoms and post traumatic behaviors
- Minimizing the scars of trauma
- Corrections of any misunderstandings and self-blame
- Restoration of hope regarding the future
- Establishing a renewed sense of trust in oneself and the world
- Developing perspective and distance regarding the trauma

Summary

Helping children recover from trauma is a family matter. It is important to maintain an open discussion of the trauma and recognize the feelings of all family members. Focus on the immediate needs of the children, and take a one-day-at-a-time approach. Find and use support systems outside of the family. Always maintain a positive image of your children as healers and survivors.

Resource for Parents

Monahon, C. (1993). *Children and trauma: A parent's guide to helping children heal.* New York: Lexington Books.

Position Statement: School Violence

Children and youth are the victims of more crimes than any other age group in the United States today. Violence against children in any setting is disturbing when it occurs at school, it is especially destructive, and swift action must be taken to ensure the safety of all students and the staff who care for them. The National Association of School Psychologists resolves to help rid America's schools of the destructive influences of violence in all its forms. This can be accomplished through prevention programs, through direct assistance to victims of school violence, through efforts to reduce the incidence of future violence by perpetrators, and through joining other community groups to sponsor anti-violence initiatives.

Violence in schools violates fundamental assumptions that society holds about the role of schooling in the lives of children and youth. When parents leave their sons and daughters at the schoolhouse door each day, they trust that their children will be cared for and safe. When violence occurs at school, this trust is broken in profound and permanent ways. For this reason, NASP believes that schools are rightfully held to a stricter standard than are other segments of society.

School violence threatens the physical, psychological, or emotional well-being of students and school staff. These threats may occur on school grounds or at school-sponsored activities, and they include but are not limited to physical assaults with and without weapons, bullying, and social isolation. To reduce school violence, schools must ensure that no harm comes to anyone on school campuses at any time. To achieve this goal, efforts must be made to reduce obvious aggressive and illegal behaviors as well as other behaviors that, while not illegal, may damage a students development and negatively affect school climate.

Creating Safe Schools

Schools must maintain campuses that are safe and conducive to learning. NASP believes that efforts to create safe schools can take many forms. Essential actions include but are not limited to intervening with aggressive students, implementing victim support programs, establishing school-wide violence prevention programs, and improving school climate.

Intervening with Aggressive Students

As a result of public demands to respond punitively to threats of violence at school through "zero-tolerance" programs, schools often focus disciplinary actions on perpetrators of violence. Policies that focus only on catching and punishing violent behaviors fall far short of the goal of creating a safe school environment As alternatives to practices such as corporal punishment and ceasing educational services, NASP promotes the use of positive methods of school discipline such as crisis intervention and the application of behavior management principles and strategies. Schools must also make efforts to modify the behavior of students who have engaged or are at risk of engaging in violent behavior. NASP strongly supports systematic efforts to teach social skills and self-control to children and youth as part of a school-wide plan to create a safe and healthy climate conducive to learning.

Implementing Victim Support Programs

Meeting the needs of victims appears self-evident However, survey data show that most schools respond to antisocial and aggressive behaviors through disciplinary action against the perpetrators, while neglecting to provide appropriate support and counseling for victims. Children who have been the victims of school violence perceive schools as failing to protect them, and as a result they may feel threatened and unsafe while at school. These children display many characteristics common to individuals with Post Traumatic Stress Disorder, including blocked learning and symptoms of serious emotional problems. NASP strongly supports the availability of counseling and recovery programs for victims of school violence.

Establishing School-Wide Violence Prevention Programs

NASP encourages the implementation of programs designed to teach peacemaking, peer mediation, and conflict resolution. Such programs are natural bridges between interventions that focus on individual change and those seeking to change the ecology of the school at the organizational level.

Improving School Climate

A comprehensive program to reduce school violence includes efforts to affect the general climate of the school itself. Such programs may not focus on specific violent behaviors directly but seek to change the conditions that are, directly or indirectly, conducive to violent acts. Individualized instruction and remedial support where needed can reduce academic failure and frustration that may contribute to violence. Programs to decrease racism and other forms of intolerance, increase appreciation of diversity, and improve levels of trust can also decrease violence by creating a climate of acceptance and understanding and by improving the quality of the relationships among and between students and staff.

Although school violence may engender a desire to discipline the aggressors harshly, NASP urges school personnel to temper disciplinary responses with efforts to promote cooperation, positive social skills, and peaceful means of resolving conflicts. Addressing school violence must go beyond increasing campus security and establishing procedures to apprehend and punish students who have violated school rules. A comprehensive campaign to end school violence must also encompass efforts to increase support, trust, and caring among students and staff.

Role of the School Psychologist

First and foremost, school psychologists can take a leadership role in encouraging schools to develop a comprehensive approach to violence reduction. School psychologists are trained to a) respond to crises spawned by violence; b) counsel victims; c) implement prevention and intervention programs designed to reduce aggressive behaviors among youths and others; and d) consult with school staff implementing social skills programs and other programs designed to teach peaceful ways to resolve conflicts. These are essential components of a comprehensive school safety plan.

Summary

NASP recognizes that violent acts, wherever they occur, have complex origins and consequences. Efforts to reduce violence at school, therefore, must be multi-faceted. A successful program will ensure the ongoing safety of all students and staff both by creating conditions that discourage violence and by responding quickly and effectively when violence occurs. To be truly comprehensive, however, a violence reduction program will seek to influence student attitudes toward violence, teach students and school staff effective conflict resolution skills, and work to create a climate that promotes tolerance and understanding among students and staff. Such a program will be most effective when blended within broader violence prevention efforts involving local law enforcement, juvenile probation, public health personnel, and other parent and community groups. When an entire community commits itself to reducing violence, the future health and well-being of its children and youth can only be enhanced.

—Adopted by the NASP Delegate Assembly, July 14, 1996

Supporting Information

Furlong, M. J., & Morrison, G. M. (Eds.) (1994). Mini-Series: School Violence. *School Psychology Review, 23,* 139–262.

Furlong. M. J., Babinksi, L, Poland, S., Munoz, J., & Boles, S. (1996). Factors associated with school psychologists' perceptions of campus violence. *Psychology in the Schools, 33,* 29–38.

Furlong, M. J., Chung, A., Bates, M. & Morrison, R. (1995). Profiles of non-victims and multiple victims of school violence. *Education and Treatment of Children, 18,* 282–298.

For further information about NASP or the role of the school psychologist in preventing and intervening with school violence, contact NASP at 4340 East West Highway #402, Bethesda, MD 20814; or call (301) 657-0270.

APPENDIX B: RAISING CHILDREN TO RESIST VIOLENCE: WHAT YOU CAN DO[1]

Research has shown that violent or aggressive behavior is often learned early in life. However, parents, family members, and others who care for children can help them learn to deal with emotions without using violence. Parents and others can also take steps to reduce or minimize violence.

This brochure is designed to help parents work within the family, school, and community to prevent and reduce youth violence.

Suggestions for Dealing with Children

Parents play a valuable role in reducing violence by raising children in safe and loving homes. Here are suggestions that can help. You may not be able to follow each one exactly, but if you do your best, it will make a difference in your children's lives.

Give your children consistent love and attention.

Every child needs a strong, loving, relationship with a parent or other adult to feel safe and secure and to develop a sense of trust. Without a steady bond to a caring adult, a child is at risk for becoming hostile, difficult, and hard to manage. Behavior problems and delinquency are less likely to develop in children whose parents are involved in their lives, especially at an early age.

It's not easy to show love to a child all the time. It can be even harder if you are a young, inexperienced, or single parent, or if your child is sick or has special needs. If your baby seems unusually difficult to care for and comfort, discuss this with your child's pediatrician, another physician, a psychologist, or a counselor. He or she can give you advice and direct you to local parenting classes that teach positive ways to handle the difficulties of raising children.

It is important to remember that children have minds of their own. Children's increasing independence sometimes leads them to behave in ways that disappoint, anger, or frustrate you. Patience and a willingness to view the situation through the children's eyes, before reacting, can help you deal with your emotions. Do your best to avoid responding to your children with hostile words or actions.

Make Sure Your Children Are Supervised

Children depend on their parents and family members for encouragement, protection, and support as they learn to think for themselves. Without proper supervision, children do not receive the guidance they need. Studies report that unsupervised children often have behavior problems.

- Insist on knowing where your children are at all times and who their friends are. When you are unable to watch your children, ask someone you trust to watch them for you. Never leave young children home alone, even for a short time.
- Encourage your school-aged and older children to participate in supervised after-school activities such as sports teams. tutoring programs, or organized recreation. Enroll them in local community programs, especially those run by adults whose values you respect.
- Accompany your children to supervised play activities and watch how they get along with others. Teach your children how to respond appropriately when others use insults or threats or deal with anger by hitting. Explain to your children that these are not appropriate behaviors, and encourage them to avoid other children who behave that way.

Show Your Children Appropriate Behaviors By the Way You Act

Children often learn by example. The behavior, values, and attitudes of parents and siblings have a strong influence on children. Values of respect, honesty, and pride in your family and heritage can be important sources of strength for children, especially if they are confronted with negative peer pressure, live in a violent neighborhood, or attend a rough school.

Most children sometimes act aggressively and may hit another person. Be firm with your children about the possible dangers of violent behavior. Remember also to praise your children when they solve problems constructively without violence. Children are more likely to repeat good behaviors when they are rewarded with attention and praise.

You can teach your children nonaggressive ways to solve problems by

- Discussing problems with them,
- Asking them to consider what might happen if they use violence to solve problems, and
- Talking about what might happen if they solve problems without violence.

This kind of "thinking out loud" together will help children see that violence is not a helpful solution.

Parents sometimes encourage aggressive behavior without knowing it.

For example, some parents think it is good for a boy to learn to fight. Teach your children that it is better to settle arguments with calm words, not fists, threats, or weapons.

Help your children learn constructive, nonviolent ways to enjoy their free time. Teach them your favorite games, hobbies, or sports, and help them develop their own talents and skills, Read stories to younger children, take older children to the library, or tell family stories about admired relatives who have made the world a better place.

Don't Hit Your Children

Hitting, slapping, or spanking children as punishment shows them that it's okay to hit others to solve problems and can train them to punish others in the same way they were punished.

Physical punishments stop unwanted behavior only for a short time. Even with very harsh punishment, children may adapt so that it has little or no effect. Using even more punishment is equally ineffective.

Nonphysical methods of discipline help children deal with their emotions and teach them nonviolent ways to solve problems, Here are some suggestions:

- Giving children "time out"—making the children sit quietly, usually 1 minute for each year of age (this is not appropriate for very young children),
- Taking away certain privileges or treats.
- "Grounding"—not allowing the children to play with friends or participate in school or community activities (this is only appropriate for older children or adolescents).

Punishment that involves taking away privileges or "grounding" should be consistently applied for realistic, brief periods.

Children need to feel that if they make mistakes, they can correct them. Show them how to learn from their errors. Help them figure out what they did wrong and how they can avoid making similar mistakes in the future. It is especially important not to embarrass or humiliate your child at these times. Children always need to feel your love and respect.

A positive approach to changing behaviors is to emphasize rewards for good behavior instead of punishments for bad behavior. Remember that praise and affection are the best rewards.

Be Consistent About Rules and Discipline

When you make a rule, stick to it. Children need structure with clear expectations for their behavior. Setting rules and then not enforcing them is confusing and sets up children to "see what they can get away with."

Parents should involve children in setting rules whenever possible. Explain to your children what you expect, and the consequences for not following the rules. This will help them learn to behave in ways that are good for them and for those around them.

Make Sure Your Children Do Not Have Access to Guns

Guns and children can be a deadly combination. Teach your children about the dangers of firearms or other weapons if you own and use them. If you keep a gun in your home, unload it and lock it up separately from the bullets. Never store firearms where children can find them, even if unloaded.

Don't carry a gun or a weapon. If you do, this tells your children that using guns solves problems.

Try to Keep Your Children From Seeing Violence in the Home or Community

Violence in the home can be frightening and harmful to children. Children need a safe and loving home where they do not have to grow up in fear. A child who has seen violence at home does not always become violent, but he or she may be more likely to try to resolve conflicts with violence.

Work toward making home a safe, nonviolent place, and always discourage violent behavior between brothers and sisters. Keep in mind as well that hostile, aggressive arguments between parents frighten children and set a bad example for them.

If the people in your home physically or verbally hurt and abuse each other, get help from a psychologist or counselor in your community. He or she will help you and your family understand why violence at home occurs and how to stop it.

Sometimes children cannot avoid seeing violence in the street, at school, or at home, and they may need help in dealing with these frightening experiences. A psychologist or counselor at school or a religious leader are among those who can help them cope with their feelings.

Try to Keep Your Children from Seeing Too Much Violence in the Media

Seeing a lot of violence on television, in the movies, and in video games can lead children to behave aggressively. As a parent, you can control the amount of violence your children see in the media. Here are some ideas:

- Limit television viewing time to 2 hours a day.
- Make sure you know what TV shows your children watch, which movies they see, and what kinds of video games they play.
- Talk to your children about the violence that they see on TV shows, in the movies, and in video games. Help them understand how painful it would be in real life and the serious consequences for violent behaviors.
- Discuss with them ways to solve problems without violence.

Teach Your Children Ways to Avoid Becoming Victims of Violence

It is important that you and your children learn to take precautions against becoming the victims of a violent crime. Here are some important steps that you can take to keep yourself and your children safe:

- Teach your children safe routes for walking in your neighborhood
- Encourage them to walk with a friend at all times and only in well-lighted, busy areas.
- Stress how important it is for them to report any crimes or suspicious activities they see to you, a teacher, another trustworthy adult, or the police. Show them how to call 911 or the emergency service in your area.
- Make sure they know what to do if anyone tries to hurt them: Say "no," run away, and tell a reliable adult.
- Stress the dangers of talking to strangers. Tell them never to open the door to or go anywhere with someone they don't know and trust.

Help Your Children Stand Up Against Violence

Support your children in standing up against violence. Teach them to respond with calm but firm words when others insult, threaten, or hit another person. Help them understand that it takes more courage and leadership to resist violence than to go along with it.

Help your children accept and go along with others from various racial and ethnic backgrounds. Teach them that criticizing people because they are different is hurtful, and that name-calling is unacceptable. Make sure they understand that using words to start or encourage violence—or to quietly accept violent behavior—is harmful. Warn your child that bullying and threats can be a set-up for violence.

An Extra Suggestion for Adults

Take Care of Yourself and Your Community

Stay involved with your friends, neighbors, and family. A network of friends can offer fun, practical help, and support when you have difficult times. Reducing stress and social isolation can help in raising your children.

Get involved in your community and get to know your neighbors. Try to make sure guns are not available in your area as well. Volunteer to help in your neighborhood's anticrime efforts or in programs to make schools safer for children. If there are no programs like this nearby, help start one!

Let your elected officials know that preventing violence is important to you and your neighbors. Complain to television stations and advertisers who sponsor violent programs.

Encourage your children to get involved in groups that build pride in the community, Such as those that organize clean-ups of litter, graffiti, and run-down buildings. In addition to making the neighborhood a safer place, these groups provide a great opportunity for parents, children, and neighbors to spend time together in fun, safe, and rewarding activities.

Potential Warning Signs

Parents whose children show the signs listed below should discuss their concerns with a professional, who will help them understand the children and suggest ways to prevent violent behavior.

Warning Signs In the Toddler and Preschool Child

Has many temper tantrums in a single day or several lasting more than 15 minutes and often cannot be calmed by parents, family members, or other caregivers

Has many aggressive outbursts, often for no reason

Is extremely active, impulsive, and fearless

Consistently refuses to follow directions and listen to adults

Does not seem attached to parents; for example, does not touch, look for, or return to parents in strange places

Frequently watches violence on television, engages in play that has violent themes or is cruel toward other children

Warning Signs in the School-Aged Child

Has trouble paying attention and concentrating

Often disrupts classroom activities

Does poorly in school

Frequently gets into fights with other children in school

Reacts to disappointments, criticism, or teasing with extreme and intense anger, blame, or revenge

Watches many violent television shows and movies or plays a lot of violent video games

Has few friends and is often rejected by other children because of his or her behavior

Makes friends with other children known to be unruly or aggressive

Consistently does not listen to adults

Is not sensitive to the feelings of others

Is cruel or violent toward pets or other animals

Is easily frustrated

Warning Signs in the Preteen or Teenaged Adolescent

Consistently does not listen to authority figures

Pays no attention to the feelings or rights of others

Mistreats people and seems to rely on physical violence or threats of violence to solve problems

Often expresses the feeling that life has treated him or her unfairly

Does poorly in school and often skips class

Misses school frequently for no identifiable reason

Gets suspended from or drops out of school

Joins a gang, gets involved in fighting, stealing, or destroying property

Drinks alcohol and/or uses inhalants or drugs

Index